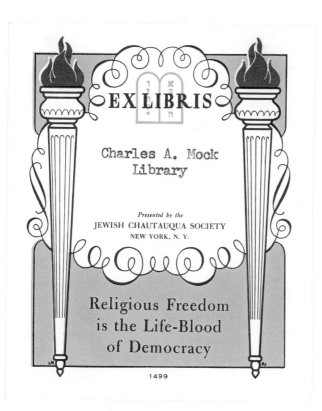

Aspects of the
RELIGIOUS
BEHAVIOR
OF
American Jews

Aspects of the
RELIGIOUS
BEHAVIOR
OF
American Jews

by Charles S. Liebman

KTAV PUBLISHING HOUSE, INC.

NEW YORK

Library of Congress Cataloging in Publication Data

Liebman, Charles S
  Aspects of the religious behavior of American Jews, See Slip.

  Three essays originally published in the American
Jewish year book, 1965, 1968, 1970.
  Includes bibliographical references.
    1. Judaism—United States. 2. Rabbinical seminaries—
United States. 3. Orthodox Judaism—United States. 4.
Reconstructionist Judaism. I. Title.
BM205.L538   296'.0973   74-546
ISBN 0-87068-242-3

MANUFACTURED IN THE UNITED STATES OF AMERICA

TABLE OF CONTENTS

FOREWORD VII

INTRODUCTION IX

THE TRAINING OF AMERICAN RABBIS 1

ORTHODOXY IN AMERICAN JEWISH LIFE 111

RECONSTRUCTIONISM IN AMERICAN JEWISH LIFE 189

FOREWORD

The Jewish tradition recognizes two kinds of scholarship: that of the *baqi,* the expert with wide and thorough knowledge; and of the *ḥarif,* who is acute in analysis. Of course, the best scholarship combines both qualities—for example, Charles Liebman's studies in the *American Jewish Year Book:* "Orthodoxy in American Jewish Life" (Vol. 66, 1965), "The Training of American Rabbis" (Vol. 69, 1968), and "Reconstructionism in American Jewish Life" (Vol. 71, 1970). Professor Liebman provides information that is important and original, and for that alone his readers can say *dayyenu,* it would have sufficed us. But he gives even more. He has asked the right questions; he has known when to be historical, when sociological, when theological; and to his analysis he brings a mind at once disciplined and imaginative.

Nor is there anything of the hidden persuader about him. His concerns and his values are out in the open.

The editors of the *Year Book* congratulate themselves for having published such work, and KTAV for making it available in one volume.

MORRIS FINE
MILTON HIMMELFARB

'Erev Rosh Hashanah 5734

INTRODUCTION

Preparation of this introduction gave me occasion to reread all the essays in their entirety; something I have not done since their initial publication. In an orgy of self-abuse I decided to read them all in one sitting. I thought this might provide a better perspective for their evaluation. I cannot recommend my example to others. There is more than a problem of tediousness involved. The essays are not an integrated whole. They require shifts in perspective and focus. They are written on quite disparate topics. But precisely because I do believe that there is an essential unity to the essays which is not overt, I would like to consider them together. After that I will consider each essay separately.

The essays are all behavioral. That is, they all focus on the activity and attitudes of American Jews rather than on the formal institutions of American Jewry. But the framework or the rubric under which American Jewish behavior is treated is an institutional one. There are a number of studies which attempt to treat the attitudes and behavior of American Jews. There are also some studies—fewer in number and generally poorer in quality—which attempt to treat the organizational-institutional life of American Jewry. What we sorely lack are studies which focus on Jewish behavior in an institutional context. A model for such studies is Marshall Sklare's *Conservative Judaism: An American Religious Movement,* published in a revised edition by Schocken in 1972. But we have all too few such studies.

Most authors who describe American Jewish life tend to choose one perspective to the exclusion of the other. Each has its own justification. Jewish life is disorganized, but American Jews are organized. There is a multiplicity of organizations and movements and institutions in American Jewish life which deserve understanding not only because they are

there, not only by virtue of their successes and failures, but also because
they absorb an enormous amount of the energy and resources of
American Jews. Hence a study of Jewish institutions and organizations
is legitimate and important. Indeed, it is unfortunate that we do not
have more such studies.

Paradoxically, important as these institutions are for the understanding of American Jews, one would be misled by focusing exclusively
upon them. The structure, activity and ideological orientations of American Jewish institutions ('ideology' would be too presumptuous a term)
are irrelevant to that which many if not most American Jews consider
as really important, since the private Jewish life of most American Jews
occupies a greater and more significant part of their life space than does
their public Jewish life. Furthermore, the institutional and organizational
multiplicity—the presumed pluralism of American Jewish life—is somewhat misleading because it conceals the essential unity, along with a
degree of apathy, that is far more characteristic of Jewish attitudes and
behavior.

Consequently, what we really need are studies which provide both
detailed description of Jewish institutional life and the meaning of the
institution for its members and audience. This is what, in retrospect, I
was attempting in my essays, although I was self-conscious about it only
in the final section of my essay on Reconstructionism. While I resist the
temptation of giving myself marks on each essay, I would like to call the
reader's attention to the final section of this last essay, which in my
opinion is the most important statement I have to make about religion
in general and American Jewish religious life in particular. That section
is incorporated into and expanded in "The Religion of American Jews,"
which appeared in my *The Ambivalent American Jew,* published in
1973 by the Jewish Publication Society.

The most satisfying aspect of the essays to me, personally, is that my
own biases hardly find expression, except where they are clearly labeled.
I had deep convictions about almost every idea, group, movement, and
institution which I treated. Over the years, my own values and convictions have changed, but after rereading the essays I do not believe that
I dealt unfairly with any group or idea; nor would I today, despite the
different convictions which I now hold, treat any person, group or idea
differently.

There is one exception. Instead of first presenting the Reconstructionist point of view, and then perhaps subjecting it to my critique, I

hardly permit a statement of their point of view to be made before I take issue with it. In retrospect I realize that it was not really Reconstructionism or Mordecai Kaplan that I was arguing with. This deserves some explanation.

If my essays have merit it is because I was able to empathize with the individuals and institutions I wrote about. My effort was to identify myself with the individuals and institutions so closely that, at least for a brief period, I was able to understand *their* behavior by asking myself how *I* would behave or how *I* would perceive a situation. When I was convinced I could do that, I was satisfied that my research was complete. For brief periods of my life, therefore, I was a whole variety of Orthodox Jews, a rabbinical student at a number of different seminaries, and a Reconstructionist. But I was also a Reconstructionist in another sense. As I indicated in my essay, most American Jews are, behaviorally though not institutionally, reconstructionists (in the lower-case). This was true of myself as well. It was really not with Reconstructionism that I was conducting an argument in my essay. It was with myself and, in a more general sense, with American Jews.

Each essay, though all are concerned with the religious life of American Jews, has its own institutional focus. Yet in each essay the material covered is broader than is suggested by the title. The essay on Orthodoxy discusses aspects of Conservative Judaism. The essay on Reconstructionism has a great deal to say about Reform and Conservative Judaism, about religious life between the two world wars, and especially about the Jewish Theological Seminary. The essay on rabbinical training touches on the broader aspects of all three denominations in Jewish life.

No amount of pleasure or self-indulgence at seeing these essays reprinted can conceal the fact that they are not quite timeless. First of all, things have changed even in the few years since they were written. Secondly, some of the things that should have been treated, even within the confines of each topic, were omitted. Let me consider each essay in its turn.

The essential outlines of American Orthodoxy, as presented in the first essay, have remained unchanged. Obviously the details of the number of day schools, or synagogue members, or the size of organizational budgets have changed. But the structure of American Orthodoxy has remained the same. Indeed, even my prediction that questions of dogma within Orthodoxy would ultimately be raised with "explosive consequences" has not come about in the decade since the article was written, nor are there as many signs now as there were then that such a challenge will be raised.

In discussing the development of American Orthodoxy the essay indicates that the synagogue rabbi replaced the communal rabbi in importance because, among other reasons, the synagogue replaced the community as a focus of Jewish identity. It seems obvious that the synagogue has declined in importance in the life of American Jews in the last decade, that to some extent it has been replaced by the community and communal activity. But a corollary return of the communal rabbi to the American scene has not taken place. Rather, local lay leaders, especially Federation of Jewish Philanthropy leaders, have assumed greater importance. This is connected to both the decline of the overt importance of "religion" in American Jewish life and the increased importance of ostensibly "secular" activity—especially support for Israel.

The most serious omission in the essay on Orthodoxy has to do with the attitudes of Orthodox Jews toward Israel and the divisions within Orthodoxy concerning Israel. I have tried to rectify the first omission in "American Jews and Israel" in my *The Ambivalent American Jew,* where I also discuss Israel's role in American Jewish life. Additionally, much attention is given to the divisions within American Orthodoxy concerning Israel and Orthodox efforts to affect Israel in two chapters of a book I am now preparing on the influence of Diaspora Jewry in shaping Israel's public policy.

Any study of American Orthodoxy today would have to devote more attention to the phenomena of the "hippie Orthodox," the attraction of Hasidism for seemingly alienated and radical Jewish youth, and the interest of many young Jews in traditional Judaism. However faddish and temporary this phenomenon may be—and I am of the opinion that it is of no lasting consequence nor will it affect Orthodoxy itself, as it might if enough such young people over a long enough period of time really joined its ranks—it is an indication of the kinds of currents that are to be found among some young Jewish people today, and therefore deserves to be treated.

Finally, the Americanization of Orthodoxy receives insufficient attention. It is easy to see that modern Orthodoxy underwent a process of acculturation and there is a temptation to juxtapose the two wings of Orthodoxy and suggest that one is simply more Americanized than the other. This still leaves us with a problem of defining "Americanization" and of explaining the consequences of the decline of "Americanization" as an American and Jewish value. However, the right wing of American Orthodoxy—the Sectarian Orthodox, as I label them in the essay—have also undergone a process of Americanization, which is far more obvious to me today from the perspective of a resident of Israel observing Israeli Orthodoxy. The process of this Americanization and its expression are, however, far more subtle among the sectarians than among the modern Orthodox.

The essay on Orthodoxy begins with a statement of its limitations— insufficient attention to phenomena which could not be dealt with because of limitations of time and space. Unfortunately, the vacuum in our knowledge of American Orthodoxy remains unfilled. No serious essay, much less book, on contemporary Orthodoxy has appeared since the publication of my essay. The number of publishers who are looking for such a manuscript suggests that market consideration are not the impediment.

The essay on rabbinical training is the most time-bound. Three important changes have taken place since it was written. First, dissatisfaction with rabbinical training at the major American seminaries has increasingly been expressed by rabbis and rabbinical students. My essay touched off some of this expression by eliciting a great deal of public and private comment. While almost all the comment was favorable, I believe that many who praised it abused my conclusions. In a symposium sponsored by *Judaism* (fall 1969) I found myself in the paradoxical position of defending rabbinical seminaries against what I thought was unfair criticism, some of which relied upon my own essay. I will quote part of my statement there as a balance to what some have inferred from my essay.

It does not seem to me that we can meaningfully discuss rabbinical training or the role of the rabbi in the community, unless we have some agreement on the meaning and value of Judaism. One central aspect of Judaism is the primacy of the textual tradition and of Jewish text within Jewish life. This means that there is an insignificance—virtually an utter insignificance—in such courses as New Testament or psychotherapy or cultural anthropology or in sociology of the ghetto or in Buddhism or Hinduism. Certainly, such courses are utterly insignificant before the rabbinical student has a basic knowledge and understanding of the Jewish texts and of the Jewish tradition. It would be hypocritical of me if I said that

I do not think people ought to know about or read about Hinduism and Buddhism and Islam and cultural anthropology and psychotherapy. Fine! But to introduce this into a rabbinical school curriculum? At the expense of what? Of a basic knowledge of Jewish sources?

... Secondly, I do not think the seminaries—or, for that matter, Judaism—are open to just any kind of idea, or to any form of experimentation, or to a *total* variety of Jewish experiences. It also seems to me that if the price that Judaism and Jews have to pay for this today is the alienation of most intellectuals or of radical college youth, then let us pay the price.

... The faults of American Judaism are not necessarily attributable to the seminaries. I do not think we can blame the state of American Judaism on the conditions within rabbinical seminaries. If the picture of American Judaism today is a very dismal one—and I believe it is—if the future of American Judaism looks very grim—and I think it does—that is in great part because we live in an essentially hostile environment.... the American culture at its best, not at its worst (I'm not talking about drugs and extreme Right or Left), is hostile to Judaism and to basic Jewish values. Consequently, the most meaningful response that the seminary can make to this kind of environment is basically defensive. By and large, for all their faults—and there is, as I repeat, much to criticize in the seminaries—this has been their response.

A second change that has taken place since my essay was written is in the leadership of both the Reform and Conservative institutions. And lastly, the changes on the college campus with respect to Jewish life have meant that some rabbinical students now come out of a different environment and that the college student seeking a more intensive Jewish environment has other options. It seems likely that the newly established Reconstructionist Rabbinical College, the various experiments in Jewish communal living and study in *chavurot* and *batim* in or around a number of college campuses, the development of the Jewish Free Universities, and the introduction of Judaic studies in so many American colleges and universities an likely to have consesequences for the kinds of students whom the seminaries recruit, the students' expectations of the seminaries, and the students' career orientations.

Of all these factors I want to single out only the growth of Judaica departments in American colleges and Universities. (Two important articles on this question are Jacob Neusner's "Studies in Judaism: Modes and Contexts," *Journal of the American Academy of Religion* [June 1969], and "Two Settings for Jewish Studies," *Conservative Judaism* [Fall 1972]. My essay indicates that the better rabbinical students were oriented toward non-rabbinical careers. With the growth of Judaica departments one might have anticipated a number of developments. First, there would be an increased loss of seminary faculty members to better paying or more academically prestigious universities. Secondly, there would be a drop in the number of rabbinical students, since at least some of those oriented to a scholarly career might prefer university Ph.D. programs to seminaries. Thirdly, there would be a drop in the absolute number of seminary students who choose rabbinical careers because of the increased opportunities for university careers in Judaica.

Informants tell me that none of these developments has taken place. Perhaps this is because the pool of rabbinical students has grown. Perhaps it is because Judaica departments still cannot provide scholarly training superior in quality to that of the rabbinical seminaries. Perhaps it is still too early for these developments to have taken place. What has happened is that increased numbers of rabbinical graduates have enrolled in Ph.D. programs in universities, although the tendency to do so predates the great expansion of university departments of Judaica.

The essay on rabbinical training mentions the opportunities that seminaries offer for study in Israel. Since then the HUC-JIR has greatly expanded its Israel program.

There is one important addition to the empirical literature on rabbinical institutions which should be noted—the study by Theodore I. Lenn *et al., Rabbi and Synagogue in Reform Judaism,* commissioned by the Central Conference of American Rabbis and published in 1972. The best article to come to my attention on the chavurot is Stephen C. Lerner's "The Havurot," *Conservative Judaism* (spring 1970). Since publication of that article new chavurot have sprung up. These, along with the Jewish Free Universities and the growth of Jewish houses on college campuses, have not received systematic study, but their development, problems, successes, and failures can be followed on the pages of the new periodical *Sh'ma.*

I have already commented on the Reconstructionist essay. Obviously, for one who wishes to follow current developments, there is no substitute for the *Reconstructionist* magazine.

Greater and purer souls may have mixed feelings about republication of their essays—I am delighted. One reason is that they will reach a different and newer audience. Publication of a feature article in the *American Jewish Year Book* assures the author of an instant public. But only scholars read past volumes of the *Year Book*. Instant recognition, therefore, is followed by relative neglect. But there is a growing number of students interested in contemporary Jewish life. I hope these essays will stimulate some of them to retrace my steps, to correct my errors, to bring matters up to date, and to address themselves to questions which have not received sufficient attention.

I cannot conclude without an expression of gratitude to my friend Jacob Neusner. He suggested the idea of republication in early 1973 and communicated with me, with Ktav publishers, and with the editors of the *American Jewish Year Book*. To Neusner's other manifold talents we must now add that of impresario.

THE TRAINING OF AMERICAN RABBIS*

by CHARLES S. LIEBMAN

PREFACE • MAJOR RABBINICAL SEMINARIES • STUDENTS •
FACULTY • CURRICULUM • SOCIALIZATION • SUMMARY
• PERSONAL CONCLUSION

PREFACE

THIS IS PRIMARILY a study of the three American institutions
having the largest rabbinical training programs. It is not a study of any
institution in its entirety, but rather of that part of each school which
prepares students for ordination. In evaluating the findings and observa-
tions, the reader should bear in mind that this is an analytical study and
therefore, by definition, critical; that a microscopic view of any social
institution inevitably magnifies its weaknesses; that parts, when observed
in isolation from the whole, may appear distorted.

The major rabbinical institutions, Yeshiva University (YU), the Jew-
ish Theological Seminary of America (JTS), and Hebrew Union College-
Jewish Institute of Religion (HUC-JIR) have trained the majority of
American congregational rabbis. They are the fountainhead of American
Jewish scholarship and religious leadership.

The seminaries must be rated positively, also, in any comparative sense.
They are superior in many respects to Catholic and Protestant semina-

* I am most grateful to a number of people who read an earlier draft and made
suggestions, particularly to Rabbis Eugene Borowitz, Neil Gillman, Robert Hirt, and
Aaron Lichtenstein. Professors David Weiss and Meyer Simcha Feldblum read the
section on methods of Talmudic study and made many helpful comments. I am
also indebted to the students, faculty, and administration of the rabbinical seminaries, who were most cooperative and gracious in extending their hospitality and
answering my questions.

1

ries.[1] This should not cloud the fact that the Christians have shown far greater concern than the Jews with self-evaluation and criticism; Catholic and Protestant seminaries, one Jewish faculty member noted, are today characterized by renewal and change. The hallmarks of Jewish seminaries, on the other hand, are tradition and continuity.

To use another basis for comparison, rabbinical seminaries to some extent have failed to prepare rabbis adequately for the pulpit; but Ph.D. programs in American universities do not even attempt to prepare candidates for college teaching, though most of their graduates will enter this profession. The relationship between a rabbinical curriculum and the rabbinate is certainly less remote than, let us say, the training of teachers in large cities and the conditions which they find in large-city classrooms. In all educational institutions, sociological, psychological, and ideological pressures create a gap between curriculum and the role for which the student is being prepared.

There are defects attendant upon the kind of bureaucracy needed to run institutions as complex as our colleges, universities, and seminaries. There are also cultural lags between what a professor has learned and what a student wants to learn. The demand for scholarship is necessary for, but not always compatible with, good teaching and counseling. A religious seminary, in particular, must balance its desire for an outstanding teaching and research faculty and its requirement that the faculty members accept the values of the institution. The contingent problems must be recognized, but they can never be entirely overcome. Readers should therefore not judge the rabbinical seminaries too harshly; many of their dilemmas are insoluble.

Finally, any bias in this report is on the side of criticism rather than of praise. The public-relations department of each seminary can be relied upon to extol its glories.

*   *   *

[1] Some recent studies of Protestant and Catholic seminaries include: H. Richard Niebuhr, Daniel Day Williams, and James Gustafson, *The Advancement of Theological Education* (New York, 1957); Keith R. Bridston and Dwight W. Culver, eds., *The Making of Ministers* (Minneapolis, 1964); Keith R. Bridston and Dwight W. Culver, *Pre-Seminary Education* (Minneapolis, 1965); Walter D. Wagoner, *The Seminary: Protestant and Catholic* (New York, 1966); Charles R. Feilding, "Education for Ministry" (*Theological Education*, Autumn 1966; entire issue). The last book, in particular, will be read with profit by those interested in the training of clergymen, Christian or Jewish.

The rabbi is the most important figure in American Jewish life today. Recent years have witnessed the growing importance of Jewish scholars, educators, and professional administrators of large Jewish organizations. Jewish philanthropists have always been leaders in the Jewish community, and political leaders, too, have sometimes been recognized as spokesmen for the Jewish community, or some of its parts. But while individual scholars, educators, administrators, philanthropists, or even politicians may assume leadership positions and preeminence in Jewish life, none is as important as the rabbi. None has as direct and immediate contact with American Jews as the rabbi. None is exposed to as many facets of the Jew as the rabbi. And all leaders, to a greater or lesser extent, depend upon the rabbi to mobilize the Jewish community in support of the goals or programs they seek to achieve.

Perhaps most significantly, the rabbi is the only figure in Jewish life who can command leadership, deference, even awe, by virtue of an ascribed title. Sociologists distinguish between ascribed and achieved status. Ascribed status inheres by virtue of the position held or the role performed, achieved status by virtue of demonstrated abilities. In Jewish community leadership, the rabbi alone has a title or position having ascribed status. It is of no small interest, therefore, to understand why and how one becomes a rabbi.

MAJOR RABBINICAL SEMINARIES

The first successful rabbinical school in America, Hebrew Union College, was founded in 1875 by Isaac Mayer Wise, the leader of American Reform Judaism.[2] According to Samuel S. Cohon, the term "Union" expressed the founder's hope "to have one theological school for all Jews of the country"[3]—at least for all but the "ultra-orthodox," to use Cohon's formulation. HUC created the American Jewish image of the

---

[2] On the history of HUC see Samuel S. Cohon, "The History of Hebrew Union College," *Publications of the American Jewish Historical Society,* September 1950, pp. 17–55; David Philipson, "History of the Hebrew Union College 1875–1925," *Hebrew Union College Jubilee Volume* (Cincinnati, 1925), pp. 1–70; James G. Heller, *Isaac Mayer Wise: His Life, Work and Thought* (New York, 1965); Moshe Davis, "Jewish Religious Life and Institutions in America," in Louis Finkelstein, ed., *The Jews: Their History, Culture and Religion* (third ed.; Philadelphia, 1960), pp. 488–587. Stanley F. Chyet, *Hebrew Union College—Jewish Institute of Religion: 1947–1967* (Cincinnati, 1967), presents a brief survey of its recent history.
[3] *Loc. cit.,* p. 24.

rabbi as an urbane, cultured religious leader. Later seminaries have sought or have been forced to emulate this model.

The hope for a single rabbinical school was short-lived. In 1886 the Jewish Theological Seminary of America was organized to train rabbis for the more traditional segment of the community.[4] In 1950 HUC merged with the Jewish Institute of Religion, founded in 1922 in New York City by Stephen S. Wise as a nondenominational seminary to prepare rabbis for Reform, Conservative, and Orthodox congregations.[5] JIR had a strong Zionist and Hebraic orientation that was lacking in HUC until after World War II. The merger was resisted by certain groups within the Reform movement who felt that JIR influence would pull HUC to the right religiously, and by some JIR alumni and faculty who opposed a dilution of JIR's nondenominationalism.

While subtle differences still distinguish the Cincinnati and New York Reform centers, and more overt differences in curriculum emphasis and religious outlook separate HUC-JIR from JTS,* both resemble a certain type of rabbinical school that had already developed in Central Europe and was later to extend to Eastern Europe as well. This was the rabbinical seminary, as distinct from the yeshivah.[6]

At the yeshivot the exclusive subject of study was Talmud (occasionally interspersed with ethical tracts), and the method of study was the examination of sacred texts and accompanying commentaries which, in varying degree, were also sacred. This meant that the text (*peshaṭ*) and,

---

[4] On the history of JTS see Moshe Davis, *The Emergence of Conservative Judaism* (Philadelphia, 1963); *id.*, "Jewish Religious Life and Institutions in America," *loc. cit.*; Herbert Parzen, *Architects of Conservative Judaism* (New York, 1964); Marshall Sklare, *Conservative Judaism* (Glencoe, Ill., 1955).

[5] On JIR see Stephen S. Wise, *Challenging Years* (New York, 1949), pp. 129–42.

* For convenience, a glossary of abbreviations is appended to this article on p. 112.

[6] Unfortunately we have no adequate history of rabbinical institutions or yeshivot in Europe. Some of the available material includes Jacob Mann, "Modern Rabbinical Seminaries and Other Institutions of Jewish Learning," in *Central Conference of American Rabbis Yearbook* (Cincinnati, 1925), pp. 295–310; Zevi Scharfstein, *History of Jewish Education in Modern Times* (3 vols., Hebrew; New York, 1945–49), particularly vols. 1 and 3; Samuel K. Mirsky, ed., *Jewish Institutions of Higher Learning in Europe: Their Development and Destruction* (Hebrew; New York, 1956), and two survey articles by Abraham Menes, "The Yeshivot in Eastern Europe," in *The Jewish People; Past and Present* (New York, 1948), Vol. 2, pp. 108–118, and "Patterns of Jewish Scholarship in Eastern Europe," in *The Jews: Their History, Culture, and Religion, op. cit.*, pp. 376–426. Some material is also available in Dov Katz, *The Musar Movement: Its History, Personalities, and Methods* (5 vols., Hebrew; Tel Aviv, 1953).

for the most part, the commentary were regarded as authoritative. Memorization of the text, while not necessarily demanded, was regarded with some deference. Though the methods of study in the various yeshivot differed, they all had a basic orientation toward the text. They were also concerned with the personal religious and ethical conduct of the students and sought to prepare *talmide hakhamim,* masters of the Talmud (literally, disciples of the wise). Yeshivah students desiring positions as communal rabbis obtained *semikhah,* or ordination, upon mastering certain portions of the *Shulhan 'Arukh* (the last definitive code of Jewish law, compiled in the sixteenth century) and the accompanying commentaries, which were prerequisite for dealing with the practical questions of religious law that might arise. In modern times *semikhah* was a certificate given by a recognized rabbi to a student, attesting to the latter's expertness in Jewish law. One's *semikhah,* therefore, was only as good as the rabbi who conferred it. Some young men sought *semikhah* from a number of rabbis. Others, though eminent as *talmide hakhamim,* might never bother to obtain the *semikhah.* The European yeshivah was a place where one studied to become a master of Talmud. At best, ordination was secondary.

The rabbinical seminary, as opposed to the yeshivah, arose from a felt need for institutions that would train rabbis in skills other than, or in addition to, the mastery of Talmud. The best known of the European seminaries were the Jewish Theological Seminary of Breslau, founded in 1854 under the leadership of Zacharias Frankel, father of the "historical school" which was the ideological precursor of American Conservative Judaism, and the Hochschule (at various times Lehranstalt) für die Wissenschaft des Judentums, whose leading faculty member when it opened in Berlin in 1872 was Abraham Geiger, one of the pillars of Reform Judaism.

These and other rabbinical seminaries were established to train rabbis in what was called the *Wissenschaft des Judentums* (literally, science of Judaism). They sought to give the rabbinical student familiarity with Jewish culture in a broad sense—Bible, Talmud, Midrash, history, rabbinical literature. They also undertook to train him in the scientific method of study, the dispassionate examination and understanding of Jewish texts in a manner no different from the examination of other ancient texts. In 1873 Israel (Azriel) Hildesheimer founded in Berlin the Rabbinerseminar für das orthodoxe Judentum, a seminary for the training of Orthodox rabbis. It differed from the other, non-Orthodox seminaries in religious standards, ideology, and some parts of the curriculum, but not in its recognition that the education a rabbi required was more than just Talmud, and that the method of study, at least for subjects other than Talmud, should be patterned after that employed by universities. Thus, in Europe Orthodox, Reform, and more or less Conservative rabbinical seminaries coexisted with traditional yeshivot, and were distinguishable from them in curriculum, method, and purpose.

The more crucial distinction was that, at least in the non-Orthodox seminaries, the Wissenschaft des Judentums was more than a method. It was a program deriving from 19th-century romanticism and historicism, which turned to the Jewish past.[7] The motives of its founders are still disputed. It would appear that many sought to demonstrate the nobility of their own heritage in an effort to further the cause of Jewish emancipation and to gain admission to Christian society. Indeed, some of the early founders and supporters of the Wissenschaft movement apostatized. For many the science of Judaism was also a program for the reform of Judaism. If, the argument ran, one can objectively understand the nature, origin, and development of Jewish history and Jewish law, one is in a position to reform or modernize Judaism by retaining what is basic or essential and abandoning what simply accrued through superstition or accident of time or place. Thus, the Wissenschaft movement provided students in the rabbinical seminaries with a method and ideology, making study purposeful beyond the mere accumulation of facts. It is true that Moritz Steinschneider, the bibliographer and orientalist whose life work was to demonstrate the important contributions of the Jews to the sciences and general culture of the Middle Ages, was reported to have seen his task as nothing more than giving the Jewish past "an honorable burial"; [8] but Geiger wrote:

> We need men able to demonstrate how Judaism developed gradually to its present state; that . . . much of it . . . originates in a historical period and can therefore also be rejected when times change. We need men who know how to oppose the views of ignorant reformers and the malicious mockery of non-Jews.[9]

Frankel, more religiously conservative than Geiger, saw in Wissenschaft "a means to establish harmony between the theory and practice

---

[7] Gershon Scholem, *Mi-tokh hirhurim 'al hokhmat Yisrael* ("Reflections on the Wissenschaft des Judentums"; Luah Ha-arez, Tel Aviv, 1944), pp. 94–112.

[8] *Ibid.*, p. 102.

[9] In *Zeitschrift für die Wissenschaft des Judentums*, 1823, pp. 11–12, quoted in Adolph Kober, "The Jewish Theological Seminary of Breslau and 'Wissenschaft des Judentums,' " *Historia Judaica*, Oct. 1954, p. 87.

of Judaism through scholarly reasonableness." [10] However naive, misguided, and thoroughly 19th-century the optimism about the science of Judaism may have been, however faulty the assumption of some that a more or less desacralized religious tradition would remain an object of sufficient interest to merit reform, the new approach made of the European rabbinical seminaries places where Jewish scholarship and the possibilities of Jewish life were self-evidently interrelated.

JTS and HUC-JIR, while in many respects patterned after the European rabbinical seminary, have rejected its program. They are committed to the scientific study of Judaism, but their science is not directed to any systematic effort of reform. Indeed such an effort is impossible in the absence of any systematic theology or social theory at both institutions. The result may be a purer science but the price is the students' feeling of separation between teaching and research, on the one hand, and the needs of the Jewish community, on the other.

The Rabbi Isaac Elchanan Theological Seminary (RIETS), now a division of Yeshiva University, was founded in 1897.[11] Although its certificate of incorporation stated as its objectives "to promote the study of the Talmud and to assist in educating and preparing students of the Hebrew faith for the Hebrew Orthodox Ministry," [12] RIETS was modeled after the traditional European yeshivah, not the rabbinical seminary. During the early years student-administration tension arose from the students' desire for a general cultural education to supplement Talmud. This, they felt, would give them more adequate preparation for the rabbinate. The administration resisted, and reprisals against the students led to a student strike in 1908 as well as to conversations between student leaders and JTS regarding the possibility of transferring to that institution.[13] What the students sought was a supplement to Talmud, particu-

---

[10] Albert Lewkowitz, "The Significance of 'Wissenschaft des Judentums' for the Development of Judaism," *ibid.,* p. 83.

[11] On the history of Yeshiva University see Jacob I. Hartstein, "Yeshiva University; Growth of Rabbi Isaac Elchanan Theological Seminary," *American Jewish Year Book,* Vol. 48 (1946–47), pp. 73–84, and Gilbert Klaperman, "Yeshiva University: Seventy-Five Years in Retrospect," *American Jewish Historical Quarterly,* Vol. LIV (1964), pp. 5–50; 198–201. In 1916 RIETS merged with a school for young boys, Yeshivat Etz Chaim, founded in 1886. Consequently YU, an outgrowth of RIETS, had its origins in 1886; as a school for advanced talmudic study it began only in 1897.

[12] *Ibid.,* p. 49.

[13] Gilbert Klaperman, *The Beginning of Yeshiva University: The First Jewish University in America* (Yeshiva University, unpublished doctoral dissertation, 1955).

larly courses in secular subjects, not a change in the manner of teaching Talmud, which was what JTS had to offer. With a change in administration and the growth of Yeshiva College, with its secular curriculum, as well as the later founding of the Bernard Revel Graduate School (BRGS) for general Jewish subjects, additional courses became available. However, RIETS itself remained virtually untouched.

Talmudic study in RIETS represents the heart of the rabbinical program, which, in content and method, is a replica of that of the European yeshivah. Thus, each year a tractate of the Talmud with traditional commentaries is studied, but without an introduction to the tractate; without an effort to understand the historical or social circumstances in which the various layers of material were produced and later edited; even without a serious effort to explore whether the received text is accurate, and how to deal with any errors or variants that may have entered into it.

There are, of course, programmatic implications in YU's method of study. It assumes that the Talmud and its traditional commentaries are authoritative, that the material in its essence is transcendent in origin, and that the commentaries in and to the Talmud evolved as a logical exegesis of the text, and are independent of time or place. The first task of the student is to understand the text and commentaries and, more creatively, to resolve any contradiction in the text or in the interpretations of the traditional commentators. While this method of study presents problems of its own, it is automatically invested with meaning and relevance as long as the Talmud retains its traditional religious significance for the student.

American rabbinical seminaries, in the more generic sense of the term, include all institutions preparing men for ordination. The discussion here will focus specifically on the student, the faculty, the administration, and the formal and informal programs reflecting their desires, capacities, and values. The influence of the general environment on each seminary's program is only indirect, for it is filtered through these three groups. Of external groups having a special interest in a particular seminary—the large financial contributors, the boards of trustees, the rabbinic alumni, and the congregational movements—only the rabbinic alumni exercise some direct influence. Thus far, however, their pressure for the expansion of courses in practical rabbinics has been fairly successfully resisted by the seminaries.

In almost all instances the data on rabbinical students, presented here are based on a questionnaire [14] distributed to all first- and last-year rabbinical students at YU, JTS, and HUC-JIR, and supplemented by personal interviews with selected students at each institution. Over 70 per cent of the students in question at each institution returned the questionnaire in time for inclusion in the analysis. Unless otherwise stated, our statistics on students are based on these returns.

RABBINICAL STUDENTS

Excluding special students and those on leave in the spring semester of 1967, there were 98 rabbinical students at YU, 143 at JTS, 45 at HUC-JIR, New York, and 128 at HUC-JIR, Cincinnati. Counting only full-time resident students, in 1967 there were at YU 40 first- and 25 last-year students; at JTS 36 first- and 22 last-year students; at HUC-JIR, New York, 13 first- and 7 last-year students, and at HUC-JIR, Cincinnati, 36 first- and 24 last-year students. First-year students are those who entered the rabbinical program in September 1966, and last-year students those who expected to be ordained by the summer of 1967. At JTS and HUC-JIR not all first-year students are actually in the freshman year of study.

Age, Place of Birth, and Marital Status

All rabbinical seminaries require a college degree for entrance, and most students enter rabbinical school immediately after college graduation. Among the first-year students at each institution, 70 per cent or more were between the ages of 21 and 23. The length of the program is not uniform between seminaries, and within JTS and HUC-JIR there are variations depending upon the students' previous Jewish education. Consequently, the age of last-year students varies. Most of those at YU were between 24 and 26 years old, and most at JTS and HUC-JIR between

---

[14] The questionnaire was designed with the assistance of Robert Hirt, director of new communities, Community Service Division, YU; Neil Gillman, registrar of the School of Judaica, JTS, and Eugene Borowitz, professor of education and Jewish religious thought, HUC-JIR, New York; and in consultation with Robert Katz, professor of human relations, HUC-JIR, Cincinnati. In New York the questionnaire was distributed to the students by the author, Rabbis Gillman and Borowitz, and in Cincinnati by Rabbi Kenneth Roseman, assistant dean. The questionnaires were filled out anonymously, and returned by each student individually to the AMERICAN JEWISH YEAR BOOK.

Editor's Note: Copies of the questionnaire may be obtained by writing to the *American Jewish Year Book.*

27 and 29. Whereas most of the first-year students were single, 50 per cent of the last-year students at YU and the large majority of such students at the other institutions were married. Ninety-one per cent, or more, of the rabbinical students at each institution were born in the United States.

Family Background

Differences in the students' family backgrounds were marked. The fathers of only 35 per cent of the students at YU were born in the United States, 22 per cent more having come here by the age of 13. Comparable figures for JTS were 55 and 19 per cent; for HUC-JIR, New York, 69 and 15 per cent; and for HUC-JIR, Cincinnati, 83 and 7 per cent. The differential proportion of foreign-born parents was related to differences in paternal occupation and family income (Tables 1 and 2).[15]

TABLE 1. FATHERS' PRINCIPAL OCCUPATION
(Per cent)

	YU	JTS	HUC-JIR (New York)	HUC-JIR (Cincinnati)
Owner or manager	20	33	46	57
Doctor or lawyer	2	9	0	10
Rabbi	11	12	8	2
Other Jewish professional	11	5	0	0
Other professional or technical worker	18	16	23	10
Sales worker	18	12	23	12
Other white-collar worker	11	5	0	5
Craftsman or operative	9	9	0	5
	n*=45	n=43	n=13	n=42

° Number in the sample.

TABLE 2. COMBINED INCOME OF PARENTS IN 1966
(Per cent)

	YU	JTS	HUC-JIR (New York)	HUC-JIR (Cincinnati)
Father deceased or retired	13	18	23	8
Under $7,000	20	5	8	2
7,000-8,999	24	5	8	10
9,000-10,999	11	10	8	18
11,000-12,999	7	10	15	12
13,000-14,999	7	17	0	10
15,000 or more	18	35	38	40
	n*=45	n=40	n=13	n=40

° Number in the sample.

---

15 On differences in income among Jewish laymen, see Charles S. Liebman, "Changing Social Characteristics of Orthodox, Conservative, and Reform Jews," *Sociological Analysis,* Winter 1966, pp. 210–22.

YU students came from homes appreciably lower in income and occupational status. Differences between other seminaries are less marked; though, taking occupational status and income together, HUC-JIR, Cincinnati, was on a higher level than its New York branch. Also of interest is that a distinctively large percentage of Cincinnati students came from homes where the father's principal occupation was business rather than a technical field or the Jewish or general professions. This suggests the possibility that Cincinnati students came from richer but less intellectual homes.

Differences also appeared between first- and last-year students at each institution. Beginning students, particularly at YU and JTS, came from homes whose combined family income was above that of last-year students. Table 3 facilitates comparison by indicating the percentage of students coming from homes where the combined family income was under $7,000 and from homes where it was above $15,000.

TABLE 3. PARENTS' INCOME BY SEMINARY YEAR
(Per cent)

	YU		JTS		HUC-JIR (New York)		HUC-JIR (Cincinnati)	
	First year	Last year	First year	Last year	First year	Last year	First year	Last year
Under $7,000	18	24	4	12	12	0	18	6
15,000 or more	21	12	52	12	44	25	32	50

Students were asked about their fathers' synagogue affiliation the year before they entered rabbinical school. Eighty-five per cent of YU fathers belonged to Orthodox and 11 per cent to Conservative synagogues. Most fathers of JTS students were affiliated with Conservative (69 per cent), some with Orthodox (19 per cent), and none with Reform synagogues; 10 per cent were unaffiliated. Most fathers of HUC-JIR students were affiliated with Reform (54 per cent in New York and 69 per cent in Cincinnati), some with Conservative (15 per cent in New York and 17 per cent in Cincinnati), and almost none with Orthodox synagogues; some (23 per cent in New York and 10 per cent in Cincinnati) were not affiliated with any synagogue.

At YU, fathers of first-year students were less likely to be affiliated with Conservative synagogues (3 per cent) than fathers of last-year students (24 per cent). At JTS, fathers of first-year students were less likely to be affiliated with Orthodox synagogues (17 per cent) than fathers of last-year students (22 per cent). At HUC-JIR (New York and Cincinnati combined) fathers of first-year students were less likely to be affiliated with Conservative synagogues (12 per cent) than those of last-year students (22 per cent). Everywhere, fathers of first-year students were more likely to be affiliated with synagogues of their sons' seminary denomination than fathers of last-year students.

The questionnaire also asked students to check a statement best describing the religious environment of their homes, without regard to synagogue affiliation (Table 4). Almost all YU students came from Orthodox

TABLE 4. RELIGIOUS ENVIRONMENT OF STUDENTS' HOMES
(Per cent)

	YU	JTS	HUC-JIR (New York)	HUC-JIR (Cincinnati)
Orthodox and observant	63	10	8	2
Orthodox, but not ritually meticulous	22	5	8	5
Right-wing Conservative	7	31	0	2
Conservative	4	36	8	10
Reconstructionist	0	0	0	0
Right-wing Reform	0	0	15	12
Reform	0	0	31	46
Religiously indifferent, but strongly Jewish	2	12	15	17
Generally indifferent to Judaism ...	2	7	15	4
	n*=46	n=42	n=13	n=41

* Number in the sample.

homes; two-thirds of JTS students came from Conservative homes and, of the rest, more from religiously indifferent than from Orthodox homes; slightly more than half of HUC-JIR students came from Reform, almost a quarter from religiously indifferent, and 20 per cent from either Orthodox or Conservative homes. The pattern for both JTS and HUC-JIR is to attract more students from homes which are to their left than to their right on the religious spectrum. We therefore find that at least 70 per cent of JTS and HUC-JIR students described themselves as more observant in ritual practice than their fathers, whereas only 4 per cent of the YU students so described themselves.

A comparison of first- and last-year students revealed the following: At YU a higher proportion of first-year students came from Orthodox, and fewer from Conservative homes, At JTS a higher proportion of first-year students came from Conservative, but fewer from right-wing Conservative homes. At HUC-JIR, a higher proportion of first-year students came from Reform, and fewer from Conservative or religiously indifferent homes. These findings bear out the basic tendency of seminaries to re-cruit increasingly from homes reflecting their particular religious outlook. This reflects a nearly fully accomplished Americanization or accultura-tion of all the mainstream varieties of American Judaism.

Educational

How much students are able to accomplish at the seminary depends in good part on their educational backgrounds, both Jewish and secular.

FORMAL JEWISH EDUCATION

Almost all YU students (87 per cent) had had nine years or more of Jewish education before entering college, and almost all received it in all-day schools. Ninety-five per cent did their undergraduate work at YU, which means an additional four years of Jewish study. Thus, every stu-dent in the rabbinical program entered with an extensive background in Jewish studies which, however, was largely in Talmud.

The virtually exclusive concentration on Talmud in the RIETS pro-gram, at both the college and rabbinical levels, and in the high-school studies of most students who ultimately enter the rabbinical program, precludes intensive study of Bible, Jewish history, Hebrew literature, and the rabbinical literature. Although rabbinical students have spent a major portion of their lives in Jewish studies, their knowledge of these subjects is far below the level YU critics of the yeshivah curriculum consider adequate. On the other hand, it may be argued that since Talmud is the Oral Law, and the Oral Law is the substance of Judaism, students who know Talmud know Judaism, and that what they do not know is only what different people, groups, and generations have had to say *about* Judaism. So goes the reasoning of those who defend the Jewish curriculum of most YU rabbinical students before their rabbinical program.

At JTS 74 per cent of the students had at least nine years of Jewish studies before college entrance, but only 41 per cent received most of their education in all-day schools; 47 per cent in supplementary after-noon schools, and 9 per cent in Sunday schools. Thirty per cent of the students at JTS had no formal program of Jewish studies while at college. In other words, a substantial number of students entered JTS with a good deal less than the best Jewish educational background.

The situation is far more serious at HUC-JIR, New York and Cincin-nati. Of all students at the two centers, 54 per cent and 49 per cent, respectively, had at least nine years of Jewish education before college;

but of these, 62 per cent and 72 per cent, respectively, received most of this education in Sunday schools; and 77 per cent and 72 per cent, respectively, received no formal Jewish education while at college. Moreover, only 39 per cent of all HUC-JIR students, compared with 57 per cent at JTS and 74 per cent at YU, had attended camps offering formal Jewish programs. At HUC-JIR, then, most students enter without any serious Jewish education, and this has tremendous consequences for the seminary program. The students find their pronounced weakness in Hebrew a continuing burden throughout their years at the seminary, although Hebrew is one relevant skill that HUC-JIR students could hope to master before reaching intellectual maturity.

A comparison of the Jewish educational backgrounds of first- and last-year students at YU showed no differences. At JTS, however, first-year students had less Jewish education: among first-year students, fewer had 9 years or more of Jewish education before college (57 per cent, compared with 74 per cent of last-year students); more had attended Sunday school (12 per cent compared with 5 per cent), and fewer attended all-day schools (16 per cent, compared with 42 per cent); slightly fewer (67 per cent, compared with 74 per cent) were enrolled in a formal Jewish-studies program while at college. At HUC-JIR the same situation prevailed, generally. On the whole, first-year students had less Jewish education than last-year students before and particularly during college; while at college, only 6 per cent of the first-year students, compared with 54 per cent of the last-year students, had been enrolled in some formal program of Jewish study.

INFORMAL JEWISH EDUCATION

HUC-JIR students received some informal Jewish experience as members of Jewish youth groups, to which 85 per cent of the students at the New York school and 91 per cent at Cincinnati belonged before entering college. Chief among these was the National Federation of Temple Youth (NFTY), the Reform youth group to which 67 and 72 per cent of the affiliated students in New York and Cincinnati had belonged. Most of them (69 and 74 per cent, respectively) were also members of Jewish campus groups, primarily Hillel. There was no difference in group affiliations between first- and last-year students.

At JTS 70 per cent of the students were members of Jewish groups before entering college, primarily of the two Conservative youth groups, United Synagogue Youth and Leadership Training Fellowships. Most of them (80 per cent) also belonged to Jewish campus groups. Among first-year students, affiliation with youth or college groups was more likely than among last-year students. Many YU students (51 per cent) were not members of Jewish youth groups before or during college. Bnei Akiva and Yavneh attracted most of the affiliated students.

Most rabbinical students (as many as 98 per cent at YU, and no fewer than 64 per cent at HUC-JIR, New York) had attended synagogue services regularly, at least during their last two years at college.

SECULAR EDUCATION

The secular education of the entering rabbinical students also varies with the seminary. Students were asked to list their undergraduate school or to evaluate their school's reputation. Only those responses mentioning a school that was listed in James Cass and Max Birnbaum's *Comparative Guide to American Colleges* were used in the analysis. Each school was ranked from one to four based on the listing. One signifies the highest ranking and four the lowest. Averages were then obtained for colleges from which JTS and HUC-JIR students were graduated. The JTS average was 1.9, HUC-JIR, New York 2.7, and HUC-JIR, Cincinnati, 3.0. As for their undergraduate academic averages, 48 per cent of JTS students reported B+ or better, 22 per cent B, and 30 per cent B— or below. For HUC-JIR, New York, the comparable percentages were 53, 32, and 15; for Cincinnati students, 33, 18, and 49.

It appears then that JTS students had a superior Jewish educational background as well as somewhat better academic qualifications, at least compared with Cincinnati students. HUC-JIR is raising its admission standards, and the situation may change within a few years, particularly if the number of all rabbinical seminary candidates continues to increase.

Almost all YU rabbinical students did their undergraduate work at Yeshiva College, and it is therefore misleading to compare them with others. We can, however, compare them with their fellow undergraduates. The Yeshiva College student body is highly heterogeneous in terms of intellectual capacity, for it is not the college generally, but specifically the Jewish program of studies which all students attend the entire morning and part of the afternoon, that attracts them. The admissions policy is relatively open. Whereas the best students at Yeshiva College are probably the equal of the best at any American college, its poorest students would probably have been denied admission to most good colleges.

A comparison of rabbinical-student and other Yeshiva College-student undergraduate averages indicates that the rabbinical program attracts a disproportionately high number of the best students, but an even greater disproportion of poor students. Of course, some students did poorly in college because they devoted their major effort to Jewish studies. A much higher percentage of the poorer than of the best students in the rabbinical program were likely to enter the congregational rabbinate. The same was true also at JTS.

Motives for Entering Rabbinical School

The rabbinical school may mean different things to different people. It may be viewed as a vocational or professional institution, which, unlike almost all other professional schools, also licenses its graduates. It may be regarded as preparation for an academic career, rather than for the pulpit. The career-motivated student, particularly the future congregational rabbi, will expect professionally-oriented training. His criterion for evaluating his seminary is likely to be how well it prepares him for the rabbinate. He may even be totally indifferent to the educational process, and simply look upon his attendance as time he has to spend before obtaining ordination. We do not suggest that this is the attitude of any students, at least when they enter. But if a career-oriented student comes to feel frustrated by what he considers as inadequate career preparation, he may find consolation in the thought that he is "putting in time" necessary for achieving his goal.

Alternately, the student may view the rabbinical seminary in expressive or cultural terms—as an institution where he can spend a few years in an intensely Jewish environment for the purpose of broadening his knowledge of Judaism and living a richly religious life. This type of student has very different expectations of his seminary and very different criteria for measuring its success. Thus, understanding the student's motives is important for understanding his expectations and, consequently, his evaluation of the seminary experience.

Most HUC-JIR students are professionally motivated. When asked the primary reason for enrolling in the rabbinical program, 80 per cent checked "desire for rabbinical ordination to enter the rabbinate." Consistent with this finding was that 90 per cent of the students expressed their firm or probable expectation of becoming congregational rabbis; the remaining 10 per cent were doubtful.

Many JTS and YU students stated that they had entered rabbinical school for other reasons. Only 39 per cent of the students at JTS and

22 per cent at YU said they had enrolled in order to receive ordination, while 34 and 62 per cent, respectively, said they had a "desire for a good Jewish education."

Certainly a good Jewish education is not incompatible with a rabbinical career. However, the fact that students at different seminaries chose such significantly different responses permits us to distinguish between career motivation and what may be called Jewish cultural motivation. Cultural motivation can also be distinguished from a second type of career motivation.

Eighteen and 11 per cent of JTS and YU students, respectively, listed a "desire for a scholarly education as a basis for an academic career" as the primary motivation for enrollment in rabbinical school. No student at HUC-JIR expressed this desire. Differences by year emerged only at JTS, where first-year students were more likely to have Jewish cultural motivation, and last-year students to be looking toward ordination. Whether this, in fact, was indicative of a change in the type of student entering JTS, or whether the JTS student develops an inclination for the rabbinical career while at the seminary and subordinates his former motivation, must remain an open question. The absence of more detailed data permits only conjecture.

Impressions gained by recruiters and admission officers, as well as conversations with the rabbinical students, contributed to a clearer understanding of the reasons for differences in responses. The career-oriented students at HUC-JIR want to become rabbis—Jewish professionals who "help people." Alternative careers for many Reform rabbinical students or young men planning to attend a Reform seminary are social work or teaching. But the rabbinate is particularly attractive because of its higher rewards, its potential for community leadership, and its opportunity for helping people within a Jewish context. Students were asked about aspects of the rabbinate that appeal to them most. To 70 per cent of the first-year HUC-JIR students it was the opportunity to preserve Judaism, to serve as leaders in the Jewish community, and to help people find faith. Only 16 per cent chose the opportunity to teach Torah, or to study and think. These views undergo some change during the seminary years.

At the other end of the spectrum it was to be expected that the primarily academically-minded YU students would show a preference for pursuits deriving from the study of the Talmud and sacred texts. Forty-five per cent of the first-year students checked the opportunity to teach

Torah or the opportunity to study and think as the most attractive aspects of the pulpit rabbinate.

The entering JTS student is more ambivalent than either the YU or HUC-JIR student. He too is desirous of a good Jewish education (33 per cent of the first-year students checked teaching Torah or the opportunity to study and think as the most attractive aspects of the congregational rabbinate), but he is also more career-oriented than the YU student. Moreover, the JTS student, more than the HUC-JIR and far more than the YU student, expects to find in the seminary solutions to problems troubling him with regard to faith, the meaning and nature of Judaism, the message of Judaism in the modern world, and the role of the rabbi. In a sense, the JTS student has the most serious cultural expectations and makes more ambitious intellectual and religious demands of his institution than other rabbinical students. And because JTS cannot always satisfy these demands, its students are the most dissatisfied of all rabbinical students.

A consideration of the manner in which the seminaries meet the expectations of their entering students and the changes that students undergo during their period of residence requires examination of formal and informal education and socialization in the various rabbinical institutions. Here the faculty and its relation to the students play an important role.

FACULTY

In general, rabbinical students have high regard for the teaching ability and scholarship of their faculty. At YU 30 per cent of the students believed the scholarship of most of their instructors to be outstanding, and 51 per cent good. Comparable figures for JTS were 66 and 30 per cent; for HUC-JIR, 51 and 44 per cent.

At both YU and JTS most of the permanent faculty members have never served as congregational rabbis. At HUC-JIR a much higher proportion, if not most, of the instructors had been ordained at HUC-JIR and served in the pulpit, though usually for a brief period. In no seminary, however, do more than a few instructors regard themselves as rabbis. In fact, with one or two exceptions, no instructor with both an earned doctorate and ordination uses the title rabbi. This is not necessarily a reflection of the relative status of academia and pulpit at the seminaries; at HUC-JIR the status of the congregational rabbi is equal to that of the faculty. Rather, the faculty members themselves, whether or not they have served in the pulpit or are members of a rabbinical body, look upon themselves primarily as members of the fraternity of Jewish scholars, not of American rabbis. (The talmudical faculty of RIETS is, of course, a special case. However, their world is that of the masters of the Talmud and the *rashe yeshivot*, not of the congregational rabbi).[16]

Until fairly recently, the mobility of Judaica scholars has been very limited. Nevertheless, nearly all who did leave their teaching post in a seminary entered other academic institutions, not the rabbinate. The prestige of faculty members comes from reading papers at scholarly meetings or publication in scholarly journals, not from addressing lay or rabbinical groups or contributing to rabbinical journals. Consequently, the faculty tends to favor courses and programs of studies modeled on university liberal-arts or humanities programs rather than professional-school curricula. A faculty member will typically devote his energies to the potential scholars rather than to the future rabbis among his students. And the very fact that they are teaching in what might be viewed as a quasi-vocational institution leads faculty members to draw a careful distinction between their own teaching and scholarship, on the one hand, and what is oriented toward practical rabbinics, on the other.

It is important to understand this because much of the dissatisfaction and tension in the seminaries stems from the program's scholarly orientation. We will suggest reasons for this orientation, some of which apply to particular institutions, especially JTS. However, it should be remembered that more important than any unique institutional and environmental factors pushing for a scholarly program are the faculty members' identity and self-image.

CURRICULUM

Orthodox Yeshivot

STUDY OF TALMUD

Students at Orthodox yeshivot study Talmud to the almost total exclusion of all other subjects. It is a vast corpus of law, theology, philosophy, story, and history, comprising sixty tractates. Our printed editions in-

---

[16] For a discussion of the consequences of this aloofness of the talmudical academy leaders from the world of the Orthodox rabbi see Immanuel Jakobovits, "Survey of Recent Halakhic Periodical Literature," *Tradition*, Winter 1965-Spring 1966, pp. 95–101.

clude basic commentaries on the text. The traditional yeshivah method of Talmud study, in Orthodox institutions everywhere, invests study with deep religious significance. Ideally, study of Talmud becomes an immersion into halakhah, which lies at the heart of Judaism. It is a method very different from that used in the study of any other subject matter. At its best, it is an act of devotion as well as study, and may generate both emotional and intellectual religious commitment. It separates the world of the Talmud and the Oral Law from other aspects of life.

However, the YU student lives and studies in other worlds as well, and for the more secularized and less religiously devoted, the dichotomy evokes a sense of the irrelevance of Talmud and *halakhah*. For the more devoted students it creates a feeling that *halakhah* coexists with, but does not engage, the world. Thus there is failure to recognize the close interrelationship between *halakhah* and life, or the fact that *halakhah* cannot exist in a vacuum separated from the other social and psychological reality of man. While the rabbinical student, with eyes focused on a future career in the practicing rabbinate, already begins to struggle with this dualism, the life of the teacher of Talmud at a rabbinical institution, particularly of advanced courses, provides some escape from this dualism. It generates, at least superficially, a sense of the possibility of living in the halakhic rather than in the secular world. The price exacted is an inability to communicate meaningfully not only with the vast majority of Jews who reject the assumptions about the importance of *halakhah,* but also with those among the Orthodox who refuse to accept the reality of a halakhic world separated from any other reality.

Although to students of YU especially, the Talmud is a living document, some of them see little connection between it and other aspects of their lives. Of course, the same may be said about other textual studies at other rabbinical seminaries. The fact that a text is studied "scientifically" does not necessarily make it meaningful or relevant, particularly to students with non-scholarly career motivations. In one respect, Talmud at RIETS is more meaningful and relevant than most other academic subjects at other rabbinical institutions, since it is certainly pertinent to some aspects of the student's religious life. But from another point of view, this only exacerbates the problem. Bible, or Midrash, or Hebrew literature may be instructive, but nobody really expects it to be a way of life. Nor do these subjects make such demands. But if Talmud is in fact the Oral Law, then for the Orthodox student it is the essence of Judaism; and if it does not have meaning or significance for the totality of one's life, then a gap is perceived. In this respect, the problem of Talmud for the YU student is paradigmatic for the problem of Judaism in America. If one believes that Judaism is what it claims to be, one must believe as a matter of faith that it has something to say to the total situation of man. Still, one is not quite sure what it does have to say. Furthermore, even if one knows what Judaism has to say, there still remains the problem of how many are prepared to listen.

SECTARIAN YESHIVOT

Our study was directed only to YU, as the largest institution for the training of rabbis. There are many other advanced yeshivot where students may prepare for ordination but, except for the Hebrew Theological College (HTC) at Skokie, Ill., whose program is similar to that of YU, they are under sectarian Orthodox auspices.[17] The best known among these are Mesifta Tifereth Jerusalem, Yeshivah Torah Vodaath, Yeshivah Ner Israel, Rabbinical Seminary of America, Rabbi Chaim Berlin Yeshivah, Rabbinical College of Telshe, Beth Medrash Govoha of America, and the Rabbi Jacob Joseph School and Mesifta. Most of these institutions offer almost exclusively courses in Talmud, with Codes added one or two years before ordination.

Ten or fifteen years ago, a sizeable number of students from each of these institutions entered the congregational rabbinate. Today all these schools combined yield a bare handful who do so. Some may not have a single student in any one year who will enter the congregational rabbinate; some yeshivot actually discourage students from becoming congregational rabbis. In part, this situation results from the scarcity of vacancies in synagogues having *mehizot* (partitions separating men and women during prayer, required by Jewish law), and in part from a feeling that a congregational rabbi must necessarily compromise his religious principles when catering to the demands of his congregation. In consequence, graduates of these yeshivot are attracted to Jewish education, where the need for their services is more demonstrable and their private lives more their own. But most students do not even choose Jewish education, and those who do often combine teaching with the congregational rabbinate. The fact is that most students in these yeshivot attend college at night. Those who receive a college degree find alternative careers in

---

[17] For a more detailed listing and some discussion of these and similar types of institutions see Charles S. Liebman, "Orthodoxy in American Jewish Life," *American Jewish Year Book,* Vol. 66 (1965), pp. 21–97.

the secular world less demanding and financially more rewarding. They also appreciate the freedom to practice their religion intensely, without interference by the Jewish community.

Among the yeshivot offering studies besides Talmud and Codes as part of the *semikhah* program, a few provide a course in homiletics; but none has the elaborate programs or entrance requirements found at YU or HTC.

Since its founding in 1922 HTC has ordained some 350 rabbis, of whom about 90 are now serving in pulpits and 10 as either Hillel rabbis or civilian chaplains. In HTC, too, the proportion of ordained rabbis who enter the pulpit has declined in the last decade. At present no more than one or two graduates do so each year. In 1967 there were 18 students in the *semikhah* program, which had just been changed from a two- to a three-year course of study. Unlike all other Orthodox seminaries, with the exception of YU, HTC requires an undergraduate college degree from those who seek ordination. (The institution itself is a liberal-arts junior college which hopes eventually to expand into a four-year college). It also requires a Bachelor of Hebrew Letters (B.H.L.) degree from its candidates for ordination, given after satisfactory completion of required courses in Bible, history, Hebrew language and literature, philosophy, and education, as well as electives in such subjects as Zionism, Jewish music, Jewish art, and the Apocrypha.

To those who believe that a rabbi must be firmly rooted in all aspects of Jewish culture and civilization, besides having a comprehensive knowledge of Talmud, the program at HTC appears very desirable. It is of interest that the nontalmudic Jewish studies are called *hokhmat Yisrael*, literally "wisdom of Israel" but in fact the Hebrew equivalent of Wissenschaft des Judentums, a term of opprobrium in most of the yeshivah world.

The president of HTC, Dr. Simon Kramer, stresses in principle the importance of *hokhmat Yisrael* as part of the rabbinical curriculum. Yet the program has its problems. The students do not take their extratalmudical studies seriously, and devote little time to them. Class attendance is irregular and not enforced. The reason for this laxity is that the courses are considered to be not relevant to the mastery of Talmud, which is the core of the curriculum. Talmud instructors, in particular, view it as too time-consuming and unimportant. Where they acknowledge the importance of an area, such as Jewish history, they feel that it must be taught from a Jewish point of view rather than a "scientific" or neutral one. There is little communication and some degree of tension between the Talmud and *hokhmat Yisrael* faculty, and, for a variety of reasons, the system necessarily favors the Talmud faculty. Students at HTC, as at traditional yeshivot, are not there to prepare for a career, but to study Talmud. If they wanted to engage in other Jewish studies at an advanced level, they would not come to HTC. This applies to HTC even more than to YU. An instructor in Talmud who has taught at both institutions believes that the students at HTC are a more select group than those at YU. Some students attend YU because of parental pressure or because all their friends do. The Chicago area has a less religiously intense environment than New York, and therefore does not produce this kind of social pressure. Hence, students at HTC are apt to be highly motivated.

The study of Talmud is not only purposive in that the student seeks to master a text, to know it, or to be able to manipulate a sacred system; it is an expressive or emotional act, in fact the highest level of religious activity. Hence the instructor of Talmud also becomes a religious leader, and his influence is automatically more pervasive than that of instructors in other fields. Indeed, yeshivah students call their Talmud teacher "rebbe," the appellation for hasidic leaders who traditionally exercise charismatic as well as religio-legal authority. Dr. Eliezer Berkovits, who teaches at HTC, is one of the outstanding Orthodox men in Jewish philosophy, if not the outstanding one. He has pronounced and articulate opinions on contemporary issues; yet his influence over students at HTC is less than that of Talmud instructors. In 1966 Rabbi Aaron Soloveichik, younger brother of Rabbi Joseph B. Soloveitchik, left YU to become *rosh yeshivah,* or head, of the HTC talmudic faculty. Since his arrival he has had great influence, and his presence has, if anything, widened the gulf between the two Jewish programs. This is so not only because Rav Aharon (as he is known in the yeshivah world) is a great *talmid hakham,* with a particularly warm and attractive personality; his indifference, if not antagonism, to the *hokhmat Yisrael* program is all the more significant because he also holds college and law degrees from American institutions.

Rav Aharon has instituted major changes in Talmud studies, among them the systematization of the rabbinical program and its extension from two to three years. The program is now purposively organized around Codes and the relevant sections of the Talmud, for it is the primary responsibility of the Orthodox rabbi to resolve or respond to questions of Jewish law. A rabbi must know the Codes and the law, as reflected in the *Shulḥan 'Arukh* and other codes and commentaries, as well as the particular sections of the Talmud from which the Codes are derived if he is to judge what decisions in the Codes apply to the case before him. Rav Aharon has also added to the courses on Codes and Talmud those portions of the law which he thought particularly relevant to the contemporary Jewish community and the needs of the congregational rabbi. Thus, new courses dealing with Sabbath observance, marriage and divorce, and funerals and mourning, were added to encourage some students who were reluctant to enter the congregational rabbinate because they felt that they could not adequately cope with some of the more complex questions of religious law that congregants might pose. (Rav Aharon thinks that another deterrent for students was the shortage of *meḥizah* synagogues, and here there is little he can do. He has resisted pressure from the rabbinic alumni and the administration that he urge students to accept positions in synagogues with mixed pews in the hope of instituting *meḥizot* later on.)

The failure of the yeshivot to consider the specific needs of the Orthodox congregational rabbi was confirmed in conversations with YU students. A primary function of an Orthodox rabbi is to decide questions of Jewish law—to respond to private questions of congregants as to whether certain acts or procedures are permissible or prohibited under Jewish law. Students were troubled by their sense of inadequacy here. Of course, the easy way out for a conscientious but ignorant rabbi is to prohibit anything about which he is in doubt. But many students reject this alternative as unethical. The inability of Orthodox rabbinical graduates to resolve all questions of Jewish law is understandable, of course. The most complex questions were traditionally posed by less experienced and scholarly rabbis to greater authorities. But the feeling of a general inability to answer questions of religious law among the most talented and sincere young rabbinical students is a result of unsystematic and irrelevant rabbinical study programs at American seminaries. The changes instituted by Rav Aharon may therefore encourage more of his students to enter the congregational rabbinate.

Yeshiva University

GRADUATES

YU is the largest Orthodox institution for the training of rabbis, although there are institutions, such as the Beth Medrash Govoha of Lakewood, where more students are engaged in the full-time study of Talmud. YU has ordained approximately 1,050 rabbis. Of the 905 rabbinic alumni whose occupation is known, 380 are full-time congregational rabbis in good standing and 13 are military chaplains (38 per cent in all). Fifty-six other rabbinic alumni are not in good standing because they have accepted pulpits or engaged in activity not sanctioned by YU—primarily those who have joined the (Conservative) Rabbinical Assembly or accepted posts in Conservative synagogues without the approval of YU. Some 200 ordained rabbis (26 per cent) are in professions unrelated to Jewish life.

ADMISSION REQUIREMENTS

YU has a three-year program leading to ordination. Students must be enrolled in both RIETS, which is the more important part of the program, and BRGS, the graduate school for Jewish and Semitic studies. Admission requirements include a college degree (almost all students are Yeshiva College graduates) and completion of talmudic studies in the undergraduate division of RIETS, or its equivalent.

TALMUD STUDY AT RIETS

RIETS begins at the Yeshiva University High School level and extends through the rabbinical program. Since the requirement for admission to RIETS at the college level is six years of intensive study of Talmud, the norm for the student entering the rabbinical program is ten years of Talmud three to five hours a day. Many, though not all, students have this background. A few transfer to RIETS from other Jewish programs at various stages of their high-school or college careers. Reasonably alert students find that, with some effort, they can make up their deficiencies at almost any stage—a commentary on the level of proficiency of the regular students. Indeed, given the number of years spent on Talmud, knowledgeable observers are surprised at how little many students know by the time they complete their undergraduate studies.

The average student entering the rabbinical program will have covered substantial portions of about ten of the sixty tractates of the Talmud.

More ambitious students may have gone beyond that on their own, but this is not an admission requirement. The absence of quantity is not the most serious problem: after all, a Jew has a lifetime in which he is expected to devote a part of each day to study. What the all-day Jewish school should have taught the student is the ability to study Talmud by himself, an ability he is not likely to acquire later. Independent study requires mastery of a method involving general principles and categories of thought, and it is here that talmudic training is weakest (p. 21 f.). We are not applying the criterion of "scientific method" in judging talmudic study at YU. It is by YU's own criterion that the resultant knowledge of Talmud has been unsatisfactory. Some rabbis ordained by YU, fellow students maintain, find it hard to master a page of Talmud without guidance. This failure must be ascribed to a general lack of emphasis on principles and concepts by many instructors—although the chief proponent of conceptualization, Rabbi Joseph Soloveitchik, is himself professor of Talmud at YU.

There are other weaknesses, aside from lack of conceptualization and method in YU's Talmud program, that carry over into the rabbinical program. A requirement for admission is completion of the work in the undergraduate division of RIETS. But lax standards in this division permit inadequately prepared students to enter the rabbinical program. Indeed, given the shortage of rabbis and the increased demand for them, there is a pressure against raising admission standards.

RIETS itself has no systematic program. In 1955 it made an effort in this direction by extending the ordination program from two to three years and requiring the study of major parts of three sections of the *Shulḥan 'Arukh* and relevant talmudic passages. Second- and third-year classes were to be conducted in a two-year cycle by Rabbi Soloveitchik. By 1962 the program was virtually abandoned and at present the study of Codes is emphasized only in the final year of the rabbinical program. Students learn just one part of *Yoreh De'ah,* which is the portion of the *Shulḥan 'Arukh* traditionally taught in all yeshivot in preparation for ordination. About half the time is devoted to the laws of *shehiṭah* (slaughtering), although the growth of large slaughtering and kosher packing houses makes it unlikely that most rabbis will ever be called upon to decide such questions. Besides, recently ordained rabbis are probably not competent to do so anyway. The Sabbath laws, marriage and divorce laws, and laws of family life and family purity are largely neglected. In the absence of an integrated talmudic program, it sometimes happens that students learn even the few sections of the Codes that are taught without ever having studied the related portions of the Talmud.

No one at YU has major responsibility for directing the rabbinical program, or even the rabbinical program within RIETS, much less for coordinating the RIETS and BRGS curricula. The program is not structured to prepare Orthodox rabbis; in fact, it is not structured at all. Decisions about who teaches or what is to be taught are often made on the basis of the instructor's seniority or the predilections of a few. The tendency of some of the instructors to focus attention on the few gifted students and to neglect the others creates more difficulties.

STUDENT EVALUATION OF THE TALMUD PROGRAM

Despite the lack of system and concern in the Talmud program, the students are not appreciably unhappy with it. They entered the program in order to study Talmud and, for better or for worse, that is what they are doing. Students are expected to, and indeed do, supplement class lectures with personal study, alone or in groups. Forty per cent of the students reported that they spend two to three hours daily in preparation and review for their class in Talmud, and 32 per cent over three hours. Fifty-seven per cent of the students characterized these classes as exciting or enjoyable; 34 per cent said they were only fair, and 17 per cent found them dull. Finally, 82 per cent of the students thought that in general the right amount of emphasis was being given to Talmud; 16 per cent felt there was too much emphasis. Despite all shortcomings, most students today know Talmud better than a decade ago. This can be ascribed to their more intense commitment to Talmud, their greater willingness to devote extra time to their studies, and better high-school and college preparation.

THE YU KOLEL

Indicative of the improvement was the institution in 1962 of the *Kolel* special program for students desiring a more intensive study of Talmud than the rabbinical program offered. Twenty-five students were enrolled in 1967, representing about a quarter of each class. All students in the program receive fellowships and devote a minimum of four additional hours each day to the study of Talmud. The offer of financial incentives to some of the best students enhanced the status of talmudic proficiency among all rabbinical students and doubtless raised the level of talmudic study. YU feels that the *Kolel* produces at least a few potential *talmede hakhamim* each year. Students in the *Kolel* report that they are somewhat less likely than those not in the program to hold positions as congregational rabbis; among its last-year students, only 33 per cent answered "yes" or "probably" to the question whether they ever expected to do so. Most expected to teach. By contrast, 75 per cent of the non-*Kolel* last-year students expected to hold positions as congregational rabbis.

BERNARD REVEL GRADUATE SCHOOL (BRGS)

Talmud constitutes the major part of YU's rabbinical program, requiring students to spend from nine in the morning until three in the afternoon, Sunday through Thursday, attending lectures or preparing for them. However, courses other than Talmud, Codes, and homiletics have been made mandatory since 1945. For ordination students must also earn an M.A. (Master of Arts) or M.H.L. (Master of Hebrew Letters) from BRGS, or an M.S. with a major in religious education from the YU Ferkauf Graduate School of Humanities and Social Sciences. As an alternative, students may enroll in a special program in selected areas of practical *halakhah,* begun in 1966, which is however confined to a small handful. Since 81 per cent of the YU respondents were in the BRGS program, we will confine our attention to that division.

An M.A. degree is granted to any qualified student enrolled at BRGS (formally a nondenominational institution), who has completed 14 semester courses and fulfilled the thesis requirement. The degree of M.H.L., designed for the rabbinical student who wishes to enter the rabbinate, is granted only simultaneously with ordination, after the student has completed 12 semester courses as well as six credits in supplementary rabbinic training, a department which is officially under the aegis of RIETS but virtually an entity unto itself. Many students who intend to enter the rabbinate prefer an M.A. degree because its thesis requirement lends it greater academic respectability and gives them a chance to continue working toward a Ph.D. at a later date. Some students also elect to enroll in supplementary rabbinic training courses.

The supplementary rabbinic training offers courses in practical rabbinics (with field work), homiletics, Hebrew, pastoral psychology, and practical *halakhah.* The last course, the most popular, deals with Jewish law in such areas as family life, marriage and divorce, birth control, intermarriage, and burial and mourning. The most frequent complaint of students is that this one-semester course, meeting for two hours weekly, is not extensive enough to prepare them for properly fulfilling the most important responsibility of the Orthodox rabbi. The regular Talmud program contains virtually no practical *halakhah.*

BRGS offers a wide variety of courses in Bible, Jewish history, literature, philosophy, sociology, Semitics, and Middle Eastern, and rabbinic and talmudic studies. Courses in Talmud are taught in a scientific, rather than traditional, manner: texts are examined historically and critically; differences between schools of thought are systematically developed; possible changes in the text, later emendations, and errors are discussed. However, exposure to the scientific method of study apparently has relatively little impact on most students, who generally are more at home with the traditional method of study, congenial to their religious point of view. Actually, time devoted to studies at BRGS is minimal, usually two courses per semester, each meeting for two hours weekly throughout the three-year *semikhah* program.

On the whole, the students do not take the BRGS program seriously. Fifty-five per cent of the students reported its academic standards to be below what would be expected of a scholarly graduate program; none thought they were higher. Supporting this appraisal is the fact that four hours a week spent in classes are barely supplemented outside the classroom. Fifty per cent of the students reported spending less than a half hour in preparation and review for every hour of classroom work, and 25 per cent between a half hour and an hour. YU students' evaluation of their Talmud studies in RIETS was considerably more favorable, with 38 per cent rating standards below those of scholarly graduate programs, but 19 per cent rating them as better. At the same time, the majority of students approved of BRGS instructors, 56 per cent rating most of them as very effective, and only 11 per cent as ineffective.

STUDENT EVALUATION OF RABBINICAL PROGRAM

Dissatisfaction with the content of courses and level of presentation is not confined to rabbinical students at YU. In fact, the general situation at YU is somewhat less tense than at JTS or HUC-JIR because the greater part of the students' time is spent in the traditional talmudical program, toward which they are highly motivated and which they find intellectually rewarding and religiously satisfying. Nevertheless, the YU student would like to see curriculum changes, and this is particularly true for those expecting to hold positions as congregational rabbis.

Our questionnaire asked the students to evaluate the preparation they were receiving for future careers. (The reader should be clear that we are dealing here, and in later sections, with the opinions of students, who may not be in a position to judge adequately their preparation for careers not as yet begun. This report, in general, tends to reflect student more than administration or faculty views). Of those who thought it likely that they would become congregational rabbis, 43 per cent called their preparation somewhat inadequate, 28 per cent fair, and 29 per cent good. Of those who did not intend to enter the pulpit, 35 per cent thought it inadequate, 30 per cent fair, and 35 per cent good. None considered it excellent (Table 5).

TABLE 5. YU STUDENTS' EVALUATION OF CAREER PREPARATION

(*Per cent*)

	Future rabbis		Non-rabbis	
	First-year	*Last-year*	*First-year*	*Last-year*
Good	40	18	31	43
Fair	20	36	31	29
Inadequate	40	45	38	29
No answer	0	0	0	0
	n* = 10	n = 11	n = 16	n = 7

* Number in the sample.

Students were asked to indicate on a given list of study areas whether the curriculum gave too much emphasis, about the right amount, or too little to each (Table 6).

The future congregational rabbis showed far more eagerness for the introduction of new areas of study than other rabbinical students. The majority thought that, except for Talmud and education (none appeared to mind that BRGS offered no education courses), too little emphasis was given to all areas. The most frequently mentioned were Bible (86 per cent), theology and philosophy (90 per cent), and comparative religion (90 per cent). It may then be assumed that the great majority of future rabbis believe their knowledge in these areas to be inadequate. But responses to an open-ended question revealed that they were most deeply disturbed by their ignorance of practical *halakhah*, which they ascribed to the curriculum's neglect of applied Jewish law and the use of the responsa literature.

Lack of attention to Bible has always been characteristic of yeshivot. What may be unique about YU is its students' discontent with this condition. According to one student, ". . . the lack of *ḥumash* [Pentateuch] requirement . . . results in almost unspeakable ignorance of things that

TABLE 6. YU STUDENTS' EVALUATION OF CURRICULUM EMPHASES

(Per cent)

Area of Study	Future rabbis			Non-rabbis		
	Too much emphasis	About right	Too little emphasis	Too much emphasis	About right	Too little emphasis
Talmud	14	86	0	18	77	5
Bible	0	14	86	0	13	87
Midrash	0	45	55	0	67	33
Codes and Responsa literature	9	36	55	0	52	48
Liturgy	0	40	60	0	70	30
Theology and philosophy.	5	5	90	0	26	74
History	5	38	57	0	77	23
Medieval Hebrew literature	0	47	53	0	68	32
Modern Hebrew literature	0	37	63	4	70	26
Hebrew language	0	40	60	0	65	35
Contemporary Jewish community	5	47	47	0	59	41
Education	5	60	35	0	77	23
Homiletics and practical rabbinics	0	41	59	9	61	30
Psychiatry and human relations	0	40	60	0	64	36
Comparative religion ...	5	5	90	0	44	56

a good eighth-grader should know." Of course, "ignorance" is a relative term. Students at YU are unfamiliar with modern textual and philological studies of the Pentateuch, much less with critical theories. They do know the simple interpretation of a Pentateuch text—although, with the exception of Rashi, most have not systematically covered the other traditional commentators. They are less comfortable with the Prophets and Hagiographa. It should be noted that the situation at JTS is similar, although its students use critical theory in studying substantial portions of the Prophets and Hagiographa. At HUC-JIR, enormous language difficulty poses a different type of problem.

Responsibility for the ordination of rabbis with poor backgrounds in Bible must be put partly on YU's failure to integrate its rabbinical program. True, students in the *semikhah* program are required to take Bible courses at BRGS. But BRGS, which is a graduate school, offers only specialized courses in Bible, and takes for granted that its students possess the necessary background. The rabbinical student has had Bible courses in the YU undergraduate school, which, however, were confined to two hours weekly of elementary, unsystematic presentation of material, and were not taken seriously. And, whereas the outside student with a comparable background in Bible would not be admitted to BRGS, the YU student is automatically admitted.

Of course, full blame cannot be put on the school and curriculum. Gaps in program will always exist, and it may not be unreasonable to expect students to supplement the formal curriculum with independent study. They will find no shortage of books on Bible and comparative religion; and since the study of Bible is a religious commandment, they should be engaged in it in any case. If students protest their ignorance of Bible, they themselves are in part responsible. Inadequate knowledge of practical *halakhah,* on the other hand, cannot easily be made up by independent study.

On the whole, YU students are guilty of the failing for which American college youth, generally, is criticized—an unwillingness to explore fields of study beyond formal class work and course assignments. Rabbinical students, it is true, often spend part of their time working (generally as teachers in Hebrew or Sunday school) and pursuing graduate studies at other universities. In fact, one attraction of the YU rabbinical program is that students have enough free time to undertake at least a half-time graduate program elsewhere. This, in itself, is a commentary on the nature of the rabbinical program.

Jewish Theological Seminary of America

GRADUATES

Since its inception JTS has ordained 814 rabbis, of whom 702 are still active. Of these, 427 (61 per cent) are serving in pulpits, 17 as Hillel directors, and 17 as military chaplains.

VALUES

JTS has undergone many changes since its founding and later reorganization under Solomon Schechter in 1902. It has increased its courses in practical rabbinics. In the last few decades it has also increased emphasis on Talmud, and, at the same time, introduced courses and curriculum changes reflecting the relatively poor Jewish educational background of its entering students in recent years. But JTS has not changed in one important respect. If anything, it has deepened its commitment to three dominant values not easily compatible with each other: commitment to religious traditionalism, to Jewish scholarship in an atmosphere of free inquiry, and to an indigenous and acculturated Jewish religion in America—Conservative Judaism. Much of our discussion of JTS here will center on the manner in which it seeks to reconcile the conflicting demands of these values.

The normal course of rabbinical studies at JTS is five years, but in certain conditions may vary from four to six years. Students need not spend the entire time at JTS. They may receive credit for a year's work at the Jerusalem JTS center or, by special permission, elsewhere in Israel. The entering student must first enroll in the School of Judaica for one to three years, depending on the level of his Jewish knowledge. Upon completing the third-year studies at this school and passing a comprehensive examination, he receives the M.H.L. and is ready to enter the three-year Graduate Rabbinical School. (At this point some students may be asked to leave the institution.) Ordination follows completion of graduates studies.

ADMISSION REQUIREMENTS

Admission requirements are rigorous and sometimes discourage students from seeking application. For placement in the School of Judaica, a candidate must have an undergraduate college degree and pass interviews with an admissions committee, as well as subject-matter examinations in Talmud, Bible, Hebrew, Jewish history, and Jewish thought. It appears that a student with a good education in an all-day Jewish secondary school, who has done a little independent reading in Jewish thought, should qualify for admission into third-year studies.

Generally, private conversations between the applicant and a member of the admissions committee precede the formal interview and tests. Their purpose is to determine the student's interest and proficiency in Jewish studies and his ability to function as a rabbi, educator, or scholar. He may be questioned on his observance of Jewish law, although the committee is more interested in his commitment to future observance than in his past practice. The stress is on Sabbath, festivals, and *kashrut*. In this spirit, students are required to sign the following statement in the application form:

A student in the Rabbinical Department must be a member of the Jewish faith. He is expected to conduct and fashion his life according to Jewish law and tradition, including the moral standards taught by the Prophets and the Sages of Israel, the observance of the Sabbath and Festivals, daily prayers and dietary laws. It is the hope of the Faculty that each student will continually deepen his commitment to, and understanding of, Jewish faith and life.

I have read the requirements for admission to the Rabbinical Department and I believe that I am qualified to apply.

For purposes of admission, areas where Conservative norms differ from those of Orthodox Judaism—such as eating fish purchased in a non-kosher restaurant—are left ambiguous. However, JTS policy follows Orthodox rather than Conservative norms. It is noteworthy that candidates finding it difficult to choose between JTS and HUC-JIR are advised to apply to HUC-JIR.

CURRICULUM

The School of Judaica concentrates on the study of Bible texts, Hebrew, Midrash, Codes, and Talmud. About 20 hours a week are spent in classroom instruction (half of these in the study of Talmud), as compared with eight to ten hours a week in most graduate-school programs, and with the normal 15 to 16 hours a week in undergraduate schools.

The Graduate Rabbinical School also stresses Talmud, but offers additional courses in such fields as Bible, philosophy and history, which are mostly textual in nature. In addition, it offers 38 credit hours in practical rabbinics—homiletics, speech, education, pastoral psychiatry. The speech course is taken in the senior year and focuses on a sermon presented by each senior at Sabbath services in the JTS synagogue.

Pastoral psychology, the most ambitious, is taught by a group of psychiatrists. They attempt to give the students theoretical and practical experience in aspects of human behavior that may come within the rabbi's domain, and to make them aware that at a certain point the help of a professional psychiatrist may be needed. The program has recently been extended under a grant from the National Institute of Mental Health. For various reasons, however, students do not take this program seriously. A report prepared by JTS for the National Institute of Mental Health states that, according to the instructors, students feel threatened by studies which, "by emphasizing the biological and the system in the psychological, undercut moral and ethical and religious views of life and behavior determination." Students particularly "resented Pastoral Psychology because by tempting them to reach out to it, it demonstrated to them in an unwelcome way the shakiness of their religious position" —a condition resulting from a failure to integrate sufficiently their theological assumptions with those of behavioral psychiatry. Students are also aware that a few members of other departments feel "a certain hostility or perhaps even contempt for the course in Pastoral Psychology, implied rather than expressed." Other instructors "have serious questions about the value of the course" [18] although it was approved by the administration.

It is likely that those instructors treat pastoral psychology as trivial not because they feel that psychology and religion are incompatible, but rather because it is not textual in nature and is oriented toward practical rabbinics. Seminaries value scholarship more highly than professional training. At JTS, in particular, the scholar, not the rabbi, has the highest status. In consequence, while every other institution thinks of the rabbi, at least in part, as a teacher, the JTS leadership makes the role of the rabbi analogous to that of the professor in an effort to define it as scholarly. However, a clear distinction is made between the status of the congregational rabbi and the scholar.

SPECIAL PROGRAM

Students in the JTS Graduate Rabbinical School may, with permission, enroll in a "special program" permitting them to concentrate on one area of Jewish studies to the exclusion of other courses, such as practical rabbinics. When the program began in 1957 as part of the Lehman Institute, it offered only talmudic studies. The expectation was that its students would go on for Ph.D.s, and that most of them would eventually teach Judaica either at JTS or at colleges or universities.[19] It was assumed that those choosing the congregational rabbinate as a profession would become leaders of the Rabbinical Assembly, the organization of Conservative rabbis, by virtue of their greater scholarship. It was further believed that their greater exposure to Talmud would make them more traditional in religious observance. (JTS, like traditional yeshivot (p. 21 f.), looks upon the Talmud as the core of Judaism—the Oral Law, which, unlike the Bible, the Written Law, remains the unique possession of the Jews. The Talmud is considered as basic to an understanding of Jewish religion and theology, and, since the Talmud is the essence of tradition, also of Jewish history.)

---

[18] Jewish Theological Seminary of America, *Final Report For Submission To the Pilot and Special Grants Section Training and Manpower Resources Branch, National Institute of Mental Health* (mimeo., September 1966), pp. 44, 45, 22, 34.
[19] For the growing demand for Jewish scholars, see Arnold J. Band, "Jewish Studies in American Liberal-arts Colleges and Universities," *American Jewish Year Book*, Vol. 67 (1966), pp. 3–30.

Despite this high regard for talmudic scholarship, until recently JTS has been unable to produce talmudic scholars. In a sense, the problem is one of self-image, for the challenge to produce talmudic scholars comes not from outside, but rather from within JTS, which is desirous of enlarging its talmudic faculty and of countering the threat to its leaders' view of their own enterprise. JTS is simultaneously an institution of Conservative Judaism and a school for Jewish research and scholarship. Its chancellor is also the leader of the Conservative movement, and no fine distinctions between these two roles is possible. But if talmudic scholarship stands at the top of Jewish values as essential for Jewish survival, how is one to evaluate the Conservative movement, which cannot produce the leadership for survival? Since Dr. Louis Finkelstein became chancellor, about a generation ago, JTS has been placing more and more emphasis on Talmud in the curriculum, and appointed talmudists to the permanent faculty to fill vacancies in other fields. The introduction of the special program was the most ambitious move in this direction.

The program was also justified as an instrument for the preparation of future Judaica teachers; but this, in itself, does not explain why it was first exclusively devoted to Talmud, the subject in least demand at colleges and universities, or why participating students were given financial and prestige rewards. Some excluded or non-participating students have charged, no doubt unfairly, that participants were selected not so much for their intellectual competence as for their ritual observance. Student resentment abated substantially when JTS added special programs in Bible, philosophy, and, most recently, history, with fellowships made available and the possibility of substituting advanced seminars in special fields of interest for courses in practical rabbinics.

Since its inception, 46 students have completed the special program at JTS. Of these, 26 hold teaching or administrative positions in institutions of higher learning (primarily JTS), in a few cases combining this with graduate studies at other institutions in preparation for academic careers. It is too early to tell whether the special program will produce outstanding talmudists and rabbinical leaders, or religiously committed scholars in the academic world. One thing is certain: its development creates, within the student body, a group favorably disposed toward JTS's textual emphases in the curriculum and more readily socialized to the values of JTS than to those of the Conservative rabbinate.

JTS AND THE CONSERVATIVE MOVEMENT

JTS is thus committed to Conservative Judaism, Jewish scholarship at the highest level, and religious traditionalism; and its program, in the broadest sense, can be viewed as the pursuit of these values and the mitigation of the tensions among them. At JTS new programs and ideas are evolved at a more lively pace than at YU or HUC-JIR. Many are never tried; others are tried and fail. But programs and ideas that take root, regardless of origin, attempt either to promote the values of JTS or to resolve its dilemmas.

JTS is that institutional part of Conservative Judaism which trains the movement's professional leadership. The other segments of Conservative Judaism are the associations of professionals (educators, cantors, and, above all, rabbis, the latter organized in the Rabbinical Assembly [RA]) and the congregational laity, organized in the United Synagogue of America. The Reform movement has parallel institutions, as does Orthodoxy, although the latter's institutions are not so neatly divided. Yet there is a great difference between JTS's role in the Conservative movement and HUC-JIR's role in Reform, or YU's role in Orthodoxy.

JTS is more than an educational or professional institution, it is Conservatism's dominant institution and, as such, asserts the right to determine the movement's ideological-religious policy. JTS argues, for example, that it must control the Ramah and United Synagogue camping programs, or "The Eternal Light," a television series on Jewish life sponsored by the Conservative movement. This control by JTS is based on the premise that all programs must accurately reflect the teaching of tradition. It is legitimized by pressing the notion that scholarship is central to Jewish life; that a scholarly institution is best able to understand the tradition and guide its application, and that JTS, as Conservative Judaism's scholarly institution, must therefore be central to the movement and exercise the power derived from this position.

Control is maintained through creating the proper climate within JTS as well as within the Rabbinical Assembly and the United Synagogue. The rabbinical students and future rabbis are socialized to the value of scholarship and the centrality of their seminary. More importantly, a sense of group belonging develops between students, faculty, and administration, which ties everyone to JTS regardless of ideological positions. A network of personal relationships evolves between rabbis and JTS in which role distinctions are blurred: rabbis do not relate to JTS only as professionals; they always remain students, as well as rabbis, and their former instructors may continue to play the role of mentors, confidants, friends, and even father figures. Crucial for most rabbis is the personal approbation of JTS faculty members and, especially, of Dr. Finkelstein.[20]

The United Synagogue is controlled through the JTS executive leadership. The type of persons in leadership positions, their presence in the JTS building, and the nature of JTS support and supervision insure that the congregational association will not adopt an independent position. Funds for both the United Synagogue and the RA are raised in a unified campaign and allotted by JTS. Thus there can be no question that Dr. Finkelstein is the leader of Conservative Judaism. (In contrast, neither Orthodoxy nor Reform Judaism has a single leader. Orthodoxy's outstanding spokesman, when he chooses to exercise this role, is Rabbi Joseph B. Soloveitchik. As for Reform, most people, if forced to name a single spokesman, would probably think of Rabbi Maurice N. Eisendrath, president of its congregational group, the Union of American Hebrew Congregations. Neither of these is head of his movement's seminary.)

But if JTS controls the Conservative movement, then it must bear a responsibility for its religious practices. Yet, in religious ideology a gulf divides JTS from the laity and even the rabbis. The ideological leadership of JTS emanates from Dr. Finkelstein and Professor Saul Lieberman, the rector. Recognition of Professor Lieberman's leadership is based on his reputation as the leading Jewish scholar in America and, outside the traditional yeshivot, also as the foremost talmudic scholar in the world. Both Finkelstein and Lieberman are Orthodox in public behavior and professed belief. Indeed, on some questions of religious law, Lieberman's interpretation is said to be more uncompromising than the prevailing halakhic opinion within American Orthodoxy. Since the imposition of ideological and religious control by JTS on the Conservative movement would probably have created a schism, there has been decentralization of ideological control and substitution of institutional for ideological loyalty. The result is that in principle JTS asserts its right and the need to exercise control, but in practice ignores deviations among its rabbis or laymen by denying that it exercises control in the case in question.

JTS does not in fact have the authority it claims for itself and under

---

20 On the personal relationship and importance of JTS faculty and leaders to Conservative rabbis see Sklare, *op. cit.*, pp. 185–90. On the whole, Sklare sees this relationship as analogous to one of a parent (JTS) and child (rabbi), with all the mutual ambivalent emotions that go with it.

which many Conservative rabbis allegedly chafe. For instance, ideological content of "The Eternal Light" is bland and uncontroversial, and requires no control. And at the Ramah camps, which function within certain broad guidelines, the really crucial ideological issues—the relative stress on particular Jewish or universal humanitarian values—are decided by each camp director. Even within the walls of JTS, the student is permitted a great deal of latitude in defining his religious obligations. When Dr. Finkelstein proposed to distribute time clocks to all students for the automatic control of electric appliances on the Sabbath, as required in Orthodox practice but not by Conservatism, potential RA opposition was acknowledged. A compromise was reached by making these devices available to students who wish to have them, and withholding from the faculty information on who does or does not use them. RA has extensive autonomy, its law commission functions independently of, and at times contrary to, the wishes of JTS leadership. Many of RA's restrictions, therefore, are self-imposed.

JTS stands as a force for religious traditionalism in Conservatism and, as such it has prevented many deviations from Jewish law within the framework of its commitment to institutional survival. Significantly, however, its success has often been in the institutional rather than ideological sphere. Although observers believe that there is sympathy for the Reconstructionist position, at least among a small number of RA members, that movement is unable to obtain enough rabbis for its handful of synagogues. The reason is said to be that RA members are unwilling to confront the institutional wrath of JTS that serving a Reconstructionist synagogue might invoke. Yet they do not fear reprisals for nontraditional interpretation of Sabbath laws, ignoring laws of family purity, urging changes in *kashrut* requirements, or denying belief in the divine revelation of the Torah.

JTS AND ITS FACULTY

The ideological gulf between JTS and the Conservative movement with regard to the religious practices and beliefs of Conservative rabbis is not the only religious dilemma for JTS. In resolving the problem of what its Conservative identification means, JTS must also find a way to bridge the ideological gap between its leadership and many members of its faculty. All permanent faculty members are ritually observant in their public behavior, but many are far more liberal than the JTS leadership in personal practice and belief. These faculty members are not merely paid employees fulfilling their professional responsibility as teachers; they also have ideological and religious convictions, notably that Conservatism should offer real alternatives to Orthodoxy. A partial solution of this problem is JTS's attempt to replace such faculty members, when they leave or retire, with others who appear to be closer to traditional Judaism.

In greater part, ideological differences are overcome through commitment to a different value which commands perhaps the strongest loyalty at JTS—scholarship and academic freedom. It would be a gross travesty of truth to suggest that this commitment is but a device for bypassing ideological differences. At the same time, this historically deep-rooted commitment is functional in that it legitimizes JTS as the central institution of Conservative Judaism while preventing an eruption within the institution. As long as both faculty and administration agree on the primary importance of free inquiry and scholarship, they have the basis for a consensus lacking in religious ideology. Thus, for example, one justification for having had Mordecai Kaplan on the JTS faculty, despite the impact his heterodox teaching may have had on future rabbis, was that his exclusion would have constituted a breach of academic freedom.

However, free scholarly inquiry does not necessarily advance teaching. Scholarship means research and publication, for which a price must be paid. Above all, it requires an expenditure of time that often makes faculty unavailable for consultation and discussion with students. Stress on the value of scholarship also leads to reduced emphasis on more vocational courses, or even theology and philosophy. Here the particular nature of scholarship at JTS must be considered.

TEXTUAL NATURE OF THE COURSES

Scholarship at JTS, and this applies to teaching as well, is primarily text-oriented. This means that the presentation of much of the material takes the form of a careful reading and philological analysis of the text. As one of our respondents put it, students in a particular Bible class have given up hope for a discussion of the message of a Prophet that was being read, or even of the meaning of any one chapter in the Bible. They consider themselves fortunate if the instructor discusses the content of any one sentence; he is more likely to dwell on the derivation and interpretation of single words.

While students realize that mastery of the material requires technical virtuosity, this method of instruction offers little intellectual stimulus or challenge. They find it arduous and, at the same time, elementary. Fifty-nine per cent considered the academic standards of their courses to be below what they would expect in a scholarly graduate program. Among last-year students, 79 per cent held this view. Since the JTS student is generally bright and intellectually motivated in the pursuit of his secular and Jewish interests, he must find intellectual satisfaction outside JTS, or at least outside its formal program.

A number of reasons may be suggested for the emphasis on text: It is the traditional way of teaching a classical curriculum, the way the professors themselves were taught. It makes teaching easier, for knowledge of the text is the professor's stock in trade, his specialty, requiring least effort though not necessarily least time in preparation. It eliminates ideological divisiveness, because the instructor need not give a personal interpretation of the material, which might conflict with that of another instructor or of JTS leadership. The words are more important than the ideas they convey. Perhaps most importantly, mastery of the text is a necessary tool for scholarship and original research.

While compared with most young Jews or students at HUC-JIR students entering JTS have a good Jewish educational background, the instructors find them on the whole to be ignorant of some basic Jewish sources and incapable of pursuing serious independent study. A student beginning graduate work in social sciences or humanities will, within three or four years at most and at times within a year or two, be able to make a scholarly contribution to his field. Rabbinical students are unable to do so after six or seven years of study. In part, this discrepancy exists because seminarians must absorb a greater mass of material, in part because, unlike other graduate students, they work part-time in fields unrelated to Jewish scholarship and in fact are not really full-time students. Most rabbinical students will never sufficiently master the texts to do creative research. Yet knowledge of text continues to be stressed as both an essential of Jewish scholarship and the ultimate test of a religious Jew.

In this sense, too, JTS reflects the traditional yeshivah concepts of learning and study as the highest Jewish values. It also retains the traditionalist notions of the relative value of the texts, with Talmud primary and Bible secondary. JTS differs from the traditional yeshivah in the inclusion of other subject matter and in the manner of teaching texts. For the average student the stress on texts is not satisfactory, since he will never sufficiently master them or feel entirely comfortable with them. At the same time this emphasis precludes treating these texts, whether Bible,

Midrash, Talmud, or Codes, in a manner more useful to the practicing rabbi and more relevant to his Jewish concerns.

The emphasis on text, while establishing a value consensus among faculty members, also creates problems for them. It establishes a status hierarchy—or one that is perceived as such—that encourages instructors who are less textually-oriented or whose fields of interest are more peripheral to classical Jewish studies to accept posts at colleges and universities offering greater financial and status rewards. In the last decade JTS has lost a number of its most promising faculty members to other institutions, and some have never been replaced with specialists in their particular fields.

Yet the emphasis on text, as we have seen, provides a link between JTS and the Conservative movement's lay and rabbinical bodies. Separated, and even isolated, as JTS may be from the mainstream of Conservatism in religious-ideological matters, it is recognized as the foremost American institution for the pursuit of Jewish scholarship. As such, it lays claim to the support of all Jews.

STUDY OF TALMUD

The study of Talmud, or the orientation of most talmudic study at JTS, is scientific. It is a method that makes no explicit assumptions about the origin or ultimate source of the texts. It views the Talmud as an ancient text that is to be understood on its own terms, rather than by the imposition of categories of thought or general principles. Of course, this sophisticated method is not characteristic of most Talmud classes at JTS. Because of the students' lack of knowledge, the greatest effort is expended in trying to understand the simple meaning of the text. Most classes are therefore conducted on a more or less beginner's level. The distinction between the JTS and yeshivah courses does not lie in the teaching method, but rather in the goal toward which they are oriented.

Actually, not all JTS faculty are agreed on what the goal should be. Some, in fact, do not differ very much in their traditional orientation from yeshivah faculties. In the yeshivot, various approaches to the text may be, and have been, used. Since the time of the Gaon Rabbi Elijah of Vilna and his pupil Reb Hayyim of Volozhin, who in 1802 founded the Volozhin yeshivah that was the prototype of the 19th- and 20th-century Lithuanian yeshivot, the primary emphasis has been on a literal understanding of the text in the light of the early commentaries and normative halakhic practice. The text, as we have it today in its most popular printed edition, is assumed to be accurate. No one claims that variant readings or mistakes may not have intruded, but these are thought to be trivial. And while the Gaon was concerned with correcting the text, this function has rarely attracted the energies of later talmudic scholars. Primarily, the traditional method seeks to increase the student's understanding of the text so that he may know the Oral Law.

Although the study of Talmud is undertaken for its own sake rather than for the resolution of practical legal questions, it is, particularly in the Lithuanian tradition, oriented toward discovering the conceptual-legal principles in the text and in the *halakhah,* as we have it today. By assuming that such principles exist, this method runs the risk of "discovering" a principle where none may be, and of interpreting difficulties in the text to fit a preconceived notion. In fact this is the charge most frequently leveled against the Brisk tradition of study, whose outstanding proponent is Rabbi Joseph Soloveitchik, grandson of Reb Hayyim of Brisk (Brest Litovsk). There also is a pronounced tendency to ignore the nonlegal portions of the Talmud. Although no talmudist would ever admit it, the very de-emphasis of the speculative and philosophical midrashic and aggadic portions necessarily creates a hierarchy of values in which the latter take an inferior position.

The scientific method differs, though not perhaps on this last point. It is not oriented toward practical legal or halakhic application, at least manifestly. It rather attempts to uncover the text and the conditions under which the text evolved.[21] Of course, the scientific study is the application to the Talmud of a textual-philological method that can be used in the study of any text. There are various kinds of scientific method, including the linguistic and historical. Perhaps the most famous essay in English on one type of scientific approach is "The Significance of the Halacha for the Study of Jewish History," in which the late Professor Louis Ginzberg of JTS sought to explain the differences between the two great schools of early rabbinical thought, that of Hillel and of Shammai, by differences of class and socio-economic outlook and interest.[22] The

---

[21] On the scientific method, its assumptions, procedures, and goals, see Meyer S. Feldblum, "Professor Abraham Weiss: His Approach and Contribution to Talmudic Scholarship" in *Abraham Weiss Jubilee Volume* (New York, 1964) pp. 7–80.
[22] Louis Ginzberg, *On Jewish Law and Lore* (Philadelphia, 1955), pp. 77–124. Our discussion of this and other approaches is obviously not exhaustive. The scientific method has a history dating back to the Middle Ages. Orthodox scholars in America, Europe, and Israel have used it. Within the yeshivah world, however, it was either not tolerated or treated as minor.

historical and socio-economic method was developed further by Dr. Finkelstein in an exposition of the differences between the Pharisees and the Sadducees in the first edition of his *The Pharisees*.[23] (In a long introduction to a revised third edition of his book, Finkelstein rejects many of the underlying assumptions of the first edition.[24]) Scientific talmudists of today no longer believe that the evolution of the Oral Law can be understood exclusively or even primarily by reference to economic conflict and group interests—though these need to be taken into account. The socio-economic emphasis continues to find support, particularly among many Conservative and some Reform rabbis, because its assumptions suggest possibilities for radical changes in Jewish law: If particular social and economic conditions have molded Jewish law in the past, then changes in social and economic conditions should warrant changes in the law now. These assumptions, clearly, are similar to those of the classical Wissenschaft des Judentums.

A second approach to the Talmud might be called the comparative-law or comparative-institutions method, often associated with Professor Lieberman and his studies of the Greek and Hellenistic influences on Judaism.[25] It seeks to understand the text through an understanding of the institutions and modes of thought in the Greco-Roman world, in which the Talmud came into being. The rare use of the comparative method in yeshivot can be ascribed in part to their talmudists' ignorance of the classical world, and in part to the radical conclusions it can suggest—that Jewish law is not primarily a product of the rational exegesis of revealed law. Yet, in the last analysis, while an understanding of the Greco-Roman world opens up doors to the understanding of the Talmud, for the talmudist it remains ancillary.

The third approach is the text-critical method associated at JTS with Professor David Weiss, and found in Lieberman's writings. It rests on the belief that the talmudic text has undergone various changes not only since its codification but, more significantly, in the very process of formulation. Since the Talmud evolved over a period of centuries and its content was transmitted orally at first, errors crept into the text. Statements of one rabbi were attributed to another; parts of one sentence were com-

---

[23] Philadelphia, 1938.
[24] Phidadelphia, 1962, pp. xlvii–vxxxiv.
[25] Saul Lieberman, *Greek in Jewish Palestine* (New York, 1942), and *Hellenism in Jewish Palestine* (New York, 1950); see also Boaz Cohen, *Jewish and Roman Law: A Comparative Study* (New York, 1966).

bined with parts of another; arguments were not carried to their logical conclusions. The Talmud is made up of layers of material from different periods, highly condensed.

The text-critical method seeks to identify each layer, to identify authors of individual statements, and, where possible, to resolve apparent contradictions, and to reconstruct the original debates—with the aid of variant readings and interpretations in rabbinic literature. Textual criticism, then, requires an encyclopedic knowledge of Jewish sources, an accomplishment well beyond the students at JTS. Nevertheless, it is meaningful to a student who, while himself incapable of undertaking such research, can thereby begin to understand the ultimate goal of talmudic study. This understanding is important to the student in the special program.[26] The question, however, is whether he will ever reach this goal. And this poses the primary problem in motivation for Talmudic study.

The study of Talmud in the traditional yeshivah, we said, is the means to an understanding of the text or the law; it is also a form of religious experience. The religious value of study motivates the student, and his immersion in the text as an ongoing halakhic disputation, whose consequences are felt in the actual life of a Jew, reinforces his religious commitment. The characteristic price exacted by this motivation is the isolation of talmudic study from contemporary social reality and the assumption that there is a halakhic world extending from ancient Palestine to the contemporary world, which is self-contained and can exist separate from other realities.

Many Orthodox actually welcome this, as providing further incentive for involvement in the Talmud. Those who cannot accept the traditional yeshivah assumptions about the Talmud and the nature of talmudic study become alienated and choose alternative careers. Mastery of the Talmud, the *sine qua non* of religious leadership in Orthodoxy, makes religious leaders necessarily the most traditional in outlook; but this is a dilemma only for the less traditional elements within Orthodoxy. However, there is a second possible problem for Orthodoxy as a whole. If the text-critical school is right in its assumption that the received Talmud text is at some points inaccurate, then the *halakhah* which derives from these points is

---

[26] The text-critical method of study, as we noted, is also pursued in BRGS, at YU. But studies at BRGS are entirely separated from the core talmudic program at RIETS.

not the true Oral Law. How to solve that problem—if indeed it is one —must be left to the theologians.

It would appear on the surface that the text-critical approach offers an alternative method of study for students (both modern Orthodox and Conservative) who do not necessarily accept the traditional yeshivah assumptions about the Talmud. It might thus produce outstanding talmudists who are not of the religious right wing. But the matter is not so simple.

To be sure, there is nothing explicitly heterodox in the assumptions of that school. No one claims the Talmud text to be divine in origin; even the most traditional merely claim for it that it embodies the Rabbis' discovery of the unfolding Oral Law, revealed by God but written down relatively late.

Still, by uncovering the true text and demonstrating that our present text contains errors in transmission, the text-critical school might also discover that later rabbis were mistaken in their legal decisions. For its adherents this is not a serious problem. They argue that the *halakhah* today, even if at variance with the "real" Talmud, certainly has the sanctity of custom. And no one, they feel, would sensibly advocate radical halakhic change on the basis of textual emendations, for a textual change made today may be completely discredited tomorrow. There never will be absolutely convincing proof. At best, the emendations or clarifications of the critics can be used in special circumstances or in an emergency. There is, in fact, some precedent for this. The impact of the discovery of the works of a medieval talmudic commentator, Ha-Me'iri (Rabbi Menahem ben Solomon), brought no change in the *halakhah* even though, some rabbis hold, the *halakhah* today would be different if the early codifiers had had the Me'iri before them. The text-critical method, it may therefore be argued, will provide a basis for change only to the extent that its masters seek it.

Of course, this is true also of the traditional method of study. In fact, the imposition of particular categories of thought on the Talmud makes possible different interpretations of the text. It may therefore be argued that the text-critical method of study is no more radical in its implications than the traditional method. It constitutes a threat to the structure of *halakhah* only to the extent that those able to apply it may desire radical conclusions. But while the majority of Conservative rabbis might like to see more radical implications drawn, the talmudists are unwilling to do so.

It has been argued here that the scientific method is not necessarily radical. Whether or not this is so depends, in part, on initial perspective. It is possible for a Conservative Jew to view the Talmud with an open mind and even question Sinaitic revelation, yet accept the ritual law— because of a sense of obligation to, and participation in, Jewish history rather than belief in revelation and inspired exegesis. For him the text-critical approach does not present any ideological difficulty. On the contrary, he is apt to feel that that approach offers too little possibility of innovation and change in *halakhah*. If this is so, why would the student who is not deeply involved religiously want to undertake its study? The task is arduous, requiring years of concentrated work that can culminate only in the better understanding of an "ancient text."

For most committed Orthodox Jews the text-critical approach can raise serious ideological or, more properly, structural-psychological problems. They accept the *halakhah* as authoritative because they believe it to be intimately and directly related to revelation at Sinai.[27] An Orthodox Jew might accept with some equanimity the idea that a few laws may have an erroneous textual base, but the recognition of a large number of errors would cast doubt on the whole structure of authority of the *halakhah*. The quantitative would affect the qualitative.

What is more, the scientific method is *psychologically* not congenial for a traditionally-oriented student. By suggesting that rabbinic commentators have been wrong or misinformed on very fundamental questions, it can promote skepticism about the text and challenge the very essence of traditional learning, in which the religious dimension is not so much the study as the learning of the text.

Traditionalist scholars having some familiarity with the text-critical approach also argue that this method is misleading as well as dangerous; and that seeming errors in transmission are not necessarily errors but can be explained or understood—analytically, or dialectically. Essentially, however, textual criticism is too radical to attract the Orthodox, and too purely scholarly to have programmatic implications for an untraditional Jew. It remains, then, a tool for a small number of scholars in the United States and Israel.

---

[27] The fact that Orthodox scholars of the scientific school deny a traditional sanction for the application of this belief to more than a small portion of the *halakhah* is irrelevant to our concern. Such scholars are few in number.

STUDENT EVALUATION OF THE CURRICULUM

The textual orientation of the courses is the primary source of dissatisfaction among JTS students. Many found their courses uninspiring, and their preparation for the rabbinate inadequate, because problems raised by Jewish philosophy, theology, or the place of Judaism in the modern world are ignored. There was less dissatisfaction among students in the special programs, who were less likely to enter the rabbinate. Of first- and last-year JTS students, 51 and 32 per cent, respectively, thought it unlikely that they would become congregational rabbis.[28] Many of those who did not expect a congregational career were in special programs. (The existence of the special programs can suggest possibilities for alternative careers even to nonparticipating students, who otherwise might not have considered these alternatives.)

Students who did not expect to enter the congregational rabbinate (hereafter referred to as non-rabbis, although they all expected to be ordained) were less dissatisfied with the curriculum because they were less interested in solving Jewish problems than in preparing for future research. Among last-year students, 84 per cent of those intending to serve in the pulpit (hereafter referred to as future rabbis) rated academic standards as below the level they would expect in a scholarly graduate program, against 67 per cent of the non-rabbis. Their evaluations of career preparation showed significant differences between first- and last-year students, by career expectations (Table 7).

TABLE 7. JTS STUDENTS' EVALUATION OF CAREER PREPARATION

(*Per cent*)

	Future rabbis		Non-rabbis	
	First-year	Last-year	First-year	Last-year
Excellent or good	67	31	36	33
Fair	17	39	0	33
Inadequate	17	31	55	33
No answer	0	0	9	0
	n*=12	n=11	n=13	n=6

° Number in the sample.

---

[28] Our sample for the comparison of first- and last-year students by career orientation included only six last-year students who did not intend to become congregational rabbis. However, their responses generally confirmed our expectations, and we have confidence in the general validity of the finding, even though the actual, precise percentages may be unable to bear much weight.

The same pattern appeared in the students' evaluation of the relative emphases placed on different areas of the curriculum (Table 8). Thus

TABLE 8. JTS STUDENTS' EVALUATION OF CURRICULUM EMPHASES

(Per cent)

	Future rabbis			Non-rabbis		
	Too much emphasis	About right	Too little emphasis	Too much emphasis	About right	Too little emphasis
Talmud	44	52	4	12	76	12
Bible	4	64	32	0	59	41
Midrash	0	30	70	0	44	56
Codes and responsa literature	0	42	58	0	35	65
Liturgy	0	16	84	0	25	75
Theology and philosophy	4	29	67	0	44	56
History	8	60	32	0	59	41
Medieval Hebrew literature	0	30	70	0	44	56
Modern Hebrew literature	0	40	60	0	47	53
Hebrew language	4	32	64	6	29	65
Contemporary Jewish community	0	24	76	0	38	62
Education	4	52	44	14	57	29
Homiletics and practical rabbinics	16	52	32	38	31	31
Psychiatry and human relations	0	67	33	13	67	20
Comparative religion ...	0	13	87	6	19	75

the non-rabbinical students were satisfied with the emphasis on Talmud, while future rabbis thought there was too much. If we compare only last-year students, we find that more non-rabbis than future rabbis wanted greater emphasis on Hebrew language and medieval Hebrew literature, whereas, as could be expected, more future rabbis want greater emphasis on homiletics and practical rabbinics, education, and the contemporary Jewish community. On the other hand, even future rabbis were more critical of the lack of emphasis on academic subjects than on practical or professional subjects.

"RELEVANCE" OF THE CURRICULUM

The general emphasis on text at JTS is not without justification. It can be defended on the grounds of faculty preference and religious traditionalism, and as prerequisite for scholarly pursuits. It is also defended because the particular skills needed by the modern rabbi, counseling, administration, homiletics, are acquired primarily through experience and common sense. They cannot in fact be taught, nor are they particularly worthy of being taught.[29] Exposure to texts, to the basic sources of Jewish faith and knowledge, should broaden the future rabbi's outlook and make him receptive to the totality of the Jewish tradition.

This argument begs the question somewhat, since the students do not want practical rabbinics, but a more lively and provocative presentation in academically-oriented courses. Nevertheless, to those who believe in the classical Jewish tradition as both a guide to behavior and a treasure of human insight, the argument of the salutary effects of the rabbi's exposure to text has much cogency. The challenge to JTS, then, is to relate the tradition's wealth of resources to the modern rabbinical student. Whether responsibility for failure to do so lies with the faculty, the curriculum, the choice of text, or with the rabbinical student himself is another question.

The rabbinical student comes to his classical religious culture steeped in the intellectual processes and values of modern secularist society. JTS no longer attracts students from Orthodox or culturally traditionalist homes. Its student today is not very different in his intellectual outlook from the graduate of any good American college or university. He is open to religion, but his concepts of religious piety and values are as much a product of his exposure to the secular world as to his Jewish school and family life. This means, paradoxically, that the student's religious values have become christianized—because the earlier Christian culture has transferred many of its assumptions and presuppositions to the secular realm. He brings theological concerns to the seminary, but the context and language of these concerns are, at times only subtly, Christian in origin. He looks upon religious piety, theology, and social action as disjunctive, rather than conjoint with religious practice or the study of Codes.

JTS has yet to learn to cope directly with this problem. It has failed to do so not only because it prefers to shy away from the problem, but also—remarkably—because its leaders have so successfully solved the

---

29 For an analogous argument regarding the teaching of public administration, see Robert Hutchins, "Shall We Train for Public Administration? 'Impossible,'" in Dwight Waldo, ed., *Ideas and Issues in Public Administration* (New York, 1953), pp. 227–29, and Charles S. Liebman, "Teaching Public Administration: Can We Teach What We Don't Know?" *Public Administration Review,* September 1963, pp. 167–69.

problem for themselves. If Chancellor Finkelstein has one characteristic that distinguishes him from the leaders of the Orthodox seminaries, that is neither his piety, nor his scholarship, nor his fund-raising skill. It is, rather, his ability to integrate his traditionalist view of Jewish history and religion, his often simple ideas about American Jews and the American Jewish community, with an awareness and concern for universal moral values and human needs in a secular society.

Those closest to Finkelstein testify to his sincere belief in the importance of the JTS-sponsored interreligious programs, such as the Institute for Religious and Social Studies. These programs are not devices for fund raising or publicity, though they conveniently may serve this purpose. They stem, rather, from Dr. Finkelstein's conviction that Judaism has much to say to the world in its present condition about problems of both immediate and ultimate concern; that it has a distinct ethical message. This philosophy, however, and the type of public program undertaken by JTS find little reflection in the curriculum. For the chancellor, the interrelation of classical textual study and social ethics is obvious; the students can only wonder.

Hebrew Union College-Jewish Institute of Religion (HUC-JIR)

GRADUATE RABBIS

The combined Reform seminary has ordained approximately 1,200 rabbis, of whom 868 are active. Of these, 646 (74 per cent) occupy pulpits, 20 are military chaplains, and 28 Hillel rabbis.

THE NEW YORK AND CINCINNATI SCHOOLS

In 1954 the administration of HUC-JIR questioned the need for a full five-year rabbinical program in the smaller New York school on the ground that the duplication of facilities with Cincinnati was wasteful, and this no doubt was so. Plans to curtail the New York school's program were abandoned in view of strong opposition from both the Union of American Hebrew Congregations, the Reform congregational body, which wanted a New York-based institution mainly to provide student rabbis to the surrounding area, and from JIR alumni, who suspected an attempt to destroy the more traditionalist, Hebraist, and Zionist orientation of the New York center.

Differences between the New York and Cincinnati schools are still a touchy subject. There are complaints of discrimination against New York in the allocation of funds, in physical construction, filling vacancies on the faculty, and many minor matters. The beautiful campus of the Cincinnati center houses the rabbinical school as well as facilities for a variety of HUC-JIR activities. The New York center, on the other hand, has cramped quarters (which, however, are scheduled for expansion). The administration denies discrimination. It asserts that the Cincinnati center was enlarged first as part of an earlier expansion program, and that a shortage of funds did not permit execution of projected plans for New York. But there are many other, at times subtle, differences between the two schools.

While students admitted to HUC-JIR may choose either New York or Cincinnati, those in the New York school may transfer to Cincinnati, but not the other way around. Respondents differed on the reason for this policy, but there was general agreement that if students from Cincinnati were free to transfer, many would do so. There was less agreement on whether this was because students tired of dormitory life, of Cincinnati, or the Jewish atmosphere there. Some pointed out that the administration is located in Cincinnati and this, with the best intentions, necessarily limits the sense of freedom at the campus school. There is no doubt that differences between the two centers are exaggerated by some respondents, both faculty and students. But the exaggeration itself assumes reality when people believe it to be true, and act accordingly. Location has an important, if unintended, role in molding each student body.

It is only fair to report that some faculty members who have been at both institutions deny that real differences exist. Cognizant of the widespread belief within HUC-JIR that New York students are more traditional and have better Jewish backgrounds, they deny any evidence of it. Any differences suggested by the findings of this study, they argue, are peculiar to the particular classes sampled. They maintain that the existing standardization of admissions procedure and curriculum, and interchanging of faculty, have eradicated earlier distinctions. But not all say this. One teacher, ideologically identified with the Cincinnati school, put it simply: "The Jews go to New York and the Nordics to Cincinnati." These views apparently find credence elsewhere. Indeed, differences or expected differences between the centers affect the placement of rabbis; some Reform temples in the South will not accept rabbis ordained in New York.

It is a fact that students seeking a more Jewish atmosphere are attracted to the New York school. Its students are likely to come from the East, where exposure to different modes of Jewish life, ideas, and personalities is greater (though, as we have seen, the majority of students at the New York school come without much Jewish background). And they cannot avoid contact with the world around them, for the school has no dormitory facilities. Besides, some of the students who must support themselves as part-time teachers and temporary rabbis are necessarily directed outside the institution for their Jewish interests. By contrast, the Cincinnati center is more insular. Because off-campus Jewish life is generally shallow, the school can exercise a stronger influence. This continues to reflect, though less today than in the past, a midwestern American Reform tradition.

ADMISSION REQUIREMENTS

Cincinnati and New York have identical curricula, virtually identical requirements for ordination, and a single admission policy. Admission procedures are similar to those of JTS, though somewhat more elaborate, including a Rorschach test and a psychiatric interview. The Cincinnati and New York schools each has its own admissions committee, but the student may choose between the two centers after acceptance. (There is now a third center in Los Angeles, where students are offered only the first two years of study and from which they then transfer to Cincinnati.) Los Angeles students are not included in this report.

Students may be granted a year's leave of absence to attend HUC-JIR's Biblical and Archeological School in Jerusalem. At present it offers only two or three courses in rabbinics and, for this reason, the student must make up the year when he returns to the United States. Plans are under way to expand the course of study in Jerusalem so that a full year's credit can be granted.

HUC-JIR has an active program for recruiting candidates. A member of the administration is charged with the responsibility of visiting Reform temples and colleges and universities to talk to students about the possibility of study at the institution. This program, as well as the brochures prepared for recruitment purposes, stress the seminary's role in training Reform rabbis.

CURRICULUM

Most entering HUC-JIR students take an intensive eight-week Hebrew course at Cincinnati during the summer preceding their first year. The normal program leading to ordination requires five years of study, but students with good Jewish-studies backgrounds may receive advanced standing for one or, in rare cases, two years of work on the basis of written examinations. Undergraduates enrolled in some joint program of Jewish studies may expect to receive an advanced standing of one year. After the second year, students take an examination in Midrash, Bible, Talmud, modern Hebrew, liturgy, Mishnah, and commentaries. Those who successfully complete the examination are awarded the B.H.L. degree. Requirements for the M.A. degree and ordination are three more years of study, a comprehensive examination, and a written thesis.

HUC-JIR differs from both YU and JTS in its emphasis on the rabbinate as a career and on the denominational character of the school. At YU, Orthodox Judaism is assumed, Conservatism and Reform are simply ignored. At JTS, religious traditionalism is assumed, and by and large no official attention is given to the distinguishing characteristics of Orthodoxy, Conservatism, and Reform. HUC-JIR's school of education, on the other hand, offers a course in "Reform Judaism as a Way of Life," and a first-year requirement for all rabbinical students is a course called "Orientation to Reform Judaism."

HUC-JIR's stress on the practicing rabbinate is also reflected in the curriculum, although the relationship between the curriculum and the congregational rabbinate is rather complex. The course of study is based on a 1954 curriculum revision, which was a compromise between the curriculum until then in force, the interests of the faculty at that time, the subject matter some people thought a practicing rabbi must know, and past complaints.

Some 15 per cent of the courses are in practical rabbinics (human relations, education, speech, and homiletics). Students gain most of their practical experience through the required one-year service as part-time student rabbis, a program that simultaneously meets Reform Judaism's institutional needs by making available rabbis to small temples that cannot afford the services of full-time rabbis. Students also officiate and preach at HUC-JIR chapel services. The nature of these programs makes it difficult to judge exactly how much of the student's time is spent in "practical rabbinics." Some students and faculty feel that the courses in practical rabbinics impart only trivial information that deserves little serious thought and is of no practical value. But the discontent with the curriculum at HUC-JIR has nothing to do with practical rabbinics. No one disputes that students who are at the seminary to prepare for a pulpit career should be given the opportunity to take some professional or vocational courses. No one would further deny that these courses could probably be improved—though some of the criticism is based on the rather naive assumption that class work can fully prepare a rabbi to feel perfectly at ease and know precisely what to do when confronted with a practical situation.

The more critical problem is the presentation of academic subjects. Should courses in Bible, philosophy, theology, history, Talmud, have a purely scholarly approach? Or should they stress the practical by teaching future rabbis to interpret the concepts and practices of the Jewish tradition, or at least a carefully selected part of them, in a manner giving them contemporary relevance and meaning? But this is an oversimplification. The first alternative poses the problems of presenting the material to students who come with little background in Jewish history, classical texts, or Hebrew. The second alternative requires the teacher to take a philosophical or theological stand on Judaism that would permit him to offer judgments regarding the tradition and what is or is not relevant to it.

In the choice of curriculum and faculty, HUC-JIR has taken the scholarly approach. Its official position is that Jewish literature and lore are central to religion; that the rabbi must therefore also be a scholar, or at least strive to become one, even as he is engaged in his ministerial activity. For, the institution's leaders argue, the rabbi must know the sacred texts because he "can interpret modern life only in the light of Jewish literature and law," and must be able to do so authoritatively. He must, according to HUC-JIR's president, Dr. Nelson Glueck, "block off a portion of his life for creative Jewish studies," and it is the function of the seminary to prepare him for this task. To encourage such activity, in 1966 the Cincinnati school reduced the number of required courses, allowing students to take 20 per cent of their credits as electives and thereby concentrate on at least one area of study. The Cincinnati school's impressive and distinguished library offers more than adequate facilities. The leaders, then, see no contradiction between rabbinical responsibilities and scholarly activity.

But this still does not resolve all dilemmas. As one faculty member noted, there are two ways of studying Bible. You can stress the scientific method—biblical criticism and philology—to help in the scholarly understanding of the Bible. Alternately, you can study Bible with the traditional Jewish commentaries and thereby achieve the traditional Jewish perspective and understanding of the Bible. In fact, the method used actually depends on the proclivities of the instructor.

But the stress on scholarship offers no rational basis for choosing curriculum alternatives and, given the students' poor knowledge of classical Jewish sources, hard choices must be made. Because some students (and alumni) are unhappy with the general scholarly approach in the courses,[30] and others are merely seeking to acquire as much textual knowledge as they will need to function as rabbis, most students prefer instructors with an integrative-theological position, rather than a scholarly-textual one.

FACULTY

The faculty is divided by a wide range of religious belief and practice. Theological differences run the gamut from a kind of existential Orthodoxy to a thoroughgoing untraditionalism. In ritual practice, differences range from total nonobservance to basic observance of the laws of the Sabbath, *kashrut,* and prayer. Most of the faculty members are somewhere between the extremes and, at the Cincinnati school, closer to the less traditional end of the continuum. HUC-JIR is not unhappy with this diversity and is proud of its academic freedom.

The question some people ask of HUC-JIR is what are the limits of academic freedom. Dr. Glueck maintains that the institution would not hire a faculty member who did not accept the God idea, who did not think Israel is important, and who did not believe in the centrality of Judaism. The institution seeks, he says, "a proud, dedicated and passionately devoted Jew." In all other respects a faculty member has complete freedom. This provides a great deal of latitude. It permits the expression of views that even a student from a Reform home finds startling and radical in their challenge to the God idea—or in their suggestion that Reform Judaism is virtually a separate religion.

Curiously, the faculty are not entirely free from ritual obligation. Unlike the students (at least at Cincinnati), they are expected to attend chapel services on Sabbath morning and every weekday from 10:20 to 10:45, when no classes meet. Services are conducted by students, who, within certain guidelines, can organize them as they choose. The incongruity of a Reform institution requiring its faculty to attend religious services is not lost on the faculty. However, it is questionable whether this kind of subtle coercion—if such it is—is particularly religious in

---

[30] See Edgar E. Siskin, "Rabbinate and Curriculum," *CCAR Journal,* October 1967, pp. 2–5, 30.

intent. At least one outside observer, who, incidentally, was impressed and even moved by the services, found them to be as much an institutional ritual as a religious act. The impression was not of a group engaged in prayer or devotion, but rather of a group that met to reaffirm a common set of values and beliefs, if only by the very act of meeting. Of course, this too may be regarded as religion.

STUDENT EVALUATION OF CURRICULUM

The curriculum's general textual emphasis raises the problem of how the material can be mastered. The largest, most tedious obstacle is mastery of the Hebrew language, an obstacle which many students never overcome. Although the students generally know biblical Hebrew and most of them can sight-read passages from the Bible by the time of ordination, they are far from having facility in rabbinical Hebrew or, for that matter, in modern Hebrew. Most students cannot read with facility a modern like Ahad Ha'am, say, whose vocabulary and style are neither particularly difficult nor involved.

To the extent that the curriculum is purposeful, it is directed toward exposing the student to the totality of Jewish tradition so that nothing Jewish may remain foreign to him. The range of the subject matter is impressive, but the coverage has little depth. The curriculum, as one recent graduate stated, serves the function of showing the student how great an 'am-ha'arez (ignorant Jew) he is, and how likely he is to remain one. The student does not resent exposure to text, though he may feel unhappy about his inability to master it, or about the constant reminder by some faculty members of how little he knows. He would like to see more emphasis on preparation for the rabbinate, though he realizes exposure to the classical texts is part of that preparation.

To put it differently, the student at HUC-JIR wants a more challenging presentation of ideas and a greater emphasis on direct training for serving the needs of the Jewish community, as envisaged by the community (counseling, synagogue administration). On the other hand, neither the rabbinical student nor his institution believes that he must strictly adhere to congregational standards. The student comes to realize that he must also in some way, though not necessarily in ritual observance, serve as an exemplary figure in Jewish life, and this he cannot do if he is ignorant of Jewish sources.

The HUC-JIR student, perhaps more than the JTS student, is cognizant of his institution's problem—to secure both a solid classical Jewish education and a theology relevant to the modern Jew. Yet he is more passive than the JTS student. Unlike the latter, he is not apt to bring burning theological questions or problems of Jewish identity to his institution. The HUC-JIR student wants to be a rabbi so that he can help people, and he is quite prepared to defer to his institution's judgments of courses and curriculum. To be sure, he desires a change in content and emphasis—like the student at JTS, YU, or, for that matter, at any other institution of higher learning. The difference is that HUC-JIR students are not nearly as agitated about such matters as those at JTS, or even at YU. He knows that if he completes the prescribed studies he will become a rabbi, and this is his primary goal. Within this general context he expresses some dissatisfaction.

Students at HUC-JIR reported satisfaction with their career training. Forty-six per cent of the New York students rated it excellent, and 15 per cent good. At Cincinnati only 2 per cent thought it excellent, but 48 per cent considered it good. Unlike the situation at YU and JTS, the proportion of satisfied students did not diminish between the first and last years (Table 9). Yet 31 per cent of the New York students and 53

TABLE 9. HUC-JIR STUDENTS' EVALUATION OF CAREER PREPARATION

(Per cent)

	First-year	Last-year
Excellent or good	62	58
Fair	25	25
Inadequate	12	17
	n*=32	n=24

º Number in the sample.

per cent of the Cincinnati students felt that academic standards were below what they would expect in a scholarly graduate program. This could not be ascribed to lower work requirements. Students spend an average of 15 hours per week in class, and 78 per cent reported that they needed from one to three hours to prepare for every hour of class work. It is noteworthy that New York students, who must travel to school and have heavier outside work schedules, spend slightly more time in preparation and review. In general, the students registered a high opinion of ther instructors' teaching ability. Of the New York students, 85 per cent thought that most of them were very effective; only 9 per cent thought most of them ineffective. At Cincinnati, comparable figures were 49 and 7 per cent.

Striking differences between the two centers were found in student views of subjects receiving too much or too little emphasis. Since the curricula—except for the larger proportion of electives at Cincinnati—were identical, it is particularly instructive to compare the reactions of the two student bodies (Table 10). In the New York school a majority of students thought there was too little emphasis on Talmud, Codes, and comparative religion. Almost half felt this to be true also of Hebrew

TABLE 10. HUC-JIR STUDENTS' EVALUATION OF CURRICULUM EMPHASES

(Per cent)

	New York			Cincinnati		
	Too much emphasis	About right	Too little emphasis	Too much emphasis	About right	Too little emphasis
Talmud	0	46	54	5	68	28
Bible	15	69	15	14	81	5
Midrash	0	75	25	8	82	10
Codes and responsa literature	8	38	54	0	73	27
Liturgy	0	62	38	0	83	17
Theology and philosophy	0	77	23	5	62	33
History	31	69	0	5	67	29
Medieval Hebrew literature	0	77	23	7	61	32
Modern Hebrew literature	8	46	46	29	55	17
Hebrew language	8	67	25	17	66	17
Contemporary Jewish community	0	77	23	0	34	66
Education	8	77	15	10	68	22
Homiletics and practical rabbinics	8	77	15	2	50	48
Psychiatry and human relations	0	77	23	0	36	64
Comparative religion ...	0	20	80	0	15	85

literature. None believed that these subjects received too much emphasis. By contrast, a majority of the Cincinnati students found insufficient emphasis on psychiatry-human relations and the contemporary Jewish community. They agreed with the New York students on comparative religion. They were almost evenly divided on whether there was too little emphasis on homiletics and practical rabbinics.

In other words, the New York students sought greater emphasis on traditional Jewish study and modern Hebrew, while the Cincinnati students wanted greater emphasis on the more practically-oriented courses.

Cincinnati students also expressed this desire most frequently in response to an open-ended question about what, in their view, was lacking in their rabbinical training. As noted before, we are reporting student attitudes, which do not necessarily reflect student behavior. For example, students say they want more comparative religion, but few registered for the elective "Introduction to Contemporary Christian Theology" offered at the New York school. Few make even minimal efforts to acquaint themselves with other religious thought.

INFORMAL SOCIALIZATION

Not all the time a student spends at the seminary is devoted to class or class-related activity. The future rabbi's attitudes and behavior are largely shaped by his life at the seminary, and here his experiences outside the classroom are as important as his formal academic training, and probably more important. The environment, both in the formal and the informal programs, socializes the student to certain values—i.e., it brings about certain changes in his attitudes and behavior that make for a certain conformity in the student body. Generally, there was greater agreement among last-year than among first-year students on a series of questions relating to attitudes and behavior.

Here we must bear in mind that the norms to which students are socialized are not necessarily those of the seminary leadership or faculty. Indeed, many of these are determined by a kind of peer-group culture that emerges among the students, who are influenced more by fellow-students or by career orientation than by other factors or persons. At the same time, of course, students continue to live a life outside the institutional environment. Still, in answer to the question with whom they spend most of their time when not engaged in formal academic activity, no fewer than 31 per cent of the students at HUC-JIR (New York) and as many as 70 per cent at YU reported that it was spent in the company of their fellow students.

The seminary shapes its students not only by what takes place within its walls but also, we may assume, by what does not take place—by its failure to meet certain of their expectations. They prepare for the rabbinate in many ways. The religious observance and beliefs they acquire at the seminary are most likely to influence their performance as rabbis and their expectations of their congregants. The quality of the religious life found at the seminary is also important. YU is no more of a religious

THE TRAINING OF AMERICAN RABBIS / 61

sanctuary in a secular world than JTS or HUC-JIR. But the seminary necessarily has more of a sanctuary, or other-worldly, atmosphere than, let us say, the synagogue. It offers at least the possibility for a more intense religious life that may become the model for the rabbinical student and, after his ordination, the yardstick against which he can measure himself and his congregation. We may therefore assume that the absence of such a model will have consequences for the rabbi in his role as a religious leader. Future rabbis may also expect to find their ideal of what a leader should be during their intellectually formative years at the seminary.

Religion is probably conveyed more by example than by formal instruction—in the old phrase, it is caught rather than taught. The precepts of most religions, and of Judaism in particular, can be taught. But if the Jewish religion is a total way of life, if it encompasses the very essence of a man's humanity, then it must be lived. And for this the student needs exemplary figures. What qualities must such a figure have? Probably three: he must be a significant thinker, be pious (according to each student's own definition of piety), and, perhaps as a corollary, demonstrate a real concern for people, students in particular.

Students are dissatisfied with the quality of religious life at their seminaries. They feel it does not furnish them with a model. More significantly, there is no one person at any seminary whom most of the students regard as an exemplary religious figure. There are at least one or two outstanding Jewish thinkers and spokesmen on the faculty of every seminary. But some do not impress students with their piety, and in almost all cases students feel that these faculty members are virtually indifferent to their problems, needs, and concerns. Thus future rabbis develop a kind of skepticism about the very individuals to whom many in the American Jewish community look for religious leadership.

It is reasonable to assume that many of the differences in attitudes and behavior between first- and last-year students, frequently pointed up in our discussion, are determined by the seminary experiences of the students. Still, we cannot dismiss the possibility that the first- and last-year students in our sample entered the seminary with different attitudes. We have noted that first- and last-year students had somewhat different family and educational backgrounds, and it is entirely possible that these or other characteristics can account for differences. In all likelihood, background characteristics and the socialization process are interrelated, and both account for differences.

In the absence of more positive data, however, we suggest that so-cialization is the more important variable—as our study suggests, simply because changes in student attitudes and behavior are far more credibly accounted for by socialization than by family background or previous education. In fact, in some cases our findings are quite contrary to what might have been expected on the basis of family or educational back-ground alone. For our purposes we will therefore assume that differences between first- and last-year students are the consequence of socialization.

Yeshiva University

FRIENDSHIP AND ACTIVITIES

In many respects, rabbinical students at YU are integrated into the life of the undergraduate talmudical students and exposed to the same envi-ronment and to many of the same influences, not all of which are detailed here. There is one student organization for all RIETS students, both undergraduate and graduate. However, the *semikhah* student usually has family responsibilities, must seek outside employment, and occasionally pursues graduate studies or a career goal at another university at the same time. He is less integrated into student life than the undergraduate.

Students called their social relationships with other students either very pleasant (47 per cent), or pleasant (53 per cent); as noted, 70 per cent reported that most of their non-academic time was spent with fellow-students rather than with other friends or family. This proportion remains constant for first- and last-year students. Although these factors might lead us to expect heavy peer-group influence, YU has no one peer group. By the time students enter their last year, their relationships are determined by career orientation.

To a query regarding the division of their leisure-time activity be-tween Jewish and non-Jewish interests, 50 per cent of the students re-plied that it was evenly divided and 39 per cent that all or most of it was Jewish. The percentage reporting mostly non-Jewish activity in-creased slightly for last-year students.

Seventy-four per cent of the students reported that they had attended at least one opera, concert, or theater performance during the past six months. Among students who will probably enter the congregational rabbinate, there was decreasing attendance at such cultural activities (91 per cent of first-year and 73 per cent of last-year students).

INTEREST IN PERIODICAL LITERATURE

Eighty-one per cent of the students regularly read one or more Jewish periodicals. Sixty-four per cent read *Tradition,* the quarterly journal of the Rabbinical Council of America, whose articles on contemporary issues generally reflect leftist or modern Orthodox views. The second most popular journal of Jewish interest was *Commentary* (45%), a quality monthly which however does not devote the major portion of its articles to topics of specifically Jewish interest. Thirty-eight per cent of the students read or subscribed to the *Jewish Observer,* a popular monthly of the (right-wing Orthodox) Agudath Israel. The only other journal attracting at least 20 per cent of the students was *Judaism* (26 per cent), probably the outstanding nonspecialized journal of Jewish thought in America. Eleven per cent of the students regularly read at least one Israeli periodical, and 8 per cent a Yiddish paper or periodical. Only three students read the journals of the Conservative or Reform rabbinical groups. Roughly half the students read at least one non-Orthodox publication of Jewish interest—about half of these, in turn, *Commentary.* Of those who regularly read any periodical of Jewish interest, 16 per cent read one, 24 per cent two, 24 per cent three, 21 per cent four, and 16 per cent five or more.

For measuring the proportion of students interested in general journals of a certain distinction, respondents were asked whether they subscribed to or regularly read any of the following: *Harpers, Saturday Review, Atlantic Monthly, New York Review of Books, Partisan Review, Dissent, Hudson Review, Yale Review, Antioch Review,* and *Commentary.* (*Commentary,* unfortunately, was included in this question to YU students; it was excluded from the same question posed to JTS and HUC-JIR students.) Only 46 per cent responded that they subscribed to or regularly read any of these publications. It is fair to assume that had *Commentary* been excluded, the figure would have been substantially lower. Among those wishing to become congregational rabbis, last-year students (45 per cent) were less likely to read at least one of these journals than first-year students (64 per cent). This does not indicate that last-year students devoted more time to exclusively Jewish activity, for we found the opposite to be true. Last-year students, generally involved in matters of more immediate and personal concern, devote less time to intellectual pursuits in general.

To a query whether they subscribed to or regularly read any of a list of the most popular serious Christian journals—*America, Christianity and Crisis, Christian Century, Christianity Today, Commonweal,* and *National Catholic Reporter*—98 per cent replied that they did not. In light of this, it is difficult to understand the expressed interest of these students in comparative religion as a field deserving greater emphasis in the curriculum. The situation is substantially the same at other seminaries.

SOCIAL ACTION

Another question probed the students' involvement in social action during the year. Responses from future congregational rabbis showed that 45 per cent of the first-year students and 36 per cent of the last-year students had participated—all but one in action in behalf of Soviet Jewry. The fact that third-year future rabbis were less, rather than more, involved than first-year students—both in creative or cultural activity of either Jewish or secular content and in social action—may be explained by their growing concern with future careers, with matters such as the chaplaincy, and with problems of raising and supporting families. Their attitudes and behavior also undergo some changes consonant with their career expectations.

RELIGIOUS PRACTICE AND BELIEF

Students at YU reported that they were Orthodox in matters of belief and, especially, of religious practice. In a series of questions regarding belief, students were given a choice of answering that "certainly" they believe, "on the whole" they believe, they "don't know," or "on the whole" they do not believe. The only difference between first- and last-year students at YU was that fewer last-year students answered that "on the whole" they believed and more answered "certainly." Seventy-three per cent of first-year and 91 per cent of last-year students gave the answer "certainly" to the question whether they believed in a God to whom man could meaningfully pray; 73 per cent of first-year and 82 per cent of last-year students believed that God gave to Moses the Pentateuch as we know it today. The rest believed it "on the whole." It is clear, then, that YU students were not troubled about matters of personal belief and practice; they were unanimous in expressing adherence to Orthodoxy. At any rate, students had resolved any questions they once might have had by the time of their ordination.

EVALUATION OF RELIGIOUS ATMOSPHERE

The questionnaire also asked for an evaluation of the religious atmosphere of the formal program at RIETS (Table 11). Forty-eight per cent

TABLE 11. YU STUDENTS' EVALUATION OF RELIGIOUS ATMOSPHERE

(Per cent)

| | First-year | | Last-year | |
	Future rabbis	Non-rabbis	Future rabbis	Non-rabbis
Promotes religious values.	27	65	45	43
Indifferent to religious values	73	29	55	57
Hostile to religious values	0	6	0	0
	n*=11	n=17	n=11	n=7

* Number in the sample.

thought the atmosphere promoted religious values, and 50 per cent that it was "indifferent to what [they] consider to be important religious values." Last-year future rabbis were more positive in their responses than first-year future rabbis. (The significance of this change will become apparent later.)

In open-ended responses to this question many students were as critical of their fellow-students as of the institution. This was particularly true of *Kolel* and first-year students. One *Kolel* student stated: ". . . among the students themselves, I find that little emphasis is placed on the spiritual-moral aspects of religion, as opposed to ritualistic observance." Another complained of an atmosphere of religious indifference on the part of "the administration—*most* of the faculty—and unfortunately the older boys of the group. . . . Even an appreciation of *minyan* (daily communal prayer), for example, let alone attendance, is not emphasized." A last-year *Kolel* student noted that "there is the tendency to be observant of ritual, but there seems to be lacking a feeling for God." And another last-year *Kolel* student:

Most of the boys spend their hours [when they should be studying] talking about everything other than Torah. There is no religious fervor. The rabbis are indifferent to the students. As a general rule, the administration (even rabbis in the administration) is very secular-minded and secular-oriented.

A second last-year student called the religious atmosphere "more secular than religious." A third stated bluntly: "The atmosphere is hostile to my religious values . . . I feel that most of my growth in Torah comes from my own study and thinking, in spite of the institution." A first-year student's comment on his rabbinical program was: "It is a showcase of artificial religion, often without religious ethical content. . . . There is an ethical-moral gap between the 'religion' that is taught and the daily practice of students. . . ." Not all students were as negative in their comments, but of those who chose to elaborate, four were positive and 14 negative in their responses.

The students' greatest concern is not the prevailing religious atmosphere, but the lack of religious and intellectual leadership. YU, most of its students believe, lacks a *hashkafah*, a religious *Weltanschauung*. The absence of religious leadership is mentioned again and again by students in personal interviews and in replies to open-ended questions (Table 12).

TABLE 12. YU STUDENTS' PRIMARY SOURCE OF RELIGIOUS ADVICE, GUIDANCE, AND EXAMPLE

(*Per cent*)

| | First-year | | Last-year | |
	Future rabbis	Non-rabbis	Future rabbis	Non-rabbis
Fellow students	0	22	18	0
Faculty	36	33	27	57
Administration	0	0	0	0
Family	18	22	27	14
Rabbi outside the institution	27	11	18	14
Other	0	0	0	0
No source	18	11	9	14
	n*=11	n=18	n=11	n=7

 º Number in the sample.

In further elaboration of this question, students were asked to select from a list, or write in, the name of the rabbi who best reflected their own religious-theological-philosophical thinking. Most significant was the finding that no more than 28 per cent of the students chose Rabbi Joseph Soloveitchik as the only such person. Yet Rabbi Soloveitchik is YU's leading religious personality; is considered by most Orthodox as the world's leading talmudist; and is the foremost leader of virtually all modern Orthodox organizations, most particularly the Rabbinical Council of America. It is to Rabbi Soloveitchik that one would expect the students to look for intellectual and religious leadership, as well as for personal guidance, and it is indeed to him that students say they would like to look.

Most YU students are aware of and concerned with the problems of religion in American Jewry. They are aware of the widespread disregard for Jewish law and agree that its authority must be maintained, but are uncertain of what can or ought to be done about it. They seek guidelines from Rabbi Soloveitchik, who is at the same time a trained philosopher, a creative thinker, and a great talmudist. They look to him also for guidance in matters relating to the political-communal aspects of Jewish life, particularly on the relationship between the Orthodox and the non-Orthodox. They seek in him, too, a personal mentor, a kind of father figure with whom they can personally identify and whom they can seek to emulate—one who also feels concern for them and their problems. In this quest most are disappointed.

The image of Rabbi Soloveitchik as an exemplary figure persists because such a figure is so desperately sought, and no one else appears to be as qualified to fill that need. Some of his earliest students found in him the kind of "rebbe" they looked for. He continues to serve as an intellectual model for most students, he does provide some personal leadership, and a few students do establish a personal relationship with him. But this only whets appetites. The "ideal" image of Rabbi Soloveitchik only deepens the disappointment, as each class of students comes to realize that he is not really the leader they desire.

To put the blame on Rabbi Soloveitchik alone would hardly be fair. He is a scholar by temperament, like many other scholars unable to make up his mind on practical matters. In its very broad outlines, his philosophy or way of life finds great resonance among the modern Orthodox, who see in it a vindication of their own involvement in the secular world. But when Rabbi Soloveitchik attempts to apply this philosophy of life to reality, his position is often indecisive, vacillating, and quite contrary to expectations. It is the Orthodox who made of Rabbi Soloveitchik a charismatic leader; he disdains this role for himself. It should be remembered that his central role in Orthodoxy subjects him to demands on his time from a host of organizations and individuals, leaving less and less time for his students.

Very broadly, Rabbi Soloveitchik's position might be described as middle-of-the-road. It acknowledges the value of secular culture and a certain openness to new ideas, while affirming the importance of talmudic scholarship and strict observance of ritual. Soloveitchik's popularity remained constant among first- and last-year students, among those who intended to enter the rabbinate and those who did not. In addition to the 28 per cent who chose him alone, 11 per cent checked both Rabbis

Soloveitchik and Emanuel Rackman, or both Rabbis Soloveitchik and Irving Greenberg, or all three.

Rackman and Greenberg represent a position to the left of Soloveitchik. They favor a more radical interpretation of Jewish law in response to contemporary Jewish problems and concerns; but more significantly, they are more outspoken on community problems. Twenty-one per cent of the students checked either Greenberg or Rackman, or both, as the rabbi best reflecting their ideological position. Among future rabbis, 18 per cent of the first-year students, as compared with 36 per cent of the last-year students, checked one or both of them. Three students (6 per cent) wrote in the name of Rabbi Norman Lamm, who probably is somewhere between the Greenberg-Rackman and Soloveitchik positions; two of them checked Soloveitchick as well.

Seventeen per cent of the students checked rabbis to the right of Soloveitchik, or both Soloveitchick and those to his right. The position to the right of Rabbi Soloveitchik may be defined as opposing secular education and cooperation between Orthodox and non-Orthodox where recognition of non-Orthodox religious positions is implied. Students not intending to enter the pulpit were more likely to identify themselves with this position. The remaining few students wrote in a variety of other names, each appearing only once.

From the students' responses it was evident that no single personality at YU is outstanding in ideological appeal. However, a definite group pattern according to career orientation emerges in the religious positions of last-year students. Among those intending to enter the rabbinate, rabbis to the left of Soloveitchik enjoyed wide popularity. Among students not intending to enter the rabbinate, none in the last year identified with rabbis to the left.

COMMUNAL AND PROFESSIONAL ATTITUDES

A similar pattern was evident in other attitudes as well. Students were asked whether relationships between Orthodoxy, Conservatism, and Reform should be closer, were all right as they are, or were too close now. Among future rabbis 27 per cent of the first-year and 64 per cent of the last-year students thought relations should be closer. Among non-rabbis 36 per cent of the first-year students and no last-year student thought relations should be closer. To the question whether they thought the Union of Orthodox Jewish Congregations (UOJC), their congregational organization, and the Rabbinical Council of America (RCA), their rabbinical one, responsive to the needs of the American Jewish community, last-year future rabbis were far more likely to say yes than first-year students. Among non-rabbis, last-year students were as critical of RCA as first-year students.

Another series of questions dealt with problems facing American Jews and attitudes toward Jewish organizations. Students were asked to indicate which, if any, of a given list of problems facing Jews deserved highest priority, and which, if any, deserved second- and third-highest priority. The responses regarding highest and lowest priority are given in Table 13.

TABLE 13. YU STUDENTS' EVALUATION OF PROBLEMS FACING
AMERICAN JEWRY

(Per cent)

	Highest priority	Little or no significance
Soviet Jewry	2	2
Strength and survival of the State of Israel *	6	0
Antisemitism in the United States	2	11
Increased dialogue and understanding between Jews and Christians	0	53
Social and ethical values of American Jews	2	2
Intellectual challenges to Judaism	6	2
State of Jewish belief	4	0
Jewish youth on the college campus	2	0
Assimilation	13	0
Intermarriage	4	0
Jewish education	38	2
Decline of religious observance and ritual practice	15	0
Greater Jewish unity	0	0
Quality of Jewish organizational life	0	0
Other or no answer	2	2
None	0	21

* Responses were received before the Middle Eastern crisis in May 1967.

Jewish education, the decline of religious observance and ritual, and assimilation were thought to deserve highest priority. For future rabbis, Jewish education became less important (from 54 to 18 per cent) between the first and last years, while problems of assimilation, intermarriage, and the strength and survival of the State of Israel became much more important. In other words, last-year future rabbis listed as deserving highest priority problems that are of general Jewish concern and least controversial. Where problems of second greatest priority were indicated, a plurality of both future rabbis and non-rabbis chose the decline of religious observance and ritual practice.

Students were asked to check the major'organizations to which they would be most willing to devote time and energy. They were also asked to indicate second and third choices, as well as the organizations of which they were most critical (Table 14).

TABLE 14. YU STUDENTS' INTEREST IN MAJOR JEWISH ORGANIZATIONS

(*Per cent*)

	Most willing to devote time and energy	*Most highly critical*
Agudath Israel	4	0
American Council for Judaism	0	72
American Jewish Committee	0	2
American Jewish Congress	0	8
Anti-Defamation League	0	2
B'nai B'rith	0	0
Bonds for Israel	0	0
Jewish Federation or local community-wide philanthropic group	0	4
Jewish Welfare Board	2	0
Labor Zionists of America	0	0
Religious Zionists of America	19	0
Torah Umesorah	47	0
United Jewish Appeal	2	0
Zionist Organization of America	0	2
Other	8	0
None	15	2

Consistently with their interest in Jewish education, YU students were most interested in Torah Umesorah, the National Society for Hebrew Day Schools. The only other agency checked by 10 or more per cent of the students was Religious Zionists of America (RZA). Last-year rabbinical students, too, were most willing to devote time to Torah Umesorah, though fewer than non-rabbis.

Among the organizations of which students were most critical, the American Council for Judaism was the overwhelming choice. It was followed by the American Jewish Congress, an organization best known in Orthodox circles for its militant opposition to federal aid to Jewish day schools. Only about half of the students checked an organization of which they were *second most* critical. Among those who did, the organizations were: the American Jewish Committee (17 per cent), B'nai B'rith (11 per cent), again the American Council for Judaism (8 per cent), and the American Jewish Congress (6 per cent). Last-year students, however, were less critical than first-year students of these secular organizations, and future rabbis less than non-rabbis. Thus last-year future rabbis were least critical of secular organizations. They were also less critical of their own rabbinical and lay organizations; more anxious for closer relations between Orthodoxy, Conservatism, and Reform; more

TABLE 15. YU STUDENTS' ASSESSMENT OF MOST ATTRACTIVE ASPECTS OF THE RABBINATE

(Per cent)

	Future rabbis	
	First-year	Last-year
Opportunity to help people find faith	27	36
Opportunity to make people more observant	18	9
Opportunity to teach Torah	18	18
Time to study and think	18	9
Comfortable living conditions	0	0
Opportunity to preserve Judaism	18	27
Opportunity to serve as leader in Jewish community.	0	0
Opportunity to serve as leader in general community	0	0
Opportunity for social action	0	0
Status of rabbi in Jewish community	0	0
Status of rabbi in general community	0	0
Other	0	0
	n*=11	n=11

° Number in the sample.

TABLE 16. YU STUDENTS' ASSESSMENT OF LEAST ATTRACTIVE ASPECTS OF THE RABBINATE

(Per cent)

	Future rabbis	
	First-year	Last-year
Necessity to listen to people's problems	0	0
Lay control over rabbi	27	27
Inadequate material conditions	0	0
Necessity to live away from large city	0	0
Necessity to preach or espouse religious beliefs and practices without being really sure of them	0	0
Necessity to compromise religious principles	9	9
Lack of privacy in personal affairs	45	18
Lack of close friends	0	0
Congregants' indifference to religious observance...	9	27
Congregants' indifference to Judaism	9	18
Other or none	0	0
	n*=11	n=11

° Number in the sample.

concerned with such broad issues as intermarriage and assimilation, and less concerned with Jewish education.

This tendency was reflected in differences between first- and last-year future rabbis regarding aspects of the rabbinate which they find most attractive. Unlike students at JTS and HUC-JIR, those at YU did not become more attracted to the specific responsibilities of the rabbinate as they neared ordination (Tables 15 and 16). The "opportunity to help people find faith" was most attractive to both first- and last-year students (27 and 36 per cent), the "opportunity to preserve Judaism" increased (18 to 27 per cent), and the "opportunity to make people more observant" and the "opportunity to study and think" decreased (18 to 9 per cent, respectively). The "opportunity to teach Torah" remained constant, at 18 per cent. Students who did not intend to become practicing rabbis found the last aspect particularly attractive (44 per cent of first-year and 57 per cent of last-year students).

To the extent that differences between first- and last-year students or between future rabbis and non-rabbis can be ascribed to changes in attitudes and opinion rather than to the predispositions with which the students entered the rabbinical program, they are produced by socialization. As the future rabbi progresses toward ordination, he becomes less critical of his rabbinical seminary, his congregational and rabbinical movements and of non-Orthodox organizations. He accepts more readily the existing pattern of Jewish life and moves his views into closer conformity with those of the Jewish community establishment. He is attracted to such ideological figures as Rabbis Rackman, Greenberg and Lamm, all vocal critics of contemporary Judaism; but the likelihood is that their appeal on the other hand, does not rest on their ideological or political views. They are successful rabbis of the largest American Orthodox congregations, who, either despite or because of their very outspokenness, move easily within the mainstream of American Jewish life. The non-rabbis, by contrast, become somewhat more sectarian in their values, their views coming closer to those of their Talmud instructors.

The YU talmudical faculty generally rejects prevailing community values. Among non-rabbis, therefore, last-year students are more likely than first-year students to look to faculty members as a source of religious inspiration. Among future rabbis, last-year students are less likely to do so than first-year students.

RABBINATE AND CHAPLAINCY PROGRAM

One of the major problems of institutional Orthodoxy is a shortage of congregational rabbis. There has been a sharp decline in the number of ordained rabbis entering the congregational rabbinate, although the number of rabbinical students has increased. Besides YU, the major Orthodox institutions that formerly provided congregational rabbis (p. 23 f.), together probably provide less than a dozen a year. Ten or twenty years ago any one of these institutions could have produced as many.

At YU, too, there has been a sharp drop in the number of students entering the rabbinate. In 1966 only two of the 16 students who received ordination became congregational rabbis—an unusually low number of an unusually small class, to be sure. The average for the past few years has been six or seven. Basically, the problem has been the greater attractiveness of other fields open to students who also have secular degrees. (Each year a handful of students may also choose to enter Jewish education. From YU's point of view, this is considered to be desirable and not competitive with the rabbinate.) However, one reason most students are unwilling to enter the rabbinate is the chaplaincy program, which can be discussed here only briefly.

The armed services each year inform the National Jewish Welfare Board (JWB) of their requirement for Jewish chaplains. JWB, in turn, assigns quotas to the Orthodox, Conservative, and Reform rabbinical movements. Until last year YU was solely responsible to RCA for meeting the quota for Orthodox chaplains, since the other yeshivot refused to participate for practical and ideological reasons. While the chaplaincy program was the cause of unhappiness and some tension at all seminaries, at YU the students' dissatisfaction over the program itself, the assigned quota, and the manner of exempting some students and selecting others to fill the quota, had reached a peak. It would not be unfair to say that for a substantial number of students, the year before ordination was poisoned by the fear of being drafted into the chaplaincy and the feeling that the school was unfair in compelling them to have chaplaincy clearance before they could be ordained.

It is not our purpose here to deal with the merits of the program or the procedures. Those responsible for the program accused students who tried to avoid the chaplaincy of shirking their duty toward their school, the Jewish people, and the United States armed forces. The students, in turn, argue that the system was unfair. In response to an open-ended question, which was asked before September 1967, most of the students suggested as a more equitable solution a compulsory two-year program for all newly-ordained students, either as chaplains or in the service of the Jewish community, as teachers, pulpit rabbis in outlying communities, and the like. The question where justice lay in the entire controversy and whether a compulsory service program was feasible, are rather complex and beyond the scope of this paper.

The chaplaincy program, the student's first real personal contact with the organized Jewish world (the YU community-service division and Orthodox rabbinical groups which have some voice in the program), is so tension-laden that it often discourages the student from entering the rabbinate. Also, to avoid being drafted, some students enrolled in graduate schools while studying at YU and, having earned an advanced degree, at times chose another career

Much of what we say here is conjecture on the part of both the interviewer and the interviewed. No one knows the precise importance of the chaplaincy program for the students' career choices, but one may safely conclude that it did not encourage students to enter the rabbinate. In September 1967 a one-year experiment was begun that put the entire chaplaincy program on a voluntary basis; students of former graduating classes, who had not fulfilled their obligations under its requirements, were relieved of any future sanctions.

DIFFERENCES BETWEEN CONGREGATIONAL AND
NON-CONGREGATIONAL RABBIS

Among first-year YU students, 37 per cent expected to be congregational rabbis at some time in their lives; among last-year students, 61 per cent. However, 73 per cent of the first-year and only 36 per cent of the last-year future rabbis looked upon the rabbinate as the most attractive career. Thus, between their first and last year, students come to find the congregational rabbinate less attractive, though a greater number become resigned to their chosen profession.

What is the impact of the student's experience on his intention of becoming a congregational rabbi? Apparently, negligible. On the whole, students do not serve as student rabbis, unless they intend to serve in the pulpit. Field service, which is voluntary at YU, is the variable that most clearly distinguishes those intending to become congregational rabbis from those who do not. Those with field experience viewed the rabbinate more favorably than those without. However, its voluntary nature does not permit an analysis of its effect on career choice. In any event, for encouraging more students to enter the rabbinate, it would be well to give them more practical experience. An organized program to accomplish that was introduced in 1965 as an elective in the supplementary rabbinics curriculum.

We have noted that students hesitate to enter the pulpit because they feel they lack the ability to answer questions of Jewish law. Did future rabbis feel equally unprepared to perform other rabbinic roles? Were they better prepared than non-rabbis? Since one of the most difficult and sensitive functions of a rabbi is comforting the mourner, we asked students how their training as a whole prepared them for this task—particularly for dealing with questions an intelligent mourner might have about the meaning of life, life after death, or God's justice.

The responses showed no differences between future rabbis and non-rabbis, but last-year students were less likely to think their training would be helpful (41 per cent) than first-year students (61 per cent). Moreover, 72 per cent of the future rabbis did not think their training would be helpful in providing an honest intellectual response. Of course, concepts such as God's justice or life after death belong more properly in the realm of academic study than of practical rabbinics. Incredibly, students reported that these subjects have no part at all in the YU curriculum, and that it is the rare instructor who chooses to discuss them informally.

The talmudic faculty of YU has at times been charged with discouraging students from entering the congregational rabbinate. The data do not support this charge, except perhaps quite indirectly. Students intending to enter the rabbinate were more likely than not to feel that they were being encouraged by the faculty. However, most students were of the opinion that the faculty is indifferent to this question or divided on it. Students uniformly asserted that they did receive such encouragement from the administration.

Nothing in the background of the students distinguished rabbis from non-rabbis, except perhaps that the rabbis were more likely to have belonged to Jewish youth groups before entering college. There were different motivations for entering rabbinical school, as well. Non-rabbis were far more likely to say they had been moved by a desire for a good Jewish education.

Jewish Theological Seminary

STUDENT ACTIVITY

Rabbinical students at JTS have an active student life. They publish a student paper; sponsor lectures and discussions; organize student participation in various social-action programs; take responsibility for placing student rabbis for the High Holy Days (including the pooling and redistribution, on the basis of an elaborate point system, of the honoraria); and show active concern with the JTS curriculum and program. Yet they are probably the most discontented student body of any seminary, particularly with regard to the curriculum. In recent years the administration has responded to student demands for representation on a joint student-faculty-administration committee to deal with a host of technical as well as more basic concerns, such as program. It is too early to tell what, if anything, will come of it.

DIFFERENCES BETWEEN CONGREGATIONAL AND
NON-CONGREGATIONAL RABBIS

Not all JTS students expect to become congregational rabbis (50 per cent of all first-year students and 68 per cent of all last-year students expected to hold such positions). At JTS all future rabbis look upon the pulpit as a lifetime career. At YU many of those who expect to enter the rabbinate are not certain they will remain in the field permanently, deliberately preparing also for careers in other fields.

The Conservative movement, like Orthodoxy, suffers from a shortage of rabbis. Unlike YU, however, JTS is less concerned about the number of students entering the rabbinate because those who do not tend to choose other fields of Jewish work. Most of the non-rabbis in fact believe that teaching at JTS or at other institutions of higher learning is the most attractive career. At YU, on the other hand, many non-rabbis leave the Jewish field altogether. Among future rabbis at JTS, half look upon the congregational rabbinate as the most attractive career, while the others are attracted to related areas such as youth work, camping, and, above all, Jewish education. Thus, at JTS, unlike YU, all students choose careers within the Jewish community.

Since non-rabbis at JTS had more scholarly aspirations than future rabbis, the question arose whether they were indeed more suited for scholarly pursuits. The responses seem to bear this out: non-rabbis reported better undergraduate averages than future rabbis and were more likely to report that they were doing considerably better or better than average at rabbinical school.

At JTS, background variables did not distinguish future rabbis from non-rabbis. No differences in Jewish education, youth-group membership, or Jewish-camping experience were apparent. Among first-year students, non-rabbis were more likely than future rabbis to have been enrolled in a formal program of Jewish studies while in college, but this was not true of last-year students. While future rabbis were more likely to have attended synagogue regularly before entering college, there were no consistent differences between them and non-rabbis in the influence any one rabbi may have had on them at the time. Neither group was more likely to have a rabbi in the immediate family. Most students came from Conservative homes, and only a handful of non-rabbis and none of the future rabbis from homes where parents had no synagogue affiliation.

Differences in students' career choices must therefore be ascribed to scholarly interest and motivation, not to any one background factor. The students who wished to become congregational rabbis felt strengthened in their choice by the encouragement of the administration, but believed the faculty to be indifferent to their career plans. On the other hand, the typical non-rabbi believed that his instructors had a positive interest in his making the best career choice for himself.

FRIENDSHIP AND ACTIVITIES

Students evaluated their relationships with other students as either very pleasant (46 per cent) or pleasant (51 per cent); first-year students and future rabbis were more likely to report "very pleasant" relationships. Here differences between first- and last-year students can be explained by the fact that last-year students tended to spend more time with their families than with their friends.

To a query on division of their leisure time between Jewish and non-Jewish activity, 47 per cent of the students reported that their time was evenly divided. Of the remaining students, about half reported their activity as mostly Jewish, and the others as mostly non-Jewish. There were no differences by year. More non-rabbis than rabbis stated that most of their leisure-time activity was Jewish, and more rabbis than non-rabbis said it was mostly non-Jewish. Almost every student had attended an opera, concert, or theater performance during the past six months.

INTEREST IN PERIODICAL LITERATURE

The most widely read journal of Jewish interest at JTS was *Conservative Judaism*, the quarterly of the Rabbinical Assembly; 62 per cent of the students said they read it regularly. Then followed *Commentary* (58 per cent), *Midstream*, a quality monthly publication sponsored by the Jewish Agency's Herzl Foundation (47 per cent), and *Judaism* (42 per cent). Thirty-one per cent of the students subscribed to or regularly read some Israeli periodical, and 9 per cent read a Yiddish periodical. Four students read *Tradition* and *CCAR Journal*, the organ of the Reform Central Conference of American Rabbis. The only other journals read by 10 per cent or more of the students were the *Jewish Spectator*, a semi-popular monthly of contemporary Jewish affairs (16 per cent), and *Hadoar*, a Hebrew weekly published by the Histadruth Ivrith of America (11 per cent). Only two students said they neither subscribed to nor regularly read any periodical of Jewish interest. About a third of the students read at least *Commentary, Conservative Judaism,* and *Judaism*. Of those who regularly read a Jewish periodical, 20 per cent read one; 10 per cent, two; 25 per cent, three; 12 per cent, four; and 33 per cent, five or more. In general, interest in Jewish periodical literature increased among last-year students, future rabbis reading slightly more than non-rabbis.

Most JTS students (60 per cent) did not regularly see any of the quality periodicals of non-Jewish content (pp. 65–6; *Commentary* to be omitted); last-year students were more inclined to read some of them. The biggest variation was by career orientation: future rabbis (28 per cent) were less likely to read these journals than non-rabbis (59 per cent)—perhaps a reflection of the more scholarly interest of the latter group. Virtually no one subscribed to, or regularly read, any of the quality Christian periodicals (p. 66).

SOCIAL ACTION

Sixty-one per cent of the JTS students reported having engaged in some form of social action during the past year. Future rabbis were somewhat less likely to have done so than non-rabbis, first-year students somewhat more likely than last-year students. Most participants were involved only in behalf of Soviet Jewry; 26 per cent also in opposition to the Vietnam war. Career orientation made little difference.

RELIGIOUS PRACTICE AND BELIEF

It is well known within the Conservative movement that JTS leader-ship is strongly traditionalist in religious orientation, and has become more rather than less so in recent years. Yet its students expressed sur-prise at the degree of the school's traditionalism. One student leader re-ported that JTS had had a student faction of traditionalists when he entered school, but that it had virtually disappeared in the absence of any vocal opposition. To what extent has traditionalism pervaded the students' belief and practice? All students expected their wives to light candles on Friday evening. Eighty-one per cent attended Sabbath services regularly; 69 per cent prayed regularly, as a matter of principle. This was more true of last-year (78 per cent) than of first-year students (65 per cent). There were no differences by career orientation.

As for *kashrut* observance, 84 per cent of the students said they would eat cooked fish in a non-kosher restaurant, a practice widely accepted in the Conservative movement but not among the Orthodox. The per-centage was somewhat higher among future rabbis. Views on turning electricity on and off on the Sabbath were markedly more divergent: 58 per cent of the students reported that they would, 30 per cent that they would not, and 12 per cent that they would not if it could be avoided. (Conservative rabbis generally permit the use of electricity on the Sab-bath. Official JTS practice is not to do so.) More last-year (37 per cent) than first-year students (26 per cent) reported that they do not turn electricity on and off, more non-rabbis (39 per cent) than future rabbis (25 per cent).

The laws of family purity, best reflected in the wife's regular atten-dance at a *mikweh* (lustral bath), are basic to traditional Judaism. They are virtually ignored by Conservative rabbis. However, JTS leaders con-sider them to be important, and a High Holy Day sermon delivered at the JTS synagogue in 1965 stressed their observance. Thirty-seven per cent of the students expect their wives to attend *mikweh,* or would prefer that they do so; 58 per cent would not expect their wives to do so, or would prefer that they did not. Again, last-year students were somewhat more likely to prefer or expect observance than first-year students (45 per cent, compared with 35 per cent), and non-rabbis more than future rabbis (50 per cent, compared with 29 per cent).

In religious practice, last-year students were generally more observant than first-year students, and non-rabbis more than future rabbis. The differences between first- and last-year students may be accounted for by religious background and socialization to the seminary's pattern of religious observance. The future rabbi, however, has an additional referent —the behavior of the majority of Conservative rabbis, his future colleagues. As a result, he is less readily socialized to the seminary's practice.

The pattern is more complex in matters of belief. Sixty-eight per cent of the students were certain or thought, on the whole, that they believe in a God to whom man can meaningfully pray. Fifty-seven per cent of the first-year students and 84 per cent of the last-year students stated that they believe this. There are no differences by career orientation. The same is true for the belief that God revealed himself in some way to Moses, which 72 per cent of the students affirmed with "certainty" or "on the whole."

Regarding the belief that God revealed the Pentateuch, as we know it today, to Moses, a belief that is central to traditional Judaism but not to the Conservative movement, there was a division by career orientation. Not only do most Conservative rabbis probably reject this belief, but also it is challenged by the manner in which Bible is taught at JTS. Seventy-three per cent of the students stated that they do not believe in the revelation of the Pentateuch as we know it today to Moses; there were no differences by year. However, the proportion of future rabbis denying this belief was greater (84 per cent) than of non-rabbis (56 per cent).

Asked whether they find prayer to be a meaningful personal experience, 51 per cent of the students replied "almost always" or "often," 48 per cent "sometimes" or "never." There were only slight differences by year and career (future rabbis were more likely to say so than non-rabbis, last-year students more likely than first-year students).

STUDENT EVALUATION OF RELIGIOUS ATMOSPHERE

Students were asked to evaluate the religious atmosphere in the formal rabbinical program (Table 17).

Fifty-one per cent thought it promoted religious values, 35 per cent felt it was indifferent, and 14 per cent thought it generally was hostile or almost hostile. Advanced students were more critical of JTS's religious atmosphere than beginning students. First-year future rabbis were the most satisfied. However, at JTS, in contrast to YU, students are not more likely to accept the religious atmosphere as they advance toward

TABLE 17. JTS STUDENTS' EVALUATION OF RELIGIOUS ATMOSPHERE

	(Per cent)			
	First-year		Last-year	
	Future rabbis	Non-rabbis	Future rabbis	Non-rabbis
Promotes religious values.	75	36	46	50
Indifferent to religious values	25	45	38	17
Hostile to religious values	0	19	15	33
	n*=12	n=11	n=13	n=6

* Number in the sample.

ordination. The reason for this divergent development, we submit, is that the Conservative rabbinate is more critical of JTS than the Orthodox rabbinate of YU.

Responses to an open-ended question suggest that though non-rabbis were as critical of their institution as future rabbis, it was for different reasons. In many instances, their criticism was directed against fellow-students, or against the institution for not demanding greater religious observance of the students.

The comments reflected a wide range of opinion. Some found the atmosphere "inspiring and conducive to religious and ethical living," or felt that "the institution teaches the student to participate in movements trying to solve modern Jewish problems . . . from a Jewish point of view." Others, however, observed that "questions of the individual's growth and major social problems are mostly ignored," or that, while observance of ritual exists, there is "no orientation to issues of concern," including theology.. One student commented that at JTS, "one lives Judaism vicariously, not enthusiastically," and another that "the atmosphere is hostile to leading a full Jewish life . . ." and to Jewish study for the sake of study.

Although some students complained that JTS is too lax in matters concerning religion, most were pleased with "the liberal religious atmosphere," the religious "leeway"—that "nobody is checking up on me" and that "faculty and fellow-students instruct by example, not coercion." In response to a direct question, 74 per cent of the students thought that the standard of religious observance set by JTS was "about right"; 14 per cent thought it "too stringent," and 9 per cent "not stringent enough." Among last-year future rabbis, 23 per cent were likely to think it "too stringent."

RELIGIOUS AND INTELLECTUAL LEADERSHIP

JTS, like YU, has no model figure who alone is the religious leader for most of the students. In response to the question, "What do you feel is lacking in your rabbinical training?" one student simply wrote "a *rebbe.*" The institutional leaders of JTS are traditionalist in observance and belief and remote from the student body; the students, for their part, are too critical of their curriculum to find it possible to look upon them as their religious leaders.

The most prominent religious personality on the JTS faculty is Professor Abraham J. Heschel, but for a number of reasons JTS students are not drawn to him. True, his religious existentialism, his concern with contemporary theology, his pietistic rather than ritualistic traditionalism, and his involvement in social and political issues constitute the single most popular position. But students are usually not exposed a great deal to his thinking, for he plays only a small institutional role and does not expound his existential theology in courses most students attend. For this and more personal reasons only 18 per cent of the students chose him as the rabbi who best reflects their own religious-philosophical-theological position. Another 7 per cent checked both Heschel and Professor Seymour Siegel, a younger colleague who has stressed the need for greater theological emphasis at JTS and is also more closely identified with the JTS administration; 9 per cent checked Siegel only.

The second in popularity was Rabbi Mordecai M. Kaplan (14 per cent checked Kaplan only; an additional 7 per cent checked Kaplan together with Heschel or Siegel). Kaplan, of course, is the father of Reconstructionism. On the JTS faculty from 1909 to 1953, he exercised profound influence on the students during those years. His depersonalization of the God idea, his concern for the community of Israel, his reinterpretation of Judaism in the language of Deweyan pragmatism, and his reinvestment of major aspects of the tradition with contemporary meaning attracted many, if not most, students at JTS at one time. In recent years, however, Kaplan's position has declined in importance as a result of his retirement from JTS, the general move toward greater traditionalism in the institution and among the students, and the growing popularity of neo-Orthodoxy and religious existentialism in all religious circles. (Of course, Death-of-God theology is of even more recent vintage and may augur a new popularity for Kaplan's ideas. That is unlikely, however. New fads usually require new high priests.)

The linking by a few students of Kaplan with Heschel, or Kaplan with Siegel, suggests either ignorance of their true positions or some rather esoteric theological interpretation. Heschel, Siegel, and Kaplan, alone or in combination, attracted 61 per cent of the student body.

The remaining students were drawn to a wide variety of positions held by a great variety of individuals, ranging from the Lubavitcher Rebbe to Rabbi Richard Rubinstein, who had recently spoken at a student-sponsored JTS lecture and who comes closest, among respected rabbis, to a Death-of-God theology. Four students listed or checked rabbis neither institutionally nor historically identified with Conservatism: two, Orthodox personalities; and two, Rabbi Eugene Borowitz of HUC-JIR (in combination with Conservative rabbis). Nine per cent of the students reported that there was no one who best reflected their own religious position. This broad distribution makes it difficult to generalize about differences by year or career orientation. The biggest change by year was the decrease from first to last in the popularity of Kaplan, the single leading choice of first-year students (25 per cent).

The absence of a central religious figure was also evident in responses to the question where the students look for religious advice, guidance, and example. Twenty-three per cent looked to the faculty, 21 per cent to rabbis not connected with JTS, 19 per cent to fellow-students, and 16 per cent to their families. The breakdown by year and career is instructive (Table 18).

TABLE 18. JTS STUDENTS' PRIMARY SOURCE OF RELIGIOUS ADVICE, GUIDANCE, AND EXAMPLE

(Per cent)

	First-year		Last-year	
	Future rabbis	Non-rabbis	Future rabbis	Non-rabbis
Fellow students	18	42	8	0
Faculty	18	33	23	17
Administration	9	0	8	0
Family	9	8	31	17
Rabbi outside the institution	36	0	15	50
Other	0	8	0	17
No source	9	8	15	0
	n* = 11	n = 12	n = 13	n = 6

* Number in the sample.

The first-year future rabbi is heavily oriented toward a rabbi outside JTS (probably his family rabbi, who may have influenced him to enter JTS). As might be expected, the student abandons this referent in time; but then he finds no substitute within JTS. The non-rabbi, having a more scholarly orientation, starts with expectations of finding his source of religious guidance at the institution (fellow-students and faculty), but also looks elsewhere as he approaches his final year. Thus, though the student, or at least the non-rabbi, becomes socialized to JTS norms, the institution and its personnel do not serve him as spiritual referents.

COMMUNAL AND PROFESSIONAL ATTITUDES

Virtually all (98 per cent) agree that relations between the Orthodox, Conservative, and Reform should be closer than they now are. There was fairly even division between students who thought Conservatism put too little emphasis on ritual observance (49 per cent), and those who believed the emphasis was about right (42 per cent). Differences by year or career were negligible. Half the students felt that, on the whole, the United Synagogue of America was responding to the needs of the American Jewish community, 27 per cent thought it was not, and 23 per cent were not sure; last-year students were somewhat more sanguine than first-year students.

The difference by career was much more marked, with 63 per cent of the future rabbis, compared with 28 per cent of the non-rabbis, approving of the United Synagogue's work. The same pattern appeared in the evaluation of the Rabbinical Assembly, except that the students were in general more negative about it: 36 per cent thought that on the whole RA was responding to the needs of the Jewish community, and 39 per cent thought not. Again, last-year students were more favorable than first-year students, and future rabbis more than non-rabbis.

Students were asked about the most and least significant problem of American Jewry (Table 19). Jewish education was voted the leading problem by 42 per cent of the students, and assimilation next in importance (12 per cent). Last-year students and future rabbis were most likely to list education. Future rabbis gave second-highest priority to the problem of Jewish youth on the college campus and, again, to Jewish education. Non-rabbis were more likely to consider the situation of Soviet Jewry and the state of Jewish belief as most pressing.

Students were divided on their choice of an organization to which they would be most willing to devote time and energy (Table 20). There

TABLE 19. JTS STUDENTS' EVALUATION OF PROBLEMS FACING
AMERICAN JEWRY

(*Per cent*)

	Highest priority	*Little or no significance*
Soviet Jewry	9	2
Strength and survival of the State of Israel *	0	2
Antisemitism in the United States	0	19
Increased dialogue and understanding between Jews and Christians	0	21
Social and ethical values of American Jews	9	0
Intellectual challenges to Judaism	7	2
State of Jewish belief	9	0
Jewish youth on the college campus	2	0
Assimilation	12	0
Intermarriage	0	0
Jewish education	42	0
Decline of religious observance and ritual practice.	7	2
Greater Jewish unity	0	2
Quality of Jewish organizational life	0	17
Other or no answer	0	7
None	0	24

* Responses were received before the Middle Eastern crisis in May 1967.

TABLE 20. JTS STUDENTS' INTEREST IN MAJOR JEWISH ORGANIZATIONS

(*Per cent*)

	Most willing to devote time and energy	*Most highly critical*
Agudath Israel	0	7
American Council for Judaism	0	71
American Jewish Committee	10	0
American Jewish Congress	2	0
Anti-Defamation League	2	2
B'nai B'rith	7	0
Bonds for Israel	5	0
Jewish Federation or local community-wide philanthropic group	5	0
Jewish Welfare Board	5	0
Labor Zionists of America	2	0
Religious Zionists of America	0	0
Torah Umesorah	5	0
United Jewish Appeal	12	0
Zionist Organization of America	5	0
Other or no answer	19	5
None	21	14

was no single organization to which more than 12 per cent of the students were most willing to devote time and energy. The United Jewish Appeal was on top of the list, and the American Jewish committee next, with 10 per cent. More future rabbis (86 per cent) than non-rabbis (65 per cent) felt that they would want to work with one of the organizations. They showed particular willingness to devote time and energy to a Jewish federation, as a second choice; two students indicated they would be active in order to change its orientation and priorities. Among last-year students, 23 per cent of the future rabbis, but no non-rabbis, gave Federation as a second choice.

If we assume that most future rabbis were willing to support Federation because they approved rather than disapproved of it, the emergent JTS pattern is similar to that at YU. The future rabbi grows more willing to involve himself in the Jewish community; he accepts its institutional structure and, in the case of Federation, approves (or tolerates) its financial priorities. Twenty-one per cent of the future rabbis but only 6 per cent of the non-rabbis were not highly critical of any organization.

It has been established that future rabbis become more career-oriented as they approach ordination. To what extent does this change affect their image of the pulpit and of the rabbi's functions? The student's views on reasonable salary expectations for rabbis in their first post and for those with five years of experience (Tables 21 and 22) varied according to both year of study and career expectation. Whereas most first-year students, both future rabbis and non-rabbis, chose $7,000-8,999 as a reasonable beginner's salary, last-year students chose $9,000-10,999. A difference in the same direction was shown in the salary expected for experienced rabbis.

TABLE 21. JTS STUDENTS' EVALUATION OF A REASONABLE BEGINNING SALARY FOR A CONGREGATIONAL RABBI

(Per cent)

Salary	First-year		Last-year	
	Future rabbi	Non-rabbi	Future rabbi	Non-rabbi
Under $5,000	0	0	0	0
5,000-6,999	8	0	0	0
7,000-8,999	50	58	8	25
9,000-10,999	33	33	69	75
11,000-12,999	8	8	23	0
13,000-14,999	0	0	0	0
	n*=12	n=12	n=13	n=4

* Number in the sample.

TABLE 22. JTS STUDENTS' EVALUATION OF A REASONABLE SALARY FOR A
CONGREGATIONAL RABBI FIVE YEARS AFTER ORDINATION

(*Per cent*)

Salary	First-year Future rabbis	First-year Non-rabbis	Last-year Future rabbis	Last-year Non-rabbis
Under $7,000	0	0	0	0
7,000-8,999	0	0	0	0
9,000-10,999	8	16	0	25
11,000-12,999	42	58	0	0
13,000-14,999	33	25	62	50
15,000-17,499	17	0	38	25
17,500-20,000	0	0	0	0
	n*=12	n=12	n=13	n=4

° Number in the sample.

Another question probed student opinion of the attractions of the
pulpit rabbinate. Among future rabbis, a plurality of first-year students
(33 per cent) checked "the opportunity to preserve Judaism." No last-
year future rabbis checked this rather vague statement, and the number
citing "opportunity to serve as a leader in the Jewish community" also
decreased. Instead, the percentage of students choosing more specific
answers, such as "helping people find faith," "teaching Torah," and
"making people more observant," increased (Table 23). Future rabbis,
then, gain an increasingly specific image of their role, one that concerns
itself with people, not with community structure or ideologies.

TABLE 23. JTS STUDENTS' ASSESSMENT OF MOST ATTRACTIVE
ASPECTS OF THE RABBINATE

(*Per cent*)

	Future rabbis First-year	Future rabbis Last-year
Opportunity to help people find faith	17	23
Opportunity to make people more observant	0	15
Opportunity to teach Torah	25	31
Time to study and think	0	8
Comfortable living conditions	0	0
Opportunity to preserve Judaism	33	0
Opportunity to serve as leader in Jewish community.	25	15
Opportunity to serve as leader in general community	0	0
Opportunity for social action	0	0
Status of rabbi in Jewish community	0	0
Status of rabbi in general community	0	0
Other	0	8
	n*=12	n=13

° Number in the sample.

As for the aspects of the congregational rabbinate that students found least attractive, again future rabbis moved from the more general and communal in the first year to the more specific and, in this case, more personal just before ordination. First-year students chose such things as "lay control over the rabbi" (33 per cent), "the congregation's indifference to Judaism" (25 per cent), and "lack of privacy for myself and family" (25 per cent). Half of the last-year future rabbis disliked, above all, "lack of privacy for myself and family"; 17 per cent "preaching things one is not sure of" (Table 24).

TABLE 24. JTS STUDENTS' ASSESSMENT OF LEAST ATTRACTIVE ASPECTS OF THE RABBINATE

(*Per cent*)

	Future rabbis	
	First-year	Last-year
Necessity to listen to people's problems	0	0
Lay control over rabbi	33	17
Inadequate material conditions	0	0
Necessity to live away from large city	0	0
Necessity to preach or espouse religious beliefs and practices without being really sure of them	8	8
Necessity to compromise religious principles	0	17
Lack of privacy in personal affairs	8	50
Lack of close friends	0	0
Congregants' indifference to religious observance...	8	0
Congregants' indifference to Judaism	25	8
Other or none	0	0
	n*=12	n=12

° Number in the sample.

Part of preparing for any career is an awareness of the inadequacies of the chosen profession. A critical time for a rabbi, we know, is his confrontation with a mourner, for this is when his counsel is most earnestly sought and when the community may exercise its severest judgment of his ability. Future rabbis facing ordination were less optimistic than first-year students about their ability to answer adequately the thoughtful and intelligent mourner's questions about the meaning of life, life after death, or God's justice. There was almost unanimous agreement among students that a good rabbi should be able to answer such questions in an intellectually satisfying and honest way. About half of the future rabbis were confident that their training at JTS would be helpful in comforting the mourner. Slightly more than half were also inclined to believe that their training would help them provide an honest and satisfactory intellectual response.

HUC-JIR

The great majority (89 per cent) of HUC-JIR students expected to serve as congregational rabbis, at least at some time or other; the remaining students were "doubtful." While 71 per cent looked upon the congregational rabbinate as the most attractive career, 14 per cent preferred the position of Hillel rabbi. Only 9 per cent wanted an academic career either at HUC-JIR (4 per cent), or at some college or university (5 per cent). Since the student body was so overwhelmingly in favor of the congregational rabbinate, we will not differentiate here between future rabbis and non-rabbis. We also restricted our comparisons of first- and last-year student attitudes to the Cincinnati campus, because of the New York school's small graduating class (seven students, of whom three had failed to respond to the questionnaire in time for our analysis).

FRIENDSHIP AND ACTIVITIES

The Cincinnati and New York centers have student organizations that arrange lectures, run a bookstore (Cincinnati only), and represent student opinion on joint faculty-student committees. New York students, who usually live at a distance from their school and spend more time at part-time jobs, necessarily lead a less active student life. Thirty-one per cent of these students, compared with 60 per cent at Cincinnati, reported spending most of their leisure time with fellow-students. Almost all HUC-JIR students evaluated their relations with fellow-students as very pleasant (38 per cent; first-year students more than last-year students), or pleasant (57 per cent). Here, as at JTS and to a lesser degree at YU, most students marry before ordination. More last-year than first-year students reported spending most of their free time with their family (45 and 13 per cent, respectively). This suggests the possibility that last-year students were increasingly concerned not only with their future career, but also with the personal and familial aspects of that career— a condition prevalent among other rabbinical students as well.

The majority of the students (65 per cent) reported that their leisure time was divided about equally between Jewish and non-Jewish activity, 15 per cent that it was mostly Jewish and 20 per cent that it was mostly non-Jewish. A somewhat larger proportion of New York students indicated spending most of their leisure in non-Jewish activity. Last-year students, like future rabbis at other institutions, reported more time spent in non-Jewish activity than beginning students. Almost all students (96 per cent) stated that they had attended a concert, opera, or theater performance in the past six months.

INTEREST IN PERIODICAL LITERATURE

Responses to the query regarding Jewish journals to which students subscribed or which they read regularly showed that 20 per cent of Cincinnati and 31 per cent of New York students read none. At the Cincinnati school the most popular journal was *Commentary* (58 per cent; 7 per cent of the students read no other Jewish journal); 54 per cent read the *CCAR Journal;* next in popularity were *Midstream* (41 per cent) and *Judaism* (34 per cent). Other journals read by at least 10 per cent of the students were *Reconstructionist* (24 per cent), *Conservative Judaism* (12 per cent), *National Jewish Monthly,* a popular monthly publication of B'nai B'rith, (12 per cent), and *Tradition* (10 per cent). Two students read *Hadoar,* one an Israeli publication, and none read Yiddish periodicals.

At the New York school the reading pattern was similar, except that its students were somewhat more likely (46 per cent) to read *Judaism,* to which Rabbi Eugene Borowitz, a member of its faculty, had contributed the regular feature "Current Theological Literature" until 1966. Of the students at both schools who read a Jewish journal, 9 per cent regularly read one; 16 per cent, two; 13 per cent, three; 24 per cent, four; and 17 per cent, five or more. Responses from last-year students showed a marked increase over first-year students in the number of periodicals read.

Slightly less than half the students read one of the quality non-Jewish periodicals (p. 65 f.; omit *Commentary*). Last-year students were more likely to do so (68 per cent) than first-year students (35 per cent). Few students (17 per cent) read a quality Christian periodical (p. 66), and last-year students were no more likely to do so than others. If less than half of the students read the theological writings of a member of their own faculty and so few read a Christian periodical, some doubt must be cast on their professed interest in theology and comparative religion.

SOCIAL ACTION

More than half of the students (57 per cent) participated in some form of social action during the year. Last-year students were more likely to have done so than first-year students. (By contrast, at JTS last-year students were less likely to have done so than first-year students.) Of participants in social action, 18 per cent were involved exclusively with Soviet Jewry and 37 per cent with both Soviet Jewry and civil rights, or poverty, or the Vietnam war. Eighteen per cent were involved with civil rights or poverty, or the war in Vietnam alone.

The HUC-JIR experience, then, apparently serves to broaden the student's interest and participation in both general and Jewish affairs, as well as in social action. This is not the case at either JTS or YU, and may reflect differences in the students' image of the rabbi's role at the various seminaries—an interpretation entirely consonant with the greater tendency among HUC-JIR students to think of the rabbi as an active leader in the Jewish community.

RELIGIOUS PRACTICE AND BELIEF

In considering changes in religious observance and practices by students while they are training for the rabbinate at HUC-JIR, as elsewhere, we assume that differences between first- and last-year students are the result of the school's influence. At HUC-JIR all students but one expected their wives to light candles on Friday evening. All but one ate cooked fish in non-kosher restaurants and used electricity on the Sabbath; and all but three (5 per cent) stated that they would object if their wives attended the mikweh, or would prefer them not to.

As a matter of principle, about half the students (54 per cent), regularly attended services on the Sabbath. Last-year students were less likely to do so (45 per cent) than first-year (56 per cent). Sixty-six per cent stated that they prayed regularly, as a matter of principle—last-year students slightly less frequently than first-year students. Sixty-nine per cent believed with certainty, or on the whole, in a God to whom man can meaningfully pray; their number decreased, from 82 per cent in the first year to 50 per cent in the last. Thirty-eight per cent believed with certainty, or on the whole, that God in some way revealed himself to Moses at Sinai; 46 per cent did not. Again, there were differences between first- and last-year students—an increase of nonbelievers from 35 to 75 per cent. To sixty-two per cent prayer was almost always, or often, a meaningful personal experience; here too the number decreased in the last year. To what can the decline in belief between the first and last years be attributed? (It will be recalled that there was no such decline at YU and JTS.) Not to HUC-JIR's leadership, for faculty members describe Dr. Glueck's faith in God as simple and traditional. And while Dr. Glueck's religion is not under discussion, it is important because of the student's image of him as a strong believer in a personal God. The explanation for the growing rejection of this faith as they approach ordination probably reflects the institution's general religious atmosphere, the views of its faculty, and its curriculum.

STUDENT EVALUATION OF RELIGIOUS ATMOSPHERE

Forty-six per cent of the HUC-JIR students felt that the general religious atmosphere of the rabbinical program promotes religious values, 44 per cent that it was indifferent to what they considered to be important religious values, and 9 per cent that it was hostile to such values. Last-year students were more likely to think the atmosphere indifferent (53 per cent) than first-year students (41 per cent). Students at the New York school were generally pleased with what they thought was a liberal religious atmosphere having traditional orientation and possibility for personal development. In fact, 62 per cent, more than at any other institution, believed it promoted religious values.

Cincinnati students interpreted this question somewhat differently from other seminarians, and figures may therefore be misleading. To students at other seminaries, religious values meant either ritual practice, traditional beliefs, or ethical and moral behavior, and they based their evaluation of the school's religious atmosphere on the extent to which it promoted these. Most JTS and New York HUC-JIR students approved of the absence of coercion on students for conformity in ritual behavior, but all seminarians felt that there should be some relationship between their formal studies and religious values. Thus, students describing the atmosphere as "indifferent" to religious values were by and large criticizing their institution or their fellow-students.

This was not so at Cincinnati. Several comments by students who thought the atmosphere *promoted* religious values will serve as illustration. One called the atmosphere "more academic than religious," another noted that "there is more study than practice," others that "there have been instances of discouragement of traditional practices," or that "there is a healthy skepticism which vitiates practice to some extent—good in the long run."

Almost identical comments came from students who called the atmosphere *indifferent* to religious values. One described it as "ideal . . . one is permitted, and even compelled, to arrive at a meaningful expression of Judaism for himself," while others observed that "God doesn't seem to play much of a role in motivating students" or that "there seems to be little belief that can be translated into action." Another typical comment: "There is a marked tendency toward uninvolved academicism." Those who thought the atmosphere hostile to religious values had much the same to say. From this it follows that HUC-JIR students, unlike those at YU or JTS, do not disagree on the kind of environment the school offers, only on whether it is good or bad.

EFFECT OF RELIGIOUS ATMOSPHERE

Most entering Cincinnati students have had no exposure to any form of Judaism other than their Reform temple or youth group. As part of their first-year liturgy course, Professor Jakob Petuchowski makes it mandatory that they attend for one week morning services at an Orthodox synagogue. For most, this is their first exposure to Orthodox ritual and the only occasion to learn to put on *tefillin*. Unlike most other rabbinical students, they know little of the diversity in Jewish religious life. In the past, many students came to Cincinnati from traditionalist backgrounds. They had rejected traditionalism in favor of Reform, and wanted to become rabbis to help others do the same. In contrast, the students today have made no definite choice, because they are not really aware of alternatives. Their limited Jewish education would preclude their acceptance at YU or JTS anyway.

A student's decision to enter YU, and particularly JTS, expresses his choice of a religious role. More often than not, even among the Orthodox, he has tried out pietism, ritualism, or religious rebellion during the crucial formative years in high school, and at least subconsciously he knows a good deal about his own religiosity before entering the seminary. If this is less true of the New York Reform seminarian, he at least has the opportunity to find out while preparing for ordination. A number of students at the New York school, for example, cover their heads at the time of their ordination. This is certainly no religious command for Reform Jews, and it is not even required by the rigors of Jewish law.

Yet, covering the head may symbolize for some Reform rabbis the decision to adopt óne religious role and reject another.

Cincinnati students do not actually have this option because their background and available opportunities give them very few religious choices. They cannot keep the laws of *kashrut* or regularly worship in traditional fashion, except at considerable personal sacrifice, and they cannot even inform themselves meaningfully about differences in religious thought and practice. HUC-JIR is primarily an academic institution. In particular instances, the absence of a religious atmosphere eliminates choice and virtually dictates a pattern. Some students—though they are the exceptions—are sensitive to this situation. As one expressed it, "Opportunities are not really available for a student to *daven* [pray] traditionally or keep *kashrut,* etc., and we need that experience and freedom." On the whole, however, they accept HUC Reform not only as the best, but as the only conceivable way (Table 25).

TABLE 25. HUC-JIR STUDENTS' EVALUATION OF RELIGIOUS ATMOSPHERE

(Per cent)

	First-year	Last-year
Promotes religious values	42	43
Indifferent to religious values	45	43
Hostile to religious values	13	13
	n*=31	n=23

° Number in the sample.

The exclusive emphasis on the academic is also accepted as natural and proper. Students can in this way evaluate the atmosphere's effect on religious values as positive, while maintaining that it has nothing to do with religion. A few students are disturbed because they feel that "God is lost among humanistic and scholarly concerns," but the predominant consensus is that the absence of a religious atmosphere gives "a genuinely modern approach to the meaning of religious observance." (In New York, one HUC-JIR faculty member has suggested that students be urged to attend other Jewish institutions simultaneously or enroll in other Jewish-study programs.) Consider the striking contrast between the Israeli schools maintained by JTS and by HUC-JIR. Only the JTS program actively directs its students to explore different facets of Jewish religious life in Israel. In all fairness, one must note that JTS is in a better position to do so because it has a full program in Israel, whereas HUC-JIR offers only selected courses.

The religious baggage the student brings with him to Cincinnati is often no more than Sunday-school notions of God and Judaism and ignorance of the religious sources and tradition. Such notions of God are quickly shattered by older students, by the general atmosphere of religious skepticism, and by some of the instructors, who have strong convictions about religion and convey them to the student.

RELIGIOUS AND INTELLECTUAL LEADERSHIP

For the rabbi who best reflects their own religious-theological-philosophical position, 54 per cent at the New York school chose Rabbi Eugene Borowitz; 23 per cent Rabbi Heschel, or Borowitz and Heschel, or Borowitz and Rabbi Jakob Petuchowski, and the remaining 23 per cent selected Mordecai Kaplan. Borowitz teaches in the New York school, Petuchowski at Cincinnati. Both are theologians. Borowitz is a religious existentialist, and Petuchowski is sympathetic to that position. Both are vocal critics of what they consider to be the theological sterility of contemporary Reform, and both favor greater traditionalism in ritual observance. Both are also good writers and public speakers. Their ideologies differ somewhat; but, except for Petuchowski's outspoken opposition to Zionist ideology—and it is not to this that his followers are attracted—the differences are rather subtle.

At the Cincinnati school 26 per cent listed Petuchowski as the person who best reflects their religious position; 12 per cent Borowitz; 12 per cent, Borowitz and Petuchowski, or both in combination with Heschel; one student checked Rabbi Rackman of YU. Thus, half the students were drawn to religious leaders associated with traditionalism. Of the remaining students, 41 per cent checked individually, or in combination, the names of rabbis representing a more radical religious position: 21 per cent Alvin Reines, professor of philosophy at Cincinnati; 9 per cent Sherwin Wine, the Reform rabbi who has removed references to God from his service, or both Reines and Wine; another 9 per cent both Kaplan and Reines, and one student (2 per cent) Kaplan.

Reines is in fact more influential than the students' replies suggest. He states his position, which is little known outside a small Reform circle, in his essay "God and Jewish Theology" (published in mimeographed form by HUC-JIR in 1967). According to him, ". . . the Community of Reform Jews denies the existence of an authoritative body of knowledge or beliefs whose affirmation is obligatory upon the members of this community." Reform Judaism, he says, is a polydoxy allowing "as equally valid all opinion on the great themes of religion such as the meaning of God, the nature of man and so forth" and disallowing only those beliefs that are "inconsistent with its polydox nature, as, for example, belief in an authoritative revelation or an orthodox doctrine."

For Reines the concept "Jewish," or "Jew," is a symbol that calls upon man to respond to the meaning of God. But he is troubled by the concept because he feels that it has no meaningful referent. In his view, there is no Jewish tradition—only a "continuum of accident rather than essence." Hence, he seeks to redefine "Jewish" in such a manner, as he puts it, as to place the burden of the definition on the question asked.

Reines denies the possibility of proving the reality of God, and without such proof, he argues, one cannot proceed to intelligent discourse or communication. He then proceeds to give the concept of God what he feels is its real meaning—"the enduring possibility of being." After this, he says, one can go on to sensible theological speculation.[31]

The fact that Reines has a strong influence on HUC-JIR students has serious implication for the future relationship of Reform Judaism with other Jewish groups. Petuchowski has noted, critically:

> ... with every passing year, the ranks of the [CCAR] ... are swelled by young rabbis who enter the Reform rabbinate with the sincerely held conviction that Reform Judaism is a new religion, founded in the nineteenth century, which —more or less by historical accident—shares part of its name with the historical religion of Judaism. That new religion, called "Reform Judaism," has only one dogma, and that is the absolute freedom of the individual to think and do what he likes. (See Alvin J. Reines, "Polydoxy and Modern Judaism" in the January 1965 issue of the *CCAR Journal*.) The [CCAR] ... has not seen fit to repudiate that position, and it is not unlikely that, within the next decade or so, it might become the position of the majority of the CCAR membership.[32]

From the percentages quoted here, it would appear at first that the student body at Cincinnati is about evenly divided between radical or traditionalist rabbis, but such a conclusion would be highly misleading. It was first-year students who gave Petuchowski 48 per cent, Borowitz or both Borowitz and Petuchowski 30 per cent, and Heschel 9 per cent. No first-year student listed Reines. Among last-year students, on the

---

31 Reines has also discussed his philosophy in his "Reform Judaism," in Belden Menkus, ed., *Meet the American Jew* (Nashville, 1963), pp. 29–43, and in four articles in *CCA   ɔurnal:* "Authority in Reform Judaism" (April 1960), "Polydoxy and Modern Judaism" (January 1965), "Shabbat As a State of Being" (January 1967), and "The Future and the Holy" (October 1967).

32 Jacob J. Petuchowski, "Realism About Mixed Marriages," *CCAR Journal,* October 1966, p. 37.

other hand, 45 per cent listed Reines and 35 per cent Wine, or both Reines and Wine, or Reines and Kaplan, a dramatic difference. Among students about to be ordained, radical theology was by far more popular. One reason may be that it is the upper-classmen who have the greatest exposure to Reines, and beginners with Petuchowski. The fact that Petuchowski began teaching theology only in 1965, when the last-year students sampled here had already completed this course, may also be a factor.

The nature of the curriculum is in keeping with the position of Reines rather than of Petuchowski. One faculty member, explaining the difference between first- and last-year students, has stated:

. . . there is undoubtedly some significance in the sheer weight of required class hours which a student has to take with certain members of the faculty between the time he completes his freshman year and the time he enters the senior class.

There are three courses in philosophy (with a total of 12 hours) which the student takes with Reines himself. There are four courses in Bible (with a total of 16 hours) in a Bible department which specializes in debunking traditional notions and in undermining any belief in Revelation. There are four courses in history (with a total of 14 hours); and, here again, it should be noted that the history department is committed to economic determinism and to the eradication of the sphere of the holy from any construct of Jewish history. And, then, there are any number of electives which the students can take in the above-mentioned departments.

During that same period of time, the students . . . [have Petuchowski] for four hours of Talmud, and three hours of liturgy—both of them courses which, in view of the students' lack of background and commitment, would hardly be reckoned among the most enjoyable courses taken by our students. . . .

The academic freedom to which we, as an institution, are so dedicated, does not mean that, in terms of its curriculum and required courses, HUC is impartial as between the various theological options possible with Reform Judaism.

And another has said:

Petuchowski was given the first-year theological courses. Inasmuch as the students, in their first year, have only met Petuchowski, and have not yet been introduced to philosophic theology . . . it would account for their choosing Petuchowski's position—it is the only one with which they are familiar. Moreover, the really scientific Bible, history, etc., courses do not begin until the later years. Since . . . [Reines's] theological position is thoroughly coherent with these scientific courses, and these courses tend to make incredible Petuchowski's view, what appears to happen is that as a student matures religiously he discards the neo-Orthodox position for one that fits his increased academic and theological development. Furthermore, Petuchowski's position is much like the position that . . . the normative Reform pulpit would present, and this would tend to be the position that a student would bring with him to the College, and find supported by Petuchowski.

Despite the impact of both Petuchowski and Reines, the students look neither to them nor to other faculty members as a primary source of religious guidance, advice, or example. At Cincinnati 19 per cent of the students (somewhat more than in any other school) stated that they had no such living source; 28 per cent felt that faculty members provided this source (compared with 58 per cent in the New York school), and 21 per cent looked to a rabbi outside HUC-JIR (Table 26).

TABLE 26. HUC-JIR STUDENTS' PRIMARY SOURCE OF RELIGIOUS ADVICE, GUIDANCE, AND EXAMPLE

(*Per cent*)

	First-year	Last-year
Fellow students	13	17
Faculty	29	42
Administration	0	0
Family	10	4
Rabbi outside the institution.	19	20
Other	10	0
No source	19	17
	n*=31	n=24

* Number in the sample.

COMMUNAL AND PROFESSIONAL ATTITUDES

Student attitudes toward the Reform movement were mixed. There was almost unanimous agreement (91 per cent) that relations between Orthodox, Conservatives, and Reform should be closer; at Cincinnati all the first-year students and 80 per cent of the last-year students agreed on this point. Fifty-five per cent of the students thought that Reform rabbis put too little emphasis on ritual observance and practice, 9 per cent considered it too great, and 36 per cent thought it was about right. At Cincinnati the percentage of students who wanted more emphasis declined from 57 among beginners to 44 for last-year students.

Forty-five per cent of the students believed that, on the whole, the Union of American Hebrew Congregations was responsive to the needs of the American Jewish community. Twenty-seven per cent thought it was not. Favorable appraisal increased from 39 per cent of first-year to 55 per cent of last-year students. As for the Reform rabbinical movement (CCAR), 38 per cent of the students evaluated it positively and

29 per cent negatively. The proportion of favorable responses increased from 35 to 60 per cent between the first and last years.

According to the students, the most pressing problems of American Jews were Jewish social and ethical values, Jewish education, Jewish belief, and the intellectual challenges to Judaism (Table 27). A com-

TABLE 27. HUC-JIR STUDENTS' EVALUATION OF PROBLEMS FACING AMERICAN JEWRY

(*Per cent*)

	Highest priority	Little or no significance
Soviet Jewry	5	0
Strength and survival of the State of Israel *	0	4
Antisemitism in the United States	0	13
Increased dialogue and understanding between Jews and Christians	0	18
Social and ethical values of American Jews	27	0
Intellectual challenges to Judaism	16	5
State of Jewish belief	16	2
Jewish youth on the college campus	2	0
Assimilation	11	4
Intermarriage	2	4
Jewish education	18	4
Decline of religious observance and ritual practice.	2	9
Greater Jewish unity	0	5
Quality of Jewish organizational life	0	0
Other or no answer	2	5
None	0	27

* Responses were received before the Middle Eastern crisis in May 1967.

parison of first- and last-year responses showed only one difference: a decrease from 22 to 10 per cent in the top-priority rating of Jewish education. Second highest priority was given to "Jewish youth on the college campus" by 35 per cent of first-year and 10 per cent of last-year students. The selection of problems of little or no significance differed only by school. Thirty-eight per cent of the New York students and 12 per cent of the Cincinnati students saw no need for increased interfaith dialogue and understanding.

Table 28 shows the proportion of students most willing to devote their time and energy to each of the major American Jewish organizations;

TABLE 28. HUC-JIR STUDENTS' INTEREST IN MAJOR JEWISH ORGANIZATIONS

(*Per cent*)

Organization	Most willing to devote time and energy	Most highly critical
Agudath Israel	0	4
American Council for Judaism	0	51
American Jewish Committee	16	2
American Jewish Congress	4	2
Anti-Defamation League	16	4
B'nai B'rith	7	0
Bonds for Israel	2	4
Jewish Federation or local community-wide philanthropic group	13	2
Jewish Welfare Board	2	0
Labor Zionists of America	0	2
Religious Zionists of America	0	2
Torah Umesorah	0	0
United Jewish Appeal	11	0
Zionist Organization of America	4	5
Other or no answer	18	7
None	7	16

it also indicates the organizations of which students were most highly critical.

The most highly rated organizations were the prestigious secular agencies: the American Jewish Committee, the Anti-Defamation League, and local federations and welfare funds, which traditionally have a more Reform and German character than, for example, the American Jewish Congress. Among 'he New York students the American Jewish Committee elicited little support, and UJA the strongest (23 per cent). At Cincinnati attitudes toward the American Jewish Committee showed the most notable disparity: 37 per cent of graduating students thought it most deserving of their active involvement, as against 4 per cent of first-year students.

Among the organizations that HUC-JIR students were most likely to criticize, the American Council for Judaism again led the list. At Cincinnati the proportion of students so listing it increased from 30 per cent in the first year to 74 per cent in the last.

How does the entering HUC-JIR student's image of the pulpit compare with the graduating student's idea of his profession? Students who

TABLE 29. HUC-JIR STUDENTS' EVALUATION OF A REASONABLE
BEGINNING SALARY FOR A CONGREGATIONAL RABBI

(*Per cent*)

	First-year	Last-year
Under $5,000	0	0
5,000-6,999	6	0
7,000-8,999	25	0
9,000-10,999	47	78
11,000-12,999	22	22
13,000-14,999	0	0
	n*=32	n=23

* Number in the sample.

TABLE 30. HUC-JIR STUDENTS' EVALUATION OF A REASONABLE
SALARY FOR A CONGREGATIONAL RABBI FIVE YEARS
AFTER ORDINATION

(*Per cent*)

	First-year	Last-year
Under $7,000	0	0
7,000-8,999	3	0
9,000-10,999	12	0
11,000-12,999	34	22
13,000-14,999	25	57
15,000-17,499	19	17
17,500-20,000	6	4
	n*=32	n=23

* Number in the sample.

were close to ordination quoted a higher figure as a reasonable salary for congregational rabbis than first-year students (Tables 29 and 30); the trend was the same at YU and JTS. At Cincinnati, however, the student's concept of a reasonable starting salary was higher than at JTS, but his estimate of a reasonable salary after five years of experience was lower.

An analysis of aspects of the rabbinate regarded as most attractive pointed up differences in attitude between Cincinnati and New York students (Table 31). There were no differences by year. New York students were more likely to list "preserve Judaism," "teach Torah,"

TABLE 31. HUC-JIR STUDENTS' ASSESSMENT OF MOST ATTRACTIVE ASPECTS
OF THE RABBINATE

(Per cent)

	Cincinnati school			New York school	Total HUC-JIR
	First year	Last year	Total		
Opportunity to help people find faith	22	22	21	8	18
Opportunity to make people more observant	0	0	0	0	0
Opportunity to teach Torah ..	9	10	9	24	12
Time to study and think	4	5	5	15	7
Comfortable living conditions .	0	0	0	0	0
Opportunity to preserve Judaism	26	20	23	46	29
Opportunity to serve as leader in Jewish community	26	25	26	0	20
Opportunity to serve as leader in general community	0	0	0	0	0
Opportunity for social action .	4	5	5	0	4
Status of rabbi in Jewish community	0	0	0	0	0
Status of rabbi in general community	0	0	0	8	2
Other	9	15	12	0	9
	n*=23	n=20	n=43	n=13	n=56

⁰ Number in the sample.

and "study and think"; Cincinnati students, "serve as a Jewish leader"
or "help people find faith."

The respondents also indicated which aspects of the rabbinate they
found least attractive (Table 32). New York students were not greatly
concerned about the indifference of congregants or lack of privacy, having much stronger feelings about lay control. A comparison of first- and
last-year students showed the latter less concerned about congregants'
indifference to Judaism and about lay control, and much more troubled
by having to preach about matters in which the rabbi lacks conviction—
lack of privacy, and lack of close friends. Last-year students at HUC-
JIR, like those at JTS, revealed greater concern with the more personal
aspects of the rabbinate.

By and large, there was at HUC-JIR less disparity by year regarding
the image of rabbi and pulpit than at JTS—perhaps as a result of the
strong career orientation of all HUC-JIR students, who may have a clear
and fairly constant idea of their professional role. Illustrative of this
point is the fact that first-year students were no more likely than last-year
students to believe that a good rabbi should be able to comfort a mourner

TABLE 32. HUC-JIR STUDENTS' ASSESSMENT OF LEAST ATTRACTIVE ASPECTS
OF THE RABBINATE

(Per cent)

	Cincinnati school			New York school	Total HUC-JIR
	First year	Last year	Total		
Necessity to listen to people's problems	0	0	0	0	0
Lay control over rabbi	22	5	14	38	20
Inadequate material conditions	0	0	0	0	0
Necessity to live away from large city	0	0	0	0	0
Necessity to preach or espouse religious beliefs and practices without being really sure of them	0	15	7	8	7
Necessity to compromise religious principles	4	5	5	0	4
Lack of privacy in personal affairs	9	25	16	23	18
Lack of close friends	0	10	5	8	5
Congregants' indifference to religious observance	13	5	9	8	9
Congregants' indifference to Judaism	39	25	32	15	29
Other or none	13	10	12	0	9
	n*=23	n=20	n=43	n=13	n=56

° Number in the sample.

who raises questions of religious meaning. In general, students at HUC-JIR had greater confidence in their ability to do so than future rabbis at YU or JTS. Most last-year students also believed that their training would be helpful in comforting a mourner (87 per cent) and in providing an honest and satisfactory intellectual response (96 per cent) to his questions.

Summary

Parallels can be drawn between the three major rabbinical schools with regard to the socialization of their students. Future rabbis become more and more career-oriented, as their growing concern with the functions of the rabbi and with adjusting their personal lives to their profession indicates. Future rabbis become socialized to the values of the community and the rabbinical organizations, rather than to the values of each seminary or its faculty. Even at Cincinnati, where students accept a radical, almost revolutionary theology, most last-year students reject its implications if they run counter to accepted community norms. Hence, last-year Cincinnati students would like to see a closer relationship between Orthodoxy, Conservatism, and Reform Judaism.

The most outspoken critics, at least at YU or JTS, are the students who do not intend to enter the congregational rabbinate and who hold more right-wing religious values. However, their potential activist influence is diminished by their reluctance to become involved in Jewish organizational life.

This should not suggest that future rabbis who have reached their senior year simply accept the status quo in American Jewish life. They do not. They are not satisfied with the state of Jewish belief or with religious practice. They are concerned about the preservation of Judaism, and for most of them the inadequacy of Jewish education is a problem of major importance. But their attitude toward Jewish communal life as now constituted is one of acceptance or possibly of recognizing a need for reform, not one of rejection and advocacy of revolutionary changes. By and large, they visualized their influence as operating on the personal, not the communal, level. This, we suggest, is not because in this case the students really reject the explicit values of their seminaries or, for that matter, of their faculties. It is rather because the seminaries are in many respects quite conservative, have little to say about the Jewish community, and, if only by default, accept its basic structure.

BY WAY OF PERSONAL CONCLUSION

A chief purpose of our study was to gain insight into the rabbinical programs of the major seminaries. Our effort has been to understand and, to a lesser extent, to evaluate each institution—primarily on its own terms. But an understanding of the implications of the programs at each institution requires a more radical critique, that should begin by stepping back and seeking an overview.

The American rabbinical seminaries are, in essence, neither vocational nor professional institutions. Certainly, JTS and HUC-JIR are academic institutions that are close in character to graduate schools of arts or humanities. At the same time, each institution has its prototype in the European Jewish community: For YU it is the East European yeshivah; for JTS or HUC-JIR, the West European rabbinical seminary pursuing the study of the Wissenschaft des Judentums. None of the seminaries is actually oriented toward professional training, and in none is the training of rabbis *per se* an overriding concern. If they were greatly concerned with this training, we would be able to glean from the program of each seminary its particular image of the role of the rabbi. As it is, we can infer a rabbinical model, but not one that is consciously formulated.

The seminaries conceive the rabbi as knowing the Jewish textual tradition and, secondarily, as having some basic skills in preaching and officiating at religious and quasi-religious functions. Third in importance is his ability to do minimal counseling, and perhaps to recognize serious psychological problems in his congregants. Every rabbi can answer elementary questions of religious law, or at least know when a serious question has been asked; he has some familiarity with the sources, textual or living, which he can consult. He is, then, a good Jew not so much because he lives a good Jewish life, but in the traditional Jewish sense of *lo' 'am-ha'arez ḥasid,* the ignorant man cannot be righteous.

In the community the rabbi's primary function is to be a source of Jewish knowledge. Although the seminary may define his role as that of teacher, he has no special skills for articulating or communicating his knowledge. He is more like an encyclopedia sitting on a shelf, waiting to be consulted. In some ways, the rabbi is also viewed as director or coordinator of Jewish affairs, but primarily as a servant of the community not as a leader who initiates programs or activities for restructuring Jewish society, or even preserving Jewish tradition in modern society.

Our findings imply that the rabbinical schools envisage the rabbi as a conservative, insofar as he works within the established framework of Jewish institutions, and a traditionalist. This image, one may argue, was reasonable in the past. As long as the Talmud and the *Shulḥan 'Arukh* were the constitution of Jewish life, Judaism primarily required authoritative interpreters and teachers of the constitution. But such a Jewish community no longer exists.

One might therefore suggest that the rabbi's primary function today is to recreate a meaningful Jewish community with a meaningful constitution around which Jewish life can be organized. Some may envisage an altered community adopting entirely new consensual or authoritative symbols to replace the older code of law. Others may prefer a revision of the old code. The Orthodox, of course, would want nothing of the sort; but even here new applications of the extant codes or rabbinical traditions to contemporary life may be envisaged.

Whatever the case, if helping to create a more meaningful community were indeed the rabbi's function, he would need training that differs radically from the one he is now receiving. The seminaries would first have to explicate the goals of Jewish life, as they see it. At both YU and JTS, the goal, as implicitly understood, is the recreation of a romanticized notion of 19th-century East European Jewish life. It is a goal so patently absurd that no one really dares to voice it openly. If they were forced to give serious consideration to the problem, both YU and JTS would offer more meaningful goals. (HUC-JIR simply has no model or ideal of Jewish life.) Once such goals of Jewish life are established, it would be incumbent on each seminary to give the future rabbi an understanding of the contemporary world and of Jewish life as it exists in this world. This task cannot be discharged by undergraduate schools. American colleges, including Yeshiva College, base their instruction on the assumption that the student can gain adequate understanding of the world from a purely secular perspective. It is this assumption which probably poses the most serious problem for religious institutions. As a Protestant authority has put it:

> There is a widespread tendency for academic departments (of Bible, history, or theology) to talk about books, doctrines, movements and characters of the past, and for practical departments to talk about books, doctrines, movements and people of today, adding, perhaps, the sciences which help us understand them. This leaves a number of awkward impressions. In biblical times it is God who is presented as having once been active in delivering men from bondage, whereas in modern time it is industrial technology which appears as the great power causing the migrations of peoples or delivering men from drudgery. . . . Each of these things is true in its way, but often neither is related to the practice of the student's impending ministry. Or, as a Lutheran theologian put it to us in a study conference, Protestant biblical studies have left many people with the impression that God has never acted since Bible times.[33]

After goals are established and an understanding of the Jewish community and the world around it is imparted, seminaries can proceed with the formulation of strategy for the preservation or restructuring of the environment in consonance with their goals. This does not mean that seminaries would no longer teach Bible, or Talmud, or Midrash. It does mean that curricula no longer would distinguish between academic and practical courses. That which is not "practical" would have no place in the curriculum. Either the Jewish tradition and its texts have practical application, in which case they must be taught; or they have not, in which case they are unnecessary. If the former is true, it must be reflected in the teaching. God does not speak to the Jew in his tradition in the same

---

[33] Charles R. Feilding, "Education for Ministry," *op. cit.*, pp. 13–14.

way as to the Christian, or at least to the Protestant, in his. God is revealed to the Jew primarily through texts and law; nevertheless, He is to be found there by *contemporary* man. This is a matter of faith—the foundation for the entire spiritual enterprise of the Jew.

Here two possibilities must be considered. If the belief in a God who reveals and is revealed in the sacred texts is rejected, the texts have no intrinsic religious meaning. They may be beautiful and inspiring as reflections of the moral and literary achievements of man. As such, they can be pursued in a scholarly fashion, but not in rabbinical school which has too many pressing tasks to devote time to studies having no practical value. (This may not have been true a hundred years ago. But today, when the texts are not familiar to most Jews and at best have retained only broad symbolic meaning, the rabbi needs no more than the most superficial knowledge of their content.)

If, on the other hand, the traditional Jewish belief in the sacred texts is affirmed, the rabbi must be trained to understand the texts, the law, and the history of the Jews in order to understand what God tells us about our problems, our life, and our predicament. It is not necessary that seminaries teach Jewish philosophy, theology, ethics, or the contemporary community. It is necessary that every course and every instructor be grounded in Jewish theology, philosophy, ethics, and the contemporary community. Faculty members need not necessarily know "about" theology, philosophy, or ethics; but they must have a viable philosophy, theology, and ethic that are in harmony with those of their seminary. This means that seminaries could have no place on their faculties for instructors who do not accept the theology in which the curriculum is grounded.

Obviously, such practical courses are not identical with the "how-to-do-it" instruction for future rabbis on financing, administration, personnel, counseling, preaching, and like matters. These are useful, but peripheral, and best learned on the job. If they are offered at the seminary, they should be optional non-credit courses, clearly secondary to the institution's main function.

In theory, at least, such a program probably would have strong appeal for some people. It has the virtue of being so radical and impossible to implement that it could not conceivably be adopted by any existing seminary. It would require faculties different from any presently staffing the seminaries—faculties, in all probability, impossible to recruit. It would require an enormous degree of initiative, energy, and imagination. It would mean a complete reversal of current trends.

The rabbinical program plays an ever smaller part in the total programs of YU, JTS, and HUC-JIR; they have developed hosts of activities that are either not at all or only peripherally related to rabbinical training. Incredibly, there is not one single person in any of the institutions who has both the full-time responsibility and the authority to direct the rabbinical program. The top leaders are increasingly remote from their rabbinical schools. The major portion of their time and effort is not devoted to training or educating future rabbis, nor to raising funds exclusively for the rabbinical programs.

Thus, if a radical new program for training rabbis were desirable, a new rabbinical school would have to be established for it. But who would provide the resources for such an institution? Surely not those who heretofore have shown no interest in, or concern for, Jewish religion or the American rabbinate. Support would have to come from persons already committed to Jewish religious life. A new seminary also would have to have a theology or religious ideology. It would have to start with certain assumptions about God, revelation, the tradition, the "good life," and other matters. In short, it would have to be at least remotely denominational. The mere enumeration of these needs reveals the paucity of resources available for such an institution. If we measure each seminary against its lay and rabbinical organizations, we must come to the conclusion that there are in the community no emotional, intellectual, or religious resources capable of improving upon the job the seminary is doing now.

In the final analysis, moreover, a good case can be made against the merits of a radical reorganization of rabbinical training. Of course, one's sense of immediacy regarding the need for change depends on one's evaluation of how our rabbis are doing today and on one's assessment of the quality of Jewish life. Most people seem to feel that we are somehow managing to muddle through. Laymen are far less displeased with their rabbis than rabbis with their laymen. But even the rabbis do not noticeably support recommendations for radical changes in the community.

The entire program of radical reorganization is based on the assumption that religion can be communicated to man today—a dubious assumption, indeed. Not only does radical reorganization suggest faith in God and Torah; it also rests on the supposition that we can know the message of God and Torah for man today—a task that, in the Jewish tradition, requires prodigious scholarship and careful analysis. It also assumes the willingness of the American Jew to hear the message. But none of these conjectures may actually be true. Even if we are correct about God and Torah, and even if we can successfully extract their message for man today, there may not be anybody to listen. Most Jews in the United States live in, and accept, a condition of religious pluralism and Jewish voluntarism. The community lacks authority and power of coercion. Hence, the message of Judaism must transform each individual Jew, not his kings and princes. It must do so in the absence of the ordinary sanctions and rewards, both formal and informal, that are usually available in communities where ideological transformation has occurred. The minimal precondition, then, is dissatisfaction with the status quo. But most Jews are not dissatisfied.

To whom then is the new rabbinate or seminary to speak? In effect, only to itself. But this the seminary already does, at least by implication. The study of texts—the tradition of study for its own sake without expectation of reward or status—exists. It is stronger at some seminaries than at others, but it exists everywhere. Such study may be viewed as arid scholasticism. It may also be considered a rejection, by example if not by exhortation, of the path of contemporary Judaism.

At its best, the study of text is a call, however dim, for the Jew to come to Torah and find his own meaning there. The very arduousness of the task demands that he turn his back upon the irrelevance and emptiness of much of Jewish life today, and to reform and transform himself to the best of his abilities and virtues. The exclusive study of text further implies that the world is hopeless and the predicament of the Jew impossible; that grandiose programs of reform will not succeed because only a handful want to be reformed. It calls upon this handful to intensify the quality of their Jewish life. It suggests that Judaism has always survived and will continue to survive in the lives of a small remnant who pursue the work of God and the word of God at its source, and who can influence only by example.

This should not suggest that seminary life is grounded in such an ideal. By the most generous standard, the average quality of religious life at rabbinical seminaries cannot be called inspiring. As at other academic institutions, rivalries and jealousies exist. Students are often slighted. Masters of the Talmud are preoccupied with seniority rights and whether they teach a more or a less advanced class, while overlooking abuses before their very eyes. Promotions are vied for. Some professors yearn for publicity in the general press, and then enviously condemn successful colleagues. Some are failures who inflict their bitterness on students.

But the vision of an exemplary life exists in varying degrees at every institution. The vision—not the reality, yet the vision must precede the reality.

GLOSSARY

BRGS .....Bernard Revel Graduate School, Yeshiva University
CCAR .....Central Conference of American Rabbis (Reform)
HUC-JIR ...Hebrew Union College-Jewish Institute of Religion
JTS ....Jewish Theological Seminary
KOLEL ....Special program for more intensive study of Talmud, Yeshiva University
RA ....Rabbinical Assembly (Conservative)
RCA ......Rabbinical Council of America (Orthodox)
RIETS .....Rabbi Isaac Elchanan Theological Seminary, Yeshiva University
UAHC .....Union of American Hebrew Congregations (Reform)
UOJC .....Union of Orthodox Jewish Congregations
         United Synagogue of America (Conservative)
YU ....Yeshiva University

ORTHODOXY IN AMERICAN JEWISH LIFE[1]

by Charles S. Liebman

INTRODUCTION • DEMOGRAPHIC CHARACTERISTICS OF ORTHODOXY • EARLY ORTHODOX COMMUNITY • UNCOMMITTED ORTHODOX • COMMITTED ORTHODOX • MODERN ORTHODOX • SECTARIANS • LEADERSHIP • DIRECTIONS AND TENDENCIES • APPENDIX: YESHIVOT PROVIDING INTENSIVE TALMUDIC STUDY

THIS ESSAY is an effort to describe the communal aspects and institutional forms of Orthodox Judaism in the United States. For the most part, it ignores the doctrines, faith, and practices of Orthodox Jews, and barely touches upon synagogue life, which is the most meaningful expression of American Orthodoxy.

It is hoped that the reader will find here some appreciation of the vitality of American Orthodoxy. Earlier predictions of the demise of

---

[1] I am indebted to many people who assisted me in making this essay possible. More than 40, active in a variety of Orthodox organizations, gave freely of their time for extended discussions and interviews and many lay leaders and rabbis throughout the United States responded to a mail questionnaire. A number of people read a draft of this paper. I would be remiss if I did not mention a few by name, at the same time exonerating them of any responsibility for errors of fact or for my own judgments and interpretations. The section on modern Orthodoxy was read by Rabbi Emanuel Rackman. The sections beginning with the sectarian Orthodox to the conclusion of the paper were read by Rabbi Nathan Bulman. Criticism and comments on the entire paper were forthcoming from Rabbi Aaron Lichtenstein, Dr. Marshall Sklare, and Victor Geller, without whose assistance the section on the number of Orthodox Jews could not have been written. To all of these, and to Mrs. Ruth Gould for her editorial assistance, I am deeply grateful.

In general, Hebrew has been transliterated according to the Israeli pronunciation, but Hebrew names of institutions are usually given as the institutions themselves give them. See p. 507 for abbreviations.

Orthodox Judaism in the United States have been premature, to say the least. Orthodoxy is on the upsurge. Its inner core is growing in numbers and financial strength. It is experiencing a greater sense of confidence and purpose, but its ultimatè direction and form are still undetermined. An attempt is here made to pose the alternatives, at least for Orthodoxy's public posture.

DEMOGRAPHIC CHARACTERISTICS OF ORTHODOXY

Number of Orthodox Jews

We propose to discuss Orthodoxy, as a differentiated movement among American Jews, in institutional terms. Hence we define Orthodox Jews as all Jews who are affiliated with nominally Orthodox synagogues. Alternate definitions would include Jews who view the *halakhah* or Jewish law as an obligatory standard for all Jews; or who behave as Orthodox Jews in ritual or halakhic terms, or who define themselves as Orthodox without regard to their behavior. There are definitional problems in the first two alternatives, although an estimate is given at a later point of the number of such observant Orthodox Jews. With respect to the number of Jews who consider themselves as Orthodox, no reliable estimates can be made because we have no quantitative study of Orthodoxy in New York City. Studies made in various communities outside New York indicate that as many as a third of the Jews who consider themselves as Orthodox are not affiliated with any congregation.[2] On the other hand, these and other studies [3] show that at least a third of Jews affiliated with Orthodox synagogues outside New York City consider themselves as something other than Orthodox (usually Conservative), whereas a far smaller proportion of members of Conservative synagogues consider themselves as Orthodox.

---

[2] See, for example, *The Jewish Population of Rochester, New York, 1961* (Rochester: Jewish Community Council, 1961); Stanley K. Bigman, *The Jewish Population of Greater Washington in 1956* (Washington, D.C.: Jewish Community Council, 1957), and Albert J. Mayer, *Branches of Judaism, Synagogue and Temple Membership, and Attendance at Religious Services of the Jewish Population in the Detroit Metropolitan Area, 1956* (Detroit: Jewish Welfare Federation, 1961).

[3] For example, Leonard Reissman, *Profile of a Community; A Sociological Study of the New Orleans Jewish Community* (New Orleans: Jewish Federation, 1958); Sidney Goldstein, *The Greater Providence Jewish Community; A Population Survey* (Providence: General Jewish Community, 1964); or the series of studies by Manheim Shapiro, under the sponsorship of the American Jewish Committee, of attitudes of Jews in Miami, Memphis, Baltimore, Kansas City, and White Plains.

When the present study was undertaken in 1964, there were no reliable estimates of the number of Jews affiliated with Orthodox synagogues in the United States. With the assistance of Victor Geller and other staff members of the Community Service Division of Yeshiva University, lists of all known Orthodox synagogues were compiled for the 40 communities outside Greater New York (New York City, Westchester, Nassau, and Suffolk counties) which have 10,000 or more Jews or three or more known Orthodox synagogues. A questionnaire was sent to an Orthodox community leader, generally a practicing rabbi, in each of these communities. It listed the known Orthodox synagogues and asked the respondent to estimate the number of adult male members in each. Respondents were asked to correct the lists by removing congregations that were not at least nominally Orthodox and adding any that had been omitted, including private *minyanim* (conventicles) unaffiliated with organized synagogues. Thirty-three replies were received. Figures for the other seven communities were taken from local community studies (Detroit) or estimated by a staff member of the Community Service Division on the basis of his synagogue contacts. Estimates for all other known Orthodox synagogues in the United States outside New York City and the 40 major Jewish communities were made by Victor Geller. This included estimates for New York suburbs.

Estimates for New York City were arrived at somewhat differently because of the large number of Orthodox synagogues (approximately 800),[4] about many of which little is known.[5] Large-congregation memberships were estimated by CSD staff members most familiar with each borough. Memberships of smaller congregations in New York City were estimated by applying an arbitrary multiplier, which varied from borough to borough and neighborhood to neighborhood. In the Bronx and Queens the multiplier was 30; on the Lower East Side of Manhattan it was 100; in Brooklyn, with most of the synagogues, and particularly the small ones, it was 80.

Thus there is an estimated total of 205,640 men affiliated with the 1,603 known Orthodox synagogues in the United States.

It should be clear then that the figures given in the table are only estimates and that the margin of error is surely quite high. The method employed to make the estimates would account for formal membership only;

---

[4] The actual number of syngagogues in New York City was derived from New York City's *List of Tax-exempt Properties* for 1962.

[5] The figure of 1,103 Orthodox synagogues, presented in the 1964 *Statistical Guide for New York City,* is based on estimates by the Union of Orthodox Jewish Congregations and is not current.

TABLE 1. NUMBER OF KNOWN ORTHODOX SYNAGOGUES AND AFFILIATED MALE WORSHIPPERS IN THE UNITED STATES, BY STATE, 1964 [a]

State	Synagogues	Male Worshippers
Alabama	3	650
Arizona	2	450
Arkansas	1	300
California	57	5,415
Colorado	7	1,375
Connecticut	29	5,335
Delaware	1	700
District of Columbia	9	1,820
Florida	12	1,220[b]
Georgia	5	1,225
Illinois	64	10,132
Indiana	7	1,395
Iowa	4	565
Kansas	2	370
Kentucky	2	650
Louisiana	6	1,270
Maine	9	1,020
Maryland	43	6,440
Massachusetts	60	8,750
Michigan	28	4,212[c]
Minnesota	16	1,960
Mississippi	2	90
Missouri	15	3,725
Nebraska	3	575
New Hampshire	1	40
New Jersey	113	15,310
New York	906	100,720
New York City	809[d]	86,115
Bronx	129	12,485
Brooklyn	467	45,895
Manhattan	123	13,435
Queens	86	13,800
Richmond	4	500
Westchester, Nassau, Suffolk, and Rockland counties	42	7,530
Upstate New York	55	7,075
North Carolina	2	175
Ohio	33	8,336
Oregon	3	430
Pennsylvania	103	11,175
Rhode Island	14	1,380
South Carolina	1	375
Tennessee	6	1,875
Texas	10	1,795
Utah	1	275
Vermont	1	120
Virginia	8	1,225
Washington	5	925

TABLE 1. (Continued)

State	Synagogues	Male Worshippers
West Virginia	2	320
Wisconsin	10	1,370
Wyoming	1	75
TOTAL	1,607	204,815

ᵃ Excluding approximately 15 synagogues in downtown business districts which are used exclusively for saying *kaddish* and have no regular membership or Sabbath services, or the approximately 50 synagogues which respondents judged to lie between Orthodox and Conservative; but including *yeshivot* known to be places of worship.

ᵇ The number of regular worshippers far exceeds the number of members, but many of the worshippers are tourists in the Miami area who are presumably affiliated with synagogues in their home towns. However, the transient character of many residents probably means that membership figures for Florida are not a good criterion for estimating the strength of the local synagogues.

ᶜ Figures for Detroit were not available. The Michigan estimate of 4,212 includes 3,977 men belonging to Orthodox synagogues in Detroit, estimated on the basis of a 1956 sample survey in Albert J. Mayer, *op. cit.*, and 235 in the rest of the state, estimated by CSD staff members. As the AJYB went to press, data became available for 1963: Albert J. Mayer, *Social and Economic Characteristics of the Detroit Jewish Community: 1963* (Detroit: Jewish Welfare Federation, December 1964). They suggest that our estimate is probably too high.

ᵈ Based on estimates derived from the 1962 *List of Tax-exempt Properties.*

it does not include family members or others served by the synagogue, or people who worship there only on special occasions. If it did, the figure would be much higher.

The men referred to in the table may belong to more than one Orthodox synagogue, as indicated by two studies of dual memberships. Howard Polsky found that 91 per cent of Milwaukee Jews affiliated with Orthodox congregations belonged to only one such congregation and over eight per cent to two.[6] This means that the actual number of affiliated Orthodox Jews was only about 95 per cent of what the membership rolls would seem to indicate. In Providence, R.I.[7] the figure was 96 per cent. It can therefore be assumed that there is some duplication of members in the figures presented, but it does not appear to be substantial.

No effort was made to estimate the number of all Orthodox Jews by applying a multiplier to the total of men. Any multiplier would have to

---

[6] Howard Polsky, *The Great Defense: A Study of Jewish Orthodoxy in Milwaukee* (University of Wisconsin, unpublished doctoral dissertation, 1956), p. 275. Part of this study is summarized in Marshall Sklare, ed., *The Jews* (Glencoe, 1957), pp. 325–35.

[7] Sidney Goldstein, *op. cit.*

take into account factors beyond the scope of this paper, including these:

1. The average size of Orthodox families compared with the average size of all Jewish families in the United States, currently estimated at 3.3 by the research department of the Council of Jewish Federations and Welfare Funds.

2. The age distribution of Orthodox Jews, compared with the total Jewish population.

3. The effect on fertility of the concentration of Orthodox Jews in central cities rather than suburbs.

4. The total effect of the halakhic proscription against most types of birth control, which has contributed to an average birth rate of six to seven children per Orthodox family in Williamsburg.[8]

5. The greater propensity of people with children to affiliate with synagogues than single people or young married couples.

The (Reform) Union of American Hebrew Congregations uses a multiplier of 3.5 individuals per family as the first stage in arriving at their estimate of the number of Reform Jews; the (Conservative) United Synagogue of America uses 4.5. For institutional purposes, most organizations and movements no doubt need membership estimates, but since Orthodox data are insufficient for the purpose, the effort will not be made here.

Social Characteristics

To determine the social characteristics of the nominally Orthodox Jews, we must rely almost exclusively on data originating outside New York City. Studies of various Jewish communities have included questions on synagogue affiliation or self-identification of Orthodox, Conservative, Reform, and unaffiliated or unidentifying Jews.[9] Respondents have often been further classified by one or more such variables as age, income, education, and occupation.

All such studies have found the nominally Orthodox to be older, of more recent immigrant origin, of lower income and occupational status, and with more limited secular education than Conservative, Reform, or unaffiliated Jews. However, no published study traces the relationship of

---

8 Solomon Poll, *Hasidic Community of Williamsburg* (New York, 1962).
9 E.g., Jewish Community Council of Rochester, *op. cit.;* Stanley K. Bigman, *op. cit.;* Leonard Reissman, *op. cit.;* Jack Porter, *Differentiating Features of Orthodox, Conservative, and Reform Jewish Groups in Metropolitan Philadelphia* (Temple University, unpublished doctoral dissertation, 1958); Sidney Goldstein, *op. cit.;* Albert J. Mayer, *op. cit.,* and Marshall Sklare, Marc Vosk, and Mark Zborowski, "Forms and Expressions of Jewish Identification," *Jewish Social Studies,* July 1955, pp. 205–18.

social characteristics to denomination over time.[10] Details from a study in progress are not yet available, but it appears that the income and the educational and occupational levels of the American Orthodox Jew are rising relatively to other Jews, and that Reform is reaching into lower-middle-income levels for the first time.

EARLY ORTHODOX COMMUNITY

The demographic data on the social characteristics of the nominally Orthodox support the popular notion of the development of Orthodox and Conservative Judaism in the United States. According to this notion, the masses of East and Central European Jews who came to the United States between 1870 and 1924 were overwhelmingly Orthodox. Under the impact of economic necessity and cultural challenge, they changed. Some abandoned religion completely, a few became Reform. Some, however, and many more of their descendants, adjusted their religious tradition to the mores of contemporary America and evolved a form of worship and ritual that eventually became known as Conservative Judaism. Of course, many remained Orthodox. But these were the aged, the poor, and the poorly-educated, who established their early synagogues in the downtown areas of most large American cities. As the Jewish population gained in social status and new generations migrated outward and abandoned Orthodox practices, they left behind a residue of socially static Orthodox.[11]

There is reason to challenge this notion.[12] Unquestionably, a large group of immigrants, who conformed superficially to many Orthodox norms, were viewed as Orthodox by their "uptown" coreligionists. But a second look affords some contrary impressions. That the new immigrants founded countless small synagogues almost immediately upon arrival was not in itself evidence of religiosity. If the function of the synagogue was primarily for worship there was no need for such multiplication whereas if the primary purpose of the synagogue was to meet the social and cultural needs of small groups originating in the same European community, the multiplication is more understandable. In fact, the activity within

---

[10] A comparison of the social characteristics of Greater New York areas where new Orthodox, Conservative, or Reform synagogues were established, or existing facilities were expanded, is being prepared by the author for future publication in AJYB.

[11] The popular literature is replete with such assertions. For a scholarly study that makes this point see Howard Polsky, *op. cit.* Polsky's material is drawn from Milwaukee.

[12] I am indebted to my wife, Carol Liebman, for suggesting this line of inquiry.

these new synagogues raises serious questions about their religion. The synagogues were social forums and benevolent societies [13] adapted to the requirements of poor, unacculturated people. The oft-cited absence of decorum during the services strongly suggests that even the act of worship was perhaps a social more than a religious function, although this may have been true in Eastern Europe as well.

If the immigrants were indeed religiously motivated, the practical exigencies of strict ritual requirements would demand a *mikveh, the* lustration bath, before a synagogue. (For a discussion of *mikveh* see p. 90.) There is at least anecdotal evidence that *mikvaot* were scarce and inaccessible outside New York City, and sometimes even within it.

Talmud Torah—the study of the Jewish tradition and particularly its holy texts—and the maintenance of educational facilities certainly take halakhic precedence over the establishment of synagogues. But the new immigrants conspicuously neglected Jewish education. A survey in New York in 1908 indicated that only 28 per cent of the Jewish children between the ages of six and sixteen received even the scantiest Jewish education.[14] Until 1915 there were only two Jewish day schools in the whole country. The immigrants flocked instead to the public schools, to night classes, and to adult-education courses,[15] not only for vocational purposes but for general cultural advancement. The dangers to Orthodoxy of secular education must have been evident from the outset, but only since World War II have strong voices within the Orthodox camp been raised against college education, the institutionalization of secular knowledge.

The Young Israel movement in its infancy was frequently castigated as being "too modern" and hence non-Orthodox. But attempted mergers between Young Israel and neighboring Orthodox synagogues often failed not because of Young Israel's modernity and questionable Orthodoxy, but rather because its requirement that all congregational officers be Sabbath observers could not be met by the older, more "traditional" synagogue.

The early East European immigrants came to the United States at a

---

13 There is a vast literature on this point as well. For one of the most pertinent and interesting series of essays in English see Charles S. Bernheimer, ed., *The Russian Jew in the United States* (Philadelphia, 1905).

14 Cited among other places in Moses Rischin, *The Promised City* (Cambridge, 1962), p. 108. See also Lloyd P. Gartner, "The Jews of New York's East Side, 1890–1893," *American Jewish Historical Quarterly,* March 1964, pp. 264–78.

15 Moses Rischin, *op. cit.,* and every other study of the East European Jews in the United States.

time when traditional Judaism, even in Eastern Europe, had been thoroughly shaken by Enlightenment and secularism.[16] Even for those Orthodox who idealized religious life in Eastern Europe, the revival of traditional Judaism did not begin until the 1920s, at the end of the great wave of immigration to the United States. In fact, Agudath Israel, which represented the most traditional element in Jewish life and whose membership rose to an estimated half million in Eastern Europe, sought and failed to establish an organization in the United States in 1922 although almost all the great rabbinical leaders of Eastern Europe supported it. (Significantly, the organization did succeed in establishing a youth organization.)

There was a paucity of distinguished rabbis and scholars among the immigrants. Although an estimated 50,000 Jews immigrated from 1881 to 1885, the leading East European congregation of the time in New York had only a part-time rabbi of meager scholarship. When 26 Orthodox congregations met to choose a joint leader for New York Jewry, no American rabbi was even considered, and in 1887 the secretary to Rabbi Isaac Elhanan Spektor, the outstanding rabbinic authority of Russia, referred to American rabbinical leaders as "improper men." [17]

Those who emigrated first can be expected to have been the least traditional, whose piety was at most what Leo Baeck called *Milieu-Frömmigkeit*.[18] Willing as they were to take extended leave of family and home, they were no doubt less committed to tradition than their relatives and neighbors who came much later. When the Rabbi of Slutsk visited America and appeared at a public meeting of the Union of Orthodox Jewish Congregations during the first wave of immigration, "he chastised the assemblage for having emigrated to this *trefa* [impure] land." [19] Similarly,

---

[16] E.g., Herbert Parzen, "When Secularism Came to Russian Jewry," *Commentary*, April 1952, pp. 355–62.

[17] Abraham J. Karp, "New York Chooses a Chief Rabbi," *Publications of the American Jewish Historical Society*, March 1955, pp. 129–98.

[18] A Yiddish story relates how a small Jewish town in East Europe raised money to send a young man to America for fear that he would otherwise have married a gentile: Isaac Metzker, "To the New World," in Irving Howe and Eliezer Greenberg, eds., *A Treasury of Yiddish Stories* (New York, 1958), pp. 504–15. Another writer has noted: "After all, who went to America? Overwhelmingly, it was not the elite of learning, piety, or money but the *shnayders*, the *shusters*, and the *ferdganovim*": Milton Himmelfarb, "The Intellectual and the Rabbi," in Rabbinical Assembly of America, *Proceedings*, 1963, p. 124. See also Mark Zborowski and Elizabeth Herzog, *Life is with People* (New York, 1952), pp. 260–61, and Arthur Hertzberg, "Seventy Years of Jewish Education," *Judaism*, October 1952, p. 361.

[19] Moshe Davis, "Jewish Religious Life and Institutions in America," in Louis Finkelstein, ed., *The Jews: Their History, Culture, and Religion* (2nd ed.; New

would-be emigrants were warned to stay home and not endanger their Judaism by such renowned rabbinic authorities as the *Hafetz Hayyím*, Rabbi Israel Meir Hacohen.[20] Immigrants, often unable to separate the essential from the unessential in Judaism, would surrender an element of custom such as a beard, and then feel free to compromise everything else. Parents, brought to America by children who prepared the way, first wept for their children's violations of ritual, then adjusted. And of the older men who did go to work, most succumbed to violations of the Sabbath.[21]

The evidence suggests an absence of religious as distinct from ethnic commitment on the part of most nominally Orthodox immigrants to the United States. Thus, the rise of Conservative Judaism and secularism in American Jewish life did not entail a decision to opt out of traditional religion. It was, rather, a decision to substitute new social and cultural mores for the older ones, which had been intermingled with certain ritual manifestations.

Of course, this discussion does an injustice to those truly religious Jews who worked to build the early *mikvaot* and day schools and who sought the continuation of their authentic religious tradition in the United States. The significant fact, however, is that people of this sort represented a much smaller minority than has heretofore been imagined; and even of them or their descendants, many were attracted by the nascent Conservative movement, which they felt held greater promise for modern-day religiosity.

UNCOMMITTED ORTHODOX

Two groups of Orthodox Jews will be defined and considered in this section—the residual Orthodox and the non-observant Orthodox. The Union of Orthodox Rabbis of the United States and Canada (*Agudat Ha-rabbanim*) is treated together with the residual Orthodox only for clarity of presentation. The rabbis themselves obviously do not fall into this category.

York, 1955), I, p. 405. See also Bernard D. Weinryb, "Jewish Immigration and Accommodation to America: Research, Trends, Problems," in Moshe Davis and Isidore Meyer, eds., *The Writing of American Jewish History* (New York), p. 319, for a similar point.

20 Quoted in Lloyd P. Gartner, *The Jewish Immigrant in England, 1870–1914* (Detroit, 1960), p. 30.

21 Charles Bernheimer, *op. cit.*, pp. 158–61.

Residual Orthodox

We shall designate as residually Orthodox those remnants of the East European immigrants who remained nominally Orthodox more out of cultural and social inertia than out of religious choice. In all likelihood they still constitute the bulk of nominally Orthodox Jews in the United States; they probably determine the social image of Orthodoxy and are doubtless responsible for the statistical picture which shows a skewed distribution on the high end of the age continuum and on the low end of the income and educational continuum. The residual Orthodox represent a dying generation. Until the Second World War their children, with few exceptions, abandoned Orthodoxy. Since 1940, however, an increasing number of these, having been afforded the opportunity for a day-school education or a certain measure of social status in modern Orthodox synagogues, have become committed and practising Orthodox Jews, or have retained at least nominal affiliation with Orthodoxy.

It would be misleading to conceptualize a communal structure for the residual Jew, whose major identification came through the local synagogue. To the extent that such a structure existed, however, it was headed by the *shtot rov* or chief rabbi of each community. This was particularly true outside New York City and Chicago. Cities like Newark, N.J., Boston, Mass., Philadelphia, Pa., Baltimore, Md., Cleveland and Cincinnati, O., Milwaukee, Wis., Springfield, Mass., Rock Island, Ill., and Detroit, Mich. each had one rabbi who towered over the Orthodox community; he supervised kosher slaughtering, baking, and the processing of other foods, and presided over the local Jewish court. These were Orthodox leaders par excellence. New York and Chicago never produced a *shtot rov,* although one effort in that direction was made when Rabbi Jacob Joseph was brought from Vilna in 1888 to serve as chief rabbi of New York. The failure to organize either of the two major Jewish cities around a single rabbinic personality could be attributed to their size, Jewish diversity, and the fact that the residual Jew was not communally oriented. Nevertheless, even in New York and Chicago there were a handful of rabbis whose names were known to Orthodox Jews and who together could make some claim to leadership in the Orthodox community. These, and the lesser rabbinic personalities who revolved about them, were organized in the Union of Orthodox Rabbis, which gradually lost its ascendancy as the position of communal rabbi declined. This decline mirrored the decline of the communal rabbi's constituency, the residual Orthodox, who at one time probably constituted the majority of all Jews in the United States.

*Union of Orthodox Rabbis of the United States
and Canada (Agudat Ha-rabbanim)*

Agudat Ha-rabbanim is the oldest organization of Orthodox rabbis in the United States. Founded in 1902, it was led for many years by Rabbi Israel Rosenberg, a leading New York rabbi and a founder of Yeshiva University. Its prestige rested on the affiliation of the leading rabbis of most Jewish communities. Its members were instrumental in founding most early day schools in the United States. At the beginning of World War I they established the Central Relief Committee, which was eventually absorbed by JDC, and during the 1920s they sponsored the visit to the United States of leading European rabbinic authorities. Today, however, little remains of Agudat Ha-rabbanim's influence and prestige. Three factors contributed to its decline.

First, the role of the communal rabbi declined drastically as the Jew increasingly became congregationally rather than communally oriented. With Americanization and the growth of the YMHA, community centers, and Conservative, Reform, and finally even Orthodox synagogue centers (not to speak of country clubs and fraternal lodges), fewer and fewer Jews looked for an authoritative rabbinic figure to speak for the community. Most Jews looked for communal services that were essentially philanthropic rather than religious. An authoritative figure who could answer questions of religious law was no longer required, since such questions were now rarely asked.

The second factor accounting for the decline of the Agudat Ha-rabbanim stemmed from the nature of the Orthodox immigrants who began arriving in the late 1930s. If the communal rabbi received little support from the acculturated Jew, his position was not bolstered by the more aggressively Orthodox Jews who immigrated in the Nazi and postwar era from Poland, Hungary, and Germany. The new Orthodox immigrants did not relate to the existing network of American Jewish institutions and had little need and much distrust for Orthodox rabbis who served the function of Orthodoxy's representatives in the larger Jewish community.

Agudat Ha-rabbanim members were caught, in the midst of changing Jewish identification, between the less religious left and the more religious right, and they were unable to respond. The Yiddish-speaking, often bearded rabbi—a severe and inflexible figure—was a symbol of a past generation with which the secularized, Americanized Jew had little in common. To the new immigrant and the younger, more militant Orthodox Jew, on the other hand, that rabbi was too compromising. The *rashe yeshivot,* the Talmud scholars who headed the *yeshivot,* rose to prominence in this period, when the younger, more committed, observant Jew noted that the communal rabbi's talmudical scholarship could not equal that of his *rosh yeshivah.*

The issue which most severely damaged the image of the Agudat Harabbanim type of rabbi was *kashrut* supervision. Rightly or wrongly, an image persisted of the communal rabbi who, pressured by butchers, food processors, and slaughterers to ease *kashrut* requirements, and plagued by the indifference of Jewish consumers, lowered his standards of supervision. The Agudat Ha-rabbanim, unlike the Union of Orthodox Jewish Congregations, took no organizational responsibility for the supervision of its members and affiliates. Nevertheless, there was a feeling of distrust within the new Orthodox community toward many of the organization's members and hence toward the organization itself.

A third factor contributing to the organization's decline was its policy regarding new members. Members were required to have the qualification of *yadin yadin,* or at least be on the road to it, and this qualification demanded study beyond that offered by most American *yeshivot.* The reason for this policy—whether it was to maintain high standards or to serve some other purpose—is of no interest here; its result was to close the organization's ranks to most American-trained rabbis. (One large category of exceptions were the graduates of the Yeshivah Rabbi Israel Meyer Hacohen in Queens, N.Y., whose ordination includes *yadin yadin.*) But it was the American-trained rabbis to whom the larger, more prosperous, modern Orthodox congregations were attracted. These rabbis joined the Rabbinical Council of America, raising the status and prestige of that organization at the expense of Agudat Ha-rabbanim.

Nevertheless, Agudat Ha-rabbanim was not without resources or energy in 1964. With over 600 members and an annual budget of $25,000, it led other Orthodox groups in such activities as the successful lobbying for enactment of the New York State Sabbath Closing Law in 1963 (AJYB, 1964 [Vol. 65], p. 65). It also sponsored 'Ezrat Torah, an organization under the leadership of one of the great scholars and saintly souls of his time, Rabbi Elijah Henkin, which was concerned with welfare assistance to needy yeshivah students and Talmud scholars, particularly in Israel.

In 1960, in an obvious reaction to the changing power distribution within American Orthodoxy, Agudat Ha-rabbanim enlarged its three-member presidium to include the two most prestigious leaders of the yeshivah world, Rabbi Aaron Kotler, *rosh yeshivah* of the Beth Medrash Govoha in Lakewood, and Rabbi Moses Feinstein, *rosh yeshivah* of

Mesivta Tifereth Jerusalem and probably the leading active *posek* (halakhic authority) in Jewish life. After Rabbi Kotler's death in 1962 his position was filled by Rabbi Jacob Kamenetzky, *rosh yeshivah* of Torah Vodaath. Significantly, then, Agudat Ha-rabbanim has responded to only one challenge—the one from the right rather than the one from the left.

Nonobservant Orthodox

Having considered the residual Orthodox, we are ready to look at the second group of uncommitted Orthodox, the nonobservant.

Their number is difficult to estimate, but they surely represent a significant proportion of all nominally Orthodox Jews. They are the Jews who are affiliated with Orthodox synagogues but have no commitment to the *halakhah* or even to the rituals which the residual Orthodox practice. (Studies of Washington, D.C.,[22] Philadelphia, Pa.,[23] and Providence, R.I.,[24] to cite a few examples, indicate that anywhere from 25 to 60 per cent of Orthodox Jews do not even purchase kosher meat regularly.) Their social characteristics, too, are distinctly different from those of the residual Orthodox. They are not necessarily the aged, poor, or newest immigrant groups, whose adherence to ritual is often only a result of their inability or unwillingness to acculturate. On the contrary, they represent perhaps the most affluent element of Orthodoxy. Of course, in social characteristics some of the nonobservant may also be residual.

There are a variety of reasons why the nonobservant Orthodox affiliate with Orthodox institutions. Sometimes they affiliate because Orthodoxy exercises a monopoly in a city or a section of it. A survey of Kansas City, Mo., by the American Jewish Committee in 1961 provided an illustration of this.[25] In that city the Orthodox group was heavily weighted by members of a new synagogue in a suburb which had not yet acquired either a Conservative or Reform temple. As might be expected, a very high proportion of this synagogue's members did not consider themselves as Orthodox, and regularity of attendance was quite low. Only 40 per cent regarded themselves as Orthodox, 38 per cent as Conservative, 16 per cent as Reform, and 6 per cent as none of these. The social charac-

[22] Stanley K. Bigman, *op. cit.*, pp. 118–22.
[23] Jack Porter, "Differentiating Features of Orthodox, Conservative, and Reform Jewish Groups in Metropolitan Philadelphia," *Jewish Social Studies*, July 1963, p. 194.
[24] Sidney Goldstein, *op. cit.*, 212–13.
[25] Manheim Shapiro, *The Kansas City Survey of Jewish Attitudes* (New York: American Jewish Committee, mimeo, 1962).

teristics of the sample surveyed, as indicated by place of residence and age, corresponded to those of the nonobservant Orthodox; that is, young age and high income. Only 53 per cent of the sample stated that they purchased kosher meat and only 47 per cent that they kept two sets of dishes. The Kansas City finding led Shapiro to conclude that

> the choice of a particular branch of synagogue affiliation among American Jews today is rarely the product of a choice made on the basis of conscious analysis of theological or ideological philosophies. The decision is likely to be more closely related to such factors as geography, socio-economic positions and aspirations, distance from the immigrant generations, general impressions of the relative demands made by a particular branch of Judaism, relationships to parents and childhood experience, their own estimates of their own degree of commitment to what they assume Judaism to be, and many others.[26]

Another instance of Orthodox monopoly or near monopoly developed in New Orleans, where until 1960 there was no Conservative synagogue and the social status as well as the religious pattern of the existing Reform temples made them forbidding to many Jews.

Sometimes nonobservers are attracted to Orthodoxy by its outstanding rabbis. Some are attracted to the several Orthodox synagogues, such as Shearith Israel in New York, with distinguished historical traditions and high social status. Some join because membership fees are often lower than those of competing synagogues. Finally, there is the completely marginal Jew, who is almost indifferent about synagogue affiliation but, having been raised in an Orthodox environment, finds nostalgic satisfaction in attendance at familiar Rosh Ha-shanah and Yom Kippur services. To him, as to his coreligionist at the other end of the spectrum, Orthodoxy is "more religious" than Conservatism or Reform.

Elsewhere [27] I have indicated that there are three other forces operating today in favor of the Orthodox synagogue to counteract the more obvious anti-Orthodox trends. In fact, one can almost posit that as Conservative and Reform synagogues gain new members at the expense of Orthodoxy, countervailing forces are set in motion to restore the balance partially. These forces are religious status, small size, and community of interest.

Religious status favors Orthodoxy in an era in which religion has gained not only respectability but even intellectual recognition and some scientific assent. In a period in which affirmation of supernaturalism is no

---

[26] *Ibid.*, p. 8.
[27] Charles S. Liebman, "A Sociological Analysis of Contemporary Orthodoxy," *Judaism*, Spring 1964, p. 298.

longer a cause for embarrassment, and where one prevailing mood among the intellectual *avant-garde* is to stress individual and personal religious experience of a non-rational nature, Orthodoxy finds a receptive ear. It is a time when a Reform rabbi, writing with a tinge of envy and much sympathy about ultra-religious hasidic groups, barely conceals his disdain for his own congregants. In this atmosphere a Jew, particularly if he is middle-class, gains a certain status among Jewishly alert groups through affiliation with an Orthodox congregation. This status is inversely related to the degree to which the Orthodox congregation modernizes its service, grows in membership, and emulates the Conservative and Reform synagogues in the variety of non-sacred activities offered to the membership.

The large size of the Conservative and Reform synagogues propels some Jews to seek alternatives. The physical plant itself, no matter how artfully constructed, which is intended to seat a thousand or more worshippers, to educate hundreds of children, and to provide social and recreational activities for an entire neighborhood, may be inspiring and attractive to most people, but it will be forbidding to at least a few.

Finally, the lack of warmth and the anonymity of the large Reform and Conservative congregations suffer by contrast with the intimate feeling of community promoted by small Orthodox synagogues, independently of belief or disbelief in credal Orthodoxy.

There is one crucial difference between the residual Orthodox and nonobservant Orthodox which gives a clue to the future. The children of today's nonobservant Orthodox are far more likely to be drawn into the network of intensive and superior Talmud Torahs and all-day schools than were the children of the older residual Orthodox, who were raised when there was little opportunity for intensive Jewish education. In the older generation, the residual Orthodox were Jewishly better-educated than the nonobservant, but the reverse is true of their children.

COMMITTED ORTHODOX

It is not possible accurately to determine the number of committed Orthodox—that is Jews who strive to conduct their lives within the framework of the *halakhah*. Traditional Sabbath observance is a crude measure of committed Orthodoxy, and an educated guess puts the figure of Sabbath observers at 200,000, or approximately four per cent of American Jewry.[28]

---

[28] These estimates were made by staff members of CSD, based on figures supplied by Torah Umesorah.

Since the rest of this essay will deal with the committed Orthodox, and since even the residual and nonobservant Orthodox increasingly take their cues from that group and affiliate with their synagogues and other institutions, the word Orthodox will hereafter refer to the committed Orthodox, unless otherwise stated.

Most of the committed Orthodox are in the Greater New York area. Either by affinity or necessity they tend to be geographically clustered. The Orthodox Jew requires a variety of institutions, in addition to a synagogue, which a handful of individuals alone cannot support. He needs a *mikveh,* a reliable kosher butcher, and preferably a Sabbath-observing baker. A day school for his children, certainly at an elementary-school level and increasingly at a high-school level, is highly desirable if not essential.

Centers of Orthodoxy in New York are Washington Heights and the lower East Side in Manhattan; Boro Park, Crown Heights, Bensonhurst, and portions of Flatbush in Brooklyn; Far Rockaway and Kew Gardens-Forest Hills in Queens, and Spring Valley-Monsey in Rockland County. However, in none of these areas do all the Orthodox Jews constitute one community in a structural or even social sense.

The Monsey area might serve as an example. Monsey is approximately 35 miles from the heart of New York City. Most of its Orthodox residents —all of them committed—have moved there since 1956. On the whole, they are of similar income and almost all of them have had an intensive Jewish education. Within Monsey proper there are nine Orthodox synagogues serving roughly 850 regular adult male Sabbath-attending worshippers and their families.

There are two large elementary day schools, with about 300 students each, which serve the neighboring community of Spring Valley as well. One day school conducts its Jewish studies in Hebrew, the other in Yiddish. A third day school, under a hasidic rabbi, provides an old-world type of education for about 50 boys. In addition there are a few hasidic rabbis who train a handful of pupils on a private basis in their homes, providing a minimum of secular education. To complete the elementary educational picture there are a number of Talmud Torahs attached to Orthodox synagogues which serve primarily the non-Orthodox community, since the synagogue members themselves send their children to the day schools. A Yiddish-speaking high school for boys in Monsey proper was joined by a second, which moved to the vicinity in 1964; there is also a tradition-oriented Beth Jacob high school for girls. None of these educational facilities is used by the 60 to 70 families of hasidic followers of the Skverer Rebbe, who live in the neighboring community of New Square and sponsor an educational, social, and religious network of their own. Finally, there is the Beth Medrosh Elyon, a *kolel* (school for very advanced talmudic study, usually beyond what is required for ordination) with about 160 men, which serves a national constituency but receives strong local financial support.

The only local facilities in which almost all Orthodox Jews of Monsey are involved is a *hevra kaddisha* (burial society), the local *mikveh*, and the two local Sabbath-observing bakeries. Few communal activities involve all synagogue members or even leaders. Most of the members of one group of synagogues, predominantly American-born, college-educated, prosperous businessmen and professionals (prices of homes from $18,000 to $50,000), enroll their children in the Hebrew-speaking elementary school and then in New York City high schools, especially Yeshiva University high school. Members of a second group of synagogues, composed of a much higher percentage of foreign-born, with less secular education and of somewhat lower economic status, support the Yiddish-speaking elementary day schools and the local religious high schools. Some of these same people, however, also support the local hasidic day school, which deemphasizes secular education. Finally there is a German synagogue, many of whose members are oriented toward (the German) Adath Jeshurun of Washington Heights in New York City, and who transport their children to the day schools of that synagogue. Except for the relative absence of residual and nonobservant Orthodox and the high concentration of committed Orthodox (estimated at 30 to 35 per cent of the total Jewish community), the constellation of institutions in Monsey is similar to what it is in other Orthodox communities. The non-Orthodox of Monsey are either unaffiliated or are associated with the Conservative or Reform congregations in Spring Valley.

Orthodoxy in the Jewish Religious Spectrum

Before discussing the divisions within the Orthodox camp, it will be well to understand the nature of Orthodoxy within the totality of Jewish life.

Orthodoxy perceives itself as the only legitimate bearer of the Jewish tradition; to Orthodoxy this tradition is expressed almost exclusively in religious form (which is not to say that all elements of the tradition are necessarily religious in their essence). While Conservative and Reform see themselves as legitimate heirs to the Jewish tradition, neither claims to be its exclusive bearer. This distinction between Orthodoxy and the other denominations has analytically separable consequences which only seem to operate at cross-purposes. Since neither the Reform nor the Conservative lays claim to exclusive doctrinal "truth," they are free to cooperate with one another, with Orthodoxy, and even with secular Jewish groups; they risk only institutional losses. The doctrines of Orthodoxy, on the other hand, are more precise and are by definition beyond compromise or even the appearance of compromise. Hence Orthodoxy must be constantly on guard against appearing to surrender or water down its doctrine.

But there is a second consequence that flows from Orthodoxy's exclusive claim to the truth and its major tenet that it is the obligation of every Jew to observe the *mitzwot* (religious commandments). While Conservatives and Reformists are under no obligation to do anything about the matter, the Orthodox are doctrinally obligated to encourage the observance of Jewish law here and now. In addition, the doctrine of *ahavat Yisrael* (love of Israel), particularly as elaborated by the late Rabbi Abraham Isaac Kook, chief rabbi of Palestine until his death in 1935, impels Orthodoxy to extend itself to the non-Orthodox. If non-Orthodox Jews were unorganized, the consequences of Orthodoxy's doctrinal position would not be contradictory. It could simply undertake missions to the non-Orthodox. But when, in fact, about half of the non-Orthodox are organized in the Conservative and Reform movements, and the remainder are almost beyond reach of any religious group in Jewish life, then Orthodoxy is confronted with two mutually exclusive mandates—to promote faith and observance among non-Orthodox Jews, while giving no recognition and comfort to the only existing institutions which can reach those Jews. In practice, different groups within Orthodoxy have emphasized one mandate or the other, and most of the divisions within Orthodoxy, in practice, reflect this division. But the point to be stressed is that, with the possible exception of the Satmar *hasidim* (pp. 83–85), all Orthodox groups consider both mandates as binding. (The Satmar probably do, too, but feel that the obligation to promote observance is simply impractical in this day among all but a handful of Jews and that there own piety is not so secure as to justify undertaking "missions" to other Jews.) Hence, no matter how zealous the right wing may be in its stress on religious continuity, maximal observance, and condemnation of the non-Orthodox, it hesitates to characterize the non-Orthodox as beyond hope of redemption. And no matter how outgoing and conciliatory the left wing may be toward the nonobservant and the institutions of the non-

Orthodox, it is always restrained by its acceptance of the basic doctrinal principles as being beyond compromise.

Orthodoxy and the Demands of Society

The differences within Orthodoxy are best understood in the broad framework of the sociology of religion. While the concepts here developed are not directly applicable to Judaism, they are suggestive of differences among Jewish groups and serve heuristic purposes.

Students of religion, drawing their data primarily from the development of Christianity, have developed a typology of religions based on distinctions between church and sect. Following Yinger's refinement of Troeltsch,[28a] church and sect are defined as ideal types, that is, end points on a continuum along which religious groups can be placed and compared with one another as they approach one end or the other.

The central problems to which the church-sect dichotomy is addressed are how a religious body confronts the secular world and how it provides a religious response to the personal needs of its adherents. The *church* "recognizes the strength of the secular world and rather than either deserting the attempt to influence it or losing its position by contradicting the secular powers directly, accepts the main elements in the social structure as proximate goods." The major function of the church is its effort to insure social cohesion and order and to do so it must extend its ministry to everyone. As a result it must be willing to "compromise with the wide ranges of behavior that may be found in a society."[29]

The *sect* is a smaller group, arising from the inability of the church to meet some members' needs by virtue of its very flexibility and adaptability. The sect "repudiates the compromises of the church, preferring isolation to compromise."[30] Hence, unlike the church, it is hostile or indifferent to the secular order. It seeks primarily to satisfy individual religious needs rather than societal ones.

It is apparent that the church-sect dichotomy is not applicable in this form to Judaism today. The typology assumes a closed society in which the religious order is confronted only by the secular order and the individual needs of its members. When Judaism represented a basically closed society, before Emancipation, the dichotomy appears to have been more applicable. Where the definition of church or sect says "society," we can

---

[28a] John Milton Yinger, *Religion, Society and the Individual* (New York, 1957).
[29] *Ibid.*, p. 144.
[30] *Ibid.*, p. 146.

read "Judaism" or "Jews." Thus, the early development of hasidism appears to fit the definition of sectarian growth and development.

But religious groups within Judaism today are confronted with problems of the larger Jewish society—what we may call the secular (or non-religious) institutionalized Jewish order—as well as of the non-Jewish society, and the problems of the religious denomination are not only to adapt to Jewish society and insure social cohesion and order within Judaism, but also to adapt to general society and insure cohesion and order within *it*. Furthermore, Judaism must meet not only the individual needs of members as they arise by virtue of Jewishness, but also those that arise by virtue of membership in the general society. An effort to solve one kind of problem frequently exacerbates another. To sum up—the Christian denomination plays a double role: vis-à-vis the social order or general society, and vis-à-vis the individual needs of its membership. To the extent that the Christian denomination stresses the solution to one order of problems it raises questions for the other. Judaism faces not two but four problems. It must meet the needs or demands of the broader society and of the narrower, Jewish society. It must meet the needs that arise from an individual's problems in the general society and those that arise from his problems in the Jewish society.

Let us be specific about the nature of these problems as they have emerged in the United States.

1. To meet the needs of the general society, it is necessary to affirm the democratic political structure and to develop a symbolism (transcendental or not) for its transmission; to affirm the unity of all Americans and the primacy of American national interests and needs.

2. To meet the needs of the Jewish society, it is necessary to achieve unity among Jews and to maintain Jewish identification in a permissive gentile society; to maintain defenses against prejudice and discrimination.

3. To meet the individual's needs in the general society, it is necessary to confront the problems of good and evil, of reward and punishment, and of alienation and anomie in an urban, heterogeneous society.

4. To meet the individual's needs in Jewish society, it is necessary to interpret traditional Jewish beliefs and practices in the light of the individual's present needs and problems.

Bearing in mind these four types of demands or needs, we can classify all Jewish organizations by the problem or combination of problems to which they have addressed themselves. Each of these classifications can, in turn, be refined according to the *manner* in which the problem is approached. Within any given organization there is bound to be some conflict or tension over which problem should assume priority. A general theory of Jewish organizational life would have to take account of the manner in which social status, education, accommodation to the American milieu,, and other such factors cut across the leadership and constituent groups of each organization, determining the perspective in which problems are viewed and solutions chosen.

Our concern here is with Orthodoxy, but first we must look briefly into the Conservative and Reform groups, which today come closer than Orthodoxy to assuming the characteristics of church rather than sect. By and large, Conservatism and Reform address themselves to problems arising from societal demands. The application is made at an individual level and to individual problems, but the context out of which the problem emerges is generally societal—social cohesion and moral order—rather than individual. Until recently, Reform was more oriented towards general societal problems and Conservatism toward those of Jewish society. This is changing somewhat as Conservatism becomes more self-conscious about its role as a church and Reform, with a longer church experience, becomes more aware of the limitations of a church in reaching its membership directly.

For an illustration of the growing emphasis on a societal-church role for Conservative Judaism, the 1962 proceedings of the Rabbinical Assembly are useful. Its convention that year was devoted to the day-school movement, and the speakers stressed the reasons for developing Conservative as distinct from Orthodox day schools. One rabbi complained about the Orthodox day schools:

> In many, if not most instances, school holidays in the Yeshivot are set without any consideration for the dates of public school holidays so that Yeshiva students cannot possibly meet with or join in activities with friends who attend other schools.[31]

A Conservative educator called for mobilizing the Jewish community in behalf of day schools by stressing 11 points, most of which emphasized the compatibility of day schools with America, democracy, and even the public-school system.[32] Another rabbi, asking, "What should be distinctive about our Conservative day schools?", answered:

> First, I would say, is the principle of motivation. Our motivation is not isolationism, but preparation for Jewish living in the context of general life, in America, or anywhere else in the world. . . . Not only the civic

---

31 Rabbinical Assembly of America, *Proceedings,* 1962, p. 44.
32 *Ibid.,* pp. 54–56.

and political positions of Jews, but our understanding of the true nature of Judaism demands that we regard isolation from the general community and world culture as a goal devoutly to be shunned.[33]

A third rabbi commented:

The road to further progress in this area of our educational work is still strewn with obstacles, both major and minor. Many of the laymen have yet to be convinced that a Conservative Day School is not parochial, and does not deprive its pupils of a full experience in the American milieu. Some of our own colleagues are afraid lest an expanded Day School movement weaken our opposition to federal aid to education, and tempt us into the Orthodox camp altogether.[34]

And finally this proud boast of a fourth rabbi:

To be specific, from the very start of our Hillel Day School in Detroit, we paid more attention to American sancta than they do in any public school. That may be too categorical a statement, but we know that Thanksgiving day is roundly ignored in the public school. We glorify it, because it is one of the sancta of American life which can be glorified very naturally. . . . We find that it is possible to instill the best of our American holidays and integrating them with Jewish values, and conversely taking Jewish holidays like *Pesah* and integrating them with American overtones. . . . There is a slight diminution of daily contact with non-Jewish children, but it can be made up for by a deliberately designed integrated program.[35]

Papers delivered at the 1963 meeting of CCAR offered a striking contrast to those presented at this convention of Conservative rabbis. According to one observer, himself a Reform rabbi, it had been rumored that the 1963 convention would precipitate a theological revolution.[36] The papers were described as follows:

They focus on God where the old liberals concentrated on man. They are concerned with the authoritative claim traditional texts and traditional observance have on them. They take the concept of Halachah seriously and seek to determine what is law for them today. They do not hesitate to use religious terms which the liberals ignored or reinterpreted away, like revelation, sin, the fear of God. They, too, try to define them in a modern way but one which will not do violence to

---

[33] *Ibid.*, pp. 61–62.
[34] *Ibid.*, p. 78.
[35] *Ibid.*, p. 81.
[36] Ben Hamon, "The Reform Rabbis Debate Theology: A Report on the 1963 meeting of the CCAR," *Judaism*, Fall 1963, p. 479.

their traditional Jewish intent. One might simply describe their position as seeking to take the Jewish religion with full personal seriousness but not literally.[37]

Most pertinent to our argument is this comment by the pseudonymous author: "Reform rabbis are interested in theology today because they know that they have little else to offer the cultured, ethical man, and only a living relationship between God and Israel can justify the continued effort to remain Jewish."[38] The point is that an intellectually significant element within Reform Judaism seeks a withdrawal from Reform's church-like, societally-oriented posture. No comparable development in Conservative Judaism is noticeable.

In contrast to Conservative and Reform Judaism, much of Orthodoxy's energy has been addressed to finding solutions within a halakhic framework for individual problems arising in contemporary life. Orthodoxy has been the least church-like of all Jewish religious groups. In part this stems from the absence (until recently) of any self-consciousness. Only recently has Orthodoxy begun to define itself as a particular movement in the United States and been brought into contact with the broader society by the accelerated acculturation of its adherents and its own institutional growth. This new confrontation has raised problems that formerly did not exist for Orthodoxy or were overlooked. Thus, Orthodox leaders have been much slower than other Jewish leaders to define their attitude toward problems of civil rights or labor.

Since 1960 much of this has changed. In 1964, speaking to a Young Israel meeting in New York, Rabbi Aaron Soloveichik, one of the leading talmudic authorities in Jewish life, delivered a major address on civil rights from a halakhic perspective. In that same year a joint conference of the Industrial Union Department, AFL-CIO, and the Social Action Committee of RCA heard a series of papers by young Orthodox rabbis on religion and labor. Such developments were a portent of serious stirrings within Orthodoxy.

Reform and Conservatism, however, still are more church-like than Orthodoxy, not only in their role in the general society but also in Jewish society.The ideologists of Conservatism resemble those of Orthodoxy in the nature of their formal commitment to *halakhah* and tradition. But the practical difficulties of reconciling a corpus of law having no effective sanctions with the proclivities of modern man has resulted in varying solutions. Conservatism has increasingly, albeit slowly and often grudg-

[37] *Ibid.*, p. 480.
[38] *Ibid.*, p. 485.

ingly, found its solution in the doctrine that the *halakhah* must be molded to suit modern man's material and intellectual needs. But its left wing has long argued that the potential for change is too severely limited by the necessity to fit all changes to Jewish law. The left wing has theretofore pressed its leadership to change the law by reliance on non-legal criteria (psychology, *aggadah,* etc.). Their success on this score has been limited, but they have accepted a procedure, introduced in 1948 upon the organization of the present Committee on Jewish Law and Standards, whereby unless the law committee of RA resolves a given division by issuing a unanimous opinion, Conservative rabbis are free to uphold any contending opinion. In fact, the Conservative rabbi is bound only by his own concept of Jewish propriety in advising his membership what they can or cannot do under Jewish law. The discretion thus allowed is more abstract than real, however, since Conservative rabbis are, in fact, rarely consulted on halakhic matters. Thus, Conservative Judaism has been able to meet the Jewish societal demands of its congregants without challenging individual conduct or behavior. As one JTS professor noted in private conversation, the RA deliberates and the laity decides. The rabbis debate whether it is permitted to ride to the synagogue on the Sabbath and the laymen ride. The outcome of the Rabbinical Assembly deliberations is either a foregone conclusion or irrelevant. Thus, the Conservative movement moves closer toward our definition of a church, as indeed it must if it is to achieve universality and bring the masses of Jews under its umbrella.

Orthodoxy faces a similar problem, and some of the divisions within its camp are best understood by analyzing the different positions of Orthodox leaders and institutions as they approach the church or sect ends of the continuum. The line between the left (or church) wing of Orthodoxy and the right wing of the Conservative movement is a very thin one. In fact, it is institutional loyalty far more than ideology which separates the two groups practically, though there are other, subtle distinctions, as well.

There are two alternative explanations for the differences among the Orthodox. The first argues that the two major categories of Orthodox—modern or church Orthodox and sectarian Orthodox—differ from one another in their degree of acculturation. It is true, as we shall show, that the sectarian Orthodox tend to be of lower income, poorer secular education, and more recent immigration than the modern Orthodox. (Sociologists of religion have noted that these tend to correlate with affinity to sect rather than church among Christians as well.) But the sectarians can boast their share of outwardly acculturated adherents; the leaders of the Association of Orthodox Jewish Scientists, to be discussed below, are far more sectarian than modern in terms of their concerns and orientations. And, most significantly, acculturation must be viewed as a dependent rather than an independent variable. The large number of American-born advanced yeshivah students who attend college at night to minimize interference with their talmudic studies and value their secular education only for its vocational benefits have in a sense deliberately rejected acculturation because of their sectarian tendencies, rather than being sectarian because unacculturated.

A second explanation for the differences among the Orthodox distinguishes among them along a fundamentalism-liberalism scale. It argues that the sectarian Orthodox differ from the modern or church Orthodox by virtue of their beliefs concerning the Mosaic authorship of the Torah or the Sinaitic origin of the Oral Law. Although some modern Orthodox thinkers would consider Franz Rosenzweig's position,[39] for example, as within the framework of Orthodox belief, questions of actual dogma have not yet been broached among Orthodox leaders. When they are, as seems likely, there will be explosive consequences. Unquestionably there are Orthodox intellectuals who would like to raise the question, but with few exceptions neither they nor the fundamentalists have yet articulated exactly what they mean by Mosaic authorship or Sinaitic origin of the Oral Law.[40] It is fair to say that the entire belief structure of American

[39] Rosenzweig accepted the notion of a biblical Redactor, but saw the task of compiling the Bible as the human presentation of divine revelation. Rosenzweig's oft-quoted statement is that for him the symbol "R" does not stand for *Redactor* but for *Rabbenu* (our rabbi, our master).

[40] In one respect the argument that the written law (the Torah) and the oral law, which constitute the basis of *halakhah,* were given by God to Moses at Sinai requires no elaboration. It has always been an article of faith for the Orthodox Jew, and the meaning of the words and their historical referent seems simple enough. Biblical criticism has not challenged this belief; on the contrary, biblical criticism becomes meaningful only when this article of faith is denied. But it is this very article of faith in its plain meaning which has become "preposterous" to the modern mind. (This, of course, says nothing about the truth or falsity of the doctrine. A round world once also seemed preposterous.) That segment of American Orthodoxy which lives in the orbit of the *rashe yeshivot* does not find such a faith preposterous. It has no severe problem in reconciling its conception of God and human experience to its faith in the divine origin of Torah. That is not so for the more acculturated Orthodox Jew. The observer is perhaps forbidden to challenge a man's belief, but he is entitled to ask whether the secularly acculturated Jew truly believes in *Torah min ha-shamayim* (Torah from heaven) when the entire structure of behavior and belief of that Jew seems inconsistent with this one article of faith. Inevitably efforts will be made to reinterpret the meaning of *Torah min ha-shamayim* in an effort to resolve the inconsistency. A variety of strategies are pos-

Orthodoxy still finds verbal expression within the bounds of a rather narrow fundamentalism. Privately, the modern Orthodox admit that they simply interpret the same words to mean different things from what they mean to the sectarian Orthodox.[41] They have sought to keep the subject outside the area of controversy, making no serious effort, for example, to engage in biblical criticism, and thereby ruling out the development of any outstanding Orthodox biblical scholars in the United States. Modern Orthodoxy pays lip service to the notion that something ought to be done in this area and that aspects of biblical criticism can be incorporated into the Orthodox tradition, but no one is prepared to undertake or even encourage the work. It is sometimes acknowledged that some abandon Orthodoxy because their intellectual predispositions cannot be reconciled with traditional patterns of belief. But such losses, qualitatively important, are quantitatively insignificant. The main body of Orthodoxy in the United States appears at present to be doctrinally untroubled.

Institutions and Currents

Using the church-sect dichotomy, then, let us turn to a discussion of specific institutions and currents within Orthodoxy. As we noted in the introduction, little attention is given to synagogue practice, although it is really in the synagogue that the full variety of Orthodox types become evident in their pure form.[42] At one extreme are the *shtibl*-type synagogues. They meet in small rooms, where bearded men cover their heads with *tallitim* (prayer shawls) to pray, generally unheedful of the leader of the service, their bodies swaying. Women are separated from the men by a full-length wall in the rear, punctured by several peepholes through which a few can peer. At the other extreme are the modern edifices with spacious auditoriums. Here services are conducted by a cantor whose trained voice is carried to the ends of the hall by a microphone. Men and women are seated together, and the heart of the service is the rabbi's

---

sible. One can begin by acknowledging this as a preposterous belief and proceed to a kind of Orthodox Jewish existentialism, with the events at Sinai being the object of some "leap of faith." One can maintain that the doctrine of *Torah min ha-shamayim* has metaphysical rather than physical referents and that we are dealing with two discrete levels of meaning. One can seek to reinterpret *Torah min ha-shamayim* as meaning something less than the entire written and oral law. These and other strategies of reinterpretation will undoubtedly be undertaken.

[41] The same is true of Conservative and Reform leaders among themselves with regard to the concept of revelation.

[42] For an illustration of the variety of Orthodox synagogues in one suburban county see Jacob Sodden, *The Impact of Suburbanization on the Synagogue* (New York University, unpublished doctoral dissertation, 1962).

sermon. Although mixed seating and the use of a microphone on the Sabbath violate *halakhah,* the modern congregation considers itself as Orthodox and is in fact more likely to support many of the supracongregational institutions to be discussed below than the *shtibl.*

MODERN ORTHODOX

By modern Orthodox we mean those individuals and institutions among the committed Orthodox who tend toward the church end of the church-sect continuum. On the one hand, they seek to demonstrate the viability of the *halakhah* for contemporary life; on the other, they emphasize what they have in common with all other Jews rather than what separates them. Until recently they composed almost the entire upper-income, well-educated strata of the committed Orthodox. Many of the best-known Orthodox congregations in the United States, and most of the wealthy ones, are led by modern Orthodox rabbis.

Like the other groups within American Orthodoxy, the modern Orthodox have not produced any systematic statement of their ideology; in part, perhaps, because they shun the practical consequences of their philosophical or theological position, and in part because none has been sanctioned by eminent talmudic scholars, still acknowledged as the arbiters of ideology. To the extent, however, that the modern Orthodox have produced an ideologist, it is probably Rabbi Emanuel Rackman, although his position is not representative of all modern Orthodox Jews. He is certainly the favorite target of the Orthodox right wing, notwithstanding the private concession of at least some of its members that he has brought more people into the Orthodox fold than any other person. Rackman has published widely on *halakhah,* Jewish values, and contemporary life.[43] His concern is with understanding the meaning of the halakhic injunctions in order to find contemporary applications. In the course of his efforts he has suggested what many feel to be a radical reinterpretation of the *halakhah:*

> The Halakhah is more than texts. It is life and experience. What made the Babylonian and not the Palestinian Talmud the great guide of Jewish life in the Diaspora was not a decree or a decision but *vox populi.*

---

[43] Essays from a variety of journals were reprinted in Emanuel Rackman, *Jewish Values for Modern Man* (New York: Jewish Education Committee, 1962). See also "Israel and God: Reflections on their Encounter," *Judaism,* Summer 1962, pp. 233–41; "Halachic Progress: Rabbi Moshe Feinstein's *Igrot Moshe* on *Even Ha-Ezer,*" ibid., Summer 1964, pp. 366–73, and *Sabbaths and Festivals in the Modern Age,* in the "Studies in Torah Judaism" series (New York, 1961).

From Maimonides it would appear that it was the acceptance of the people who by custom and popular will constituted the authority. Can a Halakhic scholar lose himself in texts exclusively when the texts themselves bid him to see what practice "has become widespread among Jews," what is required socially "because of the precepts of peace," what will "keep the world aright," and many other social criteria? These standards are as much a part of the Torah as the texts themselves.[44]

Rackman is also prominently associated with the idea that Orthodox Jews, both individually and institutionally, must cooperate with the non-Orthodox. He is outspoken in his conviction that Orthodox rabbis should be free to associate with such groups as the New York Board of Rabbis (composed of Reform and Conservative as well as Orthodox rabbis) and that Orthodox groups should remain affiliated with the umbrella organization for all religious groups, the Synagogue Council of America.

Before considering the groups within which modern Orthodoxy is dominant, some comment on the sources of authority and unity within the Jewish community will be made. We will seek to demonstrate why the drive for unity, even within the organizations controlled by modern Orthodoxy, has been blunted in recent years, and what the Orthodox basis for unity has become.

Authority in the Jewish Community

There are four possible bases of authority within the Jewish community today: numbers, money, tradition, and person or charisma.

Authority of numbers is rarely exercised directly. Although organizations and institutions make some claim to authority on the basis of their numerical superiority, issues have rarely been resolved on this basis. There have been a few exceptions, the most noteworthy being the American Jewish Conference and particularly its 1943 meeting in which the sympathy of the masses of American Jews for the Zionist program was reflected in the division of votes (AJYB, 1944–45 [Vol. 46], pp. 169–70). Today almost no Jewish organization lays claim to authority within the community by virtue of its size. In part this is because no organization has a generally accepted, trustworthy membership list. More significantly, it is because no mass organization in Jewish life can even pretend to be able to mobilize its membership behind one position or another.

The most potent claim for authority in Jewish life today is exercised by money. Perhaps this was always so, but until recently the claim was exer-

---

[44] Rackman, *Sabbaths and Festivals* . . . , p. 8.

cised in alliance with religious tradition. Tradition's loss of status has resulted in the dissolution of this alliance and today those who control the purse strings, alone, usually speak for the Jewish community and decide questions within it. Although the professionals and staff members of the various organizations generally initiate policy, their authority is often determined by their access to financial resources and particularly to the few big contributors. Orthodoxy cannot accept the authority of money because it contains neither a class of large contributors nor a group of professionals with access to large contributors. In this regard, the Conservative and Reform rabbinate are in a far better, though by no means ideal, position, as they confront the "secular" Jewish institutions. The potency of money in the rest of the community, therefore, has the effect of pressuring Orthodoxy to withdraw from the community. In other words, the rule of the game in the Jewish community is that "money talks the loudest." Because Orthodoxy only loses by these rules, there is a constant pressure from within for it to leave the game unless the rules are changed. Of course, the concessions and compromises made by the Orthodox in order to play the game become unnecessary when they withdraw from it and they then move to a more intransigent right-wing position.

Orthodoxy claims the right to preserve the unity of the Jewish community by invoking the authority of tradition and charisma. With regard to the first, it claims communal support for its essentially parochial schools on the ground that these are traditional schools which simply teach Judaism as it has always been taught (in terms of content, of course, not method). This claim to legitimacy has been challenged recently, most particularly by the Conservatives. The foregoing is not meant to imply that numbers or money have only recently become sources of authority, or that tradition has lost all its force. It does mean that the weight of the different bases of authority has changed, and that Orthodoxy's claim to its exclusive access to this authority has been challenged.

The fourth possible source of authority in the Jewish community is that of person, or charisma. Jews in the United States have never produced a charismatic leader for the entire community, although Louis Marshall, Judah Magnes, Stephen Wise, and Abba Hillel Silver came close to being such leaders.

The only group within Jewish life which lays claim to charismatic leaders today is the Orthodox. Preeminent among these for the modern Orthodox is Rabbi Joseph B. Soloveitchik. RCA's claim to leadership in the general Jewish community and its belief that it ought really to exercise this leadership rest almost entirely on the fact that Rabbi Soloveitchik is its leader. RCA members consider it enormously significant that the non-Orthodox Jewish community has accorded his opinions an increasing respect. Rabbi Soloveitchik, acknowledged by most Orthodox Jews as one of the world's leading talmudic authorities, has become increasingly active in social and political life and is quite conscious of his role as a communal leader. As the descendant of the longest extant line of *gedolim,* rabbis who combined talmudic and communal authority, this could hardly be otherwise.[45]

On the other hand, the more right-wing yeshivah world (to be discussed below) rests its claim to authority on the leadership of the outstanding *rashe yeshivot* who claim the mantle of traditional as well as charismatic authority.

We turn now to those organizations in which modern Orthodoxy holds a dominant position, stressing that in none of these groups is that position exclusive.

Rabbinical Council of America (RCA)

The Rabbinical Council of America is the largest and most influential Orthodox rabbinical body in the United States. It has 830 members, all ordained by recognized rabbinic authorities. About 600 are in the active rabbinate, and most of the rest are teachers and school administrators. About half of the active rabbis were ordained at Yeshiva University's Rabbi Isaac Elchanan Theological Seminary (RIETS), and another 15 per cent at the Hebrew Theological College in Illinois. As noted below, both of these institutions represent a point of view different from that of other *yeshivot* in the United States which confer ordination. Another 20 to 25 per cent of the RCA membership come from these other American *yeshivot,* and the remaining few are from Europe.

A major controversy within RCA has centered on the question of its relationship with non-Orthodox rabbinical groups, particularly the affiliation of its members with the New York Board of Rabbis. In 1955, 11 *rashe yeshivot,* the most influential leaders of all the large academies for

---

[45] His father, Rabbi Moses Soloveitchik, was one of the great talmudic scholars in the United States in the last generation. His uncle, Reb Velvel Soloveitchik, was the *gedol ha-dor* ("the great man of his generation") of the last generation in Palestine. His grandfather, Reb Hayyim of Brisk, the famous Brisker Rav, was the leading talmudic scholar of his time, and his great-grandfather, Rabbi Joseph Beer Soloveitchik, after whom he is named, was the *rosh yeshivah* of Volozhin, the greatest talmudic academy of its time. For a biographical sketch of Rabbi Soloveitchik and a popularization of some elements of his thought see his son-in-law's article: Aaron Lichtenstein, "Joseph Soloveitchik," in Simon Noveck, ed., *Great Jewish Thinkers of the Twentieth Century.* (Washington, 1963), pp. 281–97.

142 / AMERICAN JEWISH YEAR BOOK

advanced talmudic study in the United States (except Yeshiva University and the Hebrew Theological College), issued an *issur* or prohibition against Orthodox rabbis joining organizations in which non-Orthodox rabbis were officially represented. Their position was phrased in halakhic terms as a *pesak din,* a juridical decision, but has been buttressed with the practical political argument that by officially recognizing the non-Orthodox rabbi as a rabbi, Orthodoxy accorded him a status to which he was not entitled under Jewish law and which cut the ground from under its own claim as the only legitimate bearer of the Torah tradition.

RCA referred the question to its own *halakhah* committee under the chairmanship of Rabbi Soloveitchik. At the end of 1964 the committee had not yet reported, and showed no disposition to do so as long as the *status quo* was maintained within the Jewish community.

Nevertheless, the political aspects of the question were raised on numerous occasions; in all instances the forces for separation in RCA, led by Rabbi David Hollander, were defeated, although there is a growing sympathy for the values which Hollander espouses. The opponents of separation have argued that by cooperating with the non-Orthodox they are able to restrain them from public violation of *halakhah* and are in a better position to help shape policy for the whole Jewish community. They pointed to Judaism's response to the Second Ecumenical Council (p. 128) as an example of how Orthodoxy, under the leadership of Rabbi Soloveitchik, was influential in maintaining a semblance of order among most Jewish leaders and groups on behalf of a policy which all Orthodox groups favored. Besides, they suspect that the vast majority of nominally Orthodox Jews do not see any sharp distinctions between Orthodoxy and other denominations, that a policy of separation would fail of general support, and that it would jeopardize the considerable support for Orthodox institutions that comes from non-Orthodox Jews.

Finally, and perhaps most importantly, they feel that RCA members do not view themselves as living in a community apart from the rest of American Jews. The Orthodox rabbi, particularly outside New York City, lives among and serves a non-observant constituency. In addition, he himself is likely to be American-born, a product of the American culture, which places a premium on compromise, sanctifies majority rule, and decries dogmatism.

With an annual budget of $80,000 for expenditures in the United States in 1964 and a separate budget of $15,000 for its newly established *Beth Din,* RCA maintains a manifold program.[46] It conducts welfare

---

46 All budget figures were given to the author or to CJFWF.

activities on behalf of its members, supports a variety of projects in Israel, and publishes the distinguished quarterly, *Tradition,* and a halakhic journal in Hebrew, *Hadorom.* Its house organ, the *RCA Record,* is probably the most candid organizational bulletin circulated among any American Jewish group. The *Beth Din* is concerned with family problems, offers counseling, and is engaged in developing extensive records on Jewish marriage and divorce. Its purpose is to render authoritative decisions in areas which are either halakhically or emotionally too complex for any one rabbi to handle.

RCA looks for spiritual and, more recently, political leadership to Rabbi Soloveitchik, known affectionately to his followers as the Rov (Sephardi: Rav). One can almost distinguish a Jew's religious position by the manner in which he refers to Soloveitchik. The non-Orthodox are likely to call him Rabbi Soloveitchik; the RCA modern Orthodox call him the Rov; his own students, Rebbe; and the right wing, J.B., for the first two initials of his name.

RCA has moved to the right in recent years, though not as far to the right as its separatists would like. It has continued to concern itself with communal problems but has become increasingly outspoken and antagonistic toward other groups, both religious and secular, within Jewish life. This is a result of a number of factors. The younger rabbis, particularly those from Yeshiva University, are more right-wing today in both their practice and their communal outlook than their predecessors of a decade or more ago. Secondly, as the Orthodox community has grown in numbers and risen in income and status, the rabbi has attained greater personal security and confidence in the future of Orthodoxy and has become less compromising. Thirdly, the right wing within Orthodoxy has become more acculturated. This means that it is better able to communicate with the left wing and make an impact on it. Finally, RCA has reacted to the Conservative movement's new aggressiveness.

The Conservatives have issued challenges in domains which the Orthodox believed were by tacit consent, at least, exclusively theirs. One such domain is the supervision of *kashrut.* A second is that of day schools. Conservative development of rival day schools, which the Orthodox may deplore but can hardly consider inherently objectionable, has been accompanied by increased expectation on the part of Conservative rabbis, often supported by local Jewish federations and welfare funds, of a stronger voice in the policy making of traditional Orthodox day schools. The Conservative movement, furthermore, exercises a powerful lever in the form of finances. Most Orthodox day schools outside Metropolitan

New York are dependent on federation support or contributions from large donors, many of whom are members of Conservative synagogues. Recently, the Orthodox have found that the price they must pay for the support of Conservative rabbis has gone up, at the same time that Conservatism's own increasingly militant posture has diminished its willingness to make concessions as readily as in the past.

RCA's move to the right has had the further effect of healing somewhat the breach between its modern Orthodox and sectarian elements on such questions as the development of *halakhah,* which is only indirectly related to the controversy over communal involvement. Rackman, as we have noted, is the leading advocate of radical halakhic development, but his viewpoint is almost totally isolated. Rackman elicits a sympathetic response from his colleagues when he demands that the rabbinic leaders grapple with contemporary problems and when he criticizes them for their "ivory tower" posture. But there is less sympathy with him on what the content of the response should be. As one observer put it, "The RCA rabbi doesn't want *hetterim* [lenient rulings], he only wants a good explanation for a *pesak* [a ruling]."

Union of Orthodox Jewish Congregations of America (UOJC)

Officially RCA is the rabbinical arm of the Union of Orthodox Jewish Congregations of America (UOJC), the major national congregational organization of Orthodox synagogues. UOJC is best known for its *kashrut* supervision, conducted in cooperation with RCA. Almost half of its nearly $750,000 budget is for this purpose. UOJC also provides administrative and program assistance to Orthodox congregations whether or not they are affiliated with it; provides assistance to Orthodox servicemen; publishes a popular bimonthly, *Jewish Life;* sponsors a women's division and the National Conference of Synagogue Youth, which publishes some outstanding material for young people; provides office space and at least nominal sponsorship for two other organizations, Yavneh and the Association of Orthodox Jewish Scientists (to be discussed below), and represents congregational Orthodoxy on the National Community Relations Advisory Council, the Synagogue Council of America, the National Jewish Welfare Board, and similar groups.

The forum for the controversy over Orthodox participation in non-Orthodox roof organizations has shifted in the last two years from RCA, where the separatists have been defeated, to UOJC. At its 1964 convention a resolution by the separatists was defeated, but on the ground that withdrawal would be unwarranted unless a roof organization for all Orthodox groups was first established. Toward this end, Orthodox organizations like RCA, the Religious Zionists of America, the Rabbinical Alliance of America, and Agudath Israel were invited to submit position papers on their conditions for entering a unified Orthodox organization. Agudath Israel, whose position probably best reflects that of the sectarian Orthodox, stipulated two conditions for its participation: that all members of the proposed organization withdraw from anything more than *ad hoc* participation in non-Orthodox roof organizations, and that a council of Torah authorities, composed essentially of Agudath Israel leaders, be the arbiters of the new organization. It was unlikely that the modern Orthodox would meet either of these conditions.

For many years UOJC was led by a young, Americanized, modern Orthodox element without any real constituent base among the mass of Yiddish-speaking, immigrant synagogue members. In the past decade a closer relationship has developed between Orthodox synagogues and the parent synagogue body, and UOJC has grown considerably. This is because the synagogue leadership has become more acculturated; the UOJC leadership has moved to the right, away from modernism, and the success of Conservative and Reform parent congregational bodies, as well as of Young Israel, has shown the importance of a united Orthodox synagogue body. None the less, UOJC is still not as representative of Orthodox congregations as the United Synagogue is of Conservative, or UAHC of Reform, congregations.

UOJC refuses to reveal the number of its member congregations because, they say, their definition of membership is somewhat ambiguous. Congregations whose dues are in arrears are still considered as members. UOJC has at various times claimed to serve, without regard to affiliation, 3,100 Orthodox congregations, but according to our own estimates (p. 24) there are probably no more than 1,700 synagogues in the United States which even consider themselves as Orthodox. It also claims that as the spokesman for all Orthodoxy it speaks for the 3 million Jews who, they estimate, are affiliated with the 3,100 Orthodox congregations which, they say, exist in the United States and Canada. (According to one UOJC official, there are actually 4.2 million Orthodox Jews in the United States, since by his definition all Jews who are not Conservative, Reform, or atheist are Orthodox.)

UOJC congregations range from those with mixed seating to those which go beyond the letter of the law in observing halakhic standards. Individual members include Jews from all walks of life and with a variety of opinions. Conscious of its hybrid membership and anxious not to offend any group within it, UOJC has avoided policy formulation in areas of controversy affecting internal Orthodox Jewish life and has turned much of its attention toward the broader Jewish society and the general society. Thus its resolution of 1962, repudiating its long-standing opposition to Federal aid to education, can be taken to mean that the consensus that once existed in opposition to Federal aid is no longer present.

The changing temper within the Orthodox community—the increased emphasis on halakhic observance—is reflected within UOJC. Thus, whereas status once accrued to the leaders and rabbis of congregations without *mehitzot* (barriers separating the men's and women's sections of synagogues), and a certain contempt was evident toward those "old-fashioned" congregations which still had *mehitzot* or even separate seating for men and women, the situation today is reversed. Since 1955, according to a spokesman for UOJC, some 30 synagogues which formerly had mixed seating have installed *mehitzot,* the first break in a trend which had been moving in the opposite direction since the 19th century.

Association of Orthodox Jewish Scientists (AOJS)

Although affiliated with UOJC, the Association of Orthodox Jewish Scientists (AOJS), sponsors of the quarterly *Intercom,* does not belong under the rubric of modern Orthodox. It is far less oriented toward problems of Jewish society and hardly at all to problems of the general society. It is rather concerned with problems arising out of the individual Orthodox Jew's role in the secular and scientific world. In 1964 it claimed approximately 500 members and 12 local chapters in the United States and Canada. The overwhelming majority of its members, according to its 1962 directory, are natural scientists with universities or large corporations, rather than social scientists, whom the organization has also been anxious to attract.

AOJS is preoccupied with the problem of secular education. It has never thought it appropriate to adopt a position on some of the moral issues confronting American society or American scientists as a result of the new technology and its uses, but hardly a national meeting passes in which some discussion, and usually a major address, is not devoted to the subject of the study of science or secular education in the light of the *halakhah.* It is as if the membership had to keep reassuring itself or others that their vocation is a proper one for Orthodox Jews.

Members of AOJS include some distinguished intellects, but the organization has exhibited little critical concern with the nature of American or Jewish life. In general, the natural sciences have attracted more Orthodox Jewish graduate students than the social sciences or humanities. This may be because they offer preparation for more lucrative and prestigious professions today, or because they raise fewer critical problems for Orthodox Jews. It is not difficult to dichotomize religious belief and scientific work, whereas the very assumptions of the social sciences are often thought to run counter to traditional Orthodox views. Whatever the reason, AOJS reflects the special concerns of the natural scientist and has failed to attract to its ranks the growing number of Orthodox Jews in the social sciences and the humanities who might be expected to adopt a broader and more critical approach to Jewish and general affairs.

Yavneh, National Religious Jewish Students' Association

In contrast to AOJS, Yavneh, one of the two national Orthodox collegiate bodies, exhibits great intellectual ferment and general communal concern. Founded in 1960, Yavneh had close to a thousand paid members in over 40 chapters in American colleges and universities by 1964. The founders of Yavneh were largely Yeshiva High School graduates who were dissatisfied with the complacency and lack of intellectual excitement in the Jewish community generally, and Orthodoxy particularly. A generation earlier most of them would no doubt have abandoned Orthodoxy completely. In the 1960s they chose instead to create a subcommunity within the Orthodox world that affirms the Jewish tradition but is concerned with its application to contemporary social and political problems.

Yavneh's founders were soon joined by a more conservative group of students who sought to move the organization along more traditional lines, both programmatically and organizationally; they favored, for example, abolishing mixed-swimming weekends. Yavneh chapters are usually dominated by one group or the other. All chapters, however, have attracted students from non-Orthodox homes who find in the high level of Yavneh's programs an alternative to accepting the deficiencies of the Jewish and general communities. On many campuses Yavneh has come into conflict with local Hillel groups because of its unwillingness to accept the latitudinarian *status quo.*

Although Yavneh has a higher proportion of non-Orthodox members than AOJS—as high as 25 per cent, according to some members—it is by no means non-observant. Notwithstanding their eagerness to explore the ramifications of the *halakhah,* Yavneh members share a commitment to it. Of the many seminars and classes sponsored by the organization on campuses, at national meetings, and at its special study program in Israel,

Talmud study sessions are the most popular. Yavneh's attitude is that regardless of private individual practices, *halakhah* must continue to be the public standard at least. This halakhic commitment is interesting because it may portend a future direction for American Orthodoxy. Unlike left-wing Orthodoxy, it does not call for radical reinterpretation of *halakhah*. Unlike the right, it does not demand that every Jew live his life in accordance with the halakhic prescriptions of the rabbinical authorities. Rather, it calls for an understanding of what the *halakhah* is and then a decision by the individual. In many respects this is a revolutionary outlook for an Orthodox organization, Rosenzweigian in its implication that the ultimate criterion for an individual's observance is his own judgment.

Besides its halakhic commitment, there is almost an obsession with pure intellectual activity in Yavneh. Thus, when one chapter found that many of the youth attracted to its Saturday-night discussion group came primarily for social purposes, it abolished the activity. At its 1964 national convention in New York a guest speaker, a prominent professor of philosophy and an Orthodox Jew, chose to lecture in untechnical language in the hope of making himself widely understood. An observer commented later that the speaker would have been better received had he spoken above the heads of most of the students present—they would have appreciated the compliment.

National Council of Young Israel

The Young Israel movement, with 95 synagogues and approximately 23,000 affiliated families, may be the largest single organization in American Orthodoxy. There are probably more families affiliated with the member synagogues of UOJC, but the relationship between UOJC's leadership and the members of its congregations is still so tenuous that it would be unreasonable to compare it with Young Israel, a large proportion of whose members identify closely with the movement and a few of whom are more intensely committed to the national movement than they are to their own synagogues. This is not to suggest that all or even most member families in the Young Israel are Orthodox in their personal behavior. But there is no question as to where the direction of the organization lies. In fact, only Sabbath observers are permitted to hold office in a Young Israel congregation, and synagogues remove their *mehitzot* only at the price of their charters.

Young Israel was formed in 1912 by a handful of Orthodox Americanized youth who felt themselves a part of American society, rejected many of the folkways and practices of their parents, but wished to remain Orthodox. At first the movement was nurtured intellectually by some Jewish Theological Seminary faculty members, who saw in it a hope for American Orthodoxy. As Young Israel grew, however, it dissociated itself from the nascent Conservative movement, while the Seminary became more involved with it. By the 1920s Young Israel and the Seminary had drifted apart.

Until World War II, Young Israel was a lay movement, dominated by a lay leadership. It was led by native-born, middle-class, college-educated Orthodox Jews, who in their own rather disorganized fashion stood as a bridge between Orthodoxy and the rest of the Jewish community. With modern facilities, stress on decorum in worship, and an attractive social program, Young Israel brought thousands of Jewish young people into the synagogue, many of whom were encouraged to enroll in intensive study courses or to enter *yeshivot*. (Ironically, some of them emerged from the *yeshivot* only to condemn Young Israel for not being sufficiently Orthodox.)

As late as World War II, Young Israel was looked upon as the least observant Orthodox group. This misconception was partly due to ignorance. In part, however, it reflected an awareness of Young Israel's deviations from Orthodoxy. In developing an attractive social program, for example, Young Israel had closed its eyes to such activities as mixed dancing, which few rabbinic authorities would sanction. Its lay leadership, which was not yeshivah-trained, refused to defer to an Orthodox rabbinate who, they felt, lacked secular training, sophistication, and community status comparable to theirs. Being church-oriented, it tended to lay less stress on matters of individual observance and more on Orthodoxy's role in the Jewish community.

Young Israel was among the first Orthodox organizations to seek to raise the level and dignity of *kashrut* supervision, to work with the American chaplaincy, and to lend support to Zionism, youth, and collegiate work. Its semimonthly *Young Israel Viewpoint* was, until it ran into financial difficulty and some conflicts of personalities in 1964, one of the best English-language Jewish newspapers in the United States.

Since World War II the nature of the Young Israel movement has changed. In the first place, the lay leadership has been challenged by the Council of Young Israel Rabbis, the rabbinical organization of Young Israel congregational rabbis. Native-born and acculturated, with increased sophistication and, most importantly, time and information, the postwar rabbi was able to compete with the lay leader. The very growth of the movement had created a need for greater professionalism. In addition, the expansion of membership brought a larger number of marginal affiliates, who recognized the rabbi, rather than the lay leader, as a legitimate spokesman for Jewish religious values. With increasing power at the congregational level, the rabbis were in a position to determine the effectiveness of the national program, and their cooperation became essential. As the locus of money shifted to the congregation, the layman, who viewed himself as part of a national movement seeking a national impact, was replaced by the rabbi, whose interests were more local, and status accrued to the rabbi of the largest, wealthiest, and most observant synagogue.

Another factor accounting for the changes in Young Israel has been the general move to the right within Orthodoxy—the intensification of demands for halakhic observance, which means, almost by definition, the ascendancy of the Orthodox rabbi as the halakhic authority of the congregation. This has particular significance in the case of the Young Israel rabbi, who is not typical of most Orthodox American rabbis, either European-trained or the products of Yeshiva University. The European rabbi is often disadvantaged by his lack of acculturation, and even when he fancies himself as a communal or chief rabbi, he is conscious of his utter dependence on lay approval. Yeshiva University graduates are not all of the same mold; but at least until recently they tended to be church-oriented, communally involved, and very much aware of the necessity for compromise. Rabbis ordained by other American *yeshivot,* like Torah Vodaath, Rabbi Chaim Berlin, and Rabbi Jacob Joseph, on the other hand, reject the Yeshiva University model. These Americanized, non-Yeshiva University graduates tend to be more aggressive and less compromising. About half of Young Israel's congregational rabbis are just such men; only 43 per cent are from Yeshiva University. In the borough of Queens, in New York, for example, there are 56 nominally Orthodox synagogues with 75 or more members. Fifty-five per cent of these synagogues are served by Yeshiva University rabbis. By contrast, of the nine Young Israel synagogues in Queens, only three, or 33 per cent, have Yeshiva University rabbis.

The general move to the right was perhaps more pronounced in Young Israel than elsewhere because of the influence of Dr. Samson Weiss, who served as national director of that organization from 1945 to 1956, when he moved to UOJC. It is best illustrated by the changing emphasis in Young Israel programs. The current topic of debate is whether the movement should halt its expansion efforts and concentrate instead on raising its level of education and observance. The movement has increasingly looked toward the *rashe yeshivot* of the right-wing *yeshivot* for leadership. Its national director, Rabbi Ephraim Sturm, addressing the 1963 convention, urged a united Orthodox front which would look to the *gedole Torah,* the heads of the various *yeshivot,* for direction, and be bound by their decisions not only on purely halakhic matters, but also on nonlegal matters. In recent years one synagogue has gone so far as to abolish the practice of calling to the Torah on Saturday mornings in its main sanctuary, those who do not observe the Sabbath.

Nevertheless, Young Israel has not lost its old character entirely. It still elicits a loyalty from its membership which transcends congregational attachment. Nor has the Council of Young Israel Rabbis been entirely successful in transforming many quasi-official practices. Contrary to the Council's official policy, for example, many congregations sponsor, at least unofficially, mixed dancing. Finally, changes within the adult group appear to have had little impact on the youth. The Intercollegiate Council of Young Adults, with about 1,000 members, has, in contrast to Yavneh, continued to be an essentially social organization, notwithstanding its joint efforts with Yavneh to sponsor kosher facilities on a few college campuses.

Religious Zionists of America (RZA)

The Religious Zionists of America came into being as the result of a merger in 1957 of the two Orthodox Zionist adult male groups in the United States—Mizrachi and Hapoel Hamizrachi. The women's organization of each group, as well as their respective youth groups, Mizrachi Hatzair and Bnei Akiva, have remained separate.

There are no reliable RZA membership figures. Figures of 30,000 and higher are quoted by official representatives, but other observers estimate the number at under 20,000. The organization's budget is in the neighborhood of $250,000, of which about $25,000 goes to the National Council for Torah Education (Wa'ad Ha-hinnukh Ha-torani).

RZA attracts an Orthodox Jew similar to the Young Israel members, and there is a large overlapping membership. Its most active officers and members are themselves rabbis but they play little role in the organization as rabbis. Spiritually, RZA looks to Rabbi Soloveitchik for leadership, and, as in the RCA, his influence has increased in recent years as he has become more outspoken on contemporary issues. A measure of his influence in RZA is that although many of its leaders were embarrassed by his criticisms in 1963 of the State of Israel on the missionary question, none publicly expressed his misgivings.

RZA gives political, social, and philanthropic support to Israel and to the Israeli National Religious party, with which it is affiliated. It also engages in Zionist activities in the United States and publishes a monthly magazine *Jewish Horizon* on contemporary topics, a Yiddish monthly *Mizrachi Weg,* and a Hebrew-language journal *Or Hamizrach.*

The National Council for Torah Education, which publishes two semi-annual journals, *Bitaon Chemed* in Hebrew and *Yeshiva Education* in English, is one of the two major national organizations involved in Orthodox education. The council organizes and serves day schools and Talmud Torahs. It provides a variety of educational services, assistance in teacher placement, and sponsorship of the National Association for Orthodox Education. Its stress is on Israel, Zionism, and the study of Hebrew, and it is identified with a positive approach toward secular education.

It is not clear how many day schools are actually affiliated with the National Council. It claims to have been instrumental in organizing 85, but credit is often difficult to establish. Certainly, not all of those 85 day schools are affiliated with the National Council, but the parent body does not confine its services to affiliated schools. Whatever the number of affiliates, they are fewer than those of Torah Umesorah, the other national educational agency to be discussed below.

Yeshiva University

The one institution most prominently identified with modern Orthodoxy is Yeshiva University. Indeed, the very growth of the university bespeaks the increasing concern of Orthodoxy with problems of the non-Orthodox community, both Jewish and non-Jewish. Beginning as the Rabbi Isaac Elchanan Theological Seminary (RIETS), Yeshiva University has developed or acquired 17 schools and divisions, including a new West Coast center in Los Angeles. This tremendous growth has occurred since 1940 under the leadership of its president, Samuel Belkin, who has remained singularly exempt from the public criticism directed against Yeshiva University by many in the Orthodox world. The university engages in a host of activities, including sponsorship of three Jewish periodicals and a semi-scholarly series of monographs in Judaica, "Studies in Torah Judaism." Among its other divisions are a Hebrew Teachers Institute for men and another for women, a liberal-arts college for men and one for women, graduate schools of education, social work, and science, and a medical school. The relation of some of its divisions to Orthodoxy has, at best, become tenuous. Interestingly, however, the brunt of the right-wing Orthodox attack against the institution has not been against the secular divisions but rather against the college and the Jewish divisions associated with it.

Students at the all-male college (we are not discussing Stern College for Women) are required, in addition to their regular college program, to enrol in one of three Jewish study programs; RIETS, with almost exclusive stress on Talmud and preparation for entering the three-year *semikhah* (ordination) program upon completion of undergraduate studies; the Teachers Institute for Men, with heavy stress on Talmud but a varied curriculum of Bible, history, literature, etc., all taught in Hebrew, and a Jewish-studies program for students with little or no background in Jewish studies.

The last program has been the most dramatically successful. In 1964, in its ninth year, it admitted 100 freshmen (the men's college has a total of about 750 students). The program is adapted to the needs of the students, most of whom are from non-Orthodox homes. It is led by a group of sympathetic and dedicated teachers, who produce, at the end of four years, reasonably well-educated (certainly by American Jewish standards), observant, committed Jews. Some graduates continue their studies in Hebrew and Talmud, transferring to RIETS or going on for further study in Israel. Even the severest critics of Yeshiva University have acclaimed the remarkable success of this program and are inclined to concede that no other institution within Orthodoxy is equipped to do a comparable job. The program's impact on American communities is only beginning to be felt, but inevitably its graduates will assume positions of responsibility. (In contrast to the Jewish-studies program is the Lubavitcher movement, which has also achieved a measure of success in winning youth to Orthodoxy but finds that these converts are often unable to reintegrate themselves effectively in the community from which they came.)

Contrary to popular opinion in the Orthodox world, neither the college nor RIETS espouses any particular philosophy or point of view within the Orthodox spectrum of opinion. RIETS, in particular, is almost a microcosm of the committed Orthodox world and includes among its instructors some who are out of sympathy with secular education. Both the strength and weakness of the institution, no doubt, derive from this eclectic philosophic attitude. Within its walls the whole constellation of Orthodox ideologies contend. It is probably true, however, that were

Yeshiva University to impose a definite direction, it would have the most profound repercussions within the Orthodox world. There are close to 1,000 Yeshiva University rabbinic alumni; 33 rabbis were graduated in 1963, and 28 in 1964. In 1964, 373 graduates held pulpits in nominally Orthodox congregations, 95 were in Jewish education, 65 in Jewish communal work, and 69 on the university's faculty and administrative staff. In addition, a large number of graduates of the Hebrew Teachers Institutes (for both men and women) served the Jewish community in educational and administrative positions.

As in RCA and RZA, the preeminent personality at Yeshiva University is Rabbi Soloveitchik, who teaches Talmud. At the university, however, his leadership in communal matters is not necessarily accepted by the other Talmud instructors, many of whom have also achieved eminence in the world of Talmud learning. Besides, President Belkin, a scholar in his own right, stands forth as an independent personality. Belkin, however, has been elevated above controversy in recent years and the students' image of him is somewhat hazy.

In addition to its purely educational functions, the university plays a major role in the Jewish community through its Community Service Division. The division is responsible for rabbinic and teacher placement, conducts adult-education and extension courses, provides educational services to many Talmud Torahs and youth groups, sponsors seminars for teenagers throughout the United States, and has had a hand, together with the Rabbinic Alumni Association, in sponsoring Camp Morasha, a summer camp which opened in 1964, patterned on the Conservative Ramah camps but with an Orthodox orientation.

Powered by a large staff of experienced professionals, CSD has become increasingly important as a source of information and assistance for other Orthodox bodies. Its placement activities, in particular, have so strengthened the Rabbinic Alumni that rabbis from other Orthodox *yeshivot* have sought (and been granted) associate membership in that association.

Although CSD places rabbis in non-Orthodox congregations, it draws the line at those affiliated with either the Conservative or Reform movement. It also has a relatively new policy of not placing rabbis in congregations which have *lowered* their standards of Orthodoxy. This is subject to differing interpretations. Although CSD's prominence made it the target of attack for alleged lack of Orthodox standards, few people contend that other *yeshivot* have higher standards for placing graduates. The point is made, however, that Yeshiva University, unlike other Orthodox institutions, operates from a position of prestige and financial strength, and therefore has no need to compromise. Of course, these are relative terms. With an annual operating budget of almost $30 million, a capital-fund budget of $65 million, and a deficit of $10 million, Yeshiva administrators are not always certain they can negotiate from a position of strength. CSD justifies placing rabbis in synagogues which do not conform to Orthodox standards not only as expedient but also as the only real means of bringing Jews back to Orthodoxy. It can also point to the fact that in the last few years its standards have become far more explicit and tighter than they ever were in the past, although they are still not satisfactory to a significant group of Orthodox leaders.

There are a number of people on the faculty and in the administration who are critical of Yeshiva University for other reasons. They complain about a certain intellectual complacency, an absence of thought and purpose. They feel that Yeshiva has failed not so much in providing religious standards as in providing intellectual standards. They contend that Yeshiva at times lacks a degree of Jewish and Orthodox self-respect—that there is evidence that Jewish studies and Jewish scholars are not accorded the support and distinction they deserve. The college, in particular, is criticized for not introducing courses with more specifically Jewish content; of having excessive pride in the number of its graduates who win awards, prizes, and fellowships to other graduate schools (the proportion is indeed phenomenally high), and of not taking sufficient interest in those who wish to specialize in Jewish scholarship. Nevertheless, this group of generally young and aggressive personnel remain loyal to the university as the single greatest hope for a resurgence of tradition and, indeed, the survival of American Judaism.

Hebrew Theological College (Jewish University of America)

The Hebrew Theological College, in Skokie, near Chicago, Ill., resembles Yeshiva University in many respects, although it is much smaller and its impact more regional. Established in 1921, it has ordained a total of 335 rabbis, of whom an estimated 185 are in the practicing rabbinate. However, its rabbinical program has declined in the last decade, and in 1963 only 8 rabbis were ordained and 11 teachers certified. The college has a secular division attached to it and is currently in the midst of a $5-million capital-expansion effort. Its 1964 budget was slightly over $500,000.

Sephardi Community

There are an estimated 25,000 Sephardim and 63 known Sephardi congregations—congregations which do not follow the Ashkenazi form of worship or are not of Ashkenazi descent—in the United States. They are largely of Spanish and Portuguese, Syrian, Greek, Egyptian, North African, and Yugoslav origin.

The Spanish and Portuguese, whose origin in the United States predates that of all other American Jews, are the most prestigious, and the leading Sephardi congregation is the famous Spanish and Portuguese Shearith Israel of New York. In 1963 the chief rabbi or *Hakham* of the Sephardi community of the British Commonwealth, Rabbi Solomon Gaon, was also made a rabbi of Shearith Israel, and given the responsibility for the school and authority in all matters of religious law.

Unlike the members of the large Spanish and Portuguese congregations, like Shearith Israel and Mikveh Israel of Philadelphia, Pa., those of most other Sephardi congregations are predominantly first-generation Americans. All Sephardi congregations appear to share a strong subethnic commitment to their form of worship (which differs from one group of congregations to the other), and a relative neglect of private ritual observance. (Thus, even the lay leadership of the Sephardi congregations tend to be quite lax in their religious practice. However, this has in no way affected the intensity of their desire to retain the traditional Sephardi public ritual.) The Syrians, with eight congregations in the Bensonhurst section of Brooklyn, constitute one such self-sufficient community under the leadership of their chief rabbi, Jacob Kassin. Under the initiative of Shearith Israel and its present rabbi emeritus, David de Sola Pool, a Union of Sephardic Congregations was created in 1927, but with Rabbi Pool's retirement in 1956 the organization declined. The possibility of its revitalization rests on the development of more widespread acceptance of Rabbi Gaon as spiritual leader for all Sephardi congregations in the United States.

As a minority within the American Jewish community, the Sephardi congregations face the problems of cultural dilution. Without facilities to train their own rabbis, and more importantly their own *hazzanim* (leaders of the religious service), they face danger of extinction. In 1962 they turned to Yeshiva University, which initiated a program (financed by the Sephardi community) to train religious leaders for them. (Ner Israel in Baltimore and the Mirrer Yeshiva in Brooklyn have also attracted some Sephardi students.) The Yeshiva University program is under the official direction of Rabbi Gaon. Its success depends to a large extent on its ability to recruit college-age students from within the Sephardi community.

SECTARIANS

Jewish sectarianism, unlike that of many Protestant groups, results not from the beliefs of the membership but mostly from a differing strategy as to the best way of maintaining the tradition. Thus, an organization such as Agudath Israel, which is essentially a sectarian group in the United States, was deeply involved in problems and activities of a Jewish and even a general political nature in Eastern Europe. In the United States, on the other hand, they have felt that communal participation with other Jewish groups would perforce involve a recognition of the legitimacy of non-Orthodox religious groups and institutions.

With few exceptions, the sectarian camp is of lower income, poorer education, and more recent immigration than the modern Orthodox.[47] The world of sectarian Orthodoxy is preeminently a yeshivah world, and its leaders are the *rashe yeshivot* and a few prominent hasidic rebbes. It is a mistake to think, as many even within Orthodoxy do, that the Orthodox world which has been created in this country is a replica of the European or even East European one. In fact, the *rashe yeshivot* have achieved a degree of authority in this country unparalleled in Eastern Europe, in good part because there is no counterweight to this authority here in the *shtot rov* or communal rabbi, as there was in Europe.

The years before and immediately after the Second World War brought to the United States an influx of Orthodox immigrants far more militant than those who had come earlier. They found in this country an Orthodox community largely composed of residual Orthodox and under the ostensible leadership of communal rabbis who seemed to be in despair about

---

[47] There is a vast literature on the relationship between religious sectarianism and social class indicating that among religious groups low social class correlates with sectarianism. The classic study is H. Richard Niebuhr, *The Social Sources of Denominationalism* (New York, 1929; reprinted Hamden, Conn., 1954). See also: Liston Pope, *Millhands and Preachers* (New Haven, 1942); Russell R. Dynes, "Church-Sect Typology and Socio-Economic Status," *American Sociological Review*, 1955, pp. 555–60; Donald O. Cowgill, "The Ecology of Religious Preference in Wichita," *Sociological Quarterly*, 1960, pp. 87–96; Nicholas J. Demerath, "Social Stratification and Church Involvement: The Church-Sect Distinction Applied to Individual Participation," *Review of Religious Research*, 1961, pp. 146–54, and Liston Pope, "Religion and Class Structure," *Annals of the American Academy of Political and Social Sciences*, 1948, pp. 84–91. Not all sects, however, are lower-class. Both Christian Science and the Oxford Movement were middle- and upper-class groups. See Yinger, *op. cit.*, p. 146.

the future of Orthodoxy and convinced of the necessity for compromise. They found institutions such as *kashrut* in the hands of people whom they considered as unreliable or careless. They found a bare handful of day schools and a Yeshiva University or RCA ready to accommodate themselves to secular culture. They found almost no institutions with total commitment to the Torah life which had been their world.

They began by creating their own institutions or taking over the few existing ones which they found acceptable. The first step was the creation and expansion of *yeshivot*.

In 1941 Rabbi Aaron Kotler, *rosh yeshivah* of Kletzk in Polish Lithuania, famous as a Talmud scholar and Orthodox leader, arrived in the United States intending to spend a short time here and then move on to Palestine.[48] A handful of Orthodox Jews persuaded him to stay in the United States to build Torah institutions. Reb Aharon, as he was known in the Orthodox world, assembled 20 students, mostly graduates of American *yeshivot,* many already ordained as rabbis, and established the Beth Medrash Govoha of America, in Lakewood, N.J., now also known as the Rabbi Aaron Kotler Institute for Advanced Learning (the first *kolel* in the United States). His choice of site was a deliberate attempt to isolate his students from American life and facilitate total concentration on the study of Talmud. Within a few years he was joined by some former students from Europe; by 1946 registration had risen to 100, and by 1964 to over 200.

Reb Aharon's conviction was that Torah could grow and be "experienced" in America only through *lernen* ("learning"—in the parlance of the Orthodox world, studying Talmud). According to one of Reb Aharon's former students, only "sharing the experience of the halakhic process could enable the Jew to understand the heartbeat of Judaism." The student at Lakewood lived on a small subvention from the yeshivah and whatever other financial help he got from his family or wife. Students sat and learned for as long as they wished. When they felt ready to leave the yeshivah, they left. By 1964, 90 of its former students were teachers of Talmud, 21 were school administrators, and 42 were practicing rabbis.

Reb Aharon, himself, did not confine his activity to Lakewood. He engaged in a multitude of activities where his point of view gained recognition. He served as a *rosh yeshivah* in Israel, became the head of Chinuch Atzmai (Hinnukh 'Atzmaï the independent, religious, Agudath Israel-oriented school system in Israel) upon its founding in 1952, leader of

---

[48] For a biographical sketch see Alex J. Goldman, *Giants of Faith; Great American Rabbis* (New York, 1964), pp. 257–73.

Agudath Israel in 1952, and chairman of the rabbinical administrative board of Torah Umesorah, the National Society for Hebrew Day Schools in the United States, in 1945. Though (interestingly enough) a poor fund raiser in contrast to some other *rashe yeshivot,* Reb Aharon elicited tremendous passion and dedication from those who came in contact with him. He brooked no compromise, nor did he ever question or seem to doubt his own path. He was a preeminently charismatic leader.

The influence of Reb Aharon and like thinkers extended to the higher *yeshivot* in the United States, except for Yeshiva University and the Hebrew Theological College. Thus, older institutions like Yeshivah Torah Vodaath, with its own famous *menahel* (principal) Shragai Mendlowitz,[49] or Yeshivah Rabbi Chaim Berlin under Rabbi Isaac Hutner, were caught up in the emphasis on *lernen* and separatism. In 1944 Rabbi Mendlowitz founded the Beth Medrosh Elyon in Monsey, N.Y., at first called *Esh Dat* ("Fire of Religion"), as a pilot institute for training Jewish educators to found and staff the day-school movement. Within a short period the original idea was abandoned and the institution was reorganized to make it similar to the one in Lakewood.

Advanced Yeshivot

At the heart of the sectarian Orthodox world are all the post-high-school *yeshivot* except Yeshiva University and the Hebrew Theological College. There are today approximately 4,000 men studying Talmud intensively at *yeshivot* on a post-high-school level.[50] Of these, about 825 or 20 per cent were at Yeshiva University or the Hebrew Theological College. According to the latest available figures from the 31 higher *yeshivot* in the United States, more than 250 graduates were ordained annually (not all 31 *yeshivot* give ordination); about 15 per cent of ordinations were from Yeshiva University and the Hebrew Theological College. About 600 of all post-high-school students were older than 24; and many of them were married. Many were organized in *kolelim,* which permitted them to spend the entire day studying Talmud while receiving a subvention of about $50 a week from the yeshivah. Most of the students in the *kolelim* have already been ordained or have no intention of obtaining a rabbinical degree which, in fact, has a practical value only for purposes of becoming a practicing rabbi. (Many European *rashe*

[49] Now known as Rabbi Mendlowitz, the former principal of Torah Vodaath used to refuse to use the title of Rav. His stress on the importance of Hebrew grammar and of pedagogy made him a unique figure in the yeshivah world.

[50] Figures are either from interviews or as submitted to CJFWF. All figures were for 1963–64 or later. See the Appendix.

yeshivot never had *semikhah,* which is simply a certificate attesting one's competence to decide questions of Jewish law. A scholar of renown needed no such certificate.) The very process of learning Talmud is a *raison d'être* and way of life to these men, who eventually will become *rashe yeshivot* and teachers of Talmud.

Graduates of the sectarian *yeshivot* provide the major source of staff for the day-school movement. Many of these graduates, including those with ordination, avoid the rabbinate because they neither wish nor are able to serve predominantly non-observant Orthodox memberships. By choice and absence of alternative they enter the less prestigious and more poorly paid field of Jewish education. Students from Lakewood itself have established five institutions of intensive Jewish learning at the high-school level in different parts of the United States.

Yeshivah graduates who enter Jewish education frequently supplement their talmudic training at college evening sessions, and some even take graduate courses in education. But contrary to their hopes and expectations, many of them are unprepared for the world they enter. Outside the walls of the yeshivah they meet new problems of both a secular and Jewish nature. Furthermore, there is no organization that speaks in their idiom, capable of providing help and direction for them. They continue to regard *lernen* as the highest end, but have no direction in living life short of that end. Of course this is a problem for all yeshivah graduates, not only those who choose Jewish education as their vocation. As true sectarians, they reject the communal Orthodox institutions surrounding them; their only source of leadership and guidance remains their *rosh yeshivah.*

Some yeshivah graduates do, of course, enter the rabbinate. This is a most dangerous course for a sectarian, and each has to make his own compromise with the world. A small proportion serve Reform congregations; more serve Conservative congregations, usually the smaller, less successful ones, which pay the smaller salaries. Of the majority who serve Orthodox congregations some make their peace with modern Orthodoxy, join RCA, associate themselves with the Yeshiva University Rabbinic Alumni, and are indistinguishable from Yeshiva University graduates. A few have chosen to remain isolated from the larger camp of Orthodox rabbis and are organized in the *Iggud Ha-rabbanim* (Rabbinical Alliance of America), to be discussed below.

We can consider now the institutions of the yeshivah or sectarian world, bearing in mind that the most sectarian (exclusive of the *hasidim*) are the least organized and simply continue to revolve in the orbit of their *rashe yeshivot.* We should also note that even the sectarian organizations' involvement in communal activity is not at all a reflection of the rank and file's interests or wishes.

K'hal Adath Jeshurun (Breuer Community)

Much of the preceeding discussion does not apply to K'hal Adath Jeshurun. The Breuer community, in Washington Heights, named for its rabbinic leader, represents the continuation in the United States of the separatist Orthodox community in Frankfurt established in 1849 and led by Samson Raphael Hirsch after 1851. The establishment of Hirsch's separatist community is a fascinating story but not of direct concern here.[51] The New York community, established in 1940, now has over 700 affiliated families and 1,300 adult members, mostly of German origin, and provides a day school, high school, and advanced classes in Talmud for its graduates, who, in the German tradition, are encouraged to attend college. The community sponsors a *mikveh* and provides rabbinical supervision for a host of butchers, bakers, and other food processors in the area. The leadership has maintained the strong anti-Zionism of the German period and is publicly identified with Agudath Israel.

Unlike the East Europeans, the German Orthodox separatists had already made a successful accommodation to western culture before emigrating to the new world; secular education was, indeed, a positive good in the Hirschian philosophy of Judaism. The leaders of the Breuer community might well have expected that, as the most acculturated and economically comfortable but also strictly observant and rigidly disciplined Orthodox institution in the United States, their point of view would sweep American Orthodoxy. Instead, although the community has been quite successful in establishing its own institutions, it has won few converts to its particular ideological position of both communal separatism and a positive acceptance of secular culture. On the contrary, it is on the defensive against the more parochial elements of Orthodoxy.

In part, of course, this is a result of its own decision. As a tiny minority in this country it was faced with the choice of identifying itself communally with Yeshiva University, its neighbor in Washington Heights, and the world of modern Orthodoxy, or with the European yeshivah world with which it had been aligned in Europe. It chose the latter. But in Europe, boundaries and distances separated the followers of Hirsch from the world of the Mirrer or Telshe *yeshivot,* where secular education was dis-

---

[51] The best English-language account is Herman Schwab, *History of Orthodox Jewry in Germany,* trans. Irene R. Birnbaum (London, 1950).

couraged. Even so, there were signs just before the Nazi period that some of the best talent was attracted away from Germany by these and other Lithuanian-type *yeshivot.* In the United States this continues to be the problem. The Breuer community is forced to look outside its own ranks for educational staff, and some of its teachers and administrators have a negative attitude toward secular education. Its institutions are the envy of the Orthodox world, but its future as a doctrinal community is problematical. According to some observers, the Hirschian philosophy is repeated more by rote than understanding. Having lost the Hirschian faculty for Orthodox self-criticism, the Breuer community finds itself increasingly overwhelmed by the fervor of the yeshivah world, despite some inroads by modern Orthodoxy.

National Society for Hebrew Day Schools (Torah Umesorah)

Torah Umesorah is the largest national body serving Orthodox day schools. With an active affiliated membership of some 100 schools, the organization claims to serve all Orthodox day schools without regard to affiliation. Approximately 150 principals are associated with its National Conference of Yeshiva Principals and almost 100 local PTA's are affiliated with its National Association of Hebrew Day School Parent-Teachers Associations. Torah Umesorah's annual budget is over $150,000. It publishes *Olomeinu,* a children's magazine; *The Jewish Parent; Hamenahel,* a journal for principals, and various bulletins and newsletters.

Although Torah Umesorah is staffed by one of the most competent groups of professionals in the Orthodox world, it is, nevertheless, a small body, which must operate within a framework created by *rashe yeshivot* who are somewhat disengaged from contemporary problems, a lay group of officials who tend to be rather uncritical, and a corps of teachers many of whom are untrained. A rabbinical administrative board, composed almost entirely of *rashe yeshivot,* officially dictates Torah Umesorah policy. The board was formerly led by Rabbi Aaron Kotler; since 1962 Rabbi Jacob Kamenetzky of Torah Vodaath has been chairman.

An insight into the composition of the lay leadership of Torah Umesorah is made possible by an analysis of its annual awards. Of the 19 awards given to lay leaders in 1963, 18 went to Americans. Of these, nine lived in New York City, and nine outside the city. Of those from New York, seven were contributors to the Lakewood Yeshiva, and/or Chinuch Atzmai, and/or the Beth Jacob schools (a network of girls' schools with an Agudath Israel orientation). Only one award winner was a contributor to or participant in communally-oriented activities. Of the nine award recipients outside New York, only one was a contributor to the Orthodox institutions indicated above, and eight were contributors to or participants in such communally-oriented activities as Zionist, Israeli, and UJA causes, local communal groups, and UOJC. Notwithstanding the distribution of awards between New York City and "out of town," control of the New York-centered organization is naturally in the hands of a New York or New York-oriented leadership.

In an attempt to raise the technical and ideological level of Hebrew educators, Torah Umesorah instituted teacher-training programs at Ner Israel in Baltimore in 1961 and at Torah Vodaath and Mesifta Tifereth Jerusalem in New York City in 1962 and 1964, respectively, and has cooperated with a training program of the Telshe yeshivah in Cleveland since 1964.

According to Torah Umesorah, there were in 1964 about 300 Orthodox day schools with 56,000 pupils in the United States and Canada. Some day schools had only a few grades, and a few only a kindergarten. According to data compiled by Alvin Schiff of the Jewish Education Committee of New York, there were 257 Orthodox day schools in the United States in 1963, of which 132 were in Greater New York (97 elementary schools and 35 high schools) and 125 outside (94 elementary schools and 31 high schools).[52] Figures given in this article are based upon Dr. Schiff's study, but in any case the number of day schools continues to grow. In 1935 there had been 16 day schools in New York and one in Baltimore; in 1944, 33 and 12, and in 1948 there were 56 and 55.

A number of New York City schools are in neighborhoods of declining Jewish population. This has constricted enrolment and created severe financial problems. In many day schools outside New York, too, the financial problem is critical. Often this is the consequence of inadequate community support. Sometimes the Orthodox financial base is too narrow to support the schools independently, and the wider Jewish community, as represented by federations and non-Orthodox rabbis, often demands too great a voice in school policy to make its support acceptable. The situation differs from one community to another. In many areas, as long as the secular department of the day school functions well, community support is forthcoming.[53] But where the Orthodox base of a com-

---

[52] I am indebted to Dr. Schiff for permission to see a draft of his forthcoming book, *The Jewish Day School in the United States,* to be published by the Jewish Education Committee of New York.

[53] This situation may change with the growing antagonism of Conservative leaders toward the ideology of the Orthodox day schools, but to date the Conservatives themselves have been handicapped by their own rabbis' unwillingness to

munity is quite small, day schools find difficulty in pursuing a policy of intensive Orthodoxy within the institutions' walls while projecting the image of a broad Jewish communal institution deserving of non-Orthodox support from without. In addition, while the non-Orthodox parent may be indifferent to the ideological content of the day-school program, he is not indifferent to the general personality, characteristics, and attitudes of the day-school Hebrew teacher, who is himself often the product of an "other-worldly" environment and a yeshivah where secular education was downgraded.

Of course, not all Orthodox day schools are within the orbit of Torah Umesorah, nor are they all of the same type. There are 28 hasidic day schools

. . . found mostly in the well populated areas of New York City— notably Williamsburg and Crown Heights and Boro Park to a lesser extent—now predominantly inhabited by followers of the leading Hassidic "Rebbeyim". . . . The major emphasis in these schools is upon preserving the distinct philosophy and way of living of the Hassidic group to which the pupils belong. Personal piety, with the particular and unique manner of observance of the Hassidic sect, is stressed. . . . Attention to general studies is secondary. Generally, these are studied only until the end of the compulsory school age.[54]

Within New York City, the language of instruction carries definite ideological overtones. Schools which stress Yiddish are primarily designed to prepare boys for advanced Talmud study, because Yiddish is generally the language of instruction in the advanced *yeshivot*. In addition, Rabbi Kotler is reported to have had particularly strong feelings for Yiddish and to have urged principals to abandon the use of Hebrew and substitute Yiddish instead. There are 31 elementary, non-hasidic, Yiddish-speaking schools in New York City and 19 such high schools, or a total of 50 Orthodox Yiddish day schools. The schools whose Jewish studies are in Hebrew are more likely to be of the modern Orthodox type, placing greater emphasis on Israel and some modern Hebrew literature. The current tendency is toward the use of the Sephardi (or rather, Israeli) pronunciation, although those traditional *yeshivot* which use He-

undertake the arduous task of building day schools that are potential competitors to their own synagogues and Hebrew schools for money and pupils. Even Orthodox rabbis have often been lax in the actual support of day schools. The difference, however, is that Orthodoxy contains a more dedicated and Jewishly impassioned laity, who bear much of the day-school burden without rabbinical assistance.

[54] Joseph Kaminetsky, "Evaluating the Program and Effectiveness of the All-Day Jewish School," *Jewish Education*, Winter 1956–1957, p. 41. Part of the material in this section is drawn from the same article by Torah Umesorah's national director.

brew as a language of instruction, such as the Beth Jacob schools for girls, teach the Ashkenazi pronunciation. There are 41 Hebrew-speaking Orthodox elementary schools in New York and 11 such high schools, for a total of 52 Orthodox Hebrew day schools. (Two elementary schools and one high school teach Jewish studies in English.) Of the 50 Yiddish-speaking schools in New York City, only two are coeducational, in keeping with the policy of such groups-as Torah Umesorah's rabbinical administrative board and the *rashe yeshivot* to segregate boys and girls after the fourth grade. (None of the 28 hasidic schools is coeducational.) Of the 52 Hebrew-speaking schools, 33 are coeducational, reflecting their more liberal outlook. It is fair to say that not quite half the New York City day schools are outside the orbit of the *rashe yeshivot* or the Hasidim.

Outside New York City, the division between Yiddish and Hebrew or coeducational and segregated schools is less meaningful, since there is no base of Yiddish-speaking parents, and segregating the sexes means, besides, to increase the financial burden of these generally smaller schools (average pupil enrolment 146, against 346 in New York). Thus, there are only 18 Yiddish-speaking schools outside New York City, and only 30 schools that are not coeducational.

Day-school enrolment as a percentage of total Jewish-school enrolment has grown steadily from two per cent in 1935 to nine per cent in 1964, and in Greater New York from seven per cent to 29 per cent. There is evidence, however, that day-school growth, measured as a percentage of total Jewish-school enrolment, is leveling off. There have been recent indications of a rise in high-school enrolment as a percentage of total day-school enrolment, at least in areas of large Jewish concentration. In other words, there has been no percentage increase in the number of children enrolled in day schools, but a greater percentage of elementary day-school graduates go on to Orthodox high schools. In Greater New York high-school enrolment, as a percentage of total day-school enrolment, has climbed from 14 per cent in 1956-57 to 22 per cent in 1963-64. While elementary-school enrolment barely grew in these years, even in absolute terms, high-school enrolment increased from 5,186 to 9,076, or 75 per cent. In no year was the increase less than 10 per cent.

Rabbinical Alliance of America (RAA; Iggud Ha-rabbanim)

The Rabbinical Alliance of America, founded in 1944, is composed of graduates of sectarian American *yeshivot* who were unwilling to affiliate with the Yeshiva University-dominated RCA and either were excluded from membership in the Agudat Ha-rabbanim by its *semikhah* requirements, or themselves rejected the Agudat Ha-rabbanim image. The first members of RAA were primarily from Torah Vodaath (with a few from Rabbi Jacob Joseph) and to this day placement for RAA rabbis is handled through Torah Vodaath under an arrangement reached in 1957-58, when RAA cut its formal ties with the yeshivah. Currently the membership numbers around 250, of whom about 100 are in the practicing rabbinate and most of the rest in Jewish education. Many of the practicing rabbis also teach part-time.

Structurally the organization is weak. It exists more because of dissatisfaction with the two other Orthodox rabbinic organizations than through any positive program of its own. It issues an occasional periodical, *Perspective*. Without a purposeful ideology and unable to compete with RCA in benefits or prestige, RAA is experiencing some difficulty. Its position has been further shaken by RCA's move to the right, but RAA still differentiates itself from that organization by its adherence to the separatist *issur* of the *rashe yeshivot* and its refusal to cooperate in mixed bodies of Conservative and Reform rabbis. Nevertheless, almost half the practicing rabbis in RAA are also affiliated with RCA. Spiritually the RAA is in the camp of the *rashe yeshivot*.

Agudath Israel

Agudath Israel was organized in the United States in 1939 as part of a worldwide movement, founded in Europe in 1912, which represented the largest organized force in the European Orthodox world before the Nazi period.

The widespread neglect of Agudah's growth in Europe by Jewish scholars has resulted, according to Agudah spokesmen, in a distortion of both the Agudah's position and of modern Jewish history. Historians and observers, particularly in the United States, have written from a viewpoint which regards modern Jewish history as an almost unbroken process of declining Orthodoxy and rising secularism, socialism, and Zionism. Such a perspective ruled out Orthodoxy as a subject of serious consideration, holding it to be bankrupt. Agudath Israel, on the other hand, without denying the tremendous inroads made by the non-Orthodox, contends that in the 1920s a counterrevolution began to take place in European Jewish life which was ended by the Nazi holocaust. That contemporary scholars have not even considered this claim may well be a reflection of their own biases and prejudices.[55]

---

[55] Although there is undoubtedly a paucity of data regarding the Orthodox by comparison with such groups as the Bundists, the YIVO archives in New York City

In the light of its history, one might well ask why the organization has not become a more potent force among the Orthodox in the United States. The number of members is difficult to estimate, but undoubtedly falls below 20,000, many of whom are indifferent to Agudist ideology but become members automatically by virtue of their affiliation with Agudath Israel synagogues.

All observers are of the opinion that Agudah sympathizers and potential members outnumber those presently enrolled in the organization. There are a number of reasons why the organization has not been able to reach them. First of all, Agudah arrived relatively late in the United States. An effort to establish the organization in 1922 had failed. However, the Zeirei Agudath Israel (Agudah youth) predated the parent body. It was established in 1921, and by 1940 had seven flourishing chapters in New York City,[56] one in Philadelphia, and one in Baltimore. Much of the potential leadership talent did not join the parent organization until 1949, when the adult group forced a resolution requiring that no one above the age of 28 or married could remain affiliated with the youth organization. The adult body, however, was never able to develop the *élan* and social program that were so attractive to the youth.

A second and more important reason for Agudah's weakness stems from the depoliticalization and sectarianism of the *yeshivot*. Reb Aharon and the other *rashe yeshivot* who were leaders in Agudah trained a younger generation to value only one activity, *lernen*. The result was a devaluation of and contempt for political and societal activity in the Jewish community. Thus, the yeshivah students who might have formed the nucleus for a revitalized Agudah never joined the organization; nor has the organization ever become an active communal force. Its youth organization, now firmly under the control of the parent organization, avoids controversial topics of communal concern within the Orthodox community and confines its local activities to *lernen*. This, however, is hardly

---

have an abundance of source material on the subject, much of which is simply ignored. In 1937 there were 192,000 students in Jewish schools in Poland, including vocational, Hebrew-Polish, Zionist, Yiddishist, Labor Zionist, Mizrahi, and Agudath Israel schools. (See Miriam Eisenstein, *Jewish Schools in Poland, 1919–1939* [New York 1950], p. 96.) Of these, 85,000 were in Agudah schools and 15,000 more were in *yeshivot*. Furthermore, Agudah schools were the most rapidly growing of all Jewish schools. Nevertheless, Eisenstein devotes some 70 per cent of her study to the Yiddish and Zionist schools and only about ten per cent in a chapter titled "The Ultraorthodox and Orthodox Schools," to Agudath Israel schools.

[56] For a discussion of the history of the Zeirei Agudath Israel chapter in Williamsburg and the growth of the national organization, see George Kranzler, *Williamsburg: A Jewish Community in Transition* (New York, 1961), pp. 248–86.

an attractive program to young people who spend most of their time in a yeshivah where the level of *lernen* is likely to be as high if not higher.

In an effort to reach the new generation of yeshivah graduates and educate them politically, Agudah undertook in 1963 the publication of an English-language monthly, *Jewish Observer*. It is significant that Yiddish was no longer felt to be an adequate medium of communication for this world. (Agudah has published a Yiddish monthly, *Dos Yiddishe Vort*, since 1952). *Jewish Observer* has had limited success. It has either failed or refused to enlist writers who might have aired controversial issues from which a positive Agudist position could emerge. The journal has with one exception avoided any discussion that might be offensive to any group within Agudah, and it even failed to report the sharp differences which emerged at the *Kenesiyah gedolah,* the international convention of Agudath Israel held in Jerusalem in 1964.

At the head of Agudath Israel stands the *Mo'etset gedole ha-Torah* (the Council of Torah Authorities) formerly led by Rabbi Kotler and, since 1962, by Rabbi Moses Feinstein. The extent to which the *Mo'etsah* actually makes policy for Agudah, at least in the United States, is problematical. Officially, all controversial questions on issues of a public character, whether of a halakhic or non-halakhic nature, are decided by that body. Groups both to the left and the right of Agudah charge that the *Mo'etsah* is simply a front for the professional and lay leadership—that the rabbinic sages are so removed from practical affairs that they permit themselves to be led by others. This is probably an injustice to the rabbinical leadership. It is inconceivable that men who individually spend hours deciding matters of halakhic minutiae would be indifferent to questions which they feel are of national and even international concern. What is more likely, however, is the opposite, at least in the United States. The *Mo'etsah* is handicapped by the absence of controversy. It can respond only to problems that are raised. It can act effectively only in the context of a dialogue in which its wisdom is confronted with practical exigencies and demands of the hour—in which its decisions must be weighed by practical consequences. Agudah, in the United States, has been a sectarian organization which has not challenged its own leadership and consequently has not obtained a measure of response.

Po'ale Agudath Israel (Workers of Agudath Israel)

The American section of Po'ale Agudath Israel, which exists as an independent political party in Israel, has never been an effective competitor to Agudath Israel in the United States. Its pro-Israel sympathies and positive social program might have captured the more energetic and youthful Agudists, but the organization has lacked the sanction of the *rashe yeshivot*. It has remained a small group in the United States, oriented primarily to its parent body in Israel.

Hasidim

As noted above, the original Hasidim represented a sectarian element in Jewish life. A variety of factors contributed to the rise of hasidism in the 18th century, but a discussion of its early period and its doctrines and religious expressions lies beyond the scope of this paper. We note only that the enmity between the Hasidim and the Lithuanian *mitnaggedim* was quite bitter. The Hasidim, with their particular doctrinal stresses and their original deemphasis on talmudic learning, were considered by many to lie perilously close to the outer limits of normative Judaism.

The rise of the Enlightenment, Jewish socialism, and secular Zionism occasioned a reinterpretation by the *mitnaggedim* of hasidic behavior as an aspect of piety rather than rebellion. By the 20th century there were strong ties between the Hasidim and *mitnaggedim* which resulted, finally, in the joint participation of many of their leaders in Agudath Israel.

In the United States a further blurring of ideological differences between Hasidim and *mitnaggedim* has occurred because most Hasidim retain little that makes them doctrinally unique among ultra-pious Jews. Although they cling tenaciously to some of their special customs and generally retain their traditional European dress, with few exceptions they cannot be distinguished ideologically from the *rashe yeshivot*. The one constant that remains is the notion of the *rebbe* or hasidic leader, to whom the followers attribute extraordinary qualities and around whom they cluster.

Habad, the Lubavitcher Movement

The best-known Hasidim are, of course, the followers of the Lubavitcher Rebbe.[57] It is impossible to estimate their number because, unlike

---

[57] A sympathetic portrayal of the Lubavitcher movement and a description of their rebbe and his followers is presented by a Reform rabbi in two articles: Herbert Weiner, "The Lubavitcher Movement," *Commentary*, March and April 1957. Descriptions of other hasidic groups in the United States and Israel, which attempt to capture the essence of their religious meaning and attraction, are found in other articles by Weiner. See, for example, his "Dead Hasidim," *ibid.*, March and May 1961 and "Braslav in Brooklyn," *Judaism*, Summer 1964. There is a vast literature on Hasidism and the Lubavitcher movement in particular by both observers and followers. See for example publications of their former Rebbe, Joseph I. Schneersohn, *Some Aspects of Chabad Chassidism* (New York, 1944) and *Outlines of the Social and Communal Work of Chassidism* (New York, 1953).

other hasidic groups, they are not concentrated in any one area, organized formally, or affiliated with any one institution. The Lubavitcher movement is in many respects the least sectarian of Orthodox groups although doctrinally it is among the most faithful of all hasidic groups, to the tenets of its founders. (It is also the most doctrinally sophisticated and intellectually organized of all hasidic groups.) Its unique texts are taught in its advanced *yeshivot* or in private groups, together with the standard sacred religious texts shared by all Orthodox Jews.

The relationship of its followers to the Lubavitcher movement may best be described as one of concentric circles around the Lubavitcher Rebbe, Rabbi Menahem Mendel Schneersohn, with the inner circle located predominantly, but not exclusively, in the Crown Heights section of Brooklyn, where the Rebbe lives and the headquarters of the movement is located.

Unlike other hasidic groups, the Lubavitcher have friends and sympathizers, estimated by some members of the movement to be as many as 150,000, who far outnumber the immediate coterie of followers. The overwhelming majority are said to be non-Orthodox. Many Jews seek the Rebbe's advice on personal matters and accept him as a religious guide, and he sees an estimated 3,000 people a year for personal interviews averaging 10 to 15 minutes in length.

There are 14 Lubavitcher day schools throughout the United States, besides the Central Lubavitcher Yeshiva and the Beth Rivka school for girls in New York. The total number of students in all Lubavitcher schools is about 4,000.

Outside New York City students are often from families who have little interest or concern for Orthodoxy, much less hasidic doctrine, but are attracted by the negligible tuition rates and the custodial function performed by the school. On the other hand, many followers of Habad, within and outside the city, whose homes are not close to the schools, make no particular effort to enrol their children.

The phenomenon of non-Orthodox Hasidim (President Zalman Shazar of Israel is the outstanding example) is troublesome to many in the Orthodox camp. They wonder how a presumably ultra-Orthodox leader can find such affinity with and arouse such sympathy among unobservant Jews, and whether he has not in fact compromised some essential demands of Orthodoxy in order to attract this great following. The Lubavitcher movement, however, can only be understood on its own terms, and it does in fact stand outside the Orthodox camp in many respects.

The movement does not recognize political or religious distinctions within Judaism. It has refused to cooperate formally with any identifiable organization or institution. It recognizes only two types of Jew, the fully observant and devout Lubavitcher Jew and the potentially devout and observant Lubavitcher Jew. This statement is often cited as a charming aphorism. In fact, it has tremendous social and political consequences. In every Jew, it is claimed, a spark of the holy can be found. The function of the Lubavitcher emissaries who are sent all over the world is to find that spark in each Jew and kindle it. From the performance of even a minor *mitzvah,* they argue, greater observance may follow. Thus, every Jew is recognized as sacred, but no Jew and certainly no institution outside the Lubavitcher movement is totally pure. Consequently the Lubavitcher movement can make use of allies for particular purposes without compromising its position. It can follow a policy of expediency because it never confers legitimacy on those with whom it cooperates.

One result is that sympathy for the Lubavitcher movement generally declines the further along the continuum of Orthodoxy one moves. The militantly Orthodox are continually disappointed by the independent policy which the movement pursues. This is partly due to the fact that the *rashe yeshivot* are from the tradition of the *mitnaggedim* who once bitterly opposed Hasidism and viewed its doctrines as heretical. Since the Lubavitcher are the most doctrinally faithful Hasidim, they would naturally encounter the greatest opposition. But in larger part, the antagonism is a result of the fact that Lubavitcher sectarianism is very different from other Orthodox sectarianism.

Judgment as to the success of the Lubavitcher movement depends on one's vantage point. It is indisputable that many Jews, previously untouched by Judaism, received their first appreciation of their religious faith through the missionary activity of Lubavitcher emissaries. Almost every week students from colleges all over the United States, totally removed from Judaism, visit the Central Lubavitcher Yeshiva in New York City under the prompting of a Lubavitcher representative who visited their campus. But some Orthodox observers question how many of these students who thus visit the yeshivah or pray with an *etrog* and *lulav* at the urging of a Lubavitcher representative, whom they encounter by chance on the street, in school, or in a hospital, are genuinely affected by their experience. Despite pride in its intellectual foundation, the Lubavitcher appeal today is almost exclusively emotional. More than any group in Orthodox and Jewish life, the movement offers solutions to individual problems arising not only from the Jewish condition but from man's societal condition.

The strength of the Lubavitcher movement outside the United States is also impossible to ascertain. It is believed to have the only effective Jewish organization in the Soviet Union. Before Young Israel undertook a public campaign on behalf of Soviet Jewry, its leaders consulted the Lubavitcher Rebbe because of his acknowledged expertness on Soviet Jewry. When the question arose in 1964 whether the Student Struggle for Soviet Jewry should undertake public demonstrations, many yeshivah youth, following the lead of Agudath Israel, argued that such activity would only provoke retaliation in the Soviet Union against the Jews. The student leaders consulted experts from Columbia University's Russian Institute on the point, but a decisive factor leading many students, at least at Yeshiva University, to join the demonstration was that the Rebbe did not express his disapproval.

The Rebbe continues to be accorded a certain universal deference within Orthodoxy that no other leader enjoys. When his mother died in 1964, both the Satmar Rebbe and Rabbi Soloveitchik were among those who came to "comfort the mourner." Few Orthodox Jews would expect the Lubavitcher Rebbe to do likewise in similar circumstances.

Despite the tremendous authority of the Rebbe, the Lubavitcher organization is administratively decentralized. The present Rebbe is the son-in-law of his predecessor Rabbi Joseph Schneersohn. Rabbi Schneersohn's other son-in-law, Rabbi Shemariah Gourary, exercises almost independent control of the school system. Other Lubavitcher activities, such as its publications department and youth program, are also relatively independent of one another. It is not clear to the writer whether this is by chance or design.

Klausenberger, Wischnitzer, and Other Hasidim

In addition to the Lubavitcher movement and the rebbes in the Satmar's orbit, to be discussed in the following section, there are two prominent hasidic groups which retain a strong measure of independence. The Klausenberger Hasidim, from Rumania, who still number between 200 and 300 families in the United States, have been leaving this country in growing numbers to follow their Rebbe to Israel, where he has established his own village. The Wischnitzer Rebbe, from Rumania, who has also established a center in Israel, participates in activities of Agudath Israel, with which his approximately 250 families in the United States are generally aligned. Other hasidic rebbes with followings that are ideologically associated with Agudath Israel include the Bostoner, who went from Poland to Palestine and finally to New York, the Navominsker from Poland, and the Boyoner, Kapitshinitzer, and Bluzhever from Galicia.

Satmar Hasidim and Their Allies

The Satmar community is of Hungarian origin and is the most sectarian of all Orthodox groups in the United States. By the 19th century Hungarian Orthodox Jews had gained a reputation as the most zealous opponents of the non-Orthodox and as sponsors of a school system which introduced more intensive study of Talmud, and at an earlier age, than even the traditional Lithuanian-*mitnagged yeshivot*. The community is governed by the Satmar Rebbe, Rabbi Joel Teitelbaum, head of the Central Rabbinical Congress and leader of religious and political communities which are not identical.

As rov of the religious *kehillah* (community), Rabbi Teitelbaum is final arbiter in all matters of religious law. The *kehillah* numbers about 1,200 families, located primarily in Williamsburg, with smaller branches in Boro Park and Crown Heights (all in Brooklyn).[58] Many of these families lost their rebbes to the Nazis and turned to the Satmar Rebbe when they came to the United States. The *kehillah* provides a full complement of religious and social services to its members, including welfare institutions, schools, *mikvaot,* bakeries, supervision over a variety of processed foods, and, informally, insurance and even pensions. It requires a high degree of religious conformity from its adherents, extending even to matters of dress.

The Satmar schools provide the most intensive Talmud training of all Orthodox day schools. Students begin their Jewish schooling at the age of three or four, and emphasis is on the amount of material covered. There are presently 3,500 boys and girls in the Satmar schools. Of these, some 2,200 are in the Williamsburg center.

As rebbe, political or societal arbiter, the Satmar's influence extends to a number of smaller hasidic groups of Hungarian origin, each with its own rov. These include such groups as the Tzehlemer, Szegeder, and Puper. The total, together with the Satmar's own *kehillah,* is conserva-

---

[58] There is no study on Satmar Hasidim *per se*. For general studies of Hasidim in Williamsburg, much of which is applicable to the Satmar Hasidim, see George Kranzler, *op. cit.;* Solomon Poll, *op. cit.,* and Michael Cohn, ed., *The Hasidic Community of Williamsburg, Brooklyn,* (New York: Brooklyn Childrens Museum, Occasional Papers in Cultural History, No. 4 [1963]).

tively estimated at 5,000 families.[59] The Satmar Rebbe is also recognized as religious leader of the ultrasectarian Netore Karta of Jerusalem (AJYB, 1958 [Vol. 59], pp. 387–88) who number under 200 families.

The Satmar Rebbe is the leading advocate of isolation of the Orthodox and intensification of religious observance within the community of the faithful. Unlike other hasidic groups, the Satmar do not seek converts from among other Jews. The Rebbe is a strong opponent of the State of Israel and cooperation of any kind with the authorities in Israel. The pages of *Der Yid,* the Yiddish weekly of the community, reserves some of its bitterest attacks for Agudath Israel, which, they feel, has compromised its religious principles by acknowledging the State of Israel, joining the government at one point, and developing a network of schools which, though independent of the Israeli authorities, is under their partial supervision and receives some 85 per cent of its funds from them. The Satmar community is well-disciplined, and the word of the Rebbe is almost always authoritative, although he has refused to render opinions on some matters and has thereby opened the way to various interpretations.

On rare occasions he has even been frustrated by his community. He has, for example, long been seeking a tract of land outside of Williamsburg sufficiently large to accommodate his community. According to some observers, he has been prevented from doing so not only by technical difficulties but also by the unwillingness of the entire community to leave Williamsburg. A few years ago a mirror in his home was broken by some zealots who felt it unbecoming for a rebbe's wife to use a mirror. Granted that the act had little support, it nevertheless indicated that even among the most ultra-Orthodox there were varying opinions about religious propriety.

The long-range impact of the Satmar community should not be minimized. Standing outside the mainstream of the communications network of even the Orthodox Jewish community, isolated from almost all Orthodox groups, it is easily ignored except when it erupts in some demonstration, such as picketing the Israeli consulate, which brings it to the public's attention. With 5,000 families averaging perhaps seven or eight, the Satmar community today numbers between 35,000 and 40,000 individuals.

Although its attitude toward secular education is negative, some degree

---

[59] The lowest figure was provided by a Satmar representative. Among those interviewed for this report the Satmar group was the only one whose own membership and school-enrolment estimates were lower than those hazarded by rival observers.

of acculturation is inevitable. The community has recently opened lines of communication with some personalities in Agudat Ha-rabbanim and invited Rabbi Moses Feinstein to a conference of its rabbinic body. The Satmar Rebbe was one of the half-dozen prominent sectarian leaders who delivered a eulogy at the funeral of Rabbi Kotler, while Rabbi Soloveitchik, who also attended, was not asked to speak. *Der Yid* is now distributed more widely than ever before in the yeshivah world, in an obvious effort to win the sympathy of that community. If the *kehillah* is successful in retaining the enthusiasm of its youth, it will inevitably play a more prominent role in Jewish life, and increasing numbers of Jewish leaders will have to reckon with the Satmar Rebbe.

LEADERSHIP

Orthodox institutions, as essentially religious organizations, "must rely predominantly on normative powers [as distinct from coercive or remunerative powers] to attain both acceptance of their directives and the means required for their operation." [60] Religious authority has been traditionally exercised charismatically. That is, the religious leader has been one able to "exercise diffuse and intense influence over the normative orientations of the actors." [61] But according to the value system and traditional expectations of Orthodox Jews, charisma can inhere only in a Talmud scholar. Talmud scholarship is a necessary but not sufficient condition for the exercise of maximum religious leadership or for becoming a *gadol* (plural, *gedolim*). The nature of the *gedolim* has been defined as follows:

> In Jewish life we rely completely on the collective conscience of the people that it will intuitively recognize its leaders and accept their teachings. There surely was no formal vote that thrust the Chofetz Chaim or Reb Chaim Ozer into world leadership. They emerged naturally. . . .
>
> There may be many [who] are recognized Torah scholars and yet they don't attain this wide acclaim. There is some ingredient, that transcends scholarship alone or piety alone—that makes one a Godol. Obviously, these qualities of knowledge, erudition, and piety are basic. But, over and above these there is another that is crucial and that is what we generally describe as "Daas Torah." . . . It assumes a special endowment or capacity to penetrate objective reality, recognize the

---

[60] Amitai Etzioni, *A Comparative Analysis of Complex Organizations* (New York, 1961), p. 41.
[61] *Ibid.,* p. 203.

facts as they "really" are, and apply the pertinent Halachic principles. It is a form of "Ruach Hakodesh," as it were, which borders if only remotely on the periphery of prophecy. . . . More often than not, the astute and knowledgeable community workers will see things differently and stand aghast with bewilderment at the action proposed by the "Godol." It is at this point that one is confronted with demonstrating faith in "Gedolim" and subduing his own alleged acumen in behalf of the Godol's judgment of the facts.[62]

The notion of *gedolim* is, however, becoming increasingly institutionalized, at least for the sectarian Orthodox camp. Its first formal manifestation was in the establishment by Agudath Israel of its worldwide Mo'etset Gedole Ha-torah (Council of Torah Authorities). Rabbi Aaron Kotler, until he died in 1962, was the preeminent *gedol ha-dor* (*gadol* of the generation) for the yeshivah world. The fact that he also led the *Mo'etsah* did not add to his luster. Many, even in the Mizrahi camp or in the ultra-sectarian hasidic camp to the right of Agudath Israel, recognized his eminence. Besides serving as chairman of the *Mo'etsah*, he was chairman of Torah Umesorah's rabbinical administrative board and head of Chinuch Atzmai.

With Reb Aharon's death, the vacant posts had to be filled, putting the unity of the right-wing Orthodox world to the test. In the absence of a personality comparable to Reb Aharon's, would the successors to his offices inherit authority equal to or approximating his? Would, in other words, Reb Aharon's charisma of person pass to charisma of office? Could there be "routinized charisma," so essential to organizational equilibrium, at least among religious groups?

There are three potential successors to Reb Aharon's authority among the American *rashe yeshivot*. (Only *rashe yeshivot* would be eligible since only they possess the necessary qualification of Talmud scholarship.) The most prominent candidate is Rabbi Moses Feinstein, *rosh yeshivah* of Mesifta Tifereth Jerusalem, who was elected chairman of the *Mo'etsah* and head of Chinuch Atzmai in 1962, but only vice-chairman of Torah's Umesorah's rabbinical administrative board. He is also one of five members of the Agudat Ha-rabbanim's presidium. Reb Mosheh is, as we noted, the leading *posek* (halakhic authority) of his generation. Within the world of authoritative *posekim* he is also the most lenient. His decisions, in fact, have bordered on the radical in departure from halakhic precedents to meet contemporary needs. However, greatness as

---

[62] Bernard Weinberger, "The Role of the Gedolim," *Jewish Observer*, October 1963, p. 11.

a *posek* has never by itself entitled a scholar to the highest reverence in the traditional world. Reb Mosheh is a retiring, modest, unassuming person, who, while acknowledging his role as a leader of Orthodox Judaism, none the less, unlike Reb Aharon, seeks a strong consensus on political and social questions (in contrast to religious-ritual-ethical questions) before acting.

The second outstanding *rosh yeshivah* is Rabbi Jacob Kamenetzky of Torah Vodaath, chairman of Torah Umesorah's rabbinical administrative board and a member of the *Mo'etsah*. He is also a member of the Agudat Ha-rabbanim's presidium and rose to prominence in recent years after the death of Rabbi Mendlowitz, the *menahel* of Torah Vodaath, in 1948. In a sense Rabbi Kamenetzky was pushed forward to fill the leadership post which Rabbi Mendlowitz had already endowed with a degree of charismatic authority. There are few people today, outside Torah Vodaath, who feel that he could indeed unite the other *rashe yeshivot* and the Orthodox world around his personality or office.

Finally there is the iconoclast of the yeshivah world, Rabbi Isaac Hutner, *rosh yeshivah* of Chaim Berlin. Rav Hutner's authority over his own students is unique even for a *rosh yeshivah*. He remained in the shadow of Orthodox leadership until after Reb Aharon's death, when he emerged as a forceful spokesman on a number of issues. The hierarchical relationship between himself and the other *rashe yeshivot* has not yet been clarified, but Rabbi Hutner has adopted positions on some issues contrary to theirs. He disagreed with them, for example, on the handling of the missionary situation in Israel, the controversy between the Israeli and American Youth *Pe'ilim* (activists), and the question of secular education.

There is a younger, predominantly American-born group of *rashe yeshivot* who will be assuming positions of greater authority in a few years. Torah Umesorah has given them some expression in a newly formed group called *mishnim* (deputies), which takes a somewhat active role in areas of less than crucial policy importance. Its members are becoming increasingly well known in the Orthodox world, but whether they develop sufficient independence of thought or personality to capture the admiration of the modern Orthodox as well as the sectarians remains to be seen.

The characteristics of leadership in the modern Orthodox camp are similar to those of the sectarian Orthodox. The modern Orthodox counterpart to Reb Aharon is Rabbi Joseph Soloveitchik (the Rov), and as long as the Rov remains active he will maintain his dominant positions in such organizations as RCA, RZA, Yeshiva University Rabbinic Alumni, and to a lesser extent UOJC. The future leader of the modern Orthodox world is likely to be Rabbi Soloveitchik's successor to the chairmanship of RCA's *halakhah* commission, an office which the rabbi is endowing with charismatic authority. At one time Rabbi Soloveitchik might have achieved a comparable role as spiritual mentor in Young Israel, but he rejected their overtures. (Significantly, his brother, Rabbi Aaron Soloveichik, also a renowned Talmudic scholar, has come closer to the Young Israel recently and may possibly emerge as their religious authority. On the other hand, there is great reverence for Rabbi Hutner in the Young Israel movement and particularly in the Council of Young Israel rabbis.)

Unlike Reb Aharon, the Rov assumed his leadership position only gradually. Indeed, the sectarians often charge that he never really became a leader, but is simply a front for the modern Orthodox. If that was true at one time, it certainly is no longer so, although he has been thought to change his mind on enough issues to introduce a measure of uncertainty among his own followers as to where he stands on a number of matters.

To call the Rov the leader of modern Orthodoxy is not to imply that he is always comfortable in that camp or happy with that designation. Nevertheless, his position is sharply differentiated from the sectarian *rashe yeshivot* by his positive affirmation of many elements in Western civilization (he holds a Ph.D. in philosophy from the University of Berlin) and his willingness to operate in a modern Orthodox framework. But the Rov is also part of the traditional yeshivah world. Indeed, in recent years he has moved to the right and has become more outspoken in his criticism of certain aspects of life in Israel, in his own halakhic interpretations, and in his attitude toward rabbis serving synagogues with mixed seating. The Rov may be the leader of modern Orthodoxy, but he is not really modern Orthodox. Modern Orthodoxy has yet to produce a leader from its own ranks because it still continues to acknowledge mastery of the Talmud as a qualification for leadership and yet has refused to endorse, even at Yeshiva University, a restructuring of talmudic education that would encourage bright, inquisitive minds which lack the fundamentalist positions of the *rashe yeshivot* to undertake the many years of dedicated and arduous learning required to become a talmudic authority.

Day-to-day leadership of Orthodox organizations has been assumed by professionals, almost all of whom are rabbis. The role of the professional is growing in importance, but the tremendous charismatic authority invested in the spiritual leader has contained the professional's image and often constrained his initiative.

The lay leader is left in a rather unfortunate position. He commands neither the prestige of the talmudic scholar nor the time and information of the professional. No one within the Orthodox camp really regards him very highly or takes him very seriously. Even among laymen (that is, nonprofessionals), possession of rabbinic ordination, or at least extensive Jewish education, is increasingly becoming a ticket of admission to the councils of decision making.

The only other premium is that placed on the money the layman contributes or raises, but any effort to dictate how the money should be used is resisted. However, as long as the Orthodox community contains only few men of really substantial wealth, it is inevitable that these will occupy positions of status and prestige.[63] On the other hand the growth of *yeshivot* means that Orthodoxy is producing a growing number of Jewishly educated laymen, many of whom acquire a good secular education and economically comfortable positions. This group is only beginning to make an impact on both the Orthodox and non-Orthodox Jewish community. It seems inevitable that they will play a more prominent role in all aspects of Jewish life.

DIRECTIONS AND TENDENCIES

In essence, contemporary American Orthodoxy or at least committed Orthodoxy, whence springs the leadership and direction of the community, is characterized by the growth of institutions whose origins and spirit are sectarian and who are reacting against the church-like direction of Orthodoxy in its pre-World War II period. Orthodoxy, in truth, might have been characterized in that earlier period as simply lower-class Conservative Judaism. That this is no longer the case is due to changes in both Conservatism and Orthodoxy. Orthodoxy today is defining its role in particular and differentiated terms and more than ever before sees itself as isolated from other Jews. The result has been an increased sympathy for its own sectarian wing. But the sectarians themselves have not withstood all change. As one sociologist has written, if a sect is to influ-

---

[63] One of the few Orthodox leaders who would augment the role of the laymen and argues that non-halakhic policy decisions should be made by the practicing rabbinate and lay leadership, together with the "masters of *halakhah*," is Yeshiva University's president: Samuel Belkin, *Essays in Traditional Jewish Thought* (New York, 1956), pp. 150–51.

ence the world to change, "it must itself acquire or accept the characteristics of this world to a degree sufficient to accomplish this goal." [64] It must become "of this world" and in the process it changes its definitions of what is or is not acceptable. Thus, the sectarian institutions themselves are beginning to move in a church-like direction. Strident opposition to Israel among all but the Satmar Hasidim is a thing of the past. Coeducational day schools outside New York are formally disapproved of and tacitly accepted even by the *rashe yeshivot*. Yiddish, which Reb Aharon stressed as a vehicle for maintaining tradition, has been deemphasized ever since his death.

On the other hand, the entire community is more rigid in its halakhic observance. Mixed dancing, once practiced even among Agudath Israel youth, is a thing of the past in most committed Orthodox groups. The formalistic requirements of "feminine modesty," such as covering the hair, are stressed far more than ever before. Observance of the laws of "family purity" and *mikveh,* which once seemed to be on the verge of total desuetude, are rising.[65] There are 177 public *mikvaot* in the United States—36 in the Greater New York area alone—and a number of private ones. There is even a Spero Foundation, which assists communities planning to build *mikvaot* with architectural plans, specifications, and suggestions. But, if ritually the community is more observant, even the most sectarian groups are becoming church-like or communally oriented in the problems they take cognizance of and their means of solution.[66]

Both camps, the modern Orthodox and sectarians, are growing, but the basic sources of their new-found strength are different. For the sectarians it is the young yeshivah graduates now at home in at least the superficial aspects of American culture and committed to tradition and the *rashe yeshivot.* They need not adjust completely to America because they are sufficiently well acquainted with it to be able to reject many of

---

[64] Glenn M. Vernon, *Sociology of Religion* (New York, 1962), p. 167.

[65] The observance of *mikveh,* which requires that a married woman go to a lustral bath a week (generally) after menstruation, before which she is prohibited from having marital relations, is the best single measure for determining who is a committed Orthodox Jew. To the uncommitted, it is inconceivable that so personal a matter should be subject to ritual regulation. To the committed, it is inconceivable that an aspect of life so important as marital relations should not be subject to halakhic regulation.

[66] One example can be found in the pages of the *Jewish Press,* an Orthodox weekly whose editorial position is akin to the sectarian yeshivah world but whose pages devote an increasing proportion of space to news and features of general Jewish interest.

its manifestations. For the modern Orthodox it is the *ba'ale-teshuvah,* the penitents who were raised in nonobservant homes but find in Orthodoxy an emotional or intellectual fulfillment. The first group lacks the intellectual-philosophical perspective to broaden its appeal, but while it may not expand, it will survive. The second lacks halakhic leadership and sanction for much that it reads into Orthodoxy; it lives in a half-pagan, half-halakhic world, and the personal problems of its members are more serious.

A characteristic difference between religious life today and a few years ago, particularly among the modern Orthodox, is that problems have become far more personal. In other words, the personal significance of religion has assumed increased importance over its communal significance. This has fostered increased interest in sectarianism among the ostensibly modern Orthodox, as has the right wing's courage, conviction, and sincerity. Modern Orthodoxy's appeal is dulled by the lingering suspicion of its adherents that they themselves have suffered a loss for living in a half-pagan world.

Many Orthodox Jews have been personally as well as intellectually and emotionally alienated from the non-Orthodox world through employment discrimination. Instances of observant Jews who have been denied employment in Jewish federation-supported institutions or national Jewish organizations because they are Sabbath and holiday observers are legion. And even on a more personal level, Orthodox Jews have often suffered the effects of discrimination, prejudice, and stereotyping by some non-Orthodox Jews who are prominent in Jewish educational, cultural, and communal life. Many of these Jewish leaders, themselves reared in Orthodox homes, abandoned their Orthodoxy because they believed it held no future for Judaism. The upsurge of Orthodoxy among young people bewilders them and makes them resentful. But the Orthodox who suffer at their hands are not inclined to be tolerant. Since it is the modern Orthodox who are most likely to encounter this type of discrimination, a reaction is inevitable.

Relative prosperity, a sense of alienation from other Jews, and increased concern for halakhic observance serve to unite the different groups within the Orthodox camp. But that very unity has dulled Orthodoxy's critical sense, and there is a dearth of systematic criticism to be found, even at Yeshiva University, the most likely arena. A few young faculty discussion groups meet for "lofty" intellectual purposes, but as yet their point of view has found no forceful expression. Observers note that the student body itself tends to be more right-wing than ever in the past. Jewish scholarship *per se,* which might have served as a critical tool, is only beginning to grow within Orthodoxy and still encounters fierce opposition even at Yeshiva University. Talmud study, which is as much a religious as an intellectual experience, is no substitute; it serves to awaken an awareness of tradition and a passion for religion, but not a critical faculty for the social and religious condition of Judaism in the modern world. The pages of *Tradition* have served as vehicles of criticism of the non-Orthodox Jewish world, particularly of Jewish scholarship, but even it has so far failed to develop a characteristic Orthodox response to contemporary problems, and it has ignored self-criticism. A new journal by a few students at Yeshiva University, *Gesher,* was intended to fill the gap, but its first two annual issues, in 1963 and 1964, fell short of the mark.

*　　*　　*

The only remaining vestige of Jewish passion in America resides in the Orthodox community, and it is passion and dedication, not psycho-analytic studies of divorce, which will stem the tide of intermarriage. It is significant that the Student Struggle for Soviet Jewry, the only spon-taneous movement concerned with Soviet Jews, is directed and led pri-marily by Orthodox youth, as is the only other college group recently to show signs of dynamic movement and growth, Yavneh. Whether the Orthodox community as such, however, can generate sufficient force to meet the intellectual stirrings and emotional quests in the American Jew-ish world remains to be seen. The non-Orthodox intellectual is not ready yet to embrace Torah and *halakhah* in their entirety.

But two things have changed. First, the old antagonisms to the world of Orthodoxy are gone from many intellectuals furthest removed from Orthodox life. Secondly, there is a recognition and admiration for Ortho-doxy as the only group which today contains within it a strength and will to live that may yet nourish all the Jewish world.

APPENDIX

KNOWN YESHIVOT PROVIDING INTENSIVE, POST-HIGH-SCHOOL [a] TALMUDIC STUDY IN THE UNITED STATES

Name	Location	Year founded [b]	Enrol-ment [c]	Founder	Present Rosh Yeshivah	Antecedent Yeshivah
Yeshiva University	New York City	1896	694 [d]	R. Judah David Bernstein	R. Samuel Belkin [e]; R. Joseph B. Solo-veitchik	None
Jewish University of America-Hebrew Theological College	Skokie, Ill.	1921	132 [f]	R. Saul Silber	R. Simon Kramer [g]; R. Mordecai Rogow; R. Selig Starr	None
Mesifta Tifereth Jerusalem	New York City	about 1925	111	R. Joseph Adler	R. Moses Feinstein	None
Yavne Hebrew Theo-logical Seminary	Brooklyn, N.Y.	1925	37	R. Nahum Shapiro	R. Bezalel Kaden	None
Yeshivah Torah Vodaath	Brooklyn, N.Y.	1926	240	R. Shragai Mendlowitz	R. Jacob Kamenetzky	None
Yeshivah Ner Israel	Baltimore, Md.	1933	200 [h]	R. Jacob Ruderman	R. Jacob Ruderman	None

KNOWN YESHIVOT PROVIDING INTENSIVE, POST-HIGH-SCHOOL [a] TALMUDIC STUDY IN THE UNITED STATES

Name	Location	Year founded [b]	Enrol- ment [c]	Founder	Present Rosh Yeshivah	Antecedent Yeshivah
Rabbinical Seminary of America (Yeshivah Rabbi Israel Meyer Hacohen)	Queens, N.Y.	1933	85 [1]	R. David Leibowitz	R. Enoch Leibowitz	None
Yeshivah Arugath Habosem	Brooklyn, N.Y.	1938	50 [1]	R. Levi Isaac Grunwald	R. Levi Isaac Grunwald	Arugath Habosem (Deutschkreuz, Austria)
Rabbi Chaim Berlin Yeshivah	Brooklyn, N.Y.	1939	200 [1]	R. Isaac Hutner	R. Isaac Hutner	None
Central Yeshivah Tomchei Tmimim Lubavitch	Brooklyn, N.Y.	1940	170	R. Joseph Schneerson	R. Isaac Pekarsky R. Mordecai Mentlik	Lubavitcher Yeshivah (Otwock, Poland)
Central Yeshivah Beth Joseph Rabbinical Seminary	Brooklyn, N.Y.	1941	32	R. Abraham Joffen	R. Abraham Joffen	Beth Joseph Yeshivah (Bialystok, Poland)
Rabbinical College of Telshe	Wickliffe, Ohio	1941	199	R. Hayyim Katz R. Elijah M. Bloch	R. Mordecai Gifter R. Baruch Sorotskin	Yeshivah Etz Chaim of Telshe (Telšiai, Lithuania)
Theological Seminary Yeshivath Chachmey Lublin	Detroit, Mich.	1942	39	R. Mosheh Rothenberg	R. Mosheh Rothenberg	Lublin Yeshivah (Lublin, Poland)

Institution	Location	Date	Number	Head	Associate Head	Parent Yeshivah
Beth Medrash Govoha of America	Lakewood N.J.	1943	220[l]	R. Aaron Kotler	R. Shneur Kotler	Yeshivah of Kletzk (Kletsk, U.S.S.R.)
Yeshivah Chofetz Chaim of Radun	New York City	1944	73[h]	R. Mendel Zaks	R. Mendel Zaks	Yeshivah of Radun (Radun, Poland)
Beth Medrosh Elyon (Associated with Yeshivah Torah Vodaath)	Monsey, N.Y.	1944	160	R. Shragai Mendlowitz	R. Gedaliah Schorr	Yeshivah Torah Vodaath (N.Y.)
Yeshivah Ch'san Sofer	New York City	1944	150[h]	R. Samuel Ehrenfeld	R. Gedaliah Schorr R. Samuel Ehrenfeld	Yeshivah Ch'san Sofer (Mattersdorf, Austria)
Mirrer Yeshivah	Brooklyn, N.Y.	1946	230	R. Abraham Kalmanowitz	R. Samuel Birnbaum	Mirrer Yeshivah (Mir, Poland)
Yeshivah Farm Settlement	Mount Kisco, N.Y.	1947	45[h]	R. Michael Dov Weissmandel	R. Solomon Ungar	Nitra Yeshivah (Nitra, Czecho-slovakia)
United Talmudical Academy Torah V'Yirah	Brooklyn, N.Y.	1948	300[h]	R. Joel Teitelbaum	R. Joseph Meisels R. Simeon Posen	Satmar Yeshivah (Szatmár, Hungary)
Yeshivah Bet Ha-talmid	Brooklyn, N.Y.	1949	125[h]	R. Arieh Leb Malin	R. Hayyim Wysokier	Mirrer Yeshivah (Mir, Poland)

KNOWN YESHIVOT PROVIDING INTENSIVE, POST-HIGH-SCHOOL [a] TALMUDIC STUDY IN THE UNITED STATES

Name	Location	Year founded [b]	Enrol-ment [c]	Founder	Present Rosh Yeshivah	Antecedent Yeshivah
Rabbi Jacob Joseph School and Mesifta	New York City	1950	106 [h]	R. Mendel Kravitz	R. Mendel Kravitz	None
Yeshivah Karlen-Stolin	Brooklyn, N.Y.	1950	50 [h]	R. Jochanan Perlow	R. Abraham Trup	Karlen-Stolin Yeshivah (Stolin, Poland)
Yeshivah Be'er Shmuel	Brooklyn, N.Y.	1950	100 [h]	R. Joseph Horowitz	R. Moses Horowitz	Yeshivah of Hunsdorf (Huncovce, Czechoslovakia)
Talmudical Academy of Philadelphia	Philadelphia, Pa.	1953	50 [h]	R. Samuel Kamenetsky R. Dov Schwartzman	R. Samuel Kamenetsky R. Elya Svei	Beth Medrash Govoha of Lakewood, N.J.
Boston Rabbinical Seminary	Boston, Mass.	1954	25 [h]	R. Leib Heyman	R. Leib Heyman	Beth Medrash Govoha of Lakewood, N.J.
Yeshiva Eretz Yisrael	Brooklyn, N.Y.	1955	40 [h]	R. Judah Gershuni	R. Judah Gershuni	None

Kamminetzer Yeshivah	Brooklyn, N.Y.	1960	70 [h]	R. Levi Krupenia	R. Levi Krupenia	Kamminetzer Yeshivah (Kamieniec, Poland)
Yeshivah Bet Torah	New Haven, Conn.	1960	15 [h]	R. Mordecai Yoffe	R. Mordecai Yoffe	Beth Medrash Govoha of Lakewood, N.J.
Saint Louis Rabbinical College	St. Louis, Mo.	1961	26 [h]	R. Samuel Faivelson	R. Samuel Faivelson	Beth Medrash Govoha of Lakewood, N.J.
Yeshivah Zichron Tzvi	Woodridge, N.Y.	1964	40 [i]	R. Levi Krupenia	R. Levi Krupenia	Kamminetzer Yeshivah (Brooklyn, N.Y.)

[a] The *yeshivot* listed here may have an elementary and/or high-school division, where students may spend anywhere from two or three hours to a full day. Data in the Appendix are only for the post-high-school division as well. This appendix is not exhaustive. There are undoubtedly other *yeshivot* which were inadvertently omitted. In addition, there are post-high-school students studying Talmud privately or in small groups.

[b] This refers to the year in which the post-high-school division was established. Sources are either CJFWF reports or information obtained directly from each yeshivah.

[c] Unless otherwise noted, these are the latest enrolment figures as submitted by each yeshivah to CJFWF and published in its 1964 reports.

[d] Includes the post-high-school enrolment in the Rabbi Isaac Elchanan Theological Seminary.

[e] Every instructor in Talmud in the Rabbi Isaac Elchanan Theological Seminary is called a *rosh yeshivah*. Officially Dr. Belkin, a former instructor in Talmud and now president of the University, gives the *semikhah* (ordination) and is the THE *rosh yeshivah*. Most people outside of Yeshiva University think of Rabbi Soloveitchik as THE *rosh yeshivah*.

[f] Includes 11 students in the Teachers Institute.

[g] There is no *rosh yeshivah*. Dr. Kramer is the president, Rabbi Rogow lectures to the senior class, and Rabbi Starr has the class beneath him.

[h] Figure supplied by a representative of the yeshivah.

[i] Figure by observers.

RECONSTRUCTIONISM IN AMERICAN JEWISH LIFE

by CHARLES S. LIEBMAN

NATURE OF RECONSTRUCTIONISM • ITS HISTORY AND INSTITUTIONS •
ITS CONSTITUENCY • AS IDEOLOGY OF AMERICAN JUDAISM • FOLK
AND ELITE RELIGION IN AMERICAN JUDAISM

INTRODUCTION

THE RECONSTRUCTIONIST MOVEMENT deserves more serious
and systematic study than it has been given. It has recently laid claim
to the status of denomination, the fourth in American Judaism, along
with Orthodoxy, Conservatism, and Reform. Its founder, Mordecai M.
Kaplan, probably is the most creative Jewish thinker to concern himself
with a program for American Judaism. He is one of the few intellectuals
in Jewish life who have given serious consideration to Jewish tradition,
American philosophical thought, and the experiences of the American
Jew, and confronted each with the other. Reconstructionism is the only
religious party in Jewish life whose origins are entirely American and
whose leading personalities view Judaism from the perspective of the
exclusively American Jewish experience. The *Reconstructionist* has been

Note. This study would not have been possible without the cooperation of many
Reconstructionists, friends of Reconstructionism, and former Reconstructionists.
All consented to lengthy interviews, and I am most grateful to them. I am especially indebted to Rabbi Ira Eisenstein, president of the Reconstructionist Foundation, who consented to seven interviews and innumerable telephone conversations,
supplied me with all the information and material I requested, tolerated me
through the many additional hours I spent searching for material in his office,
and responded critically to an earlier version of this study. Rabbi Jack Cohen
read the same version. He, too, pointed to several statements which, in his view,
were unfair to Reconstructionism. Finally, I am grateful to Dr. Mordecai M.
Kaplan for granting me a number of interviews.

published since 1935. There are very few serious writers in American Jewish life outside the Orthodox camp who have not at some time contributed to the magazine. Through its symposia, lectures, and discussion groups, Reconstructionism has provided one of the few platforms bringing together Jewish personalities of Conservative, Reform, Zionist, and secular Jewish orientations. In 1968 the Reconstructionist movement opened a rabbinical training school, the most ambitious non-Orthodox effort of its kind since Rabbi Stephen S. Wise founded the Jewish Institute of Religion in 1922.

The significance of Reconstructionism and the importance of studying the movement extend beyond its accomplishments. This article will suggest that an understanding of Reconstructionism is basic to an understanding of American Judaism for three reasons:

(1) Reconstructionism is really a second-generation American Jewish phenomenon. It made its appearance during the 1920's and 1930's, when many children of East European immigrants were fleeing from Judaism. Little that was new, exciting, or creative, was taking place in the Jewish community. Reconstructionism was the exception. Besides, Kaplan and his early followers were honest, self-conscious, and articulate about the condition of American Judaism. The literature of Reconstructionism opens the door to an understanding of American Judaism in that period.

(2) Understanding Kaplan's special role in the Jewish Theological Seminary and the Conservative rabbinate illuminates the conditions prevailing in the Conservative movement roughly between 1920 and 1950. In this period Reconstructionism attracted a significant proportion of the most talented and idealistic students at the Jewish Theological Seminary, who now constitute an important segment of Jewish leadership in America. Perhaps Reconstructionism was only a stage through which they passed, but it was important in their lives. One cannot understand them unless one understands Kaplan's special appeal for them.

(3) An understanding of the sociological problematics of Reconstructionism leads us to the core problematic of American Judaism— the nature of Jewish identity. We will suggest that the attitudes of most American Jews are closer to Reconstructionism than to Orthodoxy, Conservatism, or Reform, and that Reconstructionism comes closer than any other movement or school of thought to articulating the meaning of Judaism for American Jews. This raises the question why Reconstructionism today is numerically and institutionally insignificant. Its

core institution, the Reconstructionist Foundation, commands the support of fewer individuals than does any one of a dozen hasidic *rebbes*. There are a number of synagogues in the United States each of which has a larger paid membership than the Reconstructionist Foundation. The annual dinner of a fair-sized elementary *yeshivah* attracts a larger crowd than the annual Reconstructionist dinner. The disparity between the acceptance of Reconstructionist ideas and the failure of the organized movement is striking. Exploring the reasons for this disparity helps shed light on the nature of American Judaism, and on the relationship between the ideologies and institutions of American Jews.

Limitation of space does not permit a thorough analysis of Reconstructionism. Here we will briefly review its history and major ideas. A more specialized social and intellectual history remains to be written, one that will trace the impact of pragmatism, positivism, and Marxism on Jewish intellectuals, and the intellectuals' responses, in the first decades of this century. Such a history would help us to understand American Orthodoxy in that period, as well as the evolution of Conservatism, Reform, Zionism, Jewish education, and the Jewish community center. Neither does this article touch on the organized Jewish community's reaction to a new movement, its receptivity or lack of receptivity to Reconstructionist attempts to gain recognition and acceptance within the institutional framework of American Judaism.

Reconstructionism might also be considered, within the categories of religious sociology, as the germination and growth of a religious movement, with the attendant problems of relationship to a mother church, leadership and succession, routinization of charisma, and deviance.

This essay is divided into five parts. The first three deal with ideology and programs, institutions, and constituency. The last two, "Reconstructionism as the Ideology of American Judaism" and "Folk and Elite Religion in American Judaism," attempting to view American Judaism from a new perspective, present evidence for Reconstructionism's ideological success, and seek to explain its institutional failure—i.e., to show why, when so many American Jews are reconstructionists, so few are Reconstructionists. The first three sections are helpful for understanding the last two.

THE NATURE OF RECONSTRUCTIONISM

Ideology, Beliefs, and Definitions

Among themselves, Reconstructionists are not in complete agreement on matters of ideology and belief. All do agree that Mordecai Kaplan is the founder of Reconstructionism and that his writings provide the major outline of the Reconstructionist ideology and program. Our discussion will center around the ideas of Kaplan.[1]

Kaplan's critics have accused him of being a sociologist rather than a theologian, but he accepts that accusation with pride. According to Kaplan, religion is a social phenomenon, and an understanding of Judaism must begin with an understanding of the Jewish people. He lays heavy stress on the definition of terms. Following John Dewey, he defines an idea or concept, or even an institution, by its function, by its affect and effect.

The core of Kaplan's ideology is his definition of Judaism as a civilization whose standards of action are established by the Jewish people. This definition was a reaction to classical Reform Judaism, which had perceived Judaism as a set of beliefs about God and His relationship to the Jews; and to Orthodoxy, which defined Judaism by a set of laws and practices over which the living community exercised little control. To Kaplan, Judaism is a civilization that has evolved through different stages, whose common denominator is neither belief, nor tenet, nor

---

[1] The material presented in this section draws on the voluminous writings of Kaplan, with less reliance on personal interviews. The most significant of his books are *Judaism as a Civilization: Toward a Reconstruction of American Jewish Life* (New York: Macmillan, 1934; republished by Schocken, 1967); *The Meaning of God in Modern Jewish Religion* (New York: Behrman, 1937; republished by the Reconstructionist Press, 1962); *The Future of the American Jew* (New York: Macmillan, 1948; republished by the Reconstructionist Press, 1967) and *The Greater Judaism in the Making* (New York: Reconstructionist Press, 1960). For special aspects of Kaplan's thought, *A New Zionism* (New York: Herzl Press, 1955) and *Judaism Without Supernaturalism* (New York: Reconstructionist Press, 1958) are also important. The latter is a collection of previously published essays, many of which are included in the books cited above.

The most important sympathetic evaluation of Kaplan is *Mordecai M. Kaplan: An Evaluation*, edited by Ira Eisenstein and Eugene Kohn (New York: Jewish Reconstructionist Foundation, 1952), which contains an essay in intellectual autobiographical style by Kaplan. Kaplan's life and thought are also reviewed in Ira Eisenstein, "Mordecai M. Kaplan" in Simon Noveck, ed., *Great Jewish Thinkers of the Twentieth Century* (Washington: B'nai B'rith, 1963), pp. 253–279.

practice, but rather the continuous life of the Jewish people. The Jewish religion, says Kaplan, exists for the Jewish people, not the Jewish people for the Jewish religion. As he understands Judaism, he claims, this idea constitutes a Copernican revolution. While it is to be found in a number of 19th-century Jewish writers, none had pressed the point into a program of Jewish life as consistently or thoroughly as Kaplan.

Kaplan's definition of Judaism, focusing on community and people, raises the question of the Jew's relationship and responsibility to his community. To this question he suggests a variety of answers. According to Kaplan, antisemitism binds the Jews to each other despite themselves. At the same time, it arouses feelings of inferiority and humiliation in individual Jews that push them to seek an escape from the community. If only because the Jews will not find acceptance and welcome among non-Jews, it is necessary to strengthen Jewish civilization and make Jewish life more meaningful. Elsewhere Kaplan talks about the obligations imposed by Jewish birth. Each historic group, he says, has a responsibility to mankind to maintain "its own identity as a contributor to the sum of knowledge and experience." [2] Therefore it follows that each person has responsibilities to the particular historic group into which he is born.

The position Kaplan more generally espouses is that the Jew's relationship to his community is really "a matter of feeling," as ultimate as the will to live. "The will to maintain and perpetuate Jewish life as something desirable in and for itself" [3] simply exists, and Kaplan has found no better explanation or justification for its existence than anyone else. This does, however, have consequences for Reconstructionism. In the first place, it acknowledges the limitations of audience. Kaplan's message, at least in Kaplanian terms, is confined to those who begin with a sense of Jewish peoplehood—a fact which Reconstructionists themselves are reluctant to admit. Secondly, Kaplan's analysis of contemporary Judaism begins with the assertion that Jewish identity has become attenuated with the breakdown of certain traditional Jewish beliefs. According to him, Jews remained loyal to Judaism for thousands of years despite hardship and suffering because they believed that adherence to the precepts of Judaism assured them otherwordly salvation. But, says Kaplan, people no longer believe in otherwordly salvation.

---

[2] *Meaning of God . . .* , p. 96.
[3] *Judaism as a Civilization,* p. 47.

Consequently, Judaism must transform itself "into a religion which can help Jews attain this-wordly salvation." [4] In other words, Judaism must be reconstructed because otherwordly salvation, the basis upon which Jewish identity rested, is no longer tenable. But for Kaplan the present basis of Jewish identity is "a matter of feeling as ultimate as the will to live." One may ask, therefore, whether the crisis in Jewish life may have nothing to do with the loss of faith in otherwordly salvation; and whether the survival of Judaism really depends on finding a rationale for this-worldly salvation.

Even if one disagrees with Kaplan's analysis as a general statement of the Jewish condition, there is no question that he spoke directly to the predicament of many of his followers: those who, in their own lives, experienced a loss of faith in otherwordly salvation; whose ties to the Jewish people was a matter of ultimate feeling, and who sought to ground that feeling in 20th-century terms. These were the Jews whom Kaplan himself describes as unable to be "spiritually whole and happy if they repudiate their Jewish heritage," [5] but for whom the heritage was no longer as meaningful as it once had been, Reconstructionism, then, begins with a *critique* of the Jewish condition and an *affirmation* of Judaism—both more of the heart than of the mind. When Kaplan writes about the predicament of the modern Jew, he really is addressing himself to a certain kind of Jew, and to him he speaks with tremendous power and meaning. To others, he sometimes sounds trivial. The personal experiences and sentiments of his followers, not the persuasive logic of his argument, validated Kaplan's ideas.

Judaism, says Kaplan, is the civilization of the Jewish people. Like any civilization, it has a history, literature, language, social organization, folk sanctions, standards of conduct, social and spiritual ideals, aesthetic values, and religion. Influenced by the French sociologist Emile Durkheim, Kaplan states that "whatever is an object of collective concern necessarily take on all the traits of a religion." [6] Religion functions "to hold up to the individual the worth of the group and the importance of his complete identification with it." [7] Therefore it lies at the heart of every civilization. The basic, or more important, elements in the life of a civilization are called its *sancta:*

---

[4] *Meaning of God* . . . , p. viii.
[5] *Judaism as a Civilization*, p. 83.
[6] *Judaism Without Supernaturalism*, p. 216.
[7] *Judaism as a Civilization*, p. 333.

. . . those institutions, places, historic events, heroes and all other objects of popular reverence to which superlative importance or sanctity is ascribed. These *sancta*, the attitude toward life that they imply and the conduct that they inspire, are the religion of that people.[8]

The focus of the Jewish religion is salvation, which Kaplan defines as the "progressive perfection of the human personality and the establishment of a free, just and cooperative social order." [9] The desire for salvation is a constant, running throughout the Jewish tradition in its various stages of evolution. Though belief in the possibility of salvation is crucial to Kaplan's own system, it rests on faith rather than empirical reality. Without such a belief, he notes, man is unlikely to strive for salvation. According to Kaplan, there are resources in the world and capacities in man that enable him to perfect progressively his own personality and establish a free, just, and cooperative social order (i.e. to achieve salvation). The "power that makes for salvation" is what Kaplan calls God. "God is the life of the life of the universe, immanent insofar as each part acts upon every other, and transcendent insofar as the whole acts upon each part." God conforms to our experience, since "we sense a power which orients us to life and elicits from us the best of which we are capable or renders us immune to the worst that may befall us." [10]

A number of commentators have criticized Kaplan's concept of God. For Milton Steinberg, in Kaplan's definition

. . . the actuality of God is brought into question. Does God really exist or is he only man's notion? Is there anything objective which corresponds to the subjective conception? And who adds up "the sum" in "the sum total of forces that make for salvation"? Is the sum added up "out there," or in the human imagination? [11]

More caustically, he noted that Kaplan defines God as "the power which endorses what we believe ought to be." [12] Eugene Borowitz observes that, if God is an expression of hope that man may fulfill himself, He is real, but only in a subjective sense. If He corresponds to those factors in nature which make it possible for such ideals to be achieved, He may

---

[8] *Greater Judaism in the Making,* p. 460.
[9] *Future of the American Jew,* p. xvii.
[10] *Judaism as a Civilization,* p. 317.
[11] Milton Steinberg, *Anatomy of Faith* (New York: Harcourt, Brace, 1960), p. 183.
[12] *Id.,* "The Test of Time," *Reconstructionist,* February 24, 1950, p. 24.

be objectively real, but He is not a unity. God would then refer to many different forces in nature.[13]

According to Kaplan, creativity and the impulse to help others or to act justly are forces, or powers, that make for salvation. I may have a desire to help others, and this Kaplan would call an experience of God. I may also feel the urge to write a poem or to paint a picture, and, according to Kaplan, this, too, would be an experience of God. What Steinberg and Borowitz suggest is that both these experiences may be a unity only in Kaplan's mind, not in reality. Also, what I experience may not be based on any objective reality, on anything "out there," but rather on my psychological or sociological condition. By calling God a Power in the singular, Kaplan suggests that He is both a unity and an objective reality. However, his use of the term suggests other meanings. Thus, for example:

> The Jew will have to realize that religion is rooted in human nature, and that the belief in the existence of God, and the attributes ascribed to him, must be derived from and be made to refer to the experience of the average man and woman.[14]

Kaplan acknowledges a lack of clarity among his students regarding his concept of God. Indeed, he states that he himself did not fully understand the concept when he first proposed it. But the problem is of primary importance to those who take seriously the traditional Jewish belief in God and are concerned with the essence of God. It is of secondary concern to Kaplan, who is not concerned with the essence of God, which man can never know, but with the function of God in man's life. As Steinberg noted, the most serious deficiency in Kaplan's theology is that, lacking a metaphysic, "it is really not a theology at all but an account of the psychological and ethical consequences of affirming one." [15] But Kaplan does not agree that this is a deficiency. He affirms that the main problem of the Jewish religion is

> . . . not what idea of God the individual Jew must hold in order that he find his Jewish life to be an asset. Rather is it to what common purpose, which makes for the enhancement of human life, the Jews as a people are willing to be committed, and to be so passionately devoted as to see in it a manifestation or revelation of God.[16]

---

13 Eugene Borowitz, *A New Jewish Theology in the Making* (Philadelphia: Westminster, 1968), pp. 110–111.
14 *Judaism as a Civilization*, p. 306.
15 *Anatomy of Faith*, pp. 181–182.
16 *Judaism Without Supernaturalism*, p. 216.

In one sense then, the critiques of Borowitz and Steinberg are one-sided because they miss the point of Kaplan's definition. On the other hand, Kaplan's definition misses the point of their religious concerns. At the very least, Steinberg and Borowitz find Kaplan's definition of God inadequate, because irrelevant to their own questions.

However, acceptance of Kaplan's definition of God is not essential for being a Reconstructionist. Steinberg himself identified with the movement despite the more traditionalist cast of his belief in God.[17] Eugene Kohn, for many years managing editor of the *Reconstructionist* and probably more critical than Kaplan of traditional Jewish belief, has observed that, contrary to popular opinion, "there is no such thing as a Reconstructionist idea of God." [18] Yet, most books and articles published by the Reconstructionist movement accept Kaplan's point of view. Kohn himself was the subject of an earlier attack by Steinberg on precisely this point. He charged that Kohn identified Reconstructionism with the attitude that God is not a Divine Person or Absolute Being but a "Process at work in the Universe," and said that, while Kohn and

---

[17] There is some controversy as to whether Steinberg was a Reconstructionist at the time of his death. *Anatomy of Faith,* a collection of his essays published ten years after his death, the introduction to the volume by its editor Arthur A. Cohen, and the private testimony of some friends argue against Steinberg's continuing identification with Reconstructionism. On the other hand, we have Steinberg's own testimony, published a month before his death, that "the bulk of Reconstructionist theory, program, implementation seems to me to stand up under the test of the years and indeed to have been validated by it." See his "Test of Time," *loc. cit.;* also, Mordecai M. Kaplan, "Milton Steinberg's Contribution to Reconstructionism," *Reconstructionist,* May 19, 1950, pp. 9–16, and Ira Eisenstein, "Milton Steinberg's Mind and Heart," *ibid.,* October 21, 1960, pp. 9–16.

It seems clear that Steinberg remained a Reconstructionist. Evidence is the fact that his criticism of Kaplan, his refusal to participate in editing the *Reconstructionist High Holy Day Prayer Book,* and his association with Jewish existentialist thinkers came long enough before his death to have permitted him to disavow Reconstructionism, had he chosen to do so. Obviously, Steinberg was not a theological Kaplanian. But apparently other aspects of Reconstructionism—political, cultural, social, and educational—attracted him more strongly than Kaplan's theology repelled him. Indeed, shortly before his death, he agreed to a merger of his own synagogue's school with that of the Reconstructionists' Society for the Advancement of Judaism, under the joint directorship of the Reconstructionist Jack Cohen. However, the lay leaders of his synagogue objected to the merger.

[18] Eugene Kohn, "A Clash of Ideas or Words," *Reconstructionist,* February 19, 1960, p. 19.

Kaplan shared this attitude, he, Steinberg, the publication's associate editor, did not.[19]

Reconstructionism's stress on the social function of religion, rather than on its individual function (answering questions of ultimate meaning, or assisting man in confronting problems of suffering, sin, evil, and the like), also troubles some Reconstructionists. Kaplan is not indifferent to this. For example, he observes that suffering is very real, and may raise doubts not only about a supernatural God, but even about God as the Power on whom man depends for salvation. The way to deal with such doubt, Kaplan states, is "to transcend it, by focussing our attention on the reality of happiness and virtue rather than on that of misery and vice, and by thinking of the problem not in terms of speculative thought but of ethical action." [20] This statement is a clue to some of the Reconstructionists' difficulties.

The last definition of significance in Kaplan's lexicon is *organic community*. Since Judaism is a civilization, Kaplan holds, its parts can only function in interrelationship: "The organic character is maintained so long as all elements that constitute the civilization play a role in the life of the Jew." [21] Kaplan transfers this "organic" concept to the structure of Jewish communal organization which, he maintains, must also be organic:

> The basic unit of Jewish life cannot be any one agency. The entire aggregate of congregations, social service agencies, Zionist organizations, defense and fraternal bodies, and educational institutions, should be integrated into an organic or indivisible community.[22]

The notion of organic community, the creation of democratic local Jewish communal organizations and of democratically elected national leadership, was an exciting one for a number of Jewish rabbis, educators, communal workers, and even laymen in the 1930's and 1940's. It attracted to the banner of Reconstructionism people who were indifferent to its theology, but who saw in Kaplan's proposals the possibility for a structural renewal of Jewish life. Kaplan's idea of organic community is intimately related to his conception of Jewish civilization and religion. In his view, "whatever helps to produce creative social interaction

---

[19] Milton Steinberg, "A Critique of 'The Attributes of God Reinterpreted,' " *ibid.*, March 7, 1941, p. 7.
[20] *Future of the American Jew*, p. 242.
[21] *Judaism as a Civilization*, p. 515.
[22] *Future of the American Jew*, p. 114

among Jews rightly belongs to the category of Jewish religion, because it contributes to the salvation of the Jew." [23]

Kaplan distinguishes between the special, or sectional, program of Reconstructionism, with its particular religious theological formulation, and its general program, stressing the reorganization of Jewish social structure and the enrichment of all aspects of Jewish life. Presumably, one could be a Reconstructionist by accepting only the general program. In fact, the two programs are not quite readily distinguishable. As we shall see, the Reconstructionists' special and particular values have shaped their view of the general program for Judaism. Nevertheless, in the 1930's and 1940's one found in Reconstructionism, especially in the writings of Kaplan and Ira Eisenstein, a concern for Jewish communal life and a conception of what the structure of the Jewish civil community ought to be that existed in no other movement in Jewish life. The fact that Kaplan was somewhat naïve about the possibility of creating such a community, or overly formalistic about constitutional and structural aspects, must not detract from our recognition of his contribution.

Programs and Practices

Reconstructionism has more than an ideology or a set of definitions and beliefs. It has a program, practices, and ritual standards. Indeed, there is greater consistency between ideology and program in Reconstructionism than in most other groups in Jewish life. However, consistency is the hobgoblin of small minds; and since Kaplan's mind is not small, his program and ideology are not always compatible. Also, ideology and beliefs do not establish the special order of priorities, or the hierarchy of emphases, which Reconstructionists give to their programs. This hierarchy may be understood in light of our definition of Reconstructionism. Like Kaplan's definition of God, our definition of Reconstructionism points to its functions rather than to its essence. We define it as the effort to find an intellectually acceptable rationale and program that affirm the positive value of living and identifying with Judaism and Americanism.

There have been various statements of the Reconstructionist platform, all showing similarity. We will focus on the first, issued in 1935,[24] which combines a set of proposals with a statement of definitions and beliefs. It defines Judaism as a religious civilization and articulates the need for

---

[23] *Judaism as a Civilization,* p. 328.
[24] See Mordecai M. Kaplan, ed., *Jewish Reconstructionist Papers* (New York: Society for the Advancement of Judaism, 1936).

a centralized and Jewish communal organization. It also has this to say about Americanism:

> As American Jews we give first place in our lives to the American civilization which we share in common with our fellow Americans, and we seek to develop our Jewish heritage to the maximum degree consonant with the best in American life.

The platform 1) affirms the necessity for reinterpreting traditional beliefs and revising traditional practices; 2) calls for the establishment of a commonwealth in Palestine "indispensable to the life of Judaism in the diaspora," since Jewish civilization must be rooted in the soil of Palestine, and 3) declares itself opposed to fascism, and economic imperialism, "the dominant cause of war in modern times," and in favor of peace; for labor and social justice, against "an economic system that crushes the laboring masses and permits the existence of want in an economy of potential plenty," and for a "cooperative society, elimination of the profit system, and the public ownership of all natural resources and basic industries." Each of the three, belief and ritual, Zionism, and social action, deserves some elaboration.

BELIEF AND RITUAL

Reconstructionist leaders sought to reinterpret traditional beliefs and revise traditional practices through lectures, sermons, and publications. But they also engaged in two major efforts for institutional change: the development of new prayer books and the publication of a ritual guide.

As leaders of their congregation, the Society for the Advancement of Judaism, Kaplan and his associate (and son-in-law) Ira Eisenstein introduced a number of liturgical changes. In 1941 they sought a larger audience by publishing the *New Haggadah*. In 1945 they published a *Sabbath Prayer Book*, and afterward prayer books for festivals, the High Holy Days, and for daily use. In their introduction to the Sabbath prayer book, the editors—Kaplan, Eugene Kohn, Milton Steinberg, and Ira Eisenstein—argue in favor of modification to "retain the classical framework of the service and to adhere to the fundamental teachings of that tradition concerning God, man, and the world. However, ideas or beliefs in conflict with what has come to be regarded as true or right should be eliminated." [25]

---

[25] The introduction was published in the first edition of the prayer book, but was also issued as a separate pamphlet, *Introduction to the Sabbath Prayer Book* (New York, Jewish Reconstructionist Foundation, 1945); p. 9 cited here.

Reconstructionists have a tendency to identify whatever is "true or right" with their own ideology. In the *New Haggadah*,[26] the editors write that "all references to events, real or imagined, in the Exodus story which might conflict with our own highest ethical standards have been omitted." Consistently with Kaplan's ideology, all references to Jews as a chosen people, the concept of revelation of the Torah by God to Moses, the concept of a personal Messiah, restoration of the sacrificial cultus, retribution, and resurrection of the dead were excised. Some traditional passages were retained, though conflictingly with Kaplan's ideology. Here the introduction and annotations suggest how these passages are to be understood. Thus, prayers for the restoration of Israel are included, but readers are told not to construe them "as the return of all Jews to Palestine." [27] Statements to the effect that society's well-being depends on conforming to divine laws of justice and righteousness, and that the soul is immortal, are also retained, the latter to be interpreted as meaning that "the human spirit, in cleaving to God, transcends the brief span of the individual life and shares in the eternity of the Divine Life." [28]

In response to the critique that if, as the Reconstructionists say, God is the power that makes for salvation but not a supernatural power, prayer is a meaningless enterprise, Kaplan demonstrates the function or utility of prayer without regard to the object of the prayer. He argues that "life's unity, creativity and worthwhileness" are the modern equivalent of communion with God. Worship, he says,

> . . . should intensify one's Jewish consciousness . . . It should interpret the divine aspect of life as manifest in social idealism. It should emphasize the high worth and potentialities of the individual soul. It should voice the aspiration of Israel to serve the cause of humanity." [29]

We might add, parenthetically, that, according to Kaplan "the language and the atmosphere of the worship should be entirely Hebraic" [30] for the achievement of these goals.

Kaplan offers man little reason to pray, much less to pray in Hebrew. What he does, we suggest, is to offer a rationale for someone who wants

---

[26] Mordecai M. Kaplan, Eugene Kohn, and Ira Eisenstein, eds. (New York, rev. ed., 1942).
[27] *Ibid.*, p. 12.
[28] *Ibid.*, p. 14.
[29] *Judaism as a Civilization*, p. 347
[30] *Ibid.*, p. 348.

to pray anyway, but is embarrassed by what he regards as the anachronism of prayer, or the beliefs affirmed in the traditional prayer book. Kaplan provides a legitimation, not an impetus, for prayer. The rationale is meaningful only as long as the impetus is present. When impetus goes, rationale goes too. A graduate of the Jewish Theological Seminary, who reports that he never felt comfortable praying, says he felt no more comfortable when he became a Reconstructionist and used the Reconstructionist prayer book.

In their *Guide to Jewish Ritual*,[31] the Reconstructionists deny the binding character of Jewish law. Eugene Kohn has pointed to the inadequacy of any proposals that treat Jewish law as though "the traditional *Halakah* was a viable legal system capable of developing adequate norms and standards." [32]

The *Guide* views ritual not as law, but as "a means to group survival and enhancement on the one hand, and on the other, a means to the spiritual growth of the individual Jew." [33] The individual is to decide which rituals or folkways should or should not be practiced, and, in so doing, strike a balance between his own needs and those of the group:

> The circumstances of life are so different for different Jews, their economic needs and opportunities, their cultural background, their acquired skills and inherited capacities are so varied that it is unreasonable to expect all of them to evaluate the same rituals in the same way.[34]

It then follows that no stigma is attached to those who "permit themselves a wide latitude in the departure from traditional norms." The *Guide* suggests the significance of a set of rituals or a holiday, and recommends specific rituals conforming to the spirit of the system or the holiday, which can easily be observed. The *Guide* stresses that those not observing the rituals should avoid publicly flouting traditional standards where this is likely to be offensive to other Jews. But the ultimate criterion for what should be observed is the self-fulfillment of the individual. For example, the *Guide* suggests that work permitted on the Sabbath includes activity "which the individual is unable to engage in

---

31 The *Guide,* first published in 1941, called forth strong opposition from traditionalists close to the movement. It led to a break between one prominent rabbi and Reconstructionism. The edition discussed here was published by the Reconstructionist Press in 1962.
32 "The Reconstructionist—A Magazine with A Mission," *Reconstructionist,* February 18, 1955, p. 19. Kaplan makes the same point in some of his writings.
33 *Guide to Jewish Ritual,* p. 5.
34 *Ibid.,* p. 6.

during the week, and which constitutes not a means to making a living but a way of enjoying life." [35] According to the Reconstructionists, "what matters is not the ceremonial observance of the Sabbath but the extent to which these ceremonies help one to live and experience the Sabbath." [36] If one has the opportunity for a "congenial career" requiring work on the Sabbath, one need not necessarily reject it, since "observance should not involve the frustration of a legitimate and deeply felt ambition," the *Guide* states, and adds that "our will to live most happily and effectively must supersede the observance of the Sabbath." [37] In general, one celebrates the holidays by being with one's family and doing nice things.

The *Guide* is consistent with Kaplan's earliest work, which stresses that rituals or folkways, as he refers to them, should be practiced "whenever they do not involve an unreasonable amount of time, effort and expense." [38] Furthermore, he notes, the dietary and other practices are designed to enhance the Jewish atmosphere of the home and need not be observed outside the home, since they only add to inconvenience and self-deprivation, and foster the now "totally unwarranted" aloofness of the Jew.[39]

As in prayer, Reconstructionists wish to retain the basic form of Jewish ritual without its traditional rationale, and to make observance convenient. Accordingly, the Reconstructionists developed a social rationale justifying ritual in general, and a personal rationale justifying the observance of one ritual rather than another. The first is borrowed from Durkheim, and the second is based primarily on the individual's convenience. In Kaplan's understanding of Durkheim, religion is essentially a matter of observance, ceremony, and ritual, and the values attached to these acts. Ritual is central to religion and functions "to preserve the integrity of the group and to protect those *sancta,* those holy devices by which the group was enabled to survive." [40] The ritual, in turn, is sanctioned by myth. According to Steinberg, Kaplan borrowed from Ahad Ha'am the idea that Judaism, as a culture or civilization, could replace the religious myth in support of the *sancta.* In fact, the new myth has not operated successfully, and, as we will see, Reconstructionism may

[35] *Ibid.,* p. 16.
[36] *Ibid.,* pp. 17–18.
[37] *Ibid.,* p. 21.
[38] *Judaism as a Civilization,* p. 439.
[39] *Ibid.,* p. 441.
[40] Steinberg, *Anatomy of Faith,* p. 247.

thus have paved the way to ritual laxity. As early as 1944 one Reconstructionist rabbi felt called upon to emphasize that "Reconstructionism was not intended to authorize laxity of observance among practicing Jews but rather to bring Jews to whom Judaism is meaningless closer to Jewish tradition." [41] The fears expressed in 1944 reflect a continuing problem for the Reconstructionist movement.

ZIONISM

The second major plank in the practical program of Reconstructionism was the establishment of a Jewish commonwealth in Palestine. Kaplan maintained that Jewish civilization in its fullest could only be lived in Palestine, and that a condition for the renascence of Jewish civilization in the diaspora was the development of a Jewish commonwealth in Palestine. Efforts toward upbuilding Palestine were also important, according to Kaplan, because it gave Jews something to do. "Take Palestine out of the Jew's life, and the only spheres of influence that remain to him as a Jew are the synagogue and the cemetery." [42] Kaplan was later to reformulate this idea in terms of the role which "only the struggle to take root in a land can create, a collective consciousness which only a living language can beget, and common folkways which only the sharing of common practical concerns can evolve." [43]

On occasion, Kaplan also legitimized the upbuilding of Palestine in terms of a moral imperative: "It is a moral duty because it is nothing less than moral to carry out the promise implied in two thousand years of praying, the promise that, if we be given a chance to build Palestine, we shall do it." [44]

As with prayer, Kaplan's rationale for Zionism does not really proceed from any of his philosophical premises. Kaplan and his early followers were ardent Zionists. They campaigned for the cause of Israel in the 1920's, 1930's, and into the 1940's, when it was not altogether popular to do so. The pages of the *Reconstructionist* magazine blazed with editorials attacking the foes of Zionism. Although the magazine always reserved a special dislike for the Orthodox, its major villains in the 1930's and 1940's were the American Council for Judaism, Jewish Communists

---

[41] Maxwell Farber, chairman, in report of annual Reconstructionist conference, *Reconstructionist*, October 6, 1944, p. 22.
[42] *The Society for the Advancement of Judaism* (New York: SAJ, 1923), p. 11.
[43] *Future of the American Jew*, p. 141.
[44] *Society for Advancement of Judaism*, p. 12.

and fellow-travellers, and the American Jewish Committee, whose policies the *Reconstructionist*'s editors then regarded as assimilationist and anti-Zionist. Kaplan's loyalty to the upbuilding of Palestine is unquestionable. Zionism is a *religion* for many Jews, including Reconstructionists, and Kaplan seeks to give this religion a philosophical underpinning. The Zionist program of Reconstructionism is an outgrowth of its adherents' Jewish commitment, not their Reconstructionist philosophy.

However, Kaplan's Zionism is typically American. He rejects the necessity for *'aliyah* (immigration to Palestine or Israel), *kibbutz galuyot* (the ingathering of exiles in Israel), and *shelilat ha-golah* (negation of the diaspora). An editorial in the magazine attacks the Ashkenazi chief rabbi of Israel for giving "religious sanction to the mischievous policy of . . . associating the call for return of Jews to Zion with the state rather than some vague messianic period." [45] In typically American Zionist fashion, Kaplan declares that Israel must not seek *kibbutz galuyot* but should be a "haven of immigration for all Jews who are not able to feel at home in the lands where they now reside." [46] His ambitions for Palestine were modest. Jews, he felt, should be permitted to constitute a majority within a Jewish commonwealth, although they need not have exclusive responsibility for military defense and foreign policy. Before the creation of Israel many other Zionists, too, were prepared to accept such conditions, but few made a virtue of it. According to Kaplan, "relief from exclusive responsibility [in these matters] should be welcome." [47] In other words, Jews do not "require the sort of irresponsible and obsolete national sovereignty that modern nations claim for themselves." [48]

SOCIAL ACTION

The third major plank in the Reconstructionist platform deals with social action. The early programs of Reconstructionism virtually endorsed socialism, and in the 1930's and early 1940's a few members even flirted with Communism. Kaplan himself is strongly anti-Marxist in his philosophical orientation, and the movement opposes the far Left, which it perceives as anti-Zionist, assimilationist, and, in the case of the Soviet Union, anti-Jewish as well.

[45] *Reconstructionist,* November 12, 1948, p. 6.
[46] *Future of the American Jew,* p. 124.
[47] *Ibid.,* p. 125.
[48] *Ibid.*

Kaplan's belief in social amelioration is part of his religious-philosophical conviction. He holds that a primary function of religion is improving ethics,[49] that ethical discussion is equivalent to study of Torah: "Any discussion carried on for the purpose of becoming clear as to the right and wrong of a matter is Torah." [50] The particular ethical norms with which Kaplan is most concerned, those which he suggests as the central foci for the Jewish holidays, are correctives for social, rather than individual, evil.[51] He inveighs against the evil that man commits by participating in the existing social structure.

In general, there has been a diminution in the radical political rhetoric of the Reconstructionists.

Assessment of Ideology and Program

Two philosophers, former Reconstructionists, have discussed the various influences on Reconstructionism. Sidney Morgenbesser and David Sidorsky observe that Reconstructionism has been influenced by both American and European ideas.[52] They point to four major European ideas that Reconstructionism has recast into an American mold: Dubnow's emphasis on the organization and function of the local Jewish community; Ahad Ha'am's assumption that creative Jewish life outside the land of Israel depends on a community there, and his nontheological reinterpretation of Jewish values; the historical school's recognition of the natural origin and context of Judaism's most cherished institutions, and, finally, Durkheim's and Robertson-Smith's theories of religion as the expression of social life and the instrument of group cohesion and survival.

The primary influence, however, has been America. The American scene, with its political democracy, naturalistic philosophy, and pragmatic temper, has given rise to the Reconstructionist movement. At the same time, these characteristics serve as criteria by which Reconstructionism, in turn, assesses and reevaluates any current American Jewish movement.[53]

---

[49] See, for example, Mordecai M. Kaplan, *A New Approach to the Problems of Judaism* (New York: SAJ, 1924).

[50] *The Society for the Advancement of Judaism*, p. 17.

[51] See, for example, the *Meaning of God in Modern Jewish Religion*.

[52] "Reconstructionism and the Naturalistic Tradition in America," *Reconstructionist*, February 18, 1955, pp. 33–42.

[53] *Ibid.*, p. 33.

This influence is apparent in the major planks of the Reconstructionist platforms, as well as in the more detailed aspects of Reconstructionist thought. For example, *The Reconstructionist* has published articles opposing Jewish day schools because they fail to prepare students for democracy [54] and because they indoctrinate students with a particular ideology.[55] According to Kaplan, Jewish day schools are neither feasible nor desirable. They are but "a futile gesture of protest against the necessity of giving to Jewish civilization a position ancillary to the civilization of the majority." [56]

Reconstructionists accept the American environment, and seek to mold a Jewish program to fit in with it. Of special interest in this regard is Kaplan's rejection of the concept of the Jews as a "chosen people." Reinterpreting the concept of God, as Kaplan himself notes, he could have dealt with the "chosen people" in the same way—as by arguing that his conception of God does not permit of chosen peoples. Instead, he rejects the concept as undemocratic and unegalitarian. Eisenstein, in turn, suggests that though the Jews are at least unique, it is bad taste to talk about it.

We Jews have a remarkable history. In some respects we have been more preoccupied than other peoples with the belief in God and with the conception of God, with problems of life's meaning and how best to achieve life's purpose. But we should not boast about it. Humility is more befitting a people of such high aspirations. We ought not to say that God gave the Torah to us and to nobody else, particularly at a time when mankind seeks to foster the sense of the equality of peoples. We should be old enough and mature enough as a people to accept our history with dignity, without resort to comparisons which are generally odious.[57]

The American influence is in the very marrow of Reconstructionism. In his first major book Kaplan observes that "since the civilization that can satisfy the primary interest of the Jew must necessarily be the civilization of the country he lives in, the Jew in America will be first and foremost an American, and only secondarily a Jew." [58] Even on so basic a Jewish issue as intermarriage Kaplan is influenced by notions of American legitimacy. He argues that Jews cannot legitimize their objection to intermarriage since America

---

[54] Joseph Blau, "The Jewish Day School," *ibid.,* November 14, 1958, pp. 29–32.
[55] Jack Cohen, "The Jewish Day School," *ibid.,* December 26, 1958, pp. 27–28.
[56] *Judaism as a Civilization, op. cit.,* p. 489.
[57] *What Can A Modern Jew Believe* (New York: Reconstructionist Press, n.d.), p. 10 (A Reconstructionist pamphlet).
[58] *Judaism as a Civilization,* p. 216.

is certain to look with disfavor upon any culture which seeks to maintain itself by decrying the intermarriage of its adherents with those of another culture. By accepting a policy which does not decry marriages of Jews with Gentiles, provided the homes they establish are Jewish and their children are given a Jewish upbringing, the charge of exclusiveness and tribalism falls to the ground.[59]

Kaplan also strongly advocates separation of church and state. He believes that by supporting separation and helping to develop a separate religion for America, a civic religion independent of any church or of supernaturalism, Jews could make a contribution to American civilization.[60] Indeed, Kaplan's belief that church and state must be separate, but that every civilization must have its own religion to assure social cohesion and unity, makes a civic religion a necessity. In 1951 Kaplan, Eugene Kohn, and a Christian, J. Paul Williams, edited *Faith of America,* a remarkable volume published by the Reconstructionist Press. It celebrates the *sancta* of American civilization in a series of nondenominational prayers, poems, songs, literary selections, and historical documents for use by churches, synagogues, public assemblies, and patriotic societies on national holidays.

The American influence is also evident in Kaplan's definition of Judaism as a *religious* civilization. Initially, he had referred to Judaism only as a civilization—without an adjective—because, in his view, all civilizations have religion and therefore what makes Judaism different from other civilizations is not that Judaism has a religion. Judaism's content, especially its salvation orientation, makes it different. Yet Kaplan now said he had always intended to define Judaism as a *religious* civilization, and that the omission of "religious" from his earlier formulation was pure oversight. Two of Kaplan's best students, scholars of distinction, said he had added the word at their insistence. Otherwise, they asked, what distinguishes Judaism from any other civilization? Their recommendation would suggest a total misunderstanding of Kaplan. But Kaplan accepted it.

This may be an instance of semantic clarity unconsciously giving way to the goals which the early Reconstructionists set for themselves. The early Reconstructionists were philosophical, but philosophic consistency was not their ultimate value. The ultimate value was a rationale and program that would affirm the positive value of living and identifying with both Judaism and Americanism. Kaplan had to introduce the term

---

59 *Ibid.,* p. 419.
60 *Judaism Without Supernaturalism,* p. 99.

religion into his definition of Judaism because, in the last analysis, Judaism is acceptable in the American environment only as a religion, not as a civilization. Only as a religion can Judaism legitimately demand the allegiance of its followers within the American context. Thus, when Kaplan defines Judaism as a religious civilization, he utilizes a popular definition of religion, not his own.

Kaplan and Reconstructionism reflect the American experience more than does any other Jewish religious group. Reconstructionists have been aware of this. Their problem has been to transform sociological fact into theological virtue. The difficulty of this enterprise—because self-conscious social theorists make poor religious leaders—may be inherent in the very essence of religious life.

A crucial function which religion serves for its adherents is determining ultimate values. Religion tells us what is ultimately right and wrong. The skeptical sociologist may suspect that ultimate values are influenced by, if not derived from, the physical, economic, social, and political environment. The skeptic may also suspect that a religious leader who asserts ultimate values has read them *into* his religion as much as *from* it. On the other hand, the religious leader will argue that all he did was to translate the ultimate standards of the tradition into contemporary terms. Nevertheless, many religious leaders are aware of the danger that, in the process of translation, they may simply sanctify whatever the prevailing standards of society, or their subjective standards of morality, happen to be. The skeptical sociologist may argue that this is inevitable. The religious leader will argue that it is a danger against which he must struggle. He cannot accept it as inevitable without denying one of the basic functions of religion.

Kaplan wishes to be both a religious leader and a skeptical sociologist. He believes that religion must constantly undergo what he calls transvaluation. Judaism, he says, can become creative only if its true scope and character are understood, and if it assimilates, in "deliberate and planned fashion," [61] the best in contemporary civilizations, even though, as Kaplan recognizes, such *conscious* assimilation is a departure from the tradition. What Kaplan fails to realize is that when traditional values are made secondary to contemporary ones, they lose their import, and the very necessity for transvaluation loses its urgency. Secondly, by self-consciously transvaluating traditional and ultimate values into con-

---

[61] *Judaism as a Civilization*, p. 514.

temporary ones, Reconstructionism no longer has criteria for judging contemporary civilization.

As long as virtually all Reconstructionists came from the same background and environment, had a similar secular education and similar Jewish experiences, there were large areas of agreement on Jewish and ethical matters within the movement. Reconstructionists assumed that this agreement had something to do with their movement. We suggest that it did not, and that Reconstructionism may find itself increasingly divided over such issues as social action and Zionism. At present there are elements in Reconstructionism relatively unconcerned about Israel, and other elements oriented to the New-Left, even at the expense of Jewish self-interest. Reconstructionism has no intrinsic standards, as distinct from programmatic planks, to protect itself from these deviations. Indeed, there are indications that Reconstructionism itself may become transvalued, a process most compatible with its basic doctrines.

No doubt some Reconstructionists would question that the function of religion is to assert ultimate standards. They may argue that it is rather to sanctify the community's values and transmit them through symbols and rites, as well as to provide group cohesion. But these are legitimate only if one believes that the values being sanctified and transmitted are indeed inherently true. Social cohesion for the sake of cohesion, or of the self-conscious transmission of contemporary values through the use of traditional symbols for the furtherance of contemporary values, smacks of hypocrisy and sham. But, a Reconstructionist may ask, what is the alternative? If God is not a source of values and there is unwillingness to accept the authority of Torah values, how can religious leaders renew the tradition or generate new values? That question goes to the heart of the dilemma of religious liberalism. The Orthodox Jew certainly does not have the answer. He can only wonder at what he feels is a perversion of religion in the argument that Judaism must be brought "into harmony with the best ethical and social thought of the modern world" [62] when *best* can only mean what a particular writer thinks is best at a particular moment of time, or the values that happen to have been current among a group of Jewish intellectuals in the 1920s and 1930s.

The tradition is used without embarrassment as a means of strengthening group ties and legitimating the ethical values of the present. By way

---

[62] *Meaning of God in Modern Jewish Religion*, p. 358.

of illustration, Kaplan asks us to assume that research and reflection have demonstrated that the human personality must be treated as an end in itself. He then advocates drawing on the traditional values of Judaism to show that this principle has played a part "in shaping some of the most important laws and practices of the Jewish people":

> This resort to the past for the confirmation of present is not a sop to conservative minds. Ethical principles require the sanction of history . . . to show that they are in line with tendencies inherent in the very nature of man and in keeping with that character of the world which expresses itself as the power that makes for righteousness. To this end, it is necessary to select from the Jewish heritage whatever will verify the validity of the sanction which Judaism is urged to adopt.[63]

HISTORY AND INSTITUTIONS[64]

Early History

The history of Reconstructionism begins with Mordecai Kaplan. He was born in Swenziany, Lithuania, in 1881, the son of a traditional Jew and distinguished Talmudic scholar, who came to New York in 1889 at the invitation of Rabbi Jacob Joseph, the foremost Orthodox rabbi of America in the last decades of the nineteenth century, to join him as *dayyan* (rabbinical judge). Young Mordecai attended public school. He received his Jewish education in *heder,* from private tutors, and from his father. Kaplan recalls that he was strongly influenced by the Bible scholar and critic Arnold Ehrlich, a frequent visitor in his father's home. When Kaplan was 12 years old, he was enrolled in the Jewish Theological Seminary (JTS). He reports that, by the time of his ordination in 1902, at the age of 21, he questioned the Mosaic authorship of the Bible and the historicity of miracles. While attending the seminary, he graduated from City College (1900), and received his M.A. from Columbia (1902). He read widely in philosophy, psychology, sociology, and anthropology. He was particularly influenced by anthropological and sociological studies of religion, especially comparative religion, and nonsupernaturalist religious developments in the first decades of the twentieth century.[65]

---

[63] *Judaism as a Civilization,* p. 463.

[64] A history of Reconstruction still remains to be written. The material presented here draws primarily on personal interviews, as well as on material in the *Reconstructionist* and its predecessor, the *SAJ Review.*

[65] See Harold C. Weisberg, "Mordecai M. Kaplan's Theory of Religion," in *Mordecai M. Kaplan; An Evaluation,* pp. 156–162.

The first position Kaplan held was that of minister of Kehilath Jeshurun on New York's upper East Side, the most fashionable East European Orthodox congregation of its day. Kaplan was the first JTS graduate to hold a position in a New York congregation. Kehilath Jeshurun wanted an English-speaking rabbi, but was reluctant to give Kaplan the title since he did not have *semikha* (Orthodox ordination). In fact, at the urging of a prominent European rabbi who visited Kehilath Jeshurun, the congregation brought Rabbi Moses Z. Margolis from Boston to serve as its rabbi; Kaplan became his associate. On his honeymoon in Europe, in 1908, Kaplan received *semikha* from Rabbi Isaac Reines, the founder of the Mizrachi movement.

Kaplan reports that he felt increasingly uncomfortable in an Orthodox synagogue, and considered selling insurance. This, he believed, was of social value and would give him greater freedom. However, in 1909 Solomon Schechter, president of JTS, invited Kaplan to head its newly established Teachers Institute. Kaplan accepted and a year later also became professor of homiletics in the rabbinical school. Kaplan continued to hold both posts until 1946, when he became dean emeritus of the Teachers Institute. In 1947 he gave up his professorship in homiletics to become professor of philosophies of religion, a post created for him, which he held until his retirement in 1963 at the age of 82.

Kaplan's impact on his students, who were to become rabbis and educators, will be discussed later. As Samson Benderly's co-worker in the New York City Bureau of Jewish Education, Kaplan trained another group of educators, many of whom he recruited from the City College Menorah Society. Kaplan also exerted influence over Jewish social workers through his frequent lectures, articles, and books on Jewish communal affairs, and as faculty member of the Graduate School for Jewish Social Work, from 1925 until its closing in 1937.

According to Kaplan, the synagogue's function is to serve as the focal point for all Jewish life. Therefore, the synagogue had to be more than a place of worship, especially since increasing numbers of Jews felt no particular desire to worship. The synagogue had to serve as a cultural, educational, and recreational center as well, reflecting as far as possible the totality of Jewish civilization.

By 1915 New York's West Side was rapidly becoming the most fashionable place of residence for the city's Jews. A small group of Orthodox, interested in establishing a Jewish center, asked Kaplan to serve as their rabbi. The center was built on West 86th Street, and Kaplan was its rabbi until 1921.

Kaplan's relationship with the Jewish Center might well be explored by the future historians. The lay leadership was strictly Orthodox. Kaplan did not conceal his heterodoxy. His journal [66] records that he informed the founders of the Jewish Center of his position.[67] How can one then explain their request that he serve as their rabbi, or his affiliation with them until 1921?

This question is of little consequence for the history of Reconstructionism, but important for an understanding of the history of American Orthodoxy, since it reveals the attitudes of at least one important group of Orthodox Jews in the World War I period. The answer may lie in files of the Jewish Center, but its lay leader refused permission to search old records. Here we will hazard some guesses, none of them mutually exclusive.

The Jewish Center leaders simply may not have believed that anyone with traditional ordination, who was punctilious in his own ritual observances, could really be saying what Kaplan seemed to be saying. They may not have understood what Kaplan was saying. They may have felt that Kaplan's idiom, though heterodox to their own ears, was necessary to attract youth. In 1917 there were not many alternatives for a congregation that wanted an English-speaking, traditionally-ordained rabbi, who was a bright fellow, a good orator, and socially acceptable. Kaplan's first wife, Lena, came from the large, wealthy Rubin family, which was affiliated with the Jewish Center. Members of her family married into other wealthy and influential Center families. In fact, these were the families that eventually left the Jewish Center with Kaplan and founded the Society for the Advancement of Judaism (SAJ), now located on the same street as the Jewish Center, just a block away.

---

[66] Kaplan's diary or journal of his thoughts and activity, which he has kept since 1913, is an invaluable source of American Jewish history, Reconstructionism in particular. The journal cannot be seen without Kaplan's permission, which he no doubt would have granted for the purposes of this study. However, its extensive use did not seem necessary. During my interviews with Kaplan, he would refer to the journal to refresh his memory, or corroborate a point. At such times he would ask me to read aloud from it, and we would then discuss the passage in question.

[67] See also Mordecai M. Kaplan, "The Influences That Have Shaped My Life," *Reconstructionist*, June 26, 1942, p. 34. Kaplan reports that he told the founders of the Jewish Center that he was not Orthodox and did not intend to use the *Shulḥan'Arukh* as an authoritative guide.

Kaplan's conflicts with the Jewish Center laity were not confined to religious matters. From the pulpit he accused some of them of unfair treatment of their employees. In 1921 the board voted by a small margin to retain Kaplan as rabbi. He, in turn, resigned and, in January 1922, founded SAJ with 22 or 23 families.

Kaplan did not conceive of SAJ as a new synagogue. He borrowed the name from a group established earlier in the century by a few wealthy Jews to aid Judah Magnes in his efforts to organize the New York Jewish community. Kaplan envisaged an organization which would support the dissemination of his point of view. Still, his supporters had resigned from one *shul,* and now needed another. He therefore agreed to serve as their spiritual leader. From the outset, SAJ provided for societal as well as congregational members.

Kaplan refused to use the title rabbi and instead borrowed the term *leader* from the Ethical Culture Society. The *Reconstructionist* magazine, created 13 years later, was also to copy the format of the society's monthly publication. Kaplan's conception of religion and religious motivations may be better understood in the context of his sensitivity regarding Ethical Culture, which he feared because of its attraction to Jews. Also, he was deeply impressed by an incident related by Felix Adler, founder of Ethical Culture, in his autobiography: When the Torah reading is completed in the synagogue, the scrolls are raised and the congregation recites the biblical verses, "And this is the Law [Torah] which Moses put before the children of Israel [Deuteronomy 4:44] according to the word of God, in the hand of Moses [Numbers 4:37 *et passim*]." Adler, who accepted neither Divine nor Mosaic authorship of the Torah, says he could not bring himself to recite these verses, and that this was the final impetus that drove him from Judaism. Kaplan is at a loss to understand why Adler did not do what the Reconstructionist prayer book does: omit the verses and remain a Jew.

Kaplan's sensitivity about Ethical Culture can hardly be explained in terms of his experience with the first SAJ members, although some of their children may possibly have been attracted to it. Kaplan's followers were largely first- and second-generation Americans of East European descent, and successful businessmen. Most were traditional in ritual observance and observed *kashrut* in their homes. Kaplan wanted to establish SAJ on the Lower East Side in order to reach the immigrant workers who, he felt, were not served by the religious establishments. However, the SAJ members objected because they wanted a place of worship that would be reached without having to violate the Sabbath. Though they hardly were intellectuals, they had some pretension to learning. Many took courses at Cooper Union or the Educational Alliance. What drew them together were family ties, an intense personal loyalty to Kaplan, and a sense that he was saying something Jewish that was different and important.

By the end of the 1920's the membership had grown to about 150 families, most of whom resembled the founders. SAJ sponsored a number of pamphlets in which Kaplan set forth his program for the reconstruction of Jewish life. From 1922 Kaplan edited the *SAJ Bulletin,* which later became the *SAJ Review.* Of modest format, it was a forum for Kaplan and a number of JTS graduates. Many of Kaplan's articles, which he later incorporated into his books, were historical and theological in nature. But the magazine also contained many pieces on Jewish education and on the need for rethinking educational programs. Most of the contributors were identified with Conservative Judaism, and much of their writing was critical of the amorphous nature of Conservatism and bemoaned its lack of platform or the fact that it was united only by its opposition to Orthodoxy and Reform.

During this period Kaplan and his followers represented a sometimes inchoate, but generally identifiable, left wing within the Conservative movement. While Kaplan's theology was perhaps the most radical, he was publicly respectful of JTS leadership. Often at odds with Cyrus Adler, the seminary's president and Schechter's successor, Kaplan resigned from JTS in 1927. He withdrew his resignation at the urging of a committee appointed for that purpose by the Rabbinical Assembly, the organization of Conservative rabbis. Numerous efforts were made by Kaplan's followers, all of whom were affiliated with the Rabbinical Assembly, to improve the cohesion of the left wing within, or even outside, this body.[68] The pattern that was to repeat itself for many years had already evolved in the 1920's. The left wing's strength was in the practicing rabbinate, the right wing's in the Jewish Theological Seminary. The left wing, correctly or incorrectly, believed that a majority of rabbis were behind it; but it always lacked the votes. Kaplan believed that it was only a matter of time before the older, right-wing leadership disappeared and his followers would control the Conservative movement.

---

[68] Some fascinating correspondence on this matter can be found in Herman H. and Mignon L. Rubenovitz, *The Waking Heart* (Cambridge, 1967).

He opposed splitting the Rabbinical Assembly, and refused the presidency of the Jewish Institute of Religion, a nondenominational rabbinical seminary founded by Stephen S. Wise in 1922. Wise offered the presidency to Kaplan at least once: in 1927, after Kaplan had resigned from JTS and before he withdrew his resignation.

The conventional view of Reconstructionism is that it did not develop as an independent movement because Kaplan was convinced his ideology would eventually capture the Conservative movement, and because he did not relish the responsibility of organizing a new movement. This is only partially correct. It is quite true that Kaplan discouraged the formation of a separatist movement in Jewish life. It is also true that he restrained many of his followers, particularly Ira Eisenstein, from moving in that direction. But, as we shall see, Kaplan and the Reconstructionists undertook many projects, any one of which might have catalyzed Reconstructionism into a movement if it had generated real enthusiasm among more than a handful of people.

The organization of a new religious movement requires at least three elements: There must be some central personality who evokes loyalty and dedication among his followers. There must be commitment to a set of beliefs and practices which can serve to integrate the followers and establish boundaries between themselves and nonmembers. And there must be willingness on the part of the followers to transfer their loyalties from an older institution, or set of institutions, to a new one. The first dimension was always present within Reconstructionism; the second existed to a lesser extent; the third was absent. The loyalty of Kaplan's early followers and their admiration for him, even their personal adherence to his point of view, disguised the fact that most of them were quite unprepared to do more than gather periodically to honor their mentor, subscribe to his books and publication, or discuss his ideas.

Kaplan discouraged the organization of a movement in opposition to Orthodoxy, Conservatism, and Reform. But he and his closest followers certainly sought to bring Reconstructionist sympathizers together under one roof. Had Kaplan succeeded, or had there been enough such sympathizers, Reconstructionism would have become another religious denomination despite itself and despite Kaplan.

As early as 1928 a conference of rabbis, educators, and social workers was held in the Midwest to set up a national organization along the lines of SAJ. It resulted in the formation of the Mid-West Council of the Society for the Advancement of Judaism. Rabbis Felix Levy and

Max Kadushin, the educator Alexander Dushkin, and Kaplan constituted its executive committee. The success of the midwestern venture led to a similar conference in the East; but there was much greater division among its participants, some of whom were more traditional, and some more assimilationist than Kaplan. Consequently, no platform representing a consensus of the participants resulted from the second conference.

Meanwhile, through the dissemination of the *SAJ Review* and the growing influence of Kaplan's students, the ideas of Reconstructionism spread. At the close of 1928 the Beth El synagogue in Manhattan Beach, Brooklyn, adopted the SAJ platform, which tended to stress the general nature of Reconstructionism, rather than what Kaplan later was to call its sectional program. For his part, Kaplan urged that only his program, and not Conservative Judaism, could unify the Jewish people. Conservatism, he said, deals with Judaism as a religion, and religion is divisive:

> The moment you propose one mode of worship or one attitude toward observance for another, you automatically divide. These very things depend on taste, habit, and pressure of necessity. . . . A solution to the problem of Jewish life depends upon finding, or making a positive ideology which will enable Orthodox and Reform, both believers and nonbelievers, to meet in common and to work together.[69]

If Reconstructionism was not to be competitive with Conservative Judaism, that was because, in a sense, it subsumed it. (Obviously, though, if more than a handful of people had taken this idea seriously, it inevitably would have been established as a movement.)

By the end of its first decade, the nascent organization was undergoing a crisis. Kaplan found himself unable to devote sufficient time to his organizational and literary efforts. SAJ was not growing as rapidly as Kaplan had hoped, although, by the late 1920's, it had attracted a number of Zionist intellectuals and educators, such as Alexander Dushkin, Israel Chipkin, Jacob Golub, Judith Epstein, and Albert Schoolman, in addition to its earlier members. Kaplan's sense of frustration was compounded when, as a result of the 1929 depression, funds for the publication of *SAJ Review* were no longer available.

Kaplan invited Milton Steinberg and Max Kadushin to serve as his assistants, and both refused. In 1930 he invited Ira Eisenstein, a senior at JTS who had been working at SAJ since 1928 and who later became

---

[69] *SAJ Review*, January 1928; reprinted on the opening page of the first issue of the *Reconstructionist*, January 11, 1935, p. 2.

his son-in-law, to join him. Eisenstein accepted. He became assistant
leader in 1931, associate leader in 1933, and leader in 1945, when
Kaplan became leader emeritus. (The title was changed from leader to
rabbi in the 1950's.)

During the depression years a number of congregations affiliated with
SAJ by accepting its platform. Such affiliation generally occurred at the
urging of the congregation's rabbi. But most of the synagogues never
took the affiliation seriously, and, in the course of years, as the rabbi
left his pulpit or lost interest in Reconstructionism, the individual congregation would drop its affiliation. The core of the early Reconstructionist movement rested in the New York congregation which supported
Kaplan's projects and publications financially, and a small group of
sympathetic rabbis and educators around Kaplan. They included such
men as Israel Goldstein, Ben Zion Bokser, Louis Levitsky, Israel Chipkin, Abraham Duker, and Samuel Dinin. In the group closest to Kaplan
were Eugene Kohn, Milton Steinberg, and Ira Eisenstein.

Kaplan's *Judaism as a Civilization* appeared in 1934. It contained the
major premises and programs of Reconstructionism. The only matter on
which he later changed his mind, Kaplan says, was the retention of the
chosen-people doctrine, which he still accepted in 1934.

In the same year Kaplan and some of his followers agreed to launch
a successor to *SAJ Review*, which would disseminate the ideas of Reconstructionism and serve as a forum for contemporary Jewish thought. The
SAJ board agreed to act as publisher and supply office facilities. The
approval was by one vote; there was objection to the financial responsibility entailed, to the political radicalism of some among those associated
with the magazine, and a general sense of localism—opposition to divert-
ing energies from SAJ, as a congregation, to Reconstructionism, as a
national movement. The new magazine, the *Reconstructionist*, began
publication in 1935. The members of the first editorial board were strong
Zionists and Hebraists, and all but two were identified with Conservative
Judaism.

In 1936 Kaplan wrote that "Reconstructionism should become a
quality of existing Jewish institutions and movements rather than another
addition to their quantity." [70] But in the same year a *Reconstructionist*
editorial [71] invited readers to comment on whether Reconstructionism

---

[70] *Jewish Reconstructionist Papers*, p. xvi.
[71] *Reconstructionist*, November 27, 1936, pp. 3–4.

should be a new movement or a school of thought. At the first Reconstructionist dinner, held at JTS in May 1935, friends were called upon to organize Reconstructionist clubs for the study and discussion of issues of concern and to plan how to influence their fellow Jews with Reconstructionist philosophy and program. Twenty prospective leaders announced their readiness to form such clubs. They usually were formed by rabbis, existed for a few years, sponsored a project or, more likely, a discussion group, and then died out as the moving spirits changed residence or lost interest. Had the number of such groups, or the number of members within each group, grown, or the first members retained their loyalties, Reconstructionism would have inevitably become a movement.

At a summer institute, sponsored by the magazine in 1938, it was decided to expand the scope of Reconstructionism and to publish pamphlets, text books, syllabuses, and "devotional literature." A new organization, the Friends of Reconstructionism, was created to provide a financial base for the realization of these objectives, with the help of an executive director. The magazine already had 2,000 subscribers, and Eisenstein now referred to Reconstructionism as a movement, whose origin he dated from publication of *Judaism as a Civilization* in 1934.[72]

The Friends of Reconstructionism consisted of a small group of wealthy laymen from SAJ and the Park Avenue synagogue, where Milton Steinberg served as rabbi. It was dissolved in 1940, and the Jewish Reconstructionist Foundation was organized in its place. Its purpose was to act as publisher of the *Reconstructionist,* as well as of books, pamphlets, and educational material, and to encourage Jewish art. An editorial in the periodical denied that this was an effort to create a new organization. Reconstructionism, it said, seeks to influence Jewish life by infusing the existing institutions with its spirit.[73]

Associated with Reconstructionism in this period were a galaxy of Jewish rabbinical and educational personalities. In addition to those already indicated, we mention here only a few who were to leave a mark on American Jewish life: Max Arzt, Mortimer Cohen, Morris Adler, Joshua Trachtenberg, Roland Gitelsohn, and Theodore Friedman. A Reconstructionist group was formed in Chicago, whose president, in the early 1940's, was Solomon Goldman. Local members included

---

[72] Ira Eisenstein, "The Progress of Reconstructionism," *ibid.,* November 18, 1938, pp. 13–16.
[73] *Ibid.,* February 16, 1940, p. 3.

Samuel Blumenfield, Harry Essrig, Judah Goldin, Richard Hertz, Felix Levey, Judah Nadich, Maurice Pekarsky, Gunther Plaut, Charles Shulman, Jacob Weinstein, and Leo Honor. However, some of the early followers, including Max Kadushin, had already disassociated themselves from Reconstructionism; Ben Zion Bokser did so in the early 1940's.

During this period Reconstructionism had good reason to believe that it had captured the allegiance of the leading young men of the Conservative and Reform rabbinates. Growing somewhat bolder, in 1941 it published the *New Haggadah*. For this Kaplan was denounced in a letter from the JTS faculty, sent at the instigation of Professors Louis Ginzberg and Alexander Marx. It called upon him to cease his work, which was contrary to the principles of JTS. In 1945, after publication of the Reconstructionist *Sabbath Prayer Book,* another blast was leveled at Kaplan by a JTS faculty member. However, opposition to the prayer book within the Conservative movement diminished when a group of zealous Orthodox rabbis excommunicated Kaplan and burned his book in a public ceremony. Shortly thereafter, the attitude toward Kaplan at JTS changed. Moshe Davis was instrumental in convincing the JTS leadership that attacks on Kaplan were not in the institution's interest; on the contrary, his presence on the faculty demonstrated the freedom and diversity at JTS.

For his part, Kaplan remained faithful to the institution. In his later years it accorded him personal honor and recognition, though it never gave his followers, or his ideas, the place he felt they deserved, and indeed had been promised.

In 1943 the formation of Reconstructionist fellowships in different cities was recommended, under the direction of local rabbis who would interest laymen to meet frequently for study and action, and, annually, at a national convention. Eugene Kohn felt that the fellowships should appeal to Conservatives, Reform, and Zionists. The only ones that would have no place in the movement were the Orthodox, the group which, Kohn held, "by reason of its supernaturalism and dogmatic authoritarianism is so out of harmony with the whole scientific and philosophic outlook of the modern world that it is bound to diminish, although the hysteria attendant upon persecution and war may give it a new lease on life for a time." [74]

---

[74] Eugene Kohn, "A Religious Fellowship to Raise the Standards of Jewish Leadership," *ibid.,* October 18, 1943, p. 13.

The fellowships were in fact little different from the earlier Reconstructionist clubs, most of which were defunct by 1943. The new name was apparently an effort to invigorate the national movement. Within three years there were reports of Reconstructionist study groups and fellowships in Baltimore, Arlington, Alexandria, Chicago, Philadelphia, Brooklyn, Los Angeles, Oakland, Orlando, Milwaukee, and Kansas City. Rabbi Jack Cohen became director of fellowship activities. Lest there be any mistake about the intentions of Reconstructionist leaders, an editorial in the magazine observed that "with the launching of the fellowship, Reconstructionism will enter on a new phase of its career. It will cease being a mere school of thought and will emerge as an activist religious movement." [75] Kaplan himself was more hesitant about organizing as a movement rather than a school of thought. Nevertheless, even he foresaw the alignment of synagogues with Reconstructionism and, perhaps, ultimately a union of Reconstructionist congregations.[76]

The magazine continued to grow in size and to attract distinguished writers. In the late 1940's its editorial board included such disparate figures as Will Herberg and Joshua Loth Liebman, the latter much more of a Reconstructionist than the former. The major issues to which the editorials and articles were devoted included Israel, Jewish communal organization, the problem of Jewish law, and religious freedom in Israel. For Reconstructionism, the major villains were the anti-Zionists and the Orthodox. The magazine followed developments in Jewish art and music, devoting one issue annually to them.

Despite any impact the magazine may have had, the Reconstructionist movement did not grow. A Reconstructionist Youth Fellowship, formed in 1946, at first grew and then died. In December 1950 over 40 Conservative and Reform rabbis established the Reconstructionist Rabbinical Fellowship. By January 86 rabbis, as "proponents of the Reconstructionist philosophy of Judaism," had signed a statement, "A Program for Jewish Life," [77] embodying the basic Reconstructionist program. Eventually the document bore the signatures of 250 educators, social workers, and laymen, and 285 rabbis. Although the Rabbinical Fellowship membership grew to 150 within two years, little more was heard from it later. In 1957 members were urged "to become vociferous and frank

---

[75] *Reconstructionist,* January 7, 1944, p. 6.

[76] Paper read before Reconstructionist Conference: "Reconstructionism as Both a Challenging and Unifying Influence," *ibid.,* October 6, 1944, pp. 16–21.

[77] *Ibid.,* January 26, 1951, p. 24.

in their espousal of the movement so that its message would be brought forcefully to the American Jewish public." [78] Fellowships of laymen continued to spring up and disappear in cities all over the United States, but none ever attracted sizeable numbers.

In 1950 the Reconstructionist School of Jewish Studies was opened in New York, with the announcement that branches would be established in other cities. Its existence was cited as consistent with Reconstructionism's ideology that rejected the urgings of devoted followers to "become a separatist movement organized on a congregational bases like Orthodoxy, Conservatism and Reform in this country." [79] No branches were ever opened, and the New York school itself soon closed down.

Reconstructionism's hesitation to declare itself unequivocally as an independent movement continued. Eisenstein urged Kaplan to break with JTS and lead such a movement. He argued that if Jewish unity were to be Reconstructionism's first concern, it should surrender such projects as the publication of its own Haggadah and prayer book, which were divisive rather than unifying. Eisenstein's own preference was for Reconstructionism to become a separate denomination. Kaplan resisted. According to Eisenstein, those closest to the movement were frustrated by their inability to do anything for Reconstructionism. The absence of a distinctive denominational structure also diminished the interest of potential contributors. Organizational aimlessness and financial problems meant the loss of talented staff members, who found other institutions more attractive.

In 1950 Eisenstein was elected vice president of the Rabbinical Assembly, which meant automatic succession to the presidency in 1952. Kaplan saw this as a tremendous opportunity for Reconstructionism, but Eisenstein's subsequent experience only confirmed his feeling that Reconstructionism could not succeed within the framework of the Conservative movement.

However, Reconstructionism continued to develop structures which would have forced it to become a separate denomination, if they had not floundered. In 1952 the Reconstructionist Foundation resolved to establish affiliated regions and chapters throughout the United States under the direction of a national policy committee which, in turn, would select an executive board. Although "no competition with other existing organization is envisaged, no 'fourth' Jewish religious denomination is

---

[78] *Ibid.*, March 22, 1957, p. 31.
[79] Editorial, *ibid.*, October 20, 1950, p. 6.

contemplated," [80] the basis for such a movement obviously was present. A budget of $150,000 (an increase of $100,000 over the previous year) was projected. Study groups, school projects, summer camps and weekend institutes, workshops for Sabbath and holiday observances were envisaged. An organization of Jewish professionals, besides the Rabbinical Fellowship, also was proposed.

The following year the Reconstructionist Press was organized, with plans to publish works in theology, art, music, fiction, liturgy, dance, social action, social science, religion, education, and textbooks. An editorial board of over 50 rabbis, scholars, writers, and leaders was formed. The press is still in existence, but its publications have been considerably more modest than originally contemplated.

A Reconstructionist Fellowship of Congregations was organized in 1955, with four affiliated congregations—SAJ and synagogues in Skokie, Buffalo, and Indianapolis. A few months later a synagogue in Cedarhurst joined, and by 1957 three others were members. In 1958 a new Reconstructionist congregation was formed in Whitestone, N.Y., but disbanded within a short time. The Cedarhurst and Indianapolis congregations, too, ended their affiliation with the Reconstructionists.

In the 1950's there were changes in the inner circle of the movement. In 1953 Eisenstein was offered the pulpit at Anshe Emet in Chicago, where Solomon Goldman had been rabbi until his death. SAJ asked Eisenstein to stay, and he agreed on condition that it raise a substantial endowment for the Reconstructionist Foundation. This could not be accomplished, and Eisenstein went to Chicago in the hope of establishing a Reconstructionist base in the Midwest. Jack Cohen succeeded him as leader of SAJ. A series of executive directors conducted the activities of the movement, but it continued to stagnate, rousing itself only for periodic testimonials and dinners in honor of Kaplan. The movement, as some Reconstructionist said, was living off Kaplan's birthdays.

The crisis was more than financial; it was intellectual as well. Many friends of the movement felt that American Judaism had accepted its general program. Reform was no longer antagonist to Zionism and Hebrew, and accepted the concept of Jewish peoplehood. On the other hand, Zionism had ceased to be the rallying point it once was. Existentialism, inimical to Reconstructionist thinking, was the current philosophy

---

[80] *Ibid.*, October 3, 1952, p. 26.

of intellectuals. The battles of the 1920's, 1930's, and 1940's against Orthodoxy and anti-Zionism found little resonance. Reconstructionism, it appeared, had little to say to the generation of the 1950's and no longer attracted young rabbis and intellectuals. A contraction in the rabbinical base of Reconstructionism, which we will examine later, began in this period.

In Eisenstein's absence, David Sidorsky became *de facto* editor of the *Reconstructionist*. He raised its artistic, literary, and editorial standards, and attracted a large number of Jewish intellectuals as contributors. Some of them were quite marginal to the organized community, and they found in the *Reconstructionist* an outlet for Jewish expression. But from a self-interested, organizational point of view, the magazine did little more for the movement than increase its financial burden. In 1958 an executive director and fund raiser was hired at an annual salary of $15,000, which then represented a major investment for the movement. Results, however, were not satisfactory.

In 1959 Eisenstein returned to New York to become editor of the magazine and president of the Reconstructionist Foundation. He had not been successful in creating a Reconstructionist base in Chicago. Sidorsky had resigned as editor, and Kaplan, by then a widower, had married an Israeli and was expected to spend six months of each year in Israel. Eisenstein felt he was needed in New York, but his return was not unanimously hailed. Objections were directed not so much against him, as against the board, which welcomed his return as an opportunity to diminish its own activity and financial investment. The board, then as now, was composed primarily of laymen who followed the leadership of Kaplan and Eisenstein. The active members were SAJ people of long standing, relatives, and old family friends.

In 1960 the Reconstructionist Fellowship of Congregations was reorganized as the Fellowship of Reconstructionist Congregations, and a year later its name was changed to the Federation of Reconstructionist Congregations and Fellowships. (The fellowships are the local chapters, *havurot,* too small to function as synagogues.) Congregations were invited to seek affiliation with the Federation, and congregational affiliates no longer had to belong also to an Orthodox, Conservative, or Reform association. In this period its leaders began to refer to Reconstructionism as a movement rather than a school of thought, a change that was rationalized by the hardening of organizational lines in Judaism at the very time ideological walls were crumbling.[81] In 1963 the *Reconstructionist* viewed the organization's recent history as follows:

As is well known, for many years Reconstructionism was regarded by its leaders, its followers and its critics as a "school of thought." The activities were confined to the publication of the magazine and books. Since 1959, however, when Dr. Eisenstein took over the leadership of the Foundation, he has been pressing for the adoption of a more active type of program, including the establishment of agencies and institutions which would embody the ideas and concepts of the movement.[82]

Recent History

The formation of Reconstructionism as a self-conscious movement made little appreciable difference in its fortunes, and its growth continued to be sporadic. An organization for college students, *T'hiyah,* was formed in 1959, grew rapidly, and virtually ceased to function when its organizer and director, Jonathan Levine, left to lead the Conservative movement's Leadership Training Fellowship. Today, *T'hiyah* sponsors occasional seminars for college students. The women's organization of the Jewish Reconstructionist Foundation, founded in 1957, to which *T'hiyah* is responsible, sends free *Reconstructionist* subscriptions to some 500 college students.

In 1961 the Foundation announced the opening of a summer camp. The event was postponed to 1962, but the camp in fact never opened. The Rabbinical Fellowship, which had ceased functioning a few years before, was reconvened under the directorship of Paul Ritterband, but attracted only a handful of rabbis and never became a force. Ritterband left the pulpit of a Reconstructionist synagogue for academic life, and the Rabbinical Fellowship again became defunct.

The *Reconstructionist* continued, and its present circulation is 6,000. However, its quality has declined considerably in the last decade and it no longer attracts the gifted writers it once did. Part of the problem is the existence of new outlets for articles of general Jewish interest.

In 1969 there were ten member congregations of the Federation of Reconstructionist Congregations and Fellowships, the last established in 1968:

1. SAJ, founded in 1922 and located in New York City. It houses the offices of the Reconstructionist Foundation and still provides the

---

[81] "The Movement Begins to Move," *ibid.,* November 18, 1960, p. 3.
[82] *Ibid.,* May 17, 1963, p. 25.

bulk of financial support and lay leadership for the movement. When Rabbi Jack Cohen left for Israel in 1961, the synagogue could find no suitable rabbi in the United States who was willing to take the position. With the help of Wolfe Kelman, executive vice president of the Rabbinical Assembly, it invited Allen Miller from England to take its pulpit. Under Miller's leadership, SAJ almost doubled its membership to about 500 families, but the newer members lack the older members' loyalty or ties to Reconstructionism. Thus, there is a possibility of tension between those primarily congregation-oriented and those more strongly Reconstructionist-oriented.

2. A synagogue in Pacific Palisades, Calif. whose origin goes back to the early 1950's,[83] with about 175 families.

3. A synagogue in Skokie, Ill., founded in 1954, with about 800 families.

4. A synagogue in Buffalo, N.Y., founded in 1955, with about 250 families.

5. A synagogue in White Plains, N.Y., founded in 1958, with about 100 families.

6. A congregation in Great Neck, N.Y., which began holding regular services in 1959 and has about 60 families.

7. A synagogue in Montreal, Canada, founded in 1959 or 1960, with about 125 families.

8. A synagogue in Curaçao, West Indies, founded in 1963 as a merger of two older synagogues, one Orthodox and one Reform, with about 150 families and a unique history.[84]

9. A congregation in Evanston, Ill., which began holding regular services in 1966 and has about 60 families.

10. A congregation in Los Angeles, founded in the mid-1960's, which affiliated with the Federation in 1968 and has about 100 families.

Of the ten rabbis who serve these congregations (four in a part-time capacity), two were ordained in England (one Reform and one Orthodox); three at Reform institutions in America; two at JTS; one received his rabbinical training at JTS but was never ordained, and one studied at various institutions. One of the ten congregations is also affiliated

[83] Abraham N. Winokur, "A Reconstructionist Community," ibid., November 28, 1952, pp. 30–32.
[84] Simeon J. Maslin, "Reconstructionism in Curaçao," ibid., October 4, 1963, pp. 16–21.

with the Reform congregational group, four with the Conservative congregational group, and five with the Federation only.

Most of the nine *havurot,* which also are affiliated with the Federation, consist each of 10 to 15 families who meet once every two weeks for study, and gather to observe Jewish holidays. These people are generally members of other synagogues as well, but in some *havurot* almost all the members belong to one synagogue. There is a fellowship in Brooklyn, Newark, Philadelphia, Whittier, Los Angeles, and Washington, D.C. There are three in Denver.

The Federation meets annually to discuss matters of common interest and to adopt resolutions. Two are of special interest. In 1968 the Federation resolved that under certain conditions the Reconstructionist movement would consider children of mixed marriages as Jewish, even though the mother did not convert to Judaism. These conditions are that boys be circumcised and that both boys and girls receive a Jewish education and fulfill the requirements for *bar* or *bat mitzvah.* However, the parents are to be told that "in many parts of the Jewish world their children would not be recognized as Jews without undergoing the traditional forms of conversion." [85] This resolution is in accordance with proposals Kaplan made in *Judaism as a Civilization.* It is a departure from Jewish standards that constitutes a *denominational* step by Reconstructionism.

A second resolution with denominational implications, adopted in 1967, called for the establishment of a training center for Reconstructionist rabbis and teachers. Implementation of that resolution was in the hands of the Reconstructionist Foundation. In February 1968 the Foundation announced that applications would be accepted for enrollment in a new rabbinical seminary, which was to open in Philadelphia in September.

The Reconstructionist Foundation has a membership and a self-perpetuating board. The Reconstructionist Press and the magazine are activities of the board, as was the establishment of the Reconstructionist College. The college now is an independent agency, but, according to its bylaws, it must draw at least one-third of its board of governors from the Foundation board. The women's organization, of which *T'hiya* is an activity, and the Federation of Reconstructionist Congregations and Fellowships are also represented on the board. Thus, the board is a

---

[85] *Ibid.,* May 31, 1968, p. 31.

powerful instrument in shaping the institutional destinies of Reconstructionism. In turn, the board is under the influence of Ira Eisenstein, who today is the one and only institutional leader of Reconstructionism. He serves as president of the foundation, editor of the magazine, president of the college, and *de facto* editor of the press. In 1967 Arthur Gilbert, a Reform rabbi, was hired as assistant to Eisenstein in his capacity as president of the foundation and the college. (Gilbert served as Dean of the College in its first year.) Gilbert's association with the Reconstructionist movement marks the first time a distinctively Reform personality has held a position of leadership in it. The importance he ascribes to ecumenical activity, his associations with Christians, and his general style are something quite new to Reconstructionism.

Reconstructionist Rabbinical College

Reconstructionism's self-designation as a new movement in 1960, or its demand for recognition as a fourth denomination in Jewish life, received little attention in the Jewish community. As a movement, it appeared to be going nowhere. Its membership never was large and since the 1950's it had ceased to attract intellectuals. Its alternatives were either to die a quiet, dignified death—which many of its friends urged upon its leaders—or to assert itself as an independent movement through some dramatic activity.

The founding of the rabbinical school is a potential turning point in the development of Reconstructionism, in several ways. First, its graduates may serve Reconstructionist-minded congregations or provide the *havurot* with professional leaders to help them develop into congregations. Reconstructionist congregations have difficulty in finding rabbis. From time to time synagogues ask Eisenstein to recommend rabbis. In 1968 he sent an inquiry to the approximately 1,500 rabbis belonging to the Conservative and Reform rabbinical organizations, asking whether they would like to have their names referred to Reconstructionist-minded congregations. Only 60 answered yes, and many of these were not among the most successful members of the American rabbinate. Thus the college may provide professional manpower for Reconstructionism.

Second, the college is a project meaningful to the layman and may therefore be a source of financial support for the movement. It is an enterprise which, in the view of the Reconstructionists, entitles them to financial support not only from their own ranks but also from the

Jewish community at large. In turn, such support may make it possible for the movement to reach more Jews.

In its first year of operation, the college was quite successful financially. By mid-1969 it had received pledges of about $150,000 for the year, and promises of endowments of close to $200,000. Seventy per cent of the 226 pledges and 40 per cent of the actual money pledged did not come from SAJ members, indicating a response from outside the traditional Reconstructionist base.

Third, the college has introduced innovations into rabbinical training. Whether or not they prove successful, the entire Jewish community may benefit from the college's experience. For the Reconstructionists necessity proved a virtue. Since they had insufficient resources for a full-time seminary of their own, the Reconstructionists sought to link themselves in some way to another institution. They first sought a relationship with Brandeis University, suggesting that prospective students take courses in the university's department of Near Eastern studies and rabbinical courses at a Reconstructionist school to be located nearby. A price tag of $5 million, which Brandeis put on this relationship, seemed excessive to the Reconstructionist donors, and they then entered into an understanding with Temple University at Philadelphia.

The basic program of study is five years, and for those with a minimal background in Hebrew six years. (Six-year students spend their first year in Israel.) Prerequisites for admission are an undergraduate degree and acceptance into a Ph.D. program in religion at an approved institution, preferably Temple. Of the 13 first-year students, 11 were accepted at Temple and two at neighboring Dropsie College. The college itself will grant a Doctor of Hebrew Letters (D.H.L.) and rabbinical ordination to those who complete its program, the successful completion of the Ph.D. program being a requirement for the D.H.L. and rabbinical ordination. At present students must take certain courses in the field of Jewish studies which are offered at Temple, but may also choose some electives. The arrangement with Temple is a particularly happy one for the Reconstructionists, since the university's religion department is one of the largest in the United States and expects to have five permanent full-time faculty members in Jewish studies alone. Although the initial publicity of the Reconstructionists, exaggerating their tie with Temple, called forth protests from that university, relations are now extremely cordial.

The college is particularly proud of its requirement that students receive a Ph.D. in religion at a nonsectarian institution. This, it is believed, will expose them to a variety of scholars and differing points of view in an ecumenical setting. In fact, many students at other rabbinical seminaries simultaneously pursue graduate work, or at least take courses, at nonsectarian institutions. Assuming one favors such studies, the Reconstructionist innovation is the formalization of that requirement for all students and the adjustment of the institution's courses to complement those of the nonsectarian school.

The truly innovative aspect of the Reconstructionist college is its own course of study. Each of the five years is organized around a different core curriculum: biblical civilization, rabbinic civilization, medieval Jewish civilization, modern Jewish civilization, and, in the final year, contemporary civilization and specialization in an area of practical rabbinics, Jewish education, or Jewish culture. The entering class spent approximately two hours a week in a seminar on biblical civilization, where various aspects of the Bible were discussed, and every second week there was a lecture by a distinguished Bible scholar. The students also attended four-hours-a-week classes in biblical text, an increase, at their request, over the initially planned two-hour classes. The time was equally divided between Wisdom literature and the textual background to the biblical-civilization seminar. Finally, the students had a weekly two-hour seminar in Reconstructionism. All students were required to enroll in a course in biblical theology taught by Robert Gordis at Temple University, and to take one or two more elective courses at Temple or Dropsie.

A comparable program was envisaged for second-year students, organized around rabbinic civilization, i.e., the talmudic period.

There is a great deal of merit in such a program: an integrated core curriculum has an obvious advantage, and if one believes Judaism to be an evolving religious civilization, it makes sense to study the civilization as it has evolved. However, there are dangers as well: very limited time is devoted to text, which means that the students will not be able to do significant independent research or feel at home with the actual raw material of the Jewish tradition. Besides, concentration on evolutionary or developmental patterns in Judaism at the expense of text means that the instructor is superimposing his own concepts on Judaism. Students will learn *about* the Bible, *about* the Talmud, *about* the medieval commentators, rather than Bible, Talmud, and the medieval commentators. And what they learn *about* these is what the instructor thinks.

However, the argument is not all one-sided. To be sure, limited textual preparation means that the students will not be familiar with the original sources; but the textual material of Jewish civilization is so vast that most rabbinical students at other seminaries, certainly at Conservative and Reform seminaries, are never really comfortable with the original sources anyway. Of course, this too is a matter of degree. One might argue that a little ignorance is better than a great deal of ignorance. But the Reconstructionists could maintain that, whereas they have sacrificed a familiarity with source material which most students will never master in any event, their students will have acquired a knowledge of the basic patterns in Jewish life and thought. They may agree that this pattern represents a set of concepts which modern man has superimposed on Judaism, but they can say that there really is no alternative. The tradition also imposes conceptual categories on Jewish history and sacred text. The Reconstructionist patterns, they can argue, are less arbitrary because they are self-conscious and scientific. And while Reconstructionists may insist that students know what the tradition says about the Bible or Talmud or history, the college liberates the minds of the students by providing alternative explanations and more contemporary categories, or patterns, of thought. Finally, to the claim that extensive textual study is a precondition to understanding Judaism, Reconstructionists may reply that this reflects the particular bias of traditionalists.

However there is another risk to which one can point: the danger that an antiseptic scientism may be built into the program, which may arouse neither passion, loyalty, nor dedication among the students. A Jewish civilization too objectified may be emptied of its *religious* meaning. But precisely by a denial of the reality of this danger does Reconstructionism legitimize itself as a *religious movement* rather than as a *school of thought*. In addition, the Reconstructionist college introduced certain curriculum changes in the 1969–1970 academic year which, it hopes, will evoke greater commitment and fervor among its student body. Reconstructionists also may argue that though all other major seminaries stress textual scholarship, none has been outstanding in producing dedicated, well-trained rabbis. The Jewish community has little to lose from experiments in a different direction.

THE RECONSTRUCTIONIST CONSTITUENCY

A frequent and sympathetic contributor to the *Reconstructionist* once observed that Reconstructionism provides "a philosophy of life rather than a guide to living." [86] Not everybody needs or wants a "guide to living." For those who look to the Jewish tradition rather than to themselves for standards of guidance, Reconstructionism is a less than satisfactory religious expression.

Religious personalities are unlikely to be comfortable with Reconstructionism. (It is always risky to talk about a "religious personality," but the term has some intuitive meaning for most people.) Religious personalities are attracted to the *beyond,* or the totally other, as a source of values. They are attracted by the force, power, or majesty of the beyond which they are moved to worship—a concept that is foreign to Reconstructionism. They find in ritual not a force for social cohesion, but a source of excitement and a sense of power. Kaplan relies on Durkheim to explain the function of religion; but Durkheim also was aware that the meaning of the social function of religion for the observer was quite distinct from its meaning for the religious participant.

> The men who lead the religious life and have a direct sensation of what it really is . . . feel that the real function of religion is not to make us think, to enrich our knowledge, not to add to the conceptions which we owe to science . . . but rather, it is to make us act, to aid us to live. The believer who has communicated with his god is not merely a man who sees new truths of which the unbeliever is ignorant; he is a man who is *stronger*.[87]

Today there may be few religious personalities or believers, as Durkheim described them. Still, that Reconstructionism is unlikely to attract them is a problem. Many people who involve themselves in the institutional life of religion are attracted to a particular institution, or remain committed to it, because of the presence, or their belief in the presence, of such a person in it. Kaplan is certainly not a religious personality, as that term is commonly, and intuitively, understood. His own life, in the opinion of many of his former students, is not characterized by religious inner conflict. As a former admirer has put it, "he gave up supernaturalism too easily." And we have seen that Kaplan is even reluctant to grapple with problems of an individual or personal religious nature.

---

86 Max Wein, "Can Restructionism Guide Us?", *ibid.,* October 29, 1954, p. 22.
87 Emil Durkheim, *Elementary Forms of the Religious Life* (New York, 1965), pp. 463–64 (emphasis in the original).

Of course, it may be argued that Reconstructionism does not address itself to those who experience religion, but to modern man, the skeptic, the agnostic, the atheist. At a meeting of prospective members of his Reconstructionist synagogue, one rabbi distinguished between his congregation and the general Orthodox, Conservative, or Reform synagogue by asserting that the atheist could find his religious home in Reconstructionism. But the movement's literature and program are not geared to the modern skeptic. Kaplan assumes that the major religious problem is the *content* of one's belief. He dismisses supernaturalism and requires faith in the progress and goodness of man and his creative potential. According to Kaplan, "the persistent and patient application of human intelligence to life's problems will release the creativity that will solve them. Whatever ought to be can be, even though it is not at present in existence." [88] He affirms God as an expression of the belief that "what ought to be is in keeping with the very nature of things, and, secondly that what ought to be will ultimately be realized. God may therefore be defined as the Power that endorses what we believe ought to be, and that guarantees that it will be." [89] This is a strong affirmation of faith, with questionable appeal for the contemporary skeptic. He wonders less about the content of his belief than about whether he can believe at all and, if so, whether he can stake anything on his beliefs.

Reconstructionism, we suggest, can appeal neither to the religious personality nor to the skeptic. To whom does it appeal? The answer depends on how one defines Reconstructionism. In the next section (p. 68) we will define Reconstructionists as people who call themselves by that name, or who affirm a set of ideas about Judaism and God resembling those of Reconstructionist leaders. In this section we will define Reconstructionism in more institutional terms. Our question is this: who, or what kinds of Jews, have identified themselves with the Reconstructionist *movement,* even though they may not have accepted all of Kaplan's ideology or, for that matter, have not even called themselves Reconstructionists, as distinct from Orthodox, Conservative, or Reform Jews.[90]

---

[88] *Meaning of God in Modern Jewish Religion,* p. 80.

[89] *Ibid.,* pp. 323–24.

[90] Much of the material in this section draws on personal interviews. Unless otherwise noted, the term respondent refers to one of the 50 individuals interviewed in person or, occasionally, by telephone or mail. A later section relies on data derived from responses to a questionnaire. In that context "respondent" refers to a person who filled out and returned the anonymous questionnaire.

First Constituents

The early membership of SAJ, as we have noted, was composed of ritually traditional, well-to-do Jews of East European origin, who admired Kaplan without always understanding what he was saying. However, Kaplan sought from the outset to reach beyond the SAJ membership. He was, and still is, especially attracted to youth and intellectuals. SAJ provided the financial base for Reconstructionism. Its synagogue offered the possibility for liturgical experimentation. But Kaplan's significant audience were his students, primarily those of the JTS rabbinical school.

Kaplan is not a sociologist, but a philosopher making selective use of early sociological concepts. He is least sociological about Reconstructionism and the nature of his constitutency. He believes that his own ideas are accepted or rejected by virtue of their intrinsic logic or the accuracy of his facts. He assumes that people construct their religion and their lives around an ideology which they have examined. But the audiences Kaplan attracts are of a special type. He himself describes them in his first book as the future saviors of Judaism. They are those to whom

> . . . Judaism is a habit . . . Jewish modes of self-expression and association with fellow Jews are as indispensable to them as the very air they breathe. They would like to observe Jewish rites, but so many of those rites appear to them ill-adapted to the conditions and needs of our day.[91]

Steinberg puts the matter only slightly differently. With Orthodox Jews, he says,

> Reconstructionism not only has no quarrel; it has, so far as theology goes, no message. . . . it addresses itself to those who would like to make their peace with the Jewish religion but cannot; who, on matters of faith, stand at the temple doors, "heart in, head out." [92]

A writer in the old *SAJ Review* maintained the need for a movement "of modernist Judaism to appeal to intellectuals, even if it lacks the sentimentality to appeal to masses," [93] and some people believe that this is what Reconstructionism has become. But it is precisely sentimentality that Reconstructionism seeks to preserve through a new intellectual formulation.

---

[91] *Judaism as a Civilization*, p. 511.

[92] Milton Steinberg, *Partisan Guide to the Jewish Problem* (Indianapolis, 1963), p. 185 (charter edition). The book was first published in 1945.

[93] Isidor B. Hoffman, "Shall We Reckon With the Intellectuals?", *SAJ Review*, October 12, 1928.

JTS Rabbinical Students

Kaplan's rather special kind of constituency was found in disproportionately large number at JTS, between the 1920's and the end of World War II. This is reflected in the composition of JTS rabbinical alumni who are also members of the Reconstructionist Foundation. A 1968 inquiry showed 34 per cent of all living rabbinical alumni of JTS to have been ordained before 1945; correspondingly, an estimate of the year of ordination on the basis of age indicates that 59 per cent of the seminary's rabbinical alumni affiliated with the Reconstructionist Foundation were ordained before 1945. While 33 per cent of all the JTS rabbinical alumni were under 40 in 1968, only 12 per cent of the JTS rabbinical alumni in the Reconstructionist Foundation were under 40. Of the Reconstructionist Foundation members who were alumni of Hebrew Union College, the Reform rabbinical seminary in Cincinnati, 26 per cent were under 40.

Kaplan's impact at JTS before 1920 is difficult to evaluate. He certainly exercised great influence on such men as Solomon Goldman, Max Kadushin, Eugene Kohn (and his older brother Jacob ordained before Kaplan had come to JTS). But Kaplan's greatest impact came in the 1920's and lasted until the end of World War II. Beyond that, he remained a major influence until the end of the 1940's, and, even after his influence had sharply diminished, he continued to attract some students. Of course, not all students at JTS between 1920 and 1945 were Reconstructionists. The best estimate is that roughly a quarter of them became his firm followers. But in that period he influenced all students who came into contact with him to reflect self-consciously on their own predispositions and assumptions about Judaism, and he left most of them with sympathy for his general program, if not his particular theology.

The factors contributing to Kaplan's influence were student backgrounds, prevailing intellectual currents, and conditions at JTS before the end of World War II.

BACKGROUND OF JTS STUDENTS

Before 1945 virtually all JTS students came from Orthodox homes, and a majority had attended *yeshivot*. Thus JTS represented for them a break with the Judaism they had known in their homes and schools. Many report that their fathers, or fathers of fellow-students, were Orthodox rabbis. Still, many add, their parents really did not object to their attending JTS. Their parents' attitudes seemed to be that to study Talmud one should attend a *yeshivah,* and if after that one wanted to become a rabbi, one was best advised to attend JTS. Traditional Jewish law was strictly observed at JTS, at least officially. By the 1920's, however, the institution had already ordained men like Solomon Goldman, who fought with members of his own congregation to introduce changes in synagogue practices that were contrary to *halakhah,* Jewish law. It had on its faculty a Mordecai Kaplan, who preached heresy. And even the traditionalist faculty members approached the sacred texts in a spirit of critical, "scientific" inquiry, without the traditional assumptions about their authorship and meaning.

Orthodox parents not unsympathetic to their sons' enrolling at JTS suffered, on the one hand, from what may be characterized as a failure of Orthodox nerve and, on the other, from a sympathy for careerism. The East European Jews who came to this country did not represent a typical cross-section of East European Jewry.[94] Even among the rabbis, a disproportionate number were open to new styles of life and new modes of thought—after all, people with this outlook were the most likely to emigrate. In the first decades of this century they may well have despaired that Orthodoxy, as they understood it, would ever strike roots in the United States. Thus, if their sons were to become successful rabbis, serving the Jewish community and advancing their own careers, they had to acquire a good secular education and converse in the contemporary idiom; adopt middle-class manners, and be tolerant of Jews who deviated from the tradition.

Consequently, students who came to JTS with their parents' approval came from a special type of background. (Those who came without parental approval were certainly of a special sort.) Almost all students shared the following attitudes.

1) They were attached by sentiment and emotion to the Jewish people, whom they wanted to serve. In the case of some, this was associated with an element of careerism. In the 1920's and 1930's there was discrimination against Jews in employment, in the 1930's there was the depression, graduate and professional schools limited the number of Jewish entrants, universities were reluctant to hire Jews. In those

---

[94] For a discussion and elaboration of this point see Charles S. Liebman, "Orthodoxy in American Jewish Life," AMERICAN JEWISH YEAR BOOK, Vol. 66 (1965), pp. 27–30.

circumstances the rabbinate was a desirable career. It permitted the student to capitalize on a background in Jewish studies, acquired even before entering JTS. It offered at least a living wage, and often much more. Later, during the war years, when rabbinical students had draft deferments, considerations of career and draft deferment probably were in the minds of all students, but were more pronounced with some than with others. Sensitivity on this point was also stronger among some than others. The Reconstructionist students were most critical—of themselves, the institution, and the rest of the student body. An unalloyed careerist had no need to justify himself for entering the rabbinate, despite religious skepticism. It was the other students who needed to legitimize to themselves their draft deferments or their rabbinical career.

2) Most JTS students were attached, at least by sentiment, to much of traditional Jewish ritual.

3) Most of the students felt that the ritual and ideological expression of the tradition could not adequately cope with the problems of Americans Jews and their own religious problems.

4) As the students saw it, the particular failure of the tradition was the inability to come to terms with modern Western civilization. This was reflected in unaesthetic synagogues and rituals, the meaninglessness of much ritual practice, and a belief system incompatible with modern thought.

PREVAILING INTELLECTUAL CURRENTS

The second major factor in Reconstructionism's success in attracting JTS students is its compatibility with one of the dominant philosophical trends in the first part of the 20th century, Deweyan pragmatism. Positivism and Marxism also were powerful forces, but they were less directly relevant to the environment of JTS. Positivism tended to make any religious enterprise irrelevant, while Marxism made Judaism irrelevant and religion pernicious. Thus, rabbinical students could think they had no alternative but Dewey.

As we have suggested, much of Kaplan's system is Deweyan. He defines ideas, concepts, and institutions by their functions. For him, the true test of an idea is its workability. Many of Dewey's Christian followers found in his system the basis for a naturalist religion.

Another mood of the period—at least in Jewish circles—was a still dominant belief in progress. There was optimism regarding the capacity of the human mind to understand social, economic, and spiritual conditions, and continually to improve those conditions. Finally, the social climate among intellectuals and Jews, especially in New York, emphasized social action or economic justice. Their political sympathies ranged from New Deal liberalism to socialism and Communism. In this context, Reconstructionist rhetoric was in keeping with prevailing intellectual currents, but was not as radical as it sounds in retrospect.

NATURE OF JTS

The third major factor in understanding Kaplan's influence was the nature of JTS in that period, at least as the students perceived it.[95]

The curriculum stressed the study of traditional texts. While the texts were approached critically, their mastery was accepted as an end in itself. The faculty was concerned with its own research. The quality of teaching was generally poor, and most of the faculty exhibited interest only in an occasional student. Few seemed concerned with the issues of the day, Jewish or non-Jewish, or with the students. Especially frustrating was that the professors at JTS seemed not to be concerned with the reconciliation of Judaism and modern thought. Students came to JTS with the assumption that Conservative Judaism meant more than opposition to Orthodoxy and Reform. They expected JTS to have some reasoned system of thought and practice, which would permit the introduction of change into Judaism without the excesses of Reform or paving the way to assimilation. They found that virtually no one was articulating such a position and, what was worse, almost no one seemed to care.

The one striking exception was Mordecai Kaplan. Asked what attracted them to him, almost all respondents answered first: his honesty.

---

[95] We are reporting the views and perceptions of respondents interviewed in 1969 about events that occurred when they were students, ten, twenty, thirty and even forty years earlier. Also, we did not interview a random sample of alumni, but primarily those in New York City, whose names were known and who in some way were associated with Reconstructionism. However, the fact that the sample is a biased one in the sense of not being random, and that reliance is placed on remembered perceptions rather than on an examination of documents and on interviews of faculty and administration, does not necessarily mean that the perceptions are inaccurate or distorted. My own inclination is to feel that they are substantially correct, particularly in view of the virtual unanimity of all respondents, whether Reconstructionist, formerly Reconstructionist, or non-Reconstructionist.

He was honest in confronting the problems which, almost all the students agreed, were the most important. He wrestled with these problems honestly, and was willing to follow his solutions to their logical conclusions. Even those who rejected his theology expressed their gratitude to him for liberating their minds and forcing them to confront problems clearly. As a former student put it, "Other faculty were teaching texts, Kaplan was thinking thoughts."

As professor of homiletics, Kaplan had the opportunity to disseminate his heterodox ideas about the Bible and the traditional values of Judaism. He had discussed his proposed lectures with Solomon Schechter whose only comment was that Kaplan was "walking on eggs." According to Kaplan, Schechter accepted the basic tenets of biblical criticism and did not himself believe in the Mosaic authorship of the Torah. But he, and his successors at JTS, followed the pattern which had been established at the Jewish Theological Seminary of Breslau, where biblical criticism was privately accepted but not publicly taught. Many students found it hypocritical of professors to hold private views which they would not express in class, and to refuse to teach the central text of Judaism because its traditional interpretations could not be reconciled with contemporary ones. The students, therefore, appreciated Kaplan all the more because he expressed himself on matters which, at least in the early years of the Seminary, were thought to be central.

Unlike most of the faculty, Kaplan was concerned with problems of economic justice and social action. Not only did he urge political activism upon his students, he also incorporated it into his program of Judaism. Students were especially embittered at JTS's negative attitude toward the efforts of its employees to organize a local union during World War II. The issue was complex, and the merits on each side not entirely clear. But a number of students interpreted JTS behavior as exploitative of its employees, anti-union, and institutionally self-serving. Both the administration and the most prominent faculty were involved in self-justification, which many students believed to have been basically dishonest. The fact that the administration and prominent faculty were antagonistic to Kaplan at this time only raised his esteem in the eyes of the students.

Particularly as he got older, Kaplan was neither a very good teacher nor an especially warm person with whom students felt comfortable. But he had integrity; he confronted the problems of the day; he took ideas seriously, and he formulated them into a system. This leads us to a third aspect of the JTS environment that accounts for Kaplan's influence. Kaplan was the only major figure at JTS who attempted to formulate a philosophy of Judaism. Without belittling his formulations or the attraction of his particular philosophical position, one may say that Kaplan had the *only* philosophical game at JTS. This was true even in a later period, when his influence began to wane. Students could choose Abraham Heschel's theological-mystical game, Louis Ginzberg's and Saul Lieberman's halakhic-scholarship game, or Louis Finkelstein's and Simon Greenberg's institutional-eclectic game. For those attracted by a rational philosophic style, Kaplan was the only choice. When JTS students sponsored a series of debates in the 1940's between Robert Gordis and Milton Steinberg, they may have seen in Gordis a philosophical alternative to Reconstructionism. Gordis is of the opinion that as a result of the debates, Steinberg first became aware of the existence of a serious philosophical alternative to Reconstructionism within a Conservative Jewish context. But, perhaps because he was only a part-time instructor, Gordis's position did not influence the students.

Beyond style, the contents of Kaplan's formulation also was important. In the words of a former student, "Kaplan provided the only way I could continue as a functioning Jew and still retain theological doubts." His redefinition of God and his reorientation of Judaism to accent peoplehood allayed students' anxiety about their theological skepticism, rationalized their desire to retain most of the ritual tradition, and legitimized their choice of a rabbinic career, despite their religious doubts. All this was based on Dewey's philosophy and on the prevalent sociological conceptions among students of comparative religion in that period. Not all of Kaplan's followers accepted his philosophic conclusions. One respondent volunteered that he found him "unimpressive philosophically"; but they all felt that he was going about things in the right way and that "one could live with his system."

What struck the most responsive chord was Kaplan's accent on peoplehood and his commitment to Jewish survival. He built a system around that basic core of commitment. Orthodoxy, Reform, even Conservative Judaism begin with propositions concerning God and Torah about which the students have doubts. Kaplan's starting point is the Jewish people, the one *a priori* proposition the students could accept. And this justified a rabbinical career, the best means of serving the Jewish people. Also, Kaplan combines his definition of Judaism with an affirmation of American civilization. He not only sanctions, he insists that Jews live in, and affirm a loyalty to, two civilizations—the American and Judaic. This, too, the students welcomed.

As noted, Kaplan influenced all students; roughly 25 per cent (respondents' estimates varied from one period to another) identified themselves as Reconstructionists. What distinguished the Reconstructionists from the other students? Most, but not all, respondents report that the Reconstructionists, on the whole, were brighter and more ideologically and philosophically inclined. All respondents state that, on the whole, Reconstructionist students were more sensitive to moral and ethical issues, and more politically concerned. Finally, in the postwar period, when an increasing minority of students came from non-Orthodox homes, a disproportionately large number of Reconstructionist students were from Orthodox homes.

DECLINE IN INFLUENCE AT JTS

After World War II, increasing numbers of students came from Conservative backgrounds, and JTS enrollment was a break neither with their families nor their backgrounds. The affirmation of Western culture and American civilization by a Jewish thinker represented nothing terribly new or daring.

The dominant intellectual currents were religious existentialism, a skeptical attitude toward human reason, an awareness of a basic perversity in man, and a stress on the importance of "religious" experience. All this was foreign to Reconstructionism. Whereas Kaplan had no rival who proposed an alternative philosophical system, there were faculty members, like Abraham Heschel who offered alternative religious systems more in sympathy with prevailing intellectual moods. Heschel was also concerned with social and political issues, and was a champion of liberal political causes. For a variety of reasons, his popularity among the students waned after a few years. However, he did serve as a bridge between Kaplan, from whom he weaned many students, to more traditionally Jewish points of view.

In this period JTS added younger faculty members, virtually all antagonistic to Reconstructionism. Kaplan no longer represented the image of youth battling the encrusted establishment. The encrusted establishment now was the leadership of the American Jewish community, which was anti-traditional in practice and Reconstructionist in orientation, though not by identification.

In 1956 Kaplan celebrated his 75th birthday. His lectures were no longer as sharp as they once had been. He had tried, but failed, to place younger Reconstructionists on the JTS faculty. He was permitted one assistant who, however, was denied faculty status. The appointment of another Reconstructionist to the faculty was promised, but later denied because the candidate would not pledge to observe the Sabbath laws and *kashrut*. The Reconstructionist presence at JTS gradually diminished. Today Kaplan's influence stems from notions the students bring with them to JTS, rather than from currents within the institutions. In a 1967 survey of first- and last-year JTS rabbinical students, 17 per cent of first-year students, but only 10 per cent of last-year students, listed Kaplan as the single person best reflecting their own religious, philosophical, and theological positions.[96]

Among the older rabbinic alumni, very few of the once ardent Reconstructionists remained strongly committed. For some, there was gradual drifting. They became rabbis of congregations, assumed new responsibilities, and were more involved in the day-to-day problems of administration, pacifying congregants, building a religious school or a synagogue, even furthering their own careers, than in confronting the problems of their student days. But there was also gradual disaffection from the solutions offered by Kaplan. The average Conservative layman does not require a philosophic rationale for Judaism. He wants his religion to be a living experience; he wants to be touched or moved by his religion. What he does not want is to have to do much about it. Thus the modern Jew, especially the college student, may talk about hasidism as a superior mode of Jewish expression because it involves the total Jew, but he is quite ignorant of hasidism. He does not realize that one must give in order to receive. Hasidism lengthens the preliminary prayers incumbent on a Jew because it holds that before a Jew can touch the heart of the prayer and address God, he must prepare himself. Jews were more interested in Judaism after World War II than before, but they wanted to draw upon their religion emotionally without having the resources which religion could touch, or build upon. This condition presents difficulties even for Orthodox Judaism which, after all, has a notion equivalent to the Christian concept of Grace. But it is an even greater problem for Reconstructionism, with its concept of God who cannot reach out, but whom one must reach.

---

[96] Charles S. Liebman, "The Training of American Rabbis," AMERICAN JEWISH YEAR BOOK, Vol. 69 (1968), pp. 3–112, is a general report of the survey.

Reconstructionism has failed, in part, because—at least for many people and over a considerable period of time—it cannot be lived. It cannot *give*. Kaplan's followers at JTS report that for a year or two, they were able to pray as Reconstructionists. They were able to say "Blessed art Thou, God," while thinking, "Blessed are you, Power, that make for creativity, freedom, justice and salvation," but it did not last very long. The reliance on reason led some into positivism and atheism, which made the whole Reconstructionist enterprise appear trivial. Others took different paths. One respondent, who now worships in an Orthodox synagogue, found, as he grew older, that not everything in his life had to be consistent; all his actions did not have to fit into a philosophically rationalized pattern. Other respondents, even those who today still call themselves Reconstructionists, have adopted a more traditional theology. They continue to accept Kaplan's emphasis on peoplehood and his insistence on the necessity for ritual change, but not his opposition to supernaturalism.

As we have noted, Kaplan ascribes the drift of his former students from Reconstructionism to their inadequate understanding of his concept of God. In fact, Kaplan adds, he himself has arrived at an adequate understanding of it only in recent years. Eisenstein's explanation of the drift is that Reconstructionism, as a school of thought rather than a movement, does not provide a focus of activity, or an outlet for expression. Our essay suggests that this is only partly true. If Reconstructionism had had the potential for a movement in the 1930's and 1940's, it would have become one in spite of Kaplan. The young rabbis, who preached Reconstructionism from their first pulpits, would have found some echo within their congregations. The *havurot* would have grown, and not withered. Synagogues would have come together of themselves to form a union of Reconstructionist synagogues.

Reform Rabbis and Rabbinical Students

Kaplan's influence on Reform rabbis and students at Hebrew Union College—Jewish Institute of Religion was never as great as on Conservative rabbis and rabbinical students. Yet he certainly was a force among Reform Jews too. Kaplan was unknown at the Hebrew Union College (HUC) in Cincinnati during the 1920's, before the seminary merged with the Jewish Institute of Religion (JIR) in New York. He had been offered the presidency of JIR, where his ideas were especially popular. In Cincinnati Kaplan's ideas first spread with the publication

244 / american jewish year book, 1970

of *Judaism as a Civilization* in 1934. The book was widely read on the campus during the 1930's, and a small group of students called themselves Reconstructionists. The HUC students, like those of JTS, were especially attracted to Kaplan's concept of peoplehood.

In the 1930's HUC students could have looked to a number of faculty members for leadership. There were the textual scholars, traditional in their personal lives; the religious humanists who espoused social justice and universalism as opposed to Jewish particularism, and, in the congregational rabbinate, some of the great Zionist personalities of the period, preeminently Abba Hillel Silver. But the textualists did not concern themselves with social action, or with the relevance of their scholarship to contemporary Judaism. The religious humanists were anti-Zionist, and antitraditionalist in ritual. And Zionists like Silver held to a classical Reform theology.

Kaplan offered what some students found to be a happy combination of ritual traditionalism, Zionism, relevance to contemporary issues and social action, and, above all, a stress on peoplehood and a definition of Judaism as a civilization. The extent to which such a definition of Judaism posed both a real threat and a real alternative to many Reform leaders is evidenced in the fact that in 1935 Samuel Goldenson, then president of the Central Conference of American Rabbis, the Reform rabbinical group, devoted his entire presidential message to a refutation of Kaplan's major thesis, without ever mentioning by name Kaplan or his book. According to Goldenson:

> Until very recently, the average Jew and even the most cultured one looked upon Judaism as a religion. Now an entirely new interpretation is offered. Instead of being regarded and accepted as a religion, we are now asked to believe that Judaism is primarily a civilization.[97]

Unlike classical Reform, Kaplan found a place within Judaism for virtually every type of Jew, no matter how irreligious he might be or how he sought to express his affiliation. By offering a rationale for ritual, Kaplan represented a way back to the tradition for some Reform rabbis, who later were to exercise great influence on Reform Judaism. Kaplan articulated a mood that had come to be felt in Reform for a number of years; the anti-Zionism of early Reform was repudiated in the 1937 Columbus platform.

In the late 1930's the HUC student body was sharply and fairly

---

[97] "A President's Message to the Forty-Sixth Annual Convention of the Central Conference of American Rabbis," CCAR *Yearbook*, 1935, pp. 133–53.

equally divided between Zionists and leftists. The crucial issue focused on attitudes toward American intervention in the war. As long as the Nazi-Soviet pact was in force, the Left opposed American intervention. All Reform Reconstructionists were Zionists, though not all Reform Zionists were Reconstructionists. Among those Reform rabbis who considered themselves Reconstructionists, many did not accept Kaplan's denial of a supernatural God.

Kaplan's influence began to wane after the war, particularly in the 1960's, when the dominant influences at HUC were religious existentialists, such as Borowitz and Petuchowski, who were more traditional than Kaplan, and religious radicals, who denied the continuity of any meaningful Jewish tradition, and questioned whether Reform even has a place in a unified Jewish community.

Reconstructionist Following Among Rabbis

Reconstructionism has greater resonance for young Reform rabbis than for young Conservative rabbis, but its meaning is not the same for Conservatives and Reform. Eighty-two Conservative and 50 Reform rabbis are affiliated with the Reconstructionist Foundation. Of the Conservatives 15 per cent are under 40 and 27 per cent over 60. Of the Reform rabbis, 24 per cent are under 40 and 10 per cent over 60. However, many of the members do not consider themselves Reconstructionists; they affiliate out of respect for Kaplan, or a past sympathy for his ideas. Many who do consider themselves Reconstructionists agree with Kaplan on the need for an organic community, or the centrality of peoplehood (the general program of Reconstructionism), but do not accept Kaplan's theology (the "sectional" program of Reconstructionism). The *Reconstructionist,* itself, tends to express Reconstructionism's general program rather than its special or sectional program. Not even all members of the editorial board would call themselves Reconstructionist, rather than Conservative, Reform, or secularist Jews. But there are rabbis who embrace Reconstructionism in most of its particulars and consider themselves Reconstructionists, as distinct from Conservative or Reform Jews, even though they may be affiliated with Conservative or Reform rabbinical organizations.

ORGANIZATIONAL AFFILIATION OF RABBIS

An analysis was made of differences between Reconstructionist rabbis affiliated with the Conservative rabbinical group and those affiliated with the Reform one. It is part of a survey of religious ideology, which will be discussed in some detail in the section below.

Among the various groups of rabbis and Jewish lay leaders in the United States who received a questionnaire were 130 leading Orthodox, Conservative, and Reform rabbis, and 14 rabbis prominently identified with the Reconstructionist movement. All rabbis were asked to list the rabbinical organization with which they were affiliated, and to identify themselves ideologically without regard to organizational affiliation. Of the 14 Reconstructionist rabbis, 13 responded, and all identified themselves as Reconstructionists. Among 34 Reform rabbis who responded (out of 38 to whom the questionnaire was mailed), 4 identified themselves ideologically as Reconstructionists, besides, or instead of, Reform. (None of the Orthodox or Conservative rabbis did so.) Thus, a group of 17 rabbis are ideologically identified with Reconstructionism. They are not a random sample of Reconstructionist rabbis; but they are, without a doubt, representative of the majority of prominent rabbis in the United States ideologically identified with Reconstructionism. Of these 17 rabbis, 9 were also members of the Conservative and 8 of the Reform rabbinical associations. Here we will designate the first group C-R (Conservative-Reconstructionists) and the second group R-R (Reform-Reconstructionists).

These rabbis, along with the other Orthodox, Conservative, and Reform rabbis, were asked to say whether they agreed (strongly, somewhat, slightly) or disagreed (slightly, somewhat, or strongly) with 27 statements about ritual, Zionism, theology, and the relationship between Judaism and American life. From the responses one could discern distinctive Orthodox, Conservative, Reform, and Reconstructionist opinions on many, though not all, issues. There was also a typical rank-order response to most statements (though not to those concerning Zionism). Picturing the possible responses as a continuum from strong agreement to strong disagreement, we may say that, in general, Orthodox rabbis stand at one end of the continuum and Reconstructionist rabbis at the other. Conservative and Reform rabbis are in the middle: Conservatives generally to the Orthodox side and Reform to the Reconstructionist side, but closer to one another than to the two extremes.[98]

---

[98] The evidence for these last statements is not presented here because it would involve a highly technical discussion to demonstrate a point that really is peripheral to this essay. However, the point itself is of some interest. Readers desirous of pursuing the material may consult the statistical computations, as well

R-R and C-R rabbis were closer to one another in their responses than they were to Reform or Conservative, respectively, let alone to Orthodox rabbis. Nevertheless there were also distinct differences between C-R and R-R rabbis. Whereas one might have anticipated that C-R rabbis would most closely resemble Conservative rabbis, and R-R rabbis Reform rabbis, this was not the case. In most instances, R-R rabbis reflected attitudes closer to both Reform and Conservative rabbis. In other words, Reconstructionist rabbis belonging to the Conservative rabbinical group adopt a more radical position on Jewish questions than do Reconstructionist rabbis of the Reform rabbinical group.

This can be illustrated by citing some statements on which differences between C-R and R-R rabbis was greatest. (These differences were significant only at the .20 level.) C-R rabbis were less willing than R-R rabbis to accept the concept of Jews as a chosen people (Q.4 of questionnaire appended), and they disagreed more strongly than R-R rabbis with the proposition that only experts in Jewish law can interpret it with authority (Q.12). C-R rabbis agreed more strongly than R-R rabbis that the kind of Jewish life one ought to lead is a matter of individual conscience (Q.25); that Jews ought to help formulate a civic religion in which all Americans can participate (Q.27); that the primary loyalty of American Jews must be to American, rather than Jewish, culture and civilization (Q.29).

In all this, R-R rabbinical attitudes are close to those of Conservatism and Reform, whereas C-R rabbinical attitudes are close to the pure Kaplanian position. For Reform rabbis, we have suggested, Reconstructionism is a way back to the tradition. For Conservative rabbis, it would appear, Reconstructionism is a way out of the tradition. If future Reconstructionist growth occurs among Reform rather than Conservative Jews, there may be a moderation of aspects of Kaplan's religious radicalism. In that case, we would have the paradox of the Judaization of Reconstructionism through the influx of Reform Jews.

Educators and Social Workers

Reconstructionism had a special appeal not only for rabbis, but also for Jewish educators and some social workers, especially those whose Jewish identification was of a cultural-secular nature and who were un-

---

as an earlier draft of this study which discussed the relevant material in greater detail, in the offices of the AMERICAN JEWISH YEAR BOOK.

comfortable in most synagogues. It may have had a special attraction for those who realized that American Judaism was synagogue-oriented and that a Jew with no religious affiliation whatsoever was suspect. Also, educators knew Kaplan by virtue of his leadership of the JTS Teachers Institute, his activity in New York's Bureau of Jewish Education, and his speeches and publications in the field of Jewish education. Finally, older Jewish educators were often strong Hebraists, proponents of speaking Hebrew and consumers of Hebrew culture. Kaplan, personally and through SAJ, supported these activities. The Reconstructionist Press was anxious to publish educational material, and Reconstructionist leaders always placed great emphasis on education.

Not all secularist, Zionist, and Hebraist educators were sympathetic to Reconstructionism. To some of the more militant among them, Reconstructionism represented an unnecessary compromise with American values, an artificial creation. But to others it was a source of support and strength. Many educators are still identified with the Reconstructionist movement, but they tend to be of an older generation. Younger Jewish educators have different religious and cultural orientations.

Kaplan's special appeal for a third group of Jewish professionals, the Jewish social workers, goes back to 1925–37, when he served on the faculty of the Graduate School for Jewish Social Work. (The school closed in 1937 for lack of funds, after negotiations for affiliation with JTS and, later, with HUC, had come to naught.) Kaplan emphasized Jewish inclusiveness and the necessity for Jewish activity of a non-religious nature, and was concerned with communal problems and community structure. These emphases and concerns were welcomed by the more Jewishly committed social workers. Many others, however, were more sympathetic to Marxism than to Reconstructionism, to the Soviet Union than to Zion. In Kaplan's view, this large and articulate group within Jewish social work was especially dangerous because of the importance he ascribed to Jewish community centers, where these people functioned. In its early years the *Reconstructionist* published many editorials attacking the Jewish self-hatred of the Jewish Communists and their fellow-travelers, and Soviet antipathy to Zionism. According to Kaplan, these editorials were a response to the dangers from those social workers, rather than from leftists within the Reconstructionist movement.

From Professional to Lay Constituency

Among the three groups of Jewish professionals who, along with SAJ, constituted the core of Reconstructionist supporters, the rabbis were by far the largest and most influential. Perhaps they never really constituted a majority of Reconstructionists, but in the 1930's and 1940's, and even into the 1950's, Reconstructionism seemed to have had a pronounced rabbinic constitutency. This no longer is the case.

Today one can identify institutionally with Reconstructionism through affiliation with the Reconstructionist Foundation or the Federation of Reconstructionist Congregations and Fellowships. The Reconstructionist Foundation has approximately 900 paid members. Dues are $25 a year, and include a subscription to the magazine. Of the paid members, 149, or approximately 17 per cent, are rabbis. Eighty-two of these are members of the Conservative and 50 of the Reform rabbinical organization. The remaining rabbis come from a variety of places, including the Academy for Jewish Religion, a small nondenominational seminary in New York City where Eisenstein taught for a number of years. Since academy graduates are not accepted into any of the existing rabbinical organizations, some of them are especially anxious for Reconstructionism to organize its own.

As we have suggested, many, and probably most, of the rabbis affiliated with the Foundation do not consider themselves Reconstructionists, as distinct from Conservative or Reform Jews. Their membership is a tribute to Dr. Kaplan and an expression of the sympathy they had, or may still have, for Reconstructionism as a school of thought.

In 1966 the *Reconstructionist* announced that June 11 was to be declared Kaplan Shabbat in honor of his 85th birthday, and some 400 rabbis dedicated the day to its observance.[99] By contrast, the 1969 annual Reconstructionist Foundation dinner, which was dedicated to its new Reconstructionist College, was attended by only three rabbis who were paid members of the Reconstructionist Foundation, and one of them was the main speaker. This despite the fact that the dinner was held on a Sunday evening in New York City, and more than 50 rabbinical members of the Foundation live in that area. Of the 226 contributors to the Reconstructionist Rabbinical College, only 17 are rabbis.

As noted, some rabbis who identify themselves as Reconstructionists have opposed denominationalizing the movement. The launching of a

---

[99] *Reconstructionist*, June 24, 1966, pp. 34–35.

rabbinical school is embarrassing to a number of staunch friends, who are unwilling to choose between Reconstructionism and Conserva⁺ⁱ n or Reform. The movement recognizes their embarrassment but does . ˋ sympathize with it. From time to time Reconstructionism denies that it is a denomination, or is in competion with Orthodoxy, Conservatism, or Reform. However, the fact of the matter is that Kaplan has publicly declared the existence of Reconstructionism as an independent denomination.

Among those who have opposed denominationalizing Reconstructionism are also rabbis who serve member congregations of the Federation of Reconstructionist Congregations and Fellowships. The Federation, we have noted, has about 2,300 family members, but 1,300 come from two of its ten member congregations. According to the estimates of rabbis, fewer than half of the member families think of themselves as Reconstructionists. Roughly 20 per cent are affiliated with the Reconstructionist Foundation; many others receive the magazine, often at special rates, as part of an arrangement between their synagogue and the Foundation.

To many members of Federation synagogues, Reconstructionism does not represent a way of life, a broad culture and civilization, which is experienced through language, study, art, music, and ethical and political action, in addition to prayers. Rather, it is an excuse not to observe Jewish law and ritual. A number of rabbis serving Reconstructionist congregations report that, when they urge stricter observance on their congregants, the latter say it is unnecessary because they are Reconstructionists. Some rabbis comment that, in their view, the committed Reconstructionists in their synagogues have a higher secular education than the rest of the membership, but they are no more committed to, or concerned with, problems of Zionism, the general welfare of Jewry, or the United Jewish Appeal than the non-Reconstructionists. The rabbis also state that most of their Reconstructionist members come from Orthodox backgrounds. As we will see, there is reason to believe that the backgrounds of most lay Reconstructionists is traditional rather than Orthodox.

Federation synagogues differ in the extent to which Reconstructionism is part of their program. In some, the only concrete expression of affiliation, besides dues, is use of the Reconstructionist prayerbook. It is not used on all occasions in all the synagogues. Some engage in liturgical experimentation, or substitute study for traditional worship. In others, experiments of the past seem to have hardened into rituals sanctioned only by the particular congregation's tradition.

Among the Fellowships (*havurot*) there is a deeper understanding of, and appreciation for, Reconstructionism. While the individual *havurot* tend to be homogeneous, they differ in the type of members they attract. One has a generally younger professional membership with nontraditional background; a second is composed of middle-aged members from Orthodox backgrounds, who were first drawn to a Conservative synagogue but found it too impersonal and overly decorous. Members of a third *havurah* come from a Labor Zionist background.

In addition to the congregations and *havurot* which are Federation members, there are three congregations which do not belong, but whose leading members or rabbi have considered affiliation, and may yet affiliate with the Reconstructionists. Jews who call themselves Reconstructionists, or who are Reconstructionists attitudinally, but are not institutionally affiliated with the movement, will be discussed later.

Prospects

Whatever hope the Reconstructionist movement has rests with its rabbinical school, which now is a focus for the energies of its leaders. Eisenstein has observed that "people are devoted to institutions and not ideas." This, more than any other statement, distinguishes him from Kaplan in approach to Reconstructionism, and from the very forces which were attracted to Reconstructionism in the past. Eisenstein is probably correct. For, as a former Reconstructionist puts it, "Kaplan may have failed because he took theology too seriously. He kept insisting on thinking through God, but American Jews don't want to think theology, they are action-oriented." The college represents both an institution and a focus for action.

Leaders of Reconstructionism also are aware of their intellectual problems. According to one, "the movement is drawing on the past capital of Kaplan and Eisenstein." In fact, nothing of ideological significance has been written since the 1940's. Even Reconstructionists who argue that Kaplan's ideas are still valid admit the necessity for a new idiom. But Reconstructionist leaders are open to more than this. They are prepared to reformulate, and even rethink, the Reconstructionist program and philosophy. This in itself is a sign of Reconstructionism's institutionalization as a movement. After all, the proponents of a school of thought can hardly rethink and reformulate its basic program. If they did, it would become a different school of thought. The task of re-formulation is expected to be undertaken by the graduates of the college.

It is too early to predict how successful the college will be from either a broadly Jewish or a particularly Reconstructionist point of view. At this point, we can only point to some of its strengths and problem areas.

The entering class of 13 first-year students at the Reconstructionist College in 1969 came from good undergraduate colleges (two from Yale, two from Brandeis, one from Columbia, and one from Harvard), and had fine academic records, some outstanding (four were Phi Beta Kappas). Most of them had good Jewish educational backgrounds as well. They came primarily from Conservative homes. Seven had taken courses at the Hebrew University, JTS, or at a Hebrew teachers' college, as undergraduates or immediately after graduation. The remaining six had participated in Jewish life on their college campuses.

These first-year students would have been admitted to JTS or HUC-JIR. The fact that they chose the Reconstructionist College suggests that it already is able to compete with the older seminaries for talented students. Fifty applications for the entering class confirm this fact. Those who chose the Reconstructionist College were attracted by the opportunity for a Ph.D. from a secular university; but they also were attracted by the characteristics of the college itself. Among these are its deemphasis of Jewish denominationalism, which is increasingly meaning-less to most young Jews; its openness to divergent points of view or to experimentation in liturgy and ritual, and the opportunity for a variety of Jewish experiences. It is hardly likely that the older, established seminaries will ever be able to compete with the college in these respects.

On the other hand, the college may not live up to the hopes and expectations invested in it. What may seem radical, daring, and challeng-ing one year, can quickly become dull and routine the next. The Recon-structionist movement was charged by a college student (though not from its rabbinical school—which was to be established only later) with being not radical enough in religious matters.[100] The students of the college may quickly stretch the limits of the administration's or move-ment's tolerance of change. Reconstructionism has a history, an ideology, an adult constituency, all building some constraints into its program. In this respect, the college differs from a second Jewish seminary that opened its doors in 1968, the Havurat Shalom Community Seminary in

100 Raphael R. Jospe, "A Call for Radical Reconstructionism," *ibid.*, November 3, 1967, pp. 7–13.

Boston. Significantly, that seminary, whose administrative and financial conditions were far less secure than those of the Reconstructionist College but whose program was far more radical in experimentation of all kinds, admitted 11 first-year students.

Midway through their first year, Reconstructionist College students demanded abolition of grades and course requirements, such as term papers and examinations. How the college will work out these problems, and others that will continue to arise in a period of student ferment and revolution, remains to be seen. Morale among the first-year students remained high and the administration was most accommodating to their demands. But given a radical student body, the college may find itself under increased attack.

Not all, perhaps not even most, of the students who enrolled in the college did so in order to prepare for rabbinical ordination. Many enrolled in order to receive draft deferments as divinity students. Once the draft pressure on college students abates, enrollment may drop. Those who were attracted by the opportunity to combine rabbinical training with a Ph.D. may find an academic career more inviting. Since the students spend a good portion of their time in a secular academic environment, they may become socialized to the academy rather than to the rabbinate. And even those who choose to serve the Jewish community in some way may find a pulpit too confining or constricting. The synagogue today is still the center of Jewish life, but it is not "where the action is." Students may choose to work with Hillel, or with national Jewish organizations, or, to borrow a Christian term, they may choose an independent type of ministry as yet unforeseen.

Finally, some students preferring to serve in pulpits may be unable to secure one because Reconstructionist congregations cannot afford to pay them an adequate salary, and Conservative or Reform congregations prefer rabbis ordained by their own seminaries. It is possible that newly ordained rabbis of the college will have no special desire to serve Reconstructionist congregations. Indeed, after ordination they may not even consider themselves Reconstructionists. They were attracted to the college by its nondenominationalism and freedom from the constriction of the organized Jewish community. Why then should they prefer one denominational synagogue to another?

Our emphasis has been on the potential problems for the Reconstructionist movement in capitalizing on its new college as a source for leadership and growth. However, awareness of its problems should not conceal the very real potential of the college for the movement, or its very remarkable success up to the end of 1969.

RECONSTRUCTIONISM AS THE IDEOLOGY OF AMERICAN JEWS

The first section of this essay outlined the major doctrines of Reconstructionism; the second traced the institutional history of the movement, and noted its failure as an institution, by any standard criteria; the third discussed the types of people who have identified with the Reconstructionist movement, why they have been attracted, and why some end by rejecting Reconstructionism. This section takes a somewhat different look at Reconstructionism, discussing it not as an institutionalized movement but as a set of identifiable ideas, beliefs, and attitudes. We will see that Reconstructionism, viewed in this manner, has many followers. We will ask what distinguishes these Reconstructionist-minded Jews from other Jews. Finally, we will speculate on why they do not affiliate with the Reconstructionist movement, or at least identify themselves as Reconstructionists.

American Judaism and Reconstructionism

A comparison of the major values or principles of most American Jews, as gleaned from their behavior, with the major values or principles of Reconstructionism suggests that many of them are potential Reconstructionists. Here, in brief, and not necessarily in order of importance, are what this author believes to be the major ideas, symbols, and institutions arousing the deepest loyalties and passions of American Jews. At a later point we will seek to demonstrate that most American Jews share these values. Here we merely assert them:

1. There is nothing incompatible between being a good Jew and a good American, or between Jewish and American standards of behavior. In fact, for a Jew, the better an American one is, the better Jew one is. If, however, one must choose between the two, one's first loyalty is to American standards of behavior, and to American rather than to Jewish culture.

2. Separation of church and state is an absolute essential. It protects America from being controlled by religious groups; it protects Judaism from having alien standards forced upon it, and, most importantly, it protects the Jew from being continually reminded of his minority status.

Only the separation of church and state assures the existence of religiously neutral areas of life, where the status of the Jew as a Jew is irrelevant to his function.

3. The Jews constitute one indivisible people. It is their common history and experience, not a common religious belief, that define them as a people. What makes one a Jew is identification with the Jewish people, and this is not quite the same as identification with the Jewish religion. Denominational differences within Judaism must not be allowed to threaten the basic unity of the people.

4. One consequence of defining Judaism as a shared history and experience is that problems of theology are not only likely to be divisive, they are also somewhat irrelevant. On the one hand, God is not some supernatural being, some grandfather image; but, on the other hand, there is a force in the universe besides man. But whatever one's definition of God, the entire matter is not terribly crucial. There are many more important things of a Jewish nature for the Jew to do, i.e., insuring the physical and spiritual survival of the Jewish people, than to expend his energy or attention on theological matters.

5. Jewish rituals are nice, up to a point. Going to a synagogue a few times a year, or lighting candles on Friday evening, having the family together for a Seder, or celebrating a son's *bar mitzvah* are proper ways of expressing one's Jewishness and keeping the family united. But Jews cannot be expected to observe all the rituals and practices of traditional Judaism. These were suitable, perhaps, to different countries or cultures, but not to the American Jew of the 20th century. Many rituals ought to be changed; it is up to each person to decide for himself what he should or should not observe.

6. Among the major tasks facing Judaism is insuring the survival of the State of Israel. This is every Jew's obligation. But support for Israel does not necessarily mean that one must settle there, or that living outside Israel is wrong, or that living in Israel makes one a better Jew.

Reconstructionism shares these basic values, standards, and attitudes of American Jews. In fact, they constitute the bulk of the Reconstructionist program, shorn of its philosophical underpinning. As we have seen, Reconstructionism maintains that:

1. Jews must live in two civilizations or cultures, Jewish and American, but their first loyalty must be to American civilization.

2. Separation of church and state is more than merely desirable as a practical matter; it is a religious principle.

3. Judaism is defined by peoplehood, not religion. Religion must serve Jews, and not the other way around. Since religious differences tend to be divisive, the community must be organized and unified on a nonreligious basis; particular denominational identifications must be secondary to the unifying principles of one community.

4. God is the Power that makes for salvation, not a supernatural being. But a person's theology is generally unimportant, as long as he is active in some way in the Jewish community.

5. Ritual represents the folkways of the people, and should be retained for communal and personal needs. Rituals that are not functional, or that conflict with prevailing ethical standards, or that are hard to observe should be modified or abolished.

6. Jews have a religious obligation to support Israel, but they have no obligation of 'aliyah. The notion of shelilat ha-golah (negation of the diaspora) is wrong.

What, one asks, could be more Jewish-American than Reconstructionism? With some minor exceptions, it virtually embodies the major values and attitudes of American Jews. By this we do not intend to vulgarize Reconstructionism. Certainly Mordecai Kaplan, who has been so critical of American Judaism, would be the last to welcome the idea that the majority of American Jews actually accept his principles. We do not mean to imply that Kaplan, or Reconstructionism, is understood by the American Jews. Most of them surely have never heard of Kaplan, or of Reconstructionism. But we do maintain that by extracting and oversimplifying the principles of Reconstructionism one arrives at the grass-roots or folk religion of American Jews. Folk religion is often an oversimplification of a more complex religious system.

But if this is so, why is it that most Jews do not identify with Reconstructionism?

It may be argued that the other groups in American Judaism—Orthodoxy, Reform, and especially Conservatism—also embody most, if not all, these values. However, none has articulated them so explicitly as Reconstructionism, so elevated them to the status of basic principles, or so incorporated them into ideology and prayer. Only Reconstructionism really has made them into a religion. Also, the agreement with these principles among non-Reconstructionist leaders is much lower than among Reconstructionist leaders. For example, in the questionnaire mentioned above, Reconstructionist rabbis were in greater agreement than non-Reconstructionist rabbis with the statements embodying these basic values. Not all differences between Reconstructionist and non-Reconstructionist rabbis were statistically significant, but they were always in the expected direction. That is, Reconstructionist rabbis always expressed greater agreement with statements reflecting Reconstructionist ideology than did Orthodox, Conservative, and Reform rabbis. The only issue on which Reconstructionist rabbis did not stand at an extreme of the attitudinal continuum was Israel. They were more sympathetic to the role of Israel in Jewish life than were Conservative and Reform rabbis, but less than the Orthodox. This is consistent with Reconstructionist ideology, which transformed Zionism into a religious ideology earlier and more radically than Conservatism and Reform, but which, unlike Orthodoxy, adopted a position against negation of the diaspora and did not stress the religious importance of 'aliyah.

In summary: We suggested a set of major values or principles determining the behavior of American Jews. We found that these coincided with basic Reconstructionist ideology, as elaborated by Kaplan. Finally, we found that Reconstructionist rabbis were distinguishable from non-Reconstructionist rabbis by their agreement with those values or principles. In order to demonstrate the extent to which American Jews actually do accept Reconstructionist values, we will determine to what extent American Jews are in greater agreement with Reconstructionist rabbis than with Orthodox, Conservative, or Reform rabbis.

The Survey

The distribution of religious beliefs and attitudes among all American Jews, even by sampling procedures, could not be established within the limitations of this study. For this reason, it was decided to sample lay leaders of Jewish organizations, whose opinions, in the last analysis, are more crucial in determining the ideological direction of the community than a random sample of Jews, most of whom are likely to be apathetic anyway. Questionnaires were sent to presidents of all member congregations of Reform and Conservative synagogue groups. There is no listing of presidents of all Orthodox synagogues; but questionnaires were mailed to all presidents on the best available list, containing some 800 names, roughly the same number as Conservative presidents and about 150 more than Reform. The mailing reached an estimated 70 per cent of all synagogue presidents in the United States. The synagogues excluded were generally the small, unstable, or quite new.

Obtaining a sample of lay leaders from secular (nonreligious) Jewish organizations was more difficult. Two of the larger Jewish organizations, with chapters throughout the country, one an organization of men and the other of women, were approached for lists of their presidents. They were assured of anonymity, if desired. The mens' organization agreed to cooperate, but asked to remain unidentified. For purposes of presentation, we will call it the National Jewish Organization (NJO). NJO has many local chapters engaging in a variety of social, educational, pro-Israel, and Jewish-defense activities. Its membership is predominantly middle-class. The women's organization, Hadassah, unfortunately kept postponing a decision on cooperation beyond the time limit of the study and, in fact, never actually agreed or refused. Therefore, the only women respondents are the few women presidents of synagogues (less than one per cent of the total sample). Since women play an important leadership role in local Jewish organizations, their virtual absence in the sample may have biased the findings. We cannot predict whether their reactions to questions of religious ideology would be different from those of men. They might identify with Reconstructionism more than men because Reconstructionism has insisted that women be assigned religious roles, traditionally the exclusive prerogative of men, and has been more critical than any other religious group of those aspects of the tradition which discriminate against women, or relegate them to an inferior position. On the other hand, women generally tend to be religiously more conservative than men, and may therefore be in greater disagreement with attitudes reflecting Reconstructionist points of view.

The percentage of returns can be reported only with some vagueness, in part to conceal the exact number of presidents on different lists, in part because some of the organizations did their own mailing of the questionnaires, and one was not certain of the precise number sent out. Approximately 40 per cent (variations from 38 to 42 per cent) of presidents of Reform congregations, Conservative synagogues, and NJO chapters returned the questionnaire, but only 16 per cent or so of Orthodox presidents. Non-Orthodox responses therefore can be treated with a great deal more confidence than Orthodox. This is a not too serious problem for us, since Reconstructionist-type responses, in which we are interested, are least likely to come from the Orthodox.

The low return from the Orthodox may be explained by the fact that they generally respond in smaller numbers than do the non-Orthodox, possibly because of their inferior secular education, the lower rate of native Americans among them, greater suspicion of questionnaires, greater demand for privacy, less confidence in the value of social-science research, or greater time pressures. Another factor may also help to account for the low return. Respondents were asked to indicate their agreement or disagreement with a series of statements. In order to correct for any tendency on the part of respondents to agree or disagree automatically with all statements, some were worded in agreement with traditional Jewish attitudes, others in disagreement. It is conceivable then that an Orthodox Jew, who is very sensitive about his traditional beliefs and is unaccustomed to responding to attitudinal statements, would have found some formulations so offensive as to refuse to respond. Thus, the actual Orthodox returns are likely to be biased in favor of the more acculturated, Americanized, secularly better educated, and religiously less sensitive—toward the religious left or modern Orthodox, rather than the right.

Finally, there always is the possibility that the questionnaires did not reach all the approximately 800 Orthodox synagogue presidents because of incorrect addresses, or for some other, similar reason.

Results

The lay leaders were presented with a set of statements which were similar to, though not identical with, those sent to the rabbis. Changes in a few questions were made on the basis of the rabbis' earlier, open-ended responses. Like the rabbis, these respondents were asked to check whether they agreed strongly, somewhat, or slightly, or disagreed slightly, somewhat, or strongly with each statement. Each answer was assigned a score from 1 (agree strongly) to 6 (disagree strongly). An average, or mean, score was then tabulated on each question for each group of rabbis, for each group of synagogue presidents, and for NJO presidents. A comparison could then be made between the attitudes of different groups of rabbis and of different groups of laymen in the six major areas of Jewish values, at least for questions that were unchanged or had only minor stylistic modifications. The tables that follow present the mean score for each group, the number of responses from each group, and the standard error of the mean. (The standard error of the mean, computed by dividing the standard deviation by the square root of the number of responses, is most useful for readers who wish to calculate tests of significance not reported here.)

1. *Judaism and Americanism.* Reconstructionist rabbis agreed most

strongly that an American Jew's first loyalty must be to American rather than Jewish culture and civilization. The mean scores of both synagogue and NJO presidents were closer to the Reconstructionist than to any other group of rabbis.

TABLE 1.

Agree or disagree: American Jews' first loyalty must be to American not Jewish culture and civilization (Q.29)

Group	Mean Score	Standard Error	Sample Size
Orthodox rabbis	5.00	.34	21
Conservative rabbis	5.37	.33	19
Reform rabbis	4.80	.28	30
Reconstructionist rabbis	4.53	.43	15
Orthodox synagogue presidents	3.23	.19	108
Conservative synagogue presidents	2.54	.11	271
Reform synagogue presidents	2.37	.11	260
All synagogue presidents	2.59	.07	656*
NJO presidents	2.36	.08	460

1.00 = agree strongly
6.00 = disagree strongly

2. *Church and state.* Reconstructionist rabbis agreed most strongly on the necessity and religious importance of separation of church and state. The mean scores of both synagogue and NJO presidents were closer to the Reconstructionist than to any other group of rabbis.

TABLE 2.

Agree or disagree: Separation of church and state is essential (Q.28)

Group	Mean Score	Standard Error	Sample Size
Orthodox rabbis	4.00	.37	22
Conservative rabbis	2.10	.44	20
Reform rabbis	2.21	.34	29
Reconstructionist rabbis	1.82	.29	17
Orthodox synagogue presidents	2.35	.18	106
Conservative synagogue presidents	1.60	.08	274
Reform synagogue presidents	1.72	.09	262
All synagogue presidents	1.76	.06	659
NJO presidents	1.73	.07	461

1.00 = agree strongly
6.00 = disagree strongly

---

* The synagogue president total in this and subsequent tables is slightly larger than the total of all Orthodox, Conservative, and Reform synagogue presidents. The difference is accounted for by synagogue presidents who failed to list their denominational affiliation, or who were affiliated with synagogues of more than one denomination.

3. *Peoplehood.*

a. *Loyalty.* Reconstructionist rabbis agreed most strongly that loyalty to the Jewish people is more important than loyalty to Judaism as a religion. Again the mean scores of both synagogue and NJO presidents were closer to the Reconstructionist than to any other group of rabbis.

TABLE 3.

Agree or disagree: Loyalty to Jewish people is more important than loyalty to Jewish religion (Q.22)

Group	Mean Score	Standard Error	Sample Size
Orthodox rabbis	5.71	.14	24
Conservative rabbis	5.62	.16	21
Reform rabbis	5.38	.19	29
Reconstructionist rabbis	3.80	.44	15
Orthodox synagogue presidents	3.98	.19	99
Conservative synagogue presidents	3.35	.11	235
Reform synagogue presidents	3.56	.11	268
All synagogue presidents	3.53	.07	673
NJO presidents	3.10	.08	481

1.00 = agree strongly
6.00 = disagree strongly

b. *Community.* Reconstructionist rabbis also agreed most strongly on the need for a single unified Jewish community with democratically selected leaders. Orthodox and Reform rabbis disagreed most strongly. In this instance, all groups of laymen were closer to Orthodox and Reform than to Reconstructionist rabbis.

TABLE 4.

Agree or disagree: There must be a single unified Jewish community in the U.S. with democratically elected leaders (Q.23)

Group	Mean Score	Standard Error	Sample Size
Orthodox rabbis	4.04	.39	26
Conservative rabbis	2.77	.38	22
Reform rabbis	3.50	.37	30
Reconstructionist rabbis	1.71	.24	17
Orthodox synagogue presidents	3.43	.21	102
Conservative synagogue presidents	3.59	.12	289
Reform synagogue presidents	4.29	.12	270
All synagogue presidents	3.83	.08	679
NJO presidents	3.77	.09	488

1.00 = agree strongly
6.00 = disagree strongly

c. *Judaism*. Reconstructionist rabbis disagreed most strongly with the statement that Judaism was best defined as a religion rather than as a culture or civilization. Orthodox rabbis agreed most strongly, and Reform followed. The mean scores of the responses of synagogue and NJO presidents were closest to Reform.

TABLE 5.

Agree or disagree: Judaism is best defined as a religion rather than a culture or civilization (Q.13)

Group	Mean Score	Standard Error	Sample Size
Orthodox rabbis	2.92	.38	24
Conservative rabbis	4.68	.40	22
Reform rabbis	3.20	.33	30
Reconstructionist rabbis	5.56	.32	16
Orthodox synagogue presidents	3.14	.20	106
Conservative synagogue presidents	3.57	.11	296
Reform synagogue presidents	3.15	.11	280
All synagogue presidents	3.35	.07	702
NJO presidents	3.50	.09	484

1.00 = agree strongly
6.00 = disagree strongly

The scores in Tables 4 and 5 suggest a problem for Reconstructionism in its appeal to American Jews. Jews are unwilling to surrender their autonomy to more centralized communal agencies. Also, whereas Jews agree that Jewish peoplehood is of a more binding character than Jewish religion, they are not willing to accept this as part of their definition of Judaism (p. 69).

d. *Jewish religion*. Finally, the mean scores of laymen on the statement that the Jewish religion must be made to serve the Jewish people rather than having the people serve religion was closest to Conservative and Reform rabbis who, in turn, stood between the Reconstructionist rabbis' strongest agreement and Orthodox rabbis' strongest disagreement.

Jews may act as though their religion must be made to serve them rather than the reverse, but they are hardly prepared to acknowledge it. This, too, has deeper implications, to which we will return in the final discussion.

4. *Theology*. Mean scores of synagogue and NJO presidents were somewhat closer to those of Reconstructionist rabbis, who agreed most

TABLE 6.

Agree or disagree: Jewish religion must serve Jews, not Jews the religion (Q.19)

Group	Mean Score	Standard Error	Sample Size
Orthodox rabbis	5.04	.34	26
Conservative rabbis	3.10	.42	20
Reform rabbis	2.79	.36	28
Reconstructionist rabbis	2.06	.28	17
Orthodox synagogue presidents	4.63	.18	105
Conservative synagogue presidents	3.65	.11	291
Reform synagogue presidents	2.94	.11	277
All synagogue presidents	3.49	.08	693
NJO presidents	3.37	.09	476

1.00 = agree strongly
6.00 = disagree strongly

strongly that God is not a supernatural being but the Power that makes for salvation.

TABLE 7.

Agree or disagree: God is Power that makes for salvation, not a supernatural being (Q.21)

Group	Mean Score	Standard Error	Sample Size
Orthodox rabbis	5.38	.34	24
Conservative rabbis	5.00	.38	20
Reform rabbis	3.93	.41	28
Reconstructionist rabbis	1.13	.09	16
Orthodox synagogue presidents	3.13	.23	100
Conservative synagogue presidents	2.30	.11	275
Reform synagogue presidents	2.29	.11	258
All synagogue presidents	2.41	.07	651
NJO presidents	2.32	.08	471

1.00 = agree strongly
6.00 = disagree strongly

Presidents also agreed somewhat more strongly with Reconstructionist rabbis, who of all rabbis agreed most strongly, that Jews are *not* a chosen people.

5. *Ritual.* Thus far, all NJO presidents have been considered one group, although we could have subdivided them into those defining themselves as Orthodox, as Conservatives, and as Reform. Had we done so, we would have found the same results as we did when subdividing synagogue presidents: While Orthodox presidents deviated from all

TABLE 8.

Agree or disagree: Jews are not a chosen people (Q.4)

Group	Mean Score	Standard Error	Sample Size
Orthodox rabbis	4.85	.41	27
Conservative rabbis	5.25	.30	20
Reform rabbis	4.97	.34	29
Reconstructionist rabbis	2.71	.42	17
Orthodox synagogue presidents	4.51	.19	111
Conservative synagogue presidents	3.54	.11	294
Reform synagogue presidents	3.33	.12	274
All synagogue presidents	3.62	.08	699
NJO presidents	3.63	.09	491

1.00 = agree strongly
6.00 = disagree strongly

other respondents, they constituted such a small part of the sample that their deviation did not affect the totals. Conservative and Reform synagogue presidents and NJO presidents who identified themselves as Conservative or Reform, gave virtually identical responses to all the statements. This does not apply to the following series of statements dealing with ritual. Consequently, in the tables that follow data are reported

TABLE 9.

Agree or disagree: Jews should observe all rituals including those having no meaning for them (Q.8)

Group	Mean Score	Standard Error	Sample Size
Orthodox rabbis	1.15	.07	26
Conservative rabbis	4.05	.39	22
Reform rabbis	5.23	.21	30
Reconstructionist rabbis	5.44	.24	16
Orthodox synagogue presidents	2.40	.16	107
Conservative synagogue presidents	4.27	.10	298
Reform synagogue presidents	5.40	.07	280
All synagogue presidents	4.43	.07	704
Orthodox NJO presidents	2.27	.26	37
Conservative NJO presidents	4.32	.10	281
Reform NJO presidents	5.20	.12	136
All NJO presidents	4.50	.08	490*

1.00 = agree strongly
6.00 = disagree strongly

---

* In this and subsequent tables the NJO total is greater than Orthodox, Conservative, and Reform NJO presidents since it includes NJO presidents who *defined* themselves as Reconstructionists, or secularists or other (see Q.3, Appendix).

for NJO as well as synagogue president sub-groups. However, the reader should bear in mind the different definitions. In the case of synagogue presidents, the denominational differences denote the different institutions which respondents lead (Q.1). In the case of NJO presidents, denominational differences denote a respondent's reply to a question asking him to define himself denominationally, without regard to synagogue affiliation (Q.3).

Respondents were asked to react to six statements which probed their attitude toward ritual. Three statements related to the determination of proper ritual behavior. Tables 9, 10, and 11 indicate the responses to these statements.

TABLE 10.

Agree or disagree: Very inconvenient rituals can be ignored (Q.18)

Group	Mean Score	Standard Error	Sample Size
Orthodox rabbis	5.37	.31	27
Conservative rabbis	5.45	.19	22
Reform rabbis	4.43	.29	30
Reconstructionist rabbis	4.00	.39	17
Orthodox synagogue presidents	5.36	.12	109
Conservative synagogue presidents	4.59	.09	298
Reform synagogue presidents	3.89	.10	276
All synagogue presidents	4.44	.06	703
Orthodox NJO presidents	5.30	.20	40
Conservative NJO presidents	4.31	.09	276
Reform NJO presidents	3.52	.16	132
All NJO presidents	4.08	.08	484

1.00 = agree strongly
6.00 = disagree strongly

Reconstructionist rabbis agreed most strongly, and Orthodox rabbis disagreed most strongly, that the individual's conscience and convenience should determine proper Jewish behavior. As was the case in response to previous statements, the responses of Orthodox laymen (synagogue and NJO presidents) were similar to those of Orthodox rabbis. Conservative laymen agreed with Conservative rabbis on two statements, and with Reconstructionists on the statement that the kind of Jewish life one should lead should be left to the individual's conscience (Q.25). Reform laymen generally were in greater agreement with Reconstructionist rabbis than with Reform rabbis.

TABLE 11.

Agree or disagree: The kind of Jewish life one should lead should be left to the individual's conscience (Q.25)

Group	Mean Score	Standard Error	Sample Size
Orthodox rabbis	3.63	.40	27
Conservative rabbis	3.50	.45	22
Reform rabbis	3.54	.35	26
Reconstructionist rabbis	2.18	.38	17
Orthodox synagogue presidents	3.18	.21	107
Conservative synagogue presidents	2.48	.10	293
Reform synagogue presidents	2.15	.09	270
All synagogue presidents	2.45	.07	690
Orthodox NJO presidents	2.85	.35	40
Conservative NJO presidents	2.03	.09	280
Reform NJO presidents	1.60	.09	136
All NJO presidents	1.93	.06	492

1.00 = agree strongly
6.00 = disagree strongly

A second aspect of attitudes toward ritual relates not to standards of proper ritual behavior but to authority and sources for ritual and ritual change. Responses to three statements on this aspect of ritual will be found in Tables 12, 13, and 14.

TABLE 12.

Agree or disagree: A fundamental principle of contemporary Judaism must be adaptation of the tradition to contemporary man (Q.9)

Group	Mean Score	Standard Error	Sample Size
Orthodox rabbis	4.56	.37	25
Conservative rabbis	1.65	.25	23
Reform rabbis	1.34	.18	29
Reconstructionist rabbis	1.12	.12	17
Orthodox synagogue presidents	3.83	.21	103
Conservative synagogue presidents	2.06	.08	294
Reform synagogue presidents	1.50	.07	277
All synagogue presidents	2.09	.06	693
Orthodox NJO presidents	3.29	.34	38
Conservative NJO presidents	1.97	.08	280
Reform NJO presidents	1.68	.11	136
All NJO presidents	1.96	.06	490

1.00 = agree strongly
6.00 = disagree strongly

TABLE 13.

Agree or disagree: Authentic guidance for Jewish behavior comes from masters of Jewish law (Q.10)

Group	Mean Score	Standard Error	Sample Size
Orthodox rabbis	1.48	.20	27
Conservative rabbis	2.78	.31	23
Reform rabbis	3.66	.32	29
Reconstructionist rabbis	5.25	.27	16
Orthodox synagogue presidents	1.74	.12	108
Conservative synagogue presidents	2.76	.09	292
Reform synagogue presidents	3.96	.10	274
All synagogue presidents	3.08	.07	693
Orthodox NJO presidents	1.72	.21	39
Conservative NJO presidents	3.08	.10	278
Reform NJO presidents	3.95	.14	134
All NJO presidents	3.27	.08	486

1.00 = agree strongly
6.00 = disagree strongly

TABLE 14.

Agree or disagree: Only experts in Jewish law can interpret it with authority, but such experts must be knowledgeable in secular culture (Q.12)

Group	Mean Score	Standard Error	Sample Size
Orthodox rabbis	2.37	.35	27
Conservative rabbis	1.55	.31	22
Reform rabbis	2.28	.32	29
Reconstructionist rabbis	3.18	.49	17
Orthodox synagogue presidents	1.91	.13	109
Conservative synagogue presidents	1.79	.07	296
Reform synagogue presidents	2.12	.09	278
All synagogue presidents	1.93	.05	702
Orthodox NJO presidents	2.16	.31	37
Conservative NJO presidents	1.90	.08	279
Reform NJO presidents	2.17	.14	132
All NJO presidents	1.99	.06	482

1.00 = agree strongly
6.00 = disagree strongly

Among rabbis, Reconstructionists were in greatest agreement that tradition must be adapted to contemporary man and that masters of the law are not the authority for change. Orthodox rabbis were generally in greatest disagreement, except for Table 14. Here it may be assumed that Orthodox rabbis demurred not at the importance of experts in the law, but rather at the declaration that the experts must also be knowledgeable in secular and non-Jewish culture. (The statement was designed to distinguish Conservative from non-Conservative attitudes, which it did among the rabbis.) In general, the attitudes of each group of laymen resembled those of their own denomination's rabbis more closely than those of any other group of rabbis.

Regarding ritual attitudes, then, non-Orthodox laymen (the vast majority of the sample) tended to agree with Reconstructionists on the behavioral dimension of how one should act, but agreed with their own rabbis on the more theoretical dimension of the sources and authority for ritual and ritual change.

6. *Israel.* As noted, no Orthodox-Conservative-Reform-Reconstructionist order existed in the rabbis' attitudes toward Israel. Orthodox rabbis were most sympathetic toward the role of Israel in Jewish life; Reconstructionists, Conservative, and Reform followed, in that order.[101] Orthodox laymen, less Zionist than Orthodox rabbis, had a mean score closest to the Reconstructionist position. Other laymen were generally closest to the position of Reform rabbis.

* * *

To sum up the findings regarding the six areas in which the major values of American Jews are expressed: In three of them, attitudes toward America, separation of church and state, and theology, presidents of Conservative and Reform synagogues and of NJO chapters were closer to Reconstructionist than Conservative, or Reform attitudes. About Israel they were closest to Reform. There was ambiguity regarding attitudes toward peoplehood and toward ritual: The lay respondents agreed with the Reconstructionist position on the primacy of the Jewish people, rather than its religion, but they disagreed with Reconstructionism on the consequences of this position. That is, they did not agree that Judaism should therefore be defined more properly in terms of peoplehood than of religion, or that religion should be made subservient to the people. Nor did they agree that, because they feel no obligation to observe meaningless or inconvenient rituals, these should be changed to suit the convenience of modern man, or that authoritative changes in ritual should be taken out of the exclusive control of "experts

---

[101] For a detailed discussion of the responses to statements on Israel see Charles S. Liebman, "The Role of Israel in the Ideology of American Jewry," *Unity and Dispersion* (Jerusalem), Winter 1970, pp. 19–26.

in the law." In simple terms, respondents agreed with the Reconstructionist rabbis on those statements which came closest to expressing behavioral norms; on statements expressing definitions, or rationalizations of behavior, they took a more traditionalist position. American Jews may act like Reconstructionists, but they neither think nor talk like them.

This is true even with regard to theological matters. Reconstructionist rabbis unanimously reported strong disagreement (6.00) with the statement that the Pentateuch (*Humash*), as we know it today, was given by God to Moses at Sinai. Conservative and Reform rabbis expressed equally strong disagreement (5.45). Conservative and Reform laymen expressed much less disagreement (3.86 and 4.47 respectively); Orthodox laymen were in agreement. The behavior of American Jews is consistent with that of practitioners of what we will call folk religion. They may deviate from the established religion in ritual, but are less likely to do so in matters of belief or doctrine (p. 95–96).

Reconstructionists' Characteristics

In most instances, therefore, laymen (except for the Orthodox) were in greater agreement with Reconstructionist rabbis than with the rabbis of their own denominations. Reconstructionist rabbis, in turn, are indeed Reconstructionist in their acceptance of the major outlines of Kaplan's position. The question then arises why, if most Jews adopt positions congruent with Reconstructionism, they neither affiliate with the movement nor identify themselves as Reconstructionists. First, however, let us explore two related questions.

Whereas the attitudes of *most* laymen on most issues were closer to Reconstructionism than to Orthodoxy, Conservatism, or Reform, this was not necessarily true of *all* laymen. We will call the Reconstructionist-minded laymen *potential* Reconstructionists, since with few exceptions they are neither affiliated nor self-identified as Reconstructionists. What characteristics, if any, distinguish potential Reconstructionists from other respondents?

Potential Reconstructionists

To isolate the potential Reconstructionists, we must cut through our former classifications. We chose from our questionnaire selected statements on which Reconstructionist rabbis significantly differed from non-Reconstructionist rabbis, and for each such statement we construct a frequency distribution for laymen. Potential Reconstructionists are defined as those who agree strongly or somewhat, or disagree strongly or somewhat, with statements to which Reconstructionist rabbis have responded with significantly greater agreement or disagreement, respectively, than non-Reconstructionist rabbis. We then examine differences between non-Reconstructionists and potential Reconstructionists with respect to the following:

a) The role of religion in their lives (Q.31); of great importance, of some, of little, or of none.

b) Secular education (Q.32).

c) Jewish education (Q.33 and 34).

d) Age (Q.35).

e) Religious environment in parents' home (Q.37).

f) Income (Q.38).

Unless otherwise noted, whenever a difference between potential Reconstructionists and non-Reconstructionists is mentioned in the discussion that follows, it is stastically significant at the .05 level.

1) *Relationship to America.* Sixty-one per cent of the respondents agree strongly, or somewhat, that a Jew's first loyalty is to American not Jewish culture and civilization (Q.29). Thus 61 per cent of the respondents to this question are potential Reconstructionists. Here the only difference between non-Reconstructionists (other respondents) and potential Reconstructionists is that 35 per cent of the potential Reconstructionists, and 45 per cent of the non-Reconstructionists, report that religion plays a very important role in their lives. There are no other statistically significant differences.

2) *Church and state.* Sixty-eight per cent of the respondents agree with the Reconstructionist position that separation of church and state is a religious value, and is also essential for harmony and fair play (Q.28). With respect to this question, therefore, 68 per cent of the respondents fall into the category of potential Reconstructionists. Forty per cent of the potential Reconstructionists, and 30 per cent of the non-Reconstructionists (the remaining respondents), report that religion plays a very important role in their lives. People to whom religion is not very important would normally be the potential Reconstructionists. Here, however, people for whom religion is not very important may also have been more inclined to deny that separation of church and state is a *religious* value: it may have been a value, a significant one, but not a religious one. The injudicious use of the word "religious" in the question

is probably responsible for the blurring of differences here, or actually for a reversal of positions between non-Reconstructionists and potential Reconstructionists.

3) *Theology.* Thirty-three per cent of the respondents agree strongly or somewhat with the Reconstructionist position that Jews are *not* a chosen people (Q.4). In this case, therefore, only 33 per cent of the respondents are potential Reconstructionists. Thirty-four per cent of these, and 46 per cent of the others, report that religion plays a very important role in their lives.

Sixty-three per cent of the respondents agree with the Reconstructionist position that God is a force making for human betterment, but not a supernatural being (Q.30). We divide the non-Reconstructionists into two groups: those believing in a personal, supernatural God (27 per cent of the respondents), whom we label supernaturalists, and those classifying themselves as agnostics, atheists, or not having any strong beliefs about God, whom we called agnostics, as a matter of convenience (10 per cent of the respondents). Thirty-eight per cent of the potential Reconstructionists report that religion plays a very important role in their lives, compared with 62 per cent of the supernaturalists and 14 per cent of the agnostics. Sixty-six per cent of the potential Reconstructionists and 62 per cent of the agnostics, but only 49 per cent of the supernaturalists, are at least college graduates. Seventeen per cent of the potential Reconstructionists and 16 per cent of the agnostics, but 27

TABLE 15.

Differences in selected characteristics between potential Reconstructionists, supernaturalists, and agnostics

| | (*Per cent*) | | |
Characteristic	Potential Reconstruc- tionists	Super- naturalists	Agnostics
Religion plays a very important role in my life	38*	62*	14*
College graduate	66	49*	62
Nine years or more of Jewish education	17	27*	16
Under age 45	37	35	49*
traditional	62	75	49*
Total number of respondents	714	311	109

° Differences significant at the .05 level.

per cent of the supernaturalists, have had nine or more years of Jewish education. Thirty-seven per cent of the potential Reconstructionists and 35 per cent of the supernaturalists, but 49 per cent of the agnostics, are below 45 years of age. Sixty-two per cent of the potential Reconstructionists and 75 per cent of the supernaturalists, but only 49 per cent of the agnostics, come from Orthodox or traditional backgrounds.

4) *Peoplehood.* Forty-seven per cent of the respondents agree strongly or somewhat with the Reconstructionists that the Jewish religion should serve the people, not the reverse (Q.19)—i.e., in this respect 47 per cent of the respondents are potential Reconstructionists. Thirty per cent of these potential Reconstructionists, compared with 50 per cent of the non-Reconstructionists, report that religion plays a very important role in their lives. Thirty-one per cent of the potential Reconstructionists, compared with 38 per cent of the others, were under the age of 45. Fifty-five per cent of the potential Reconstructionists, compared with 63 per cent of the others, came from Orthodox or traditional backgrounds.

TABLE 16.

Differences* in selected characteristics between those who agree strongly or somewhat that Jewish religion should serve Jews (potential Reconstructionists) and those who do not (non-Reconstructionists)

Characteristic	*(Per cent)* Potential Reconstructionists	Non-Reconstructionists
Religion plays a very important role in my life	33	50
Under age 45	31	38
Parents' home Orthodox or Traditional	55	63
Parents' home Orthodox or traditional	55	63
Total number of respondents	648	722

* All differences significant at the .05 level.

Forty per cent of the respondents agree strongly or somewhat that loyalty to the Jewish people is more important than loyalty to the Jewish religion (Q.22). Again, fewer of these potential Reconstructionists than of non-Reconstructionists report that religion plays a very important role in their lives (31 as against 40 per cent), but more come from Orthodox or traditional backgrounds (65 and 55 per cent, respectively).

Thirty-seven per cent of the respondents agree strongly or somewhat with Reconstructionists that it is a matter of religious urgency to create a single, unified Jewish community, with democratically elected leaders, to constitute the basic structure of Jewish life (Q.23). Fewer potential Reconstructionists are at least college graduates (50 per cent, compared with 66 per cent of the non-Reconstructionists), fewer are under the age of 45 (23 and 42 per cent, respectively), fewer have incomes of $20,000 a year or more (46 compared to 54 per cent), but more come from Orthodox or traditional backgrounds (64 compared to 56 per cent).

TABLE 17.

Differences* in selected characteristics between those who agree strongly or somewhat on the need for a centrally organized Jewish community (potential Reconstructionists) and those who do not (non-Reconstructionists)

| | (Per cent) | |
| | Potential Reconstructionists | Non-Reconstructionists |
Characteristic		
College Graduate	50	66
Under age 45	23	42
Annual income $20,000 or more	46	54
Parents' home Orthodox or traditional	64	56
Total number of respondents	466	805

° All differences significant at the .05 level.

5) *Ritual.* Seventy per cent of the respondents agree strongly or somewhat that the kind of Jewish life a person leads ought to be left to his conscience (Q.25). Once again, there are significantly fewer potential Reconstructionists than non-Reconstructionists who say that religion plays a very important role in their lives (33 and 46 per cent, respectively).

6) *Israel.* We cannot isolate the attitudes of potential Reconstructionists toward Israel, since Reconstructionist rabbis do not differ significantly from all other rabbis in their responses to statements concerning the proper role of Israel in Jewish life.

* * *

In summary, potential Reconstructionists are generally indistinguishable from other respondents in such characteristics as secular and Jewish education, age, and income. Among respondents to questions relating to peoplehood, significantly more potential Reconstructionists than non-Reconstructionists come from Orthodox or traditional homes. The most marked difference between potential Reconstructionists and others is that significantly fewer of the former report that religion plays a very important role in their lives.

Thus, examining the responses to eight statements, we find that, on the basis of four, over 60 per cent of the respondents can be classified as potential Reconstructionists. On the remaining four, the proportion of potential Reconstructionists varies from 33 to 47 per cent. Nevertheless, very few Jews identify themselves as Reconstructionists, much less affiliate. Some do. We shall use the term "Reconstructionist laymen" to refer to those respondents who, in response to a question asking them to describe their religious identification (Q.3), checked Reconstructionist.

Reconstructionist Laymen

Respondents were asked to characterize themselves by religious identification, without regard to synagogue affiliation. Fifty-one respondents (4 per cent of the total sample) identified themselves as either Reconstructionist, or Reconstructionist and Conservative (6 cases), or Reconstructionist and Reform (2 cases). This group of 51 respondents we call Reconstructionist laymen. Here we discuss their distinctive attitudes and social characteristics.

Of the 51 respondents who characterize themselves as Reconstructionists, 4 per cent are affiliated with an Orthodox synagogue, 69 per cent with a Conservative synagogue, 18 per cent with a Reform synagogue, and 10 per cent with other synagogues (perhaps synagogues affiliated with the Federation of Reconstructionist Congregations and Fellowships). Of the Reconstructionists, 57 per cent were presidents of synagogues, and 43 per cent presidents of NJO chapters.

As might be expected, attitudes of Reconstructionist laymen conform more closely to those of Reconstructionist rabbis than do the attitudes of other groups of laymen. In social characteristics, the differences between Reconstructionist and non-Reconstructionist laymen resemble differences between potential Reconstructionists and non-Reconstructionists (p. 84). Significantly fewer Reconstructionist laymen (21 per cent) report that religion plays a very important role in their lives (Q.31). The figure for the rest of the sample was 40 per cent.

The other difference between Reconstructionist laymen and non-Reconstructionists has to do with religious background (Q.37). Twenty-two per cent of the Reconstructionists report that they were raised in Orthodox and observant homes, and the proportion for Reform Jews was about the same—lower than the 31 per cent reported by the Conservatives, and considerably lower than the 70 per cent reported by the Orthodox. Reconstructionists and Reform differed in that 47 per cent of the former and 28 per cent of the latter report having been raised in traditional, but not meticulously observant homes. For the Orthodox and Conservatives, these figures are 27 and 40 per cent, respectively.

The pattern here, while statistically not significant, is nevertheless interesting. Most Reconstructionists (67 per cent) come from either Orthodox and observant homes, or traditional though not ritually meticulous ones. In this respect they are like the Orthodox and Conservative respondents, most of whom also come from either Orthodox or traditional homes. But whereas most of the Orthodox are from Orthodox homes, and only slightly more Conservatives come from traditional than from Orthodox homes, for Reconstructionists the traditional rather than the Orthodox home is clearly the norm. (Over one half of the Reform respondents come from non-Orthodox and nontraditional homes.)

TABLE 18.

Religious backgrounds of respondents (Q.37)

Home	Ortho-dox	Conserva-tive	Reform	Reconstruc-tionist
	(Per cent)			
Orthodox	70	31	20	22
Traditional	27	40	28	47
Conservative, Reform, Reconstructionist, indifferent to religion, indifferent to Judaism	3	29	52	31
Total number responding (excluding secularists and persons who did not respond to question)	151	577	406	49

The secular education of Reconstructionist laymen is comparable to that of all other groups: seventy-three per cent of the Reconstructionists, compared with 67 per cent of the total sample, reported having at least a college degree. Jewish education, too, is roughly the same for all groups, except for the Orthodox who have had appreciably more, and more intensive, Jewish education. The age distribution among all groups, except the Orthodox, is the same. Considerably more of the latter are at least 55 years of age, and considerable fewer are under 45. Reconstructionist laymen also are indistinguishable by income. Sixty-three per cent reported income of over $20,000 a year, as compared with 55 per cent of the total sample—a difference that is statistically not significant. The percentage of Reconstructionist in this income bracket is equalled by presidents of Conservative synagogues and exceeded by presidents of Reform synagogues. Among NJO presidents, fewer Reconstructionist than Orthodox, Conservative, or Reform earn more than $20,000 annually.

Thus, Reconstructionist laymen differ from non-Reconstructionists only in the role religion plays in their lives and in their religious background—not in their secular education, Jewish education, age, or income.

The distinguishing characteristics of Reconstructionist laymen are consistent with the distinguishing characteristics of potential Reconstructionists. Now we can ask why there are so many of the latter and so few of the former.

FOLK AND ELITE RELIGION IN AMERICAN JUDAISM

Reconstructionist ideology is an articulation of the folk religion of American Jews. Orthodoxy, Conservatism, and Reform represent the three *elitist* ideologies of the American Jewish religion.[102] Folk religion can be thought of as the *popular* religious culture. The elite religion is the ritual, belief, and doctrine which the acknowledged religious leaders teach to be the religion. Thus the elite religion includes rituals and ceremonials (the cult), doctrines and beliefs (ideology), and a religious organization headed by the religious leaders. Their authority, the source of their authority, and the rights and obligations of the members of the organization are part of the beliefs and ideologies of the elite religion.

When we refer to Christianity, Islam, or Judaism, or when within Judaism we distinguish Orthodoxy, Conservatism, and Reform, we are really referring to the elitist formulations of these religions or groups. But not all who identify or affiliate with a religion accept its elitist formulation in its entirety. A subculture may exist within a religion, which the acknowledged leaders ignore or even condemn, but in which many, and perhaps a majority, of the members participate. The subculture may fall into the category of folk religion.

---

[102] The discussion here reproduces in part the section on elite and folk religion in Charles S. Liebman, *The Ambivalent Jew: Politics, Religion and Family in American Jewish Life* (forthcoming).

What, we may ask, is the difference between folk religion and denominationalism? Why call folk and elite religion two aspects of the same religion, rather than two separate religions? The answer is that both share the same organization, and both recognize, at least nominally, the authoritative nature of the cult and ideology, which the elite leadership affirms. Folk religion is not self-conscious; it does not articulate its own rituals and beliefs, or demand recognition for its informal leaders. Therefore, in the eyes of the elite religion, folk religion is not a movement but an error, or a set of errors, shared by many people.

Folk religion is expressed primarily through ritual and symbol. It tends to accept the organizational structure, and is relatively indifferent to the belief structure, of the elite religion. Of course, the rituals and symbols of folk religion imply a belief system, but one tending to be mythical rather than rational and ideational, and hence not in opposition to the more complex theological elaboration of the elite religion. Where the beliefs of the folk religion are self-conscious and articulated, the elite religion may prefer to ignore them. The fact that the folk religion of American Jews affirms belief in the separation of church and state as a cardinal principle of Judaism creates no problems as long as the elite leadership does not state the opposite.

There is always some tension between folk and elite religion. The danger always exists that folk religion will become institutionalized and articulated, in which case it will become a separate religion or an officially anathematized heresy. (The history of Catholicism abounds in examples of this.) On the other hand, for many people folk religion permits a more intimate religious expression and experience. It may in fact integrate them into organizational channels of the elite religion.

Folk religion is not necessarily more primitive than elite religion. While its ceremony and ritual may evoke emotions and inchoate ideas, associated with basic instincts and emotions, its very lack of interest in ideological or doctrinal consistency makes it more flexible than elite religion. Hence folk religion can develop ceremonial responses to new needs, which may then be incorporated into the elite religion—whose leaders must find a way of rationalizing the new ritual with prevailing doctrine. Much liturgy arises from folk religion and is then incorporated into elite religion.

The absence of an articulated theological position in folk religion, and the appeal to primal instincts and emotions, does not mean that intellectuals will necessarily find it less attractive than elite religion. Quite the opposite may be true. In secular America, elite religion has been forced to retreat before the challenges of science, biblical scholarship, the relativism implicit in social science, and the entire mood of intellectual life today. The foundations of religion are most critically shaken in doctrine and belief, which often represent elitist formulations rationalizing religious organization and cult. The religious elite's problem has been that most intellectuals cannot accept dogmatic formulations purporting to be truth assertions or to have arisen independently of time and place. Intellectuals have special difficulty with elite religion. But the same intellectual currents which challenge religious doctrine can also serve to defend behavioral and even organizational forms against the onslaught of secular doctrines, such as twentieth-century positivism or eighteenth- and nineteenth-century deism. Folk religion, with its stress on customary behavior or traditional practices, may be legitimized functionally, without the prop of elitist doctrine. An intellectual may be attracted to folk religion because it provides him with comfort and solace, a sense of tradition, a feeling of rootedness, or a source of family unity. Since his world view may remain secular, from the point of view of elite religion his beliefs will be quite unsatisfactory. But, at least in the first instance, it is elite and not folk religion which is challenged by his world view.

Most East European Jews who came to the United States between 1880 and 1920 identified in some way with Orthodox Judaism, though they did not necessarily accept its elitist formulation. They acquiesced to its authority structure (recognizing the religious authority of those who were ordained in accordance with elitist standards). They even accepted, though passively, its belief structure. What they demurred at, in practice, was its elaborate ritual structure. They developed their own hierarchy of the rituals—accepting some, modifying others, and rejecting still others, on the basis of values that had little to do with the elite religion itself. Those values were, preeminantly, integration and acceptance into American society, but also ingrained customs and life styles, and superstitions of East European origin. Thus, at the turn of the century, there existed in the United States both an elite and a folk religion of Orthodox Judaism.

As the century advanced, the Orthodox folk found themselves increasingly uncomfortable. The elitist leaders were too rigid, uncompromising, and foreign in outlook. The synagogue those rabbis controlled was aesthetically unattractive. Even the belief and ideological system became increasingly intolerable, particularly as it seemed to foreclose the possibility for any modernization. As most Jews moved from older areas of Jewish settlement and established new synagogues in middle-class neighborhoods, they were physically freed from the constraints of the Orthodox elite, who tended to remain in the older neighborhoods. The Orthodox folk began withdrawing from Orthodoxy. But they neither desired nor could they articulate their own brand of Judaism. Rather, they sought a new elitist formulation with which they might be more comfortable. Some found it in Jewish organizational life outside the synagogue. Others, socially more mobile, found it in Reform. Many, probably most, found it in Conservative Judaism.

However, the folk religion cut across Conservative, Reform, and many nonreligious organizational lines. Its adherents reshaping all the institutions with which they affiliated, a greater uniformity now emerged in Jewish life. To some extent, the immigrants' children were differentially socialized by their different institutions, and a certain divisiveness resulted. But in general the homogenizing process was the more pronounced. By the end of World War II virtually all major non-Orthodox organizations expressed the six major attitudes and values of the Jewish folk (p. 68). The Orthodox alone were excluded, because only an elite or the most passive remained Orthodox.

Our special concern here is with Conservatism, which rapidly became the dominant religious institution and expression of American Jews. However, the fact that the folk identified with Conservative Judaism did not mean that they were Conservative Jews as the Conservative elite, JTS leaders and alumni, understood Conservatism. An elaboration of the differences and tensions between the rabbinate and the congregants of the early Conservative synagogues would take us too far afield, and besides much of the basic research remains to be done. Suffice it to point out here that while the folk were more traditional in some respects and less so in others, in most respects they tended to be indifferent to Conservatism's elitist formulations.

Coincident with this development, and not entirely unaffected by it, was the effort to formulate the folk religion in elitist terms. This, we suggest, is Reconstructionism. We do not suggest that Kaplan deliberately fashioned an ideology to suit the basic attitudes of most American Jews. We do suggest that this is what Reconstructionism is. But the very nature of folk religion makes it unsuitable for elitist formulation.

In an elitist formulation folk religion is often unrecognizable to the folk.

Elite religion is expressed in ideology, folk religion in ritual and symbol. Indeed, the beliefs and ideas underlying the different folk rituals may be incompatible. This becomes a problem only if one actually bothers to formulate them philosophically. Then, with their contradictions apparent, the ideologist of the folk religion seeks to adjust them. He does this by establishing the primacy of ideology over ritual and ceremony. But that negates the essence of folk religion.

The constituents of early Reconstructionism were the religious left wing among the JTS alumni. It was these men who pressed their congregations for change and innovation. It was they who insisted on seating men and women together, shortening services, abolishing the second day of festivals, introducing organ music, abolishing the priestly blessing, and, in a later period, inviting women to recite the blessings before the reading of the Torah. To the left wing these changes were consistent with their ideology and with their understanding of Judaism. They never perceived why many of their congregants, who had ceased to observe such basic Jewish practices as Sabbath and *kashrut* in their private lives, were reluctant to accept changes in the public sphere. The failure to perceive derives from the elitist assumption that authority systems, belief systems, and ritual or cultic systems within a religion must be consistent. Also, what an elitist system may consider to be superficial or secondary—food styles, recreational and leisure styles, a spouse's family background, status of Jews, the celebration of *bar mitzvah,* or funeral services—a folk system may consider to be essential.

Influenced by prevailing Western thought, the left-wing rabbis sought to modify their congregants' beliefs. Kaplan holds that God, as Judaism understands Him, does not exist, but that there are forces in the universe that help man to be good, creative, free. These Kaplan calls God. He was not the only Jew who had gone to college and stopped believing in the traditional God of Western religion. When he redefined God to his own satisfaction, that was also apparently to the satisfaction of most American Jews who had never heard of him.

Kaplan drew certain consequences from his definition: If there was no traditional God, one could not pray to Him for help or direct intervention. But what follows for Kaplan does not necessarily follow in folk religion. On may admit in one's living-room that there is no supernatural God, no miracle, no divine intervention in the affairs of men. But this, after all, is living-room talk. When a folk Jew's child is sick, or when he is concerned about the safety of Israel, or even when he is grateful and elated to be alive, he can still open his *siddur* and pray to God—not a living-room God but the traditional God. Who can say that conclusions reached in one's living-room are more compelling than what one *knows to be true* when one prays? If one has doubts as to which is the more compelling, one must reject Reconstructionism—precisely because it demands the supremacy of rational formulations of ideology. On the other hand, complete reliance on intellectual consistency, the rejection of what one's heart knows to be true, also leads to a rejection of Reconstructionism—because its very foundation lies in undemonstrable sentiments about man, progress, Judaism, Zionism. Reconstructionism is midway between religious belief and intellectual rigor, based on a minimum of axiomatic postulates. It is most likely to appeal precisely to those who waver. In fact, it has served as a two-way bridge between Jewish commitment and marginalism.

If people took seriously the intellectual formulation of their religion as a basic *Weltanschauung,* Reconstructionism might be a more significant alternative for some Jews. Certainly, its critique of Orthodoxy, Conservatism, and Reform would be more compelling. But most people today, recognize, at least implicitly, that different institutions provide them with sources of understanding or cues to proper behavior, each in a different segment of life. Neither Orthodoxy nor Conservatism nor Reform has much to say about aspects of life that most American Jews take very seriously, such as social relationships, politics, economics, and war. But most Jews do not really expect their synagogue to have anything to say about these beyond elementary moralizing. The intellectual thinness of American Judaism is a tragedy only to the elite.

There are other reasons for Reconstructionism's failure. It may be a religion by a sociologist's standards, but it is not quite a religion by American standards of what religion ought to be. After all, it denies belief in a supernatural God. The fact that most American Jews do so, too, is immaterial. For most Jews their denial is a personal attitude; but affiliation with a synagogue which accepts their own theology will cause them embarrassment. Synagogue affiliation is more than a private act. It is public identification with a major American religion, and the *American* thing to do. But how American is it if, by American standards, the synagogue is not really *religious?*

American Jews no doubt are more ethnic, or peoplehood-oriented, than religion-oriented. But only Reconstructionism makes a virtue of this, and most American Jews are not quite willing to admit to this virtue publicly. The entire basis of Jewish accommodation to America, of the legitimacy of Jewish separateness, has been that Judaism is a religion, like Catholicism and Protestantism, and that the Jews are not merely an ethnic group, like the Irish or the Italians. America tolerates Jewish afternoon or Sunday schools, interdictions on intermarriage, and a fair degree of social isolation and exclusiveness. Would these be tolerated if Jews were considered to be an ethnic group like the Irish, Italians, or even Negroes? Though there are many more Negroes than Jews in the United States, the desire of some Negro spokesmen for separatism still has not attained the legitimacy of Jewish separatism precisely because Negroes are not defined as a religious group. Although Jews may know in their hearts that their identity stems from peoplehood and ethnicity, they are reluctant to display this truth in public. This is not a matter of deluding the American public. Above all, Jews delude themselves.

Reconstructionism's response has been to redefine religion. Kaplan has argued the need to redefine the symbolic nature of American public life and to express it in a civic non-supernatural religion that all Americans could share. Thus, since every American lives in two civilizations, he would also have two religions. Jews could then acknowledge that they are a civilization rather than a religion. At the same time, it would be understandable that the Jews' civilization must also have religious expression. At this point, one suspects, the folk find themselves "turned off."

Reconstructionism's problems are compounded by the fact that its ideology has greatest appeal to the Jews least interested in synagogue activity or organized religious life. The outstanding difference between potential Reconstructionists and all other respondents, as revealed by the answers to our questionnaire, is that proportionately fewer of the former said religion plays a very important role in their lives. *De facto,* Reconstructionism is widespread among leaders of Jewish community centers and secular Jewish organizations—all of them people who have found, for expressing their Jewish and Reconstructionist values, quite acceptable alternatives to the synagogue.

Finally, once Reconstructionism institutionalized itself, once it became a denomination, it violated a cardinal principle of Jewish folk religion: the unity of the Jewish people and the consequent irrelevance of denominational distinctions. Reconstructionism can demand that its ideology be taken seriously, but it cannot make the same demand for its distinctive institutional claims without asserting that differences between itself and other denominations are significant. And this is precisely what folk religion abjures. This is also what caused special difficulty for Reconstructionism among many close friends when it decided to establish a rabbinical college.

This essay is not to be construed as an epitaph on Reconstructionism. Twenty-five years ago, the *Reconstructionist* predicted the demise of Orthodox Judaism. Orthodoxy has since experienced renewal and growth. The same may happen to Reconstructionism. It has the financial support of a number of rich people. It has a flourishing publication, and a press. It has a few dedicated leaders and a few zealous members. Its college offers the potential for recruiting new leaders and expanding the base of lay support. Should the present condition of Jews in America change; should cultural and ethnic, as distinct from religious, separatism achieve greater respectability, Reconstructionism may yet emerge as a most significant force in American Jewish life.

APPENDIX

RELIGIOUS IDEOLOGY QUESTIONNAIRE

1. With what type of synagogue (if any) are you affiliated?
   Orthodox___1. Conservative___2. Reform___3. Other (please specify)___4. None___5.
2. Are you now or have you been president of a synagogue within the past 3 years?
   Yes___1. No___2.
3. Without regard to your synagogue affiliation which of the following best describes your religious identification?
   Orthodox___1. Conservative___2. Reform___3. Reconstructionist___4. Secularist___5. Other (please specify)___6.

Please indicate in the appropriate box * whether you agree strongly, agree somewhat, agree slightly, or disagree slightly, disagree somewhat, disagree strongly with the following statements. Some statements contain two parts. Please respond to the *entire* statement; thus disagreement with one part means disagreement with the whole statement.

4. The Jews are not a "chosen people."
5. While there must be a warm fraternal relation between Jews of the U.S. and Israel, the center of American Jewish life must be *American* Judaism rather than a Jewish culture which has developed or will develop in the State of Israel.
6. Israel should become the spiritual center of world Jewry.

───────────

* Boxes for checking the degree of agreement or disagreement are eliminated here for reasons of space. For this reason, text of instruction was slightly altered.

7. A Jew who really wants to do what Judaism requires of him should move to Israel.
8. The American Jew should observe even those aspects of Jewish ritual which have no meaning or relevance to him.
9. The freedom to adapt the Jewish tradition to the situation of modern man must become a fundamental principle of contemporary Judaism.
10. The authentic guidance for what a Jew should do is to be found by consulting the masters of Jewish law.
11. I would be willing to consider a rabbi as an outstanding interpreter of Jewish tradition today even though that rabbi had never applied secular academic or "scientific" procedures to its understanding.
12. Only experts in Jewish law can interpret it with authority, but such individuals must also be conversant with currents in secular and non-Jewish culture.
13. Judaism can more appropriately be defined as a religion than a culture or civilization.
14. Support for the State of Israel is a *religious* obligation of American Jews.
15. The Pentateuch or *Chumash,* as we know it today, was given by God to Moses at Sinai.
16. The study of Bible and rabbinic texts is of greater religious value than the study of other aspects of Judaism.
17. Modern man is very different from the kind of person to whom the Torah and the Rabbis of the Talmud addressed themselves.
18. Jewish rituals which an individual finds very inconvenient to observe, can properly be ignored.
19. Jewish religion must be made to serve the Jewish people rather than having the people serve religion.
20. Jews are obligated to observe traditional Jewish laws; but just as those laws have been changed in the past they should again be changed by *experts in the law* who should assess the contemporary condition of man and make the necessary adjustment.
21. God is the power that makes for Salvation or human betterment; not a supernatural being.
22. Loyalty to the Jewish people is more important than loyalty to Judaism as a religion.
23. It is a matter of *religious urgency* to create a single unified Jewish community in each locality in the U.S. with democratically selected leaders. It is this community, linked to all other communities which must constitute the basic structure of Jewish life.
24. Although the early Reform Jews in Germany misunderstood the nature of Judaism, Judaism still owes a great debt to them.
25. The decision as to the kind of Jewish life one ought to live should be left to the individual's conscience.
26. All study dealing with the improvement of human life—social or individual—may be considered study of Torah.
27. Jews can make a vital contribution to American life by formulating American ideals and beliefs into an American or "civic religion" in which all citizens—Jews and Gentiles—can participate.
28. Separation of church and state is not only essential for the sake of harmony and fair play but also because it is a religious value.
29. Although American Jews must remain loyal to and participate in Jewish religion, culture, and civilization, their primary loyalty must be to American culture and civilization.

30. Which statement best describes your beliefs about God?
   I believe in a personal supernatural God___1.
   I believe that God is the force in life that makes for human betterment but not in a supernatural being___2.
   I consider myself an agnostic___3.
   I consider myself an atheist___4.
   I don't have very strong beliefs about God one way or the other___5.
31. Which statement best describes the role religion plays in your life?
   Very important___1. Of some importance___2. Of little importance___3. No importance___4.
32. How much general or secular education did you have?
   High school or less___1. Some college___2. College graduate___3. Post graduate or professional school___4.
33. How many years of formal Jewish education did you have?
   Less than four years___1. Four to eight years___2. Nine to twelve years___3. Over twelve years___4.
34. Where did you receive most of your formal Jewish education?
   No formal Jewish education___1. Private study___2. Sunday School___3. Talmud Torah or afternoon school___4. Yeshiva or Day School___5. Other___6.
35. What is your age?
   Under 25___1. 25–34___2. 35–44___3. 45–54___4. 55–64___5. 65 or over___6.
36. What is your sex?
   Male___1. Female___2.
37. Without regard to synagogue affiliation, which statement best describes the home in which you were raised?
   Orthodox and observant___1.
   Traditional but not meticulous in observance___2.
   Conservative___3.
   Reform___4.
   Reconstructionist___5.
   Generally indifferent to religious aspects of Judaism, but Jewish in orientation___6.
   Generally indifferent to Jewish concerns___7.
38. What was your own and your spouse's approximate combined income last year?
   Retired___1. Under $7,999___2. $8,000–9,999___3. $10,000–11,999___4. $12,000–13,999___5. $14,000–15,999___6. $16,000–17,999___7. $18,000–19,999___8. $20,000 or more___9.